The Princeton Review

550 AP®

EUROPEAN HISTORY
Practice Questions

The Staff of the Princeton Review

PrincetonReview.com

PENGUIN RANDOM HOUSE

The Princeton Review
24 Prime Parkway, Suite 201
Natick, MA 01760
E-mail: editorialsupport@review.com

Published in the United States by Random House LLC, New York, and
simultaneously in Canada by Random House of Canada Limited, Toronto.
A Penguin Random House Company.

The Princeton Review is not affiliated with Princeton University.

AP and Advanced Placement Program are registered trademarks of the
College Board, which does not sponsor or endorse this product.

ISBN: 978-0-8041-2490-4
ISSN: 2330-703X

Editor: Calvin S. Cato
Production Editor: Kathy G. Carter
Production Coordinator: Deborah A. Silvestrini

Printed in the United States of America on partially recycled paper.

10   9   8   7   6   5   4   3   2   1

Editorial

Rob Franek, Senior VP, Publisher
Casey Cornelius, VP, Content Development
Mary Beth Garrick, Director of Production
Selena Coppock, Managing Editor
Calvin Cato, Editor
Colleen Day, Editor
Aaron Riccio, Editor
Meave Shelton, Editor
Alyssa Wolff, Editorial Assistant

Random House Publishing Team

Tom Russell, Publisher
Alison Stoltzfus, Publishing Manager
Dawn Ryan, Associate Managing Editor
Ellen Reed, Production Manager
Erika Pepe, Associate Production Manager
Kristin Lindner, Production Supervisor
Andrea Lau, Designer

Acknowledgments

The Princeton Review would like to give a special thanks to Sarah Kass, Samuel Lemley, Jason Morgan, Maggie Pfeiffer, Danny Poochigian, and Christopher Stobart for their hard work on the creation of this title. In addition, The Princeton Review thanks Kathy Carter for her hard work in copy editing the content of this title.

About the Authors

Sarah A. Kass, an instructor and tutor for The Princeton Review, received her Ph.D. in clinical psychology from Saybrook University. She is currently managing editor of The New Existentialists, a weblog highlighting scholarship in existential psychology, and is a former editor and writer for The New York Times. Her work here is dedicated to her three most favorite people in the world: Judah, Bennett, and Nava Kass.

Samuel Lemley is a Ph.D. student in the Department of English at the University of Virginia. His interests include early-modern literature, bibliography, and the history of books and reading. Sam enrolled at the University of Virginia in August 2014 after earning his B.A. from the University of North Carolina and spending a post-baccalaureate year at Columbia University studying Latin and medieval paleography.

Jason Morgan studied medieval and Renaissance history at Oxford University, England and at the Catholic University of America, where he earned a B.A. in literature and an M.A. in rhetoric. He has worked in journalism at The Washington Post, as a script consultant in the film industry, and currently as an independent educator and book editor. Using a pseudonym, he has published a successful series of international mystery novels, one of which recently reached #1 in the Amazon Free Kindle Store for a day and a half.

Maggie Pfeiffer has been teaching, tutoring, and writing content for the Princeton Review since 2013. She received her B.S. in Communications from New York University with a minor in Spanish Language and Literature. She enjoys creative writing, and though she'll probably never win an Academy Award, Maggie considers her greatest accomplishment to be her one-scene cameo in a Brendan Fraser movie. She would like to thank her parents, Joe Mullen, and Leo for their assistance on this project.

Daniel Poochigian earned his B.A. from the University of California, Irvine, majoring in History and Classics and his M.A. in Classics from the University of Colorado, Boulder. He has worked for The Princeton Review since 2009, teaching, tutoring, and developing new content. He dedicates his work in this book to his family and all his teachers and professors who have helped him become the historian he is today.

Christopher C. Stobart, Ph.D. received his Bachelor of Science degrees in Biology and Chemistry from Xavier University and his Ph.D. in Microbiology and Immunology from Vanderbilt University. Since 2008, Chris has worked with countless students in The Princeton Review prep courses and through one-on-one tutoring for a variety of tests including several AP exams, the ACT, MCAT, and DAT. Chris is currently working as a postdoctoral research fellow at Emory University in Atlanta and enjoys spending is free time traveling and exploring the outdoors with his wife.

Contents

Part I
Using This Book to Improve Your AP Score

PREVIEW: YOUR KNOWLEDGE, YOUR EXPECTATIONS

Your route to a high score on the AP European History Exam depends a lot on how you plan to use this book. Start thinking about your plan by responding to the following questions.

1. What is your level of confidence about your knowledge of the content tested by the AP European History Exam?

   A. Very confident—I know it all
   B. I'm pretty confident, but there are topics for which I could use help
   C. Not confident—I need quite a bit of support
   D. I'm not sure

2. If you have a goal score in mind, circle your goal score for the AP European History Exam:

   5   4   3   2   1   I'm not sure yet

3. What do you expect to learn from this book? Circle all that apply to you.

   A. A general overview of the test and what to expect
   B. Strategies for how to approach the test
   C. The content tested by this exam
   D. I'm not sure yet

YOUR GUIDE TO USING THIS BOOK

This book is organized to provide as much—or as little—support that you need, so you can use this book in whatever way will be most helpful to improving your score on the AP European History Exam.

- The remainder of **Part I** will provide guidance on how to use this book and help you determine your strengths and weaknesses.

- **Part II** of this book
  o provides information about the structure, scoring, and content of the AP European History Exam
  o helps you to make a study plan
  o points you towards additional resources

- **Part III** of this book explores various strategies including
  - o   how to attack multiple-choice questions
  - o   how to write effective essays: document-based questions (DBQ) and free-response questions
  - o   how to manage your time to maximize the number of points available to you

- **Part IV** of this book contains practice drills covering all of the AP European History concepts you will find on the exams.

- **Part V** of this book contains practice tests.

You may choose to use some parts of this book over others, or you may work through the entire book. Your approach will depend on your needs and how much time you have. Let's now look at how to make this determination.

HOW TO BEGIN

1.   **Take the Diagnostic Test**

Before you can decide how to use this book, you need to take a practice test. Doing so will give you insight into your strengths and weaknesses, and the test will also help you make an effective study plan. If you're feeling test-phobic, remind yourself that a practice test is a tool for diagnosing yourself—it's not how well you do that matters but how you use information gleaned from your performance to guide your preparation.

So, before you read further, take the AP European History Diagnostic Test starting at page 10 of this book. Be sure to do so in one sitting, following the instructions that appear before the test.

2.   **Check Your Answers**

Using the answer key that starts on page 30, count the number of questions you got right and how many you missed. Don't worry about the explanations for now, and don't worry about why you missed questions. We'll get to that soon.

3.   **Reflect on the Test**

After you take your first test, respond to the following questions::

- How much time did you spend on the multiple-choice questions?

- How much time did you spend on each essay?

- How many multiple-choice questions did you miss?

- Do you feel you had the knowledge to address the subject matter of the essays?

- Do you feel you wrote well-organized, thoughtful essays?

4. **Read Part II of this Book and Complete the Self-Evaluation**

   As discussed on page 2, Part II will provide information on how the test is structured and scored. It will also set out areas of content that are tested.

   As you read Part II, re-evaluate your answers to the questions above. At the end of Part II, you will revisit the questions above and refine your answers to them. You will then be able to make a study plan, based on your needs and time available, that will allow you to use this book most effectively.

5. **Engage with Parts III and IV as Needed**

   Notice the word *engage*. You'll get more out of this book if you use it intentionally than if you read it passively, hoping for an improved score through osmosis.

   Part III will open with a reminder to think about how you approach questions now and then close with a reflection section asking you to think about how and whether you will change your approach in the future.

   Part IV contains drills which are designed to give you the opportunity to assess your mastery of the concepts taught in AP European History through test-appropriate questions.

6. **Take the Practice Test and Assess Your Performance**

   Once you feel you have developed the strategies you need and gained the knowledge you lacked, you should take the practice exam at the end of this book. You should do so in one sitting, following the instructions at the beginning of the test. When you are done, check your answers to the multiple-choice sections. See if a teacher will read your essays and provide feedback.

   Once you have taken the test, reflect on what areas you still need to work on, and revisit the drills in this book that address those deficiencies. Through this type of reflection and engagement, you will continue to improve.

7. **Keep Working**

As you work through the drills, consider what additional work you need to do and how you will change your strategic approach to different parts of the test.

If you do need more guidance, there are plenty of resources available to you. Our *Cracking the AP European History Exam* guide gives you a comprehensive review of all the European history topics you need to know for the exam and offers two practice tests. In addition, you can go to the AP Central website for more information about exam schedules and European history concepts.

AP European
History
Diagnostic Test

AP® European History Exam

DO NOT OPEN THIS BOOKLET UNTIL YOU ARE TOLD TO DO SO.

At a Glance

Total Time
55 minutes
Number of Questions
80
Percent of Total Grade
50%
Writing Instrument
Pencil required

Instructions

Section I of this examination contains 80 multiple-choice questions. Fill in only the ovals for numbers 1 through 80 on your answer sheet.

CALCULATORS MAY NOT BE USED IN THIS PART OF THE EXAMINATION.

Indicate all of your answers to the multiple-choice questions on the answer sheet. No credit will be given for anything written in this exam booklet, but you may use the booklet for notes or scratch work. After you have decided which of the suggested answers is best, completely fill in the corresponding oval on the answer sheet. Give only one answer to each question. If you change an answer, be sure that the previous mark is erased completely. Here is a sample question and answer.

Sample Question   Sample Answer

Chicago is a   Ⓐ ● Ⓒ Ⓓ Ⓔ
(A) state
(B) city
(C) country
(D) continent
(E) village

Use your time effectively, working as quickly as you can without losing accuracy. Do not spend too much time on any one question. Go on to other questions and come back to the ones you have not answered if you have time. It is not expected that everyone will know the answers to all the multiple-choice questions.

About Guessing

Many candidates wonder whether or not to guess the answers to questions about which they are not certain. Multiple-choice scores are based on the number of questions answered correctly. Points are not deducted for incorrect answers, and no points are awarded for unanswered questions. Because points are not deducted for incorrect answers, you are encouraged to answer all multiple-choice questions. On any questions you do not know the answer to, you should eliminate as many choices as you can, and then select the best answer among the remaining choices.

THIS PAGE INTENTIONALLY LEFT BLANK.

EUROPEAN HISTORY

SECTION I, Part A

Time—55 Minutes

80 Multiple-Choice Questions

Directions: Each of the questions or incomplete statements below is followed by five suggested answers or completions. Select the one that is best in each case, and then fill in the corresponding oval on the answer sheet.

1. Which of the following was NOT a cause of the Renaissance?

   (A) Increased trade between Italian merchants and Arabic lands
   (B) The end of the Great Schism
   (C) The end of the Black Plague
   (D) A renewed respect for medieval scholasticism
   (E) The publication of the *Decameron*, by Boccaccio

2. Italian art during the fifteenth and sixteenth centuries displayed an increased use of all of the following EXCEPT

   (A) mathematical forms
   (B) reliance upon classical models
   (C) realistic detail
   (D) nudity
   (E) plain backgrounds

3. Unlike the Italian humanists, the humanists of Northern Europe

   (A) were more accepting of simony within the Catholic Church
   (B) suffered from political nepotism
   (C) were able to benefit more immediately from the invention of the printing press
   (D) viewed peasant uprisings with anger
   (E) built grander cathedrals

4. Erasmus's *In Praise of Folly* did NOT

   (A) contribute directly to the Counter-Reformation
   (B) influence the teaching of grammar and rhetoric for more than a century after its publication
   (C) use satire to attack the abuses of the Catholic clergy
   (D) draw from classical literary forms
   (E) demonstrate that learning could be used outside a wholly religious framework

5. The Schlieffen Plan was Germany's attempt to

   (A) destroy London through constant aerial bombing
   (B) quickly defeat France in the west before turning to face Russia, which was expected to mobilize more slowly for war
   (C) continue its control of the Austro-Hungarian Empire by encouraging disagreement among its many ethnic groups
   (D) end four centuries of Habsburg domination by placing high tariffs on all imports
   (E) create a master Aryan race

6. Which of the following increased the LEAST for the people of Europe during World War I?

   (A) The marriage rate
   (B) The number of women in the workforce
   (C) Sense of national unity
   (D) The sale of munitions
   (E) Malnutrition

7. Following World War I, the Treaty of Versailles forced Germany to do all of the following EXCEPT

   (A) accept foreign occupation and demilitarize itself
   (B) pay billions in reparations
   (C) relinquish all of its overseas colonies
   (D) return the Alsace-Lorraine to France
   (E) share responsibility for the war

8. The existential confusion experienced as a result of the intellectual and scientific upheavals of the twentieth century can be seen most clearly in which of the following works of literature?

   (A) *The Stranger*, by Albert Camus
   (B) *Mein Kampf*, by Adolf Hitler
   (C) *A History of the English-Speaking Peoples*, by Winston Churchill
   (D) *Leviathan*, by Thomas Hobbes
   (E) *The Power of the Powerless*, by Vaclav Havel

GO ON TO THE NEXT PAGE.

9. The Concert of Europe disallowed all of the following popular revolts EXCEPT

   (A) Belgian Catholics against the Dutch Protestants in 1830
   (B) the February 1830 revolution in France
   (C) the Greek revolt against the Turks during the 1820s
   (D) the Polish uprising against the Prussians in 1848
   (E) the Hungarian revolution of 1848

10. Which social group is most strongly associated with using charity to address urban poverty throughout the nineteenth century?

    (A) German aristocrats
    (B) Middle-class religious women
    (C) Conservative political philosophers
    (D) Influential government bureaucrats
    (E) Skilled artisans working within the guild system

11. Until Italian unification, the island of Sicily was controlled by

    (A) the Kingdom of Valencia, centered in Barcelona
    (B) a branch of the Bourbon dynasty
    (C) the Mafia
    (D) Louis Napoleon Bonaparte
    (E) King Victor Emmanuel II

12. All of the following contributed to the unification of Germany EXCEPT

    (A) the Schleswig-Holstein Affair
    (B) the Austro-Prussian War
    (C) the Franco-Prussian War
    (D) the Compromise of 1867
    (E) the Ems telegram

13. The First Industrial Revolution was most directly responsible for

    (A) the establishment of the Alsace-Lorraine as the premier industrial region of Europe
    (B) producing the raw materials such as cotton, coffee, furs, and timber that were then exchanged for slaves
    (C) breaking the cycle of population and productivity
    (D) strengthening the manorial system
    (E) a return to subsistence agriculture

14. During the eighteenth-century triangle of trade, European traders

    (A) sent the vast majority of slaves to the present-day United States
    (B) sold primarily guns and alcohol to African tribal leaders
    (C) were spurred on by the invention of the cotton gin
    (D) brought vast amounts of sugar from Europe to the Caribbean
    (E) hailed primarily from Eastern Europe

15. Peter the Great accomplished all of the following EXCEPT

    (A) building Russia's first navy
    (B) consolidating Romanov power by buying the loyalty of the nobles
    (C) changing the legal status of all peasants and slaves into serfs
    (D) extending more civil rights to the Russian middle class
    (E) constructing a new city named for himself, St. Petersburg

16. Which of the following did NOT contribute to the growth of absolutism in France during the seventeenth century?

    (A) A lack of significant religious civil wars
    (B) The power of high-ranking Catholic clergy in the government
    (C) The construction of the Palace of Versailles
    (D) Tax codes that favored the wealthy
    (E) The growth of the private armies of the aristocrats

17. The Berlin Conference of 1885

    (A) attempted to set up guidelines for the partitioning of Africa
    (B) ignored calls for the African population to be treated humanely
    (C) was blamed for the rise of mass politics
    (D) led to the British occupation of Egypt
    (E) caused King Leopold II of Belgium to send Henry Stanley to the Congo River Basin

GO ON TO THE NEXT PAGE.

18. The Treaty of Nanking resulted in all of the following EXCEPT

    (A) the ceding of Hong Kong to Britain
    (B) the establishment of "spheres of influence" in China
    (C) immunity for foreigners to Chinese law
    (D) the prohibition of opium trade in China
    (E) the Taiping and Boxer Rebellions

19. The rift that arose between nationalism and liberalism occurred primarily as a result of

    (A) a series of contentious lectures on the political philosophy of Edmund Burke at the University of Paris in the late eighteenth century
    (B) the French aristocracy's attempts to assassinate prominent liberal leaders
    (C) the failure of liberals to retain the power that they had temporarily seized during the revolutions of 1848
    (D) disagreement over whether Poland should be re-established as a nation
    (E) hyperinflation in Germany during the Weimar Republic

20. One of the most prominent nineteenth-century utopian socialists was

    (A) Henri Comte de Saint-Simon
    (B) Edmund Burke
    (C) Charles Darwin
    (D) Georg Hegel
    (E) Thomas More

21. The Maastricht Treaty was significant because it

    (A) ended the Dutch Revolt against King Philip II of Spain in the late 1500s
    (B) attempted to regulate the price of tulip bulbs in the Netherlands in the late 1600s
    (C) secured neutrality for the Dutch during the Napoleonic Wars of the early 1800s
    (D) provided for the safe passage of Jews through Dutch territory during World War II
    (E) paved the way for the adoption of the Euro as currency in the early 2000s

22. In formulating his Uncertainty Principle, Werner Heisenberg built upon the work of all of the following physicists EXCEPT

    (A) Edward Morley
    (B) Albert Einstein
    (C) Pierre and Marie Curie
    (D) Max Planck
    (E) Max Weber

23. Stalin did NOT commit which of the following atrocities during his totalitarian rule?

    (A) Purging his internal rivals from the ranks of the Communist Party, trying them in rigged show trials, and sending them to the gulags in Siberia
    (B) Forcing his enemies' daughters to marry his trusted lieutenants
    (C) Assassinating his archrival Trotsky after he had fled to Mexico
    (D) Erasing his enemies' names from all Russian history books
    (E) Destroying villages and murdering peasants during the state collectivization of farms

24. All of the following events are related to increasing anti-Semitism in Germany from 1933 to 1945 EXCEPT

    (A) Mass book burnings
    (B) Nuremberg Laws
    (C) The publication of the *Protocols of the Elders of Zion*
    (D) *Kristallnacht*
    (E) *Einsatzgruppen*

25. Which of the following thinkers was NOT associated with empiricism?

    (A) David Hume
    (B) Francis Bacon
    (C) John Locke
    (D) Rene Descartes
    (E) Thomas Hobbes

GO ON TO THE NEXT PAGE.

26. For Spanish peasants in the sixteenth century, the most immediate effect of the policy of mercantilism was

    (A) enormous inflation
    (B) better jewelry
    (C) decentralization of power
    (D) the Spanish Armada
    (E) increased piracy

27. The doctrinal centerpiece of the Counter Reformation was

    (A) the Council of Trent
    (B) the construction of the Cathedral of Notre Dame in Paris
    (C) increased sale of indulgences
    (D) an acknowledgement of papal fallibility
    (E) the Spanish Inquisition

28. The Augsburg Confession promoted all of the following ideas EXCEPT

    (A) salvation by faith alone
    (B) the Bible as the ultimate authority
    (C) the priesthood of all believers
    (D) consubstantiation
    (E) religious services in Latin

29. During the nineteenth century, the definition of the term "middle class" expanded to include all of the following EXCEPT

    (A) merchants
    (B) clerks
    (C) bankers
    (D) factory workers
    (E) skilled artisans

30. Throughout the Industrial Revolution, advancements in manufacturing technology tended to

    (A) move from east to west
    (B) reinforce the power of the aristocrats
    (C) be adopted most swiftly by authoritarian governments
    (D) eat into factory owners' profits
    (E) be used to support Catholic ideology

31. Peasants who moved from rural agriculture into urban factories did NOT experience which of the following?

    (A) A disconnection from natural cycles
    (B) Sudden potential unemployment
    (C) Worsened health due to lack of public services
    (D) Near-compulsory child labor
    (E) Less opportunity to marry

32. The Chartist movement

    (A) wanted to reinstitute the Corn Laws
    (B) demanded salaries for members of Parliament
    (C) sought to restrict suffrage to land-owning white males
    (D) preferred open ballots
    (E) was opposed to equal constituencies

33. The primary long-term effect of the Yalta Conference in 1945 was

    (A) the Soviet Communist occupation of much of Eastern Europe
    (B) respect for Stalin's accomplishments as a mediator between the United States and England
    (C) a greater openness to new ideologies in Eastern Europe
    (D) the unification of East and West Germany
    (E) increased trust between the Poles and the Russians

34. The idea of a "collective unconscious" can be attributed to

    (A) Sigmund Freud
    (B) Adolf Hitler
    (C) Emile Durkheim
    (D) Carl Jung
    (E) Herbert Spencer

35. The policies of Francoist Spain differed from the policies of Nazi Germany in that they

    (A) used the Catholic Church to earn legitimacy
    (B) exploited strong feelings of nationalism
    (C) oppressed and murdered internal dissidents
    (D) were fiercely anti-communist
    (E) used language politics to create homogeneity

GO ON TO THE NEXT PAGE.

36. The most immediate challenge facing the daily life of the German population during the 1920s was

(A) external attacks by Poland
(B) increasing power of Jewish shopkeepers
(C) hyperinflation
(D) unwanted foreign assistance
(E) beer shortages

37. Under the guild system, artisans

(A) kept a long period of apprenticeship
(B) were quickly promoted based on merit
(C) priced flexibly based on output
(D) often worked more efficiently than the factories
(E) took less pride in their work

38. Which of the following was NOT a result of the enclosure movement in England?

(A) The cottage industry of textile production
(B) Strengthening of the feudal class system
(C) Increased wool production for export
(D) The creation of a mobile working class
(E) Political controversy

39. During the French Revolution, the tennis-court oath was

(A) An accurate reflection of the perspectives of the clergy and nobility
(B) Sworn by King Louis XVI
(C) A renewed emphasis upon athletics among the First and Second Estates
(D) A pledge by the newly created National Assembly to draft a constitution
(E) The result of agitation by the *sans-culottes*

40. In the first half of the seventeenth century, English Puritans strongly opposed

(A) The New Model Army
(B) Scottish Presbyterians
(C) The dominance of the Levellers and Diggers
(D) The use of the *Book of Common Prayer* in the Church of England
(E) The rise of Oliver Cromwell's Commonwealth

41. The German movement known as *Sturm und Drang* was a key component of

(A) Romanticism
(B) Utopian socialism
(C) Scientific socialism
(D) Anarchism
(E) Nationalism

42. The legal application of the principles of the Enlightenment was most successfully accomplished by

(A) Joseph II of Austria-Hungary
(B) Catherine the Great
(C) Napoleon Bonaparte
(D) Frederick II of Prussia
(E) Otto von Bismarck

43. All of the following exemplified growing anti-Semitism in late nineteenth century EXCEPT

(A) the Dreyfus affair
(B) Nicholas II
(C) Russian *pogroms*
(D) Theodor Herzl
(E) Edouard Drumont

44. The fundamental irony found in the "cult of domesticity" was that

(A) most women truly wanted to work outside of the home
(B) not all women wanted to join a cult
(C) it was available only to the middle and upper socioeconomic classes
(D) it made prostitution seem more attractive
(E) significant numbers of women were attending universities instead

45. John Maynard Keynes

(A) argued for deficit spending in a time of recession
(B) applied the principle of "total war" to the English state
(C) developed the first method of mass production of steel
(D) attended the Treaty of Versailles and encouraged the punishment of Germany
(E) pioneered the team of code-crackers that led to England's successful defense at the Battle of Britain

GO ON TO THE NEXT PAGE.

46. The policy of containment was first tested in

    (A) Russia
    (B) Poland
    (C) Bulgaria
    (D) Greece
    (E) Germany

47. In the post–World War II era, British decolonization occurred in all of the following regions EXCEPT

    (A) Palestine
    (B) the Falklands
    (C) Ghana
    (D) Egypt
    (E) India

48. Since the end of World War II, increased immigration from northern Africa into Europe has NOT

    (A) helped native Europeans maintain the birth rate needed for population replacement
    (B) caused an increase in reactionary attacks from natives
    (C) improved social cohesion
    (D) helped relieve a serious labor shortage
    (E) resulted in several controversial new government policies

49. Louis XIV constructed the Palace of Versailles primarily to

    (A) impress foreign leaders
    (B) intimidate French peasants
    (C) create long-term employment for skilled laborers
    (D) distract nobles from their home districts
    (E) influence interior design for centuries

50. The establishment of the Royal Society

    (A) resulted in the production of thousands of portraits of English nobility
    (B) marked a period of intense opposition from Charles II
    (C) was an attempt to correct the misguided principles of Francis Bacon
    (D) ushered in an era of monarchical support of scientific endeavors
    (E) attempted to regulate the ways by which members of Parliament were chosen

51. "Whence it is to be noted, that in taking a state, the conqueror must arrange to commit all his cruelties at once, so as not to have to recur to them every day…. Being less tasted, they will give less offence. Benefits should be granted little by little, so that they may be better enjoyed. Above all, a prince must live with his subjects in such a way that no accident of good or evil fortune can deflect him from his course…." This quotation most closely describes the philosophy of which writer?

    (A) John Locke
    (B) Baron de Montesquieu
    (C) Isaac Newton
    (D) Thomas Hobbes
    (E) Niccolo Machiavelli

52. Skepticism is primarily associated with

    (A) David Hume
    (B) Thomas Hobbes
    (C) Galileo Galilei
    (D) William Harvey
    (E) Jean-Jacques Rousseau

53. The most significant advance in nineteenth-century medicine occurred when Louis Pasteur

    (A) introduced ether as a form of anesthesia
    (B) discovered the existence of microbes
    (C) used disinfectant to sterilize surgical tables
    (D) discovered the circulation of the blood
    (E) interpreted the results of the first DNA test

54. All of the following contributed to the growth of the Industrial Revolution in England EXCEPT

    (A) wealthy centralized banks that loaned money easily to the middle class
    (B) a peasantry that was no longer tied to the land
    (C) a natural system of rivers that facilitated transportation
    (D) a powerful guild system that encouraged the growth of factories
    (E) large natural deposits of coal

GO ON TO THE NEXT PAGE.

55. Venetia finally joined the Italian unification process when

   (A) Cavour refused to unite Italy without it
   (B) Garibaldi sent his legion of "red shirts" to defend it against the Prussians
   (C) King Victor Emmanuel II received it from the Prussians in return for Italy's assistance during the Austro-Prussian War
   (D) Napoleon III offered it in exchange for allowing French troops to continue protecting the pope
   (E) the *Risorgimento* caused a popular revolt within its borders

56. The dual monarchy of Austria-Hungary

   (A) featured separate kings who nonetheless consulted with one another
   (B) fairly represented all ethnicities within the empire
   (C) was agreed to by Franz Joseph in the Compromise of 1867
   (D) imposed a single language upon the territory
   (E) helped the empire grow stronger during the nineteenth century

57. Napoleon III accomplished all of the following EXCEPT

   (A) the successful defense of Paris against the invading Prussian army of Otto von Bismarck
   (B) expansion of the French economy through cheap credit
   (C) the attempt to transform his own government into a constitutional monarchy
   (D) construction of the wide avenues for which Paris is famous today
   (E) extension of universal manhood suffrage

58. The Belle Epoque was

   (A) a weapon used by French soldiers during the Thirty Years' War
   (B) the evening stroll taken by many middle- and upper-class Europeans before dinner
   (C) the era in which many new forms of art and entertainment were supported by the *nouveau riche*
   (D) the politically uncertain period of time prior to World War I
   (E) the scientific worldview that dominated France at the beginning of the twentieth century

59. The list of new developments that allowed imperialism to flourish in the early twentieth century does NOT include

   (A) breech-loading rifles
   (B) steamships
   (C) the Suez canal
   (D) tanks
   (E) the discovery of quinine

60. The end of the Cold War and the fall of communism signaled a general European preference for

   (A) the United States
   (B) the CIA
   (C) western-style liberal democracy
   (D) economic self-determinism
   (E) affordable denim

61. During the 1990s, the former Yugoslavia initially fell into civil war because

   (A) President Slobodan Milosevic refused to support Bosnian Serbs in their pursuit of ethnic cleansing of Bosnian Muslims
   (B) various parts of Yugoslavia, such as Slovenia and Croatia, began to demand more autonomy within the federation, while Serbia itself tried to assert more federal power
   (C) negotiations at the Dayton Peace Accords broke down
   (D) the Kosovo Liberation Army attacked Serbia
   (E) NATO launched a long-term aerial bombardment of Serbia

62. The Thirty Years' War was caused by

   (A) a series of conflicts in Bavaria and Bohemia regarding the ascension of Calvinist leaders to power
   (B) Italian nobles' refusal to recant before the pope
   (C) the rescinding of the Edict of Nantes
   (D) the Moors' insistent defense of Andalusia against Christian forces from the north
   (E) the political struggle that followed the death of Elizabeth I and the end of the Tudor dynasty

GO ON TO THE NEXT PAGE.

63. The pre-eminent economic power in Europe in the seven-teenth century was

   (A) England
   (B) France
   (C) Spain
   (D) the Netherlands
   (E) the Holy Roman Empire

64. All of the following are associated with the most violent portion of the French Revolution EXCEPT

   (A) the entry of the *sans-culottes* into the conflict
   (B) the Committee on Public Safety
   (C) the Hébertists
   (D) Danton
   (E) the Directory

65. In his effort to defeat England economically, Napoleon created the

   (A) First Consul
   (B) Third Coalition
   (C) Continental System
   (D) Battle of Trafalgar
   (D) Civil Code of 1804

66. The Impressionists were a school of French painters who did NOT

   (A) accurately depict the play of light on their canvases
   (B) include Manet, Monet, Cézanne, and Renoir
   (C) follow the academic rules of painting at the time
   (D) paint outdoor scenes
   (E) use subjectivity and individual perception to a degree rarely seen before in the world of art

67. Urging Europeans to break with traditional Christian morality, which philosopher wrote the statement "God is dead"?

   (A) Martin Luther
   (B) Galileo Galilei
   (C) John Locke
   (D) Friedrich Nietzsche
   (E) Francis Fukuyama

68. The growth of the middle class in the nineteenth century did NOT result in which of the following developments?

   (A) Running water and central heating
   (B) More freedom for women
   (C) The birth of department stores
   (D) Increased travel for pleasure
   (E) The end of public executions

69. Charles Darwin's concept of "survival of the fittest" was

   (A) applied only to the evolution of plants and animals
   (B) largely uninfluential beyond the nineteenth century
   (C) used to justify imperialistic beliefs about the superiority of white European culture
   (D) considered unremarkable when it was revealed
   (E) originally a French concept from the Cartesian school of thought

70. Trench warfare marked all of the following battles EXCEPT

   (A) the Battle of the Marne
   (B) the Battle of Verdun
   (C) the Battle of the Somme
   (D) the Battle of Jutland
   (E) the Battle of Gallipolli

71. All of the following were steps along the path towards Soviet communism EXCEPT

   (A) the February Revolution
   (B) the April Theses
   (C) Lenin's series of five-year plans
   (D) collectivization of agriculture
   (E) the New Economic Policy

GO ON TO THE NEXT PAGE.

Credit: fromoldbooks.org

72. The above photo illustrates one important innovation created by the

(A) Scientific Revolution
(B) First Industrial Revolution
(C) Second Industrial Revolution
(D) Age of Revolutions
(E) Holocaust

73. One of the positive results of Mussolini's rule of Italy was

(A) his use of public works programs to improve infrastructure
(B) his establishment of secret police
(C) his tolerance of diverse political viewpoints in the national press
(D) his conquest of Ethiopia
(E) his encouragement of peasants to educate themselves in the cities

74. The three laws of planetary motion were written by

(A) Nicolas Copernicus
(B) Tycho Brahe
(C) Johannes Kepler
(D) Galileo Galilei
(E) Isaac Newton

75. The long-term causes of the Protestant Reformation did NOT include

(A) the fiscal crisis in the Church that led to widespread corruption by monks such as Tetzel
(B) the growth of the power of secular monarchs such as the Tudors
(C) the popular discontent with seemingly empty rituals of the Church
(D) the questioning of transubstantiation by John Wycliffe and Jan Hus
(E) the lay piety movement led by German peasants

76. The end of the three-field system that had dominated European agriculture since the High Middle Ages occurred as a result of

(A) the Black Plague, which decimated the native species
(B) John Kay's invention of the flying shuttle
(C) the arrival of New World crops, such as the potato, which replenished nutrients in the soil
(D) the mechanization of agriculture during the Second Industrial Revolution
(E) the invention of pesticide in the twentieth century

GO ON TO THE NEXT PAGE.

THE DOCILE HUSBAND.

Credit: *The Docile Husband*,
by John Leech, Punch magazine, 1847

77. The above cartoon mildly satirizes what convention of Victorian life?

(A) The daily stroll
(B) The traditional subservience of husbands
(C) The public display of children
(D) The domestic sphere being restricted to women only
(E) The riding crop

78. All of the following conspired to send the French Revolution into its radical phase EXCEPT

(A) the king's attempt to secretly flee to Varennes
(B) the king's calling of the Estates General
(C) the outbreak of war with Austria and Prussia
(D) the division of the National Assembly into political factions
(E) the rise of the *sans-culottes*

79. Otto von Bismarck's release of the Ems telegram was NOT

(A) designed to anger the French
(B) intended to win the sympathy of southern German states
(C) one of the causes of the Franco-Prussian War
(D) the first step towards the unification of Germany
(E) an example of *Realpolitik*

80. An early example of the opening of the Soviet Union can be seen in

(A) increased funding for the KGB
(B) lowered rates of alcoholism after the Bolshevik Revolution
(C) the Prague Spring
(D) the deportation of Alexander Solzhenitsyn following publication of *The Gulag Archipelago*
(E) Jaruzelski's seizing of power in Poland

STOP
END OF SECTION I
**IF YOU FINISH BEFORE TIME IS CALLED, YOU MAY CHECK YOUR WORK ON THIS SECTION.
DO NOT GO ON TO SECTION II UNTIL YOU ARE TOLD TO DO SO.**

GO ON TO THE NEXT PAGE.

EUROPEAN HISTORY

SECTION II

You will have 15 minutes to read the contents of this essay question booklet. You are advised to spend most of the 15 minutes analyzing the documents and planning your answer for the document-based question in Part A. You should spend some portion of the time choosing the two questions in Part B that you will answer. You may make notes in this booklet. At the end of the 15-minute period, you will be told to break the seal on the free-response booklet and to begin writing your answers on the lined pages of that booklet. Do not break the seal on the free-response booklet until you are told to do so. Suggested writing time is 45 minutes for the document-based essay question in Part A. Suggested planning and writing time is 35 minutes for each of the two essay questions you choose to answer in Part B.

BE SURE TO MANAGE YOUR TIME CAREFULLY.

Write your answers in the free-response booklet with a pen. The essay question booklet may be used for reference and/or scratchwork as you answer the free-response questions, but no credit will be given for the work shown in the essay question booklet.

DO NOT OPEN THIS BOOKLET UNTIL YOU ARE TOLD TO DO SO.

GO ON TO THE NEXT PAGE.

GO ON TO THE NEXT PAGE.

EUROPEAN HISTORY

SECTION II

Part A

(Suggested writing time—45 minutes)

Percent of Section II score—45

<u>Directions:</u> The following question is based on the accompanying Documents 1–10. (Some of the documents have been edited for the purpose of this exercise.) Write your answer on the lined pages of the free-response booklet.

This question is designed to test your ability to work with historical documents. As you analyze the documents, <u>take into account both the sources and the author's point of view</u>. Write an essay on the following topic that integrates your analysis of the documents; in no case should documents simply be cited and explained in a "laundry list" fashion. You may refer to historical facts and developments not mentioned in the documents.

1. Describe and analyze the extent to which the lives of the citizenry improved in England during the nineteenth century.

Document 1

"Dear Mr Rawlinson, Enclosed is the long promised tracing of the Regimental Hospital for £100 per bed (120 beds) which I think on the whole the best thing we have done. I need not point out to you that some alterations must be made for a Civil Hospital—with women Patients."

—Florence Nightingale, letter to Mr Rawlinson, a civil engineer, February 12, 1861

Document 2

I was married at 23, and went into a colliery when I was married. I used to weave when about 12 years old; can neither read nor write. I work for Andrew Knowles, of Little Bolton (Lancs), and make sometimes 7s a week, sometimes not so much. I am a drawer, and work from 6 in the morning to 6 at night. Stop about an hour at noon to eat my dinner; have bread and butter for dinner; I get no drink. I have two children, but they are too young to work. I worked at drawing when I was in the family way. I know a woman who has gone home and washed herself, taken to her bed, delivered of a child, and gone to work again under the week.

I have a belt round my waist, and a chain passing between my legs, and I go on my hands and feet. The road is very steep, and we have to hold by a rope; and when there is no rope, by anything we can catch hold of. There are six women and about six boys and girls in the pit I work in; it is very hard work for a woman. The pit is very wet where I work, and the water comes over our clog-tops always, and I have seen it up to my thighs; it rains in at the roof terribly. My clothes are wet through almost all day long. I never was ill in my life, but when I was lying in.

My cousin looks after my children in the day time. I am very tired when I get home at night; I fall asleep sometimes before I get washed. I am not so strong as I was, and cannot stand my work so well as I used to.

—Betty Harris, age 37, from *Parliamentary Papers*, 1842

GO ON TO THE NEXT PAGE.

Document 3

But in all times men have been prone to believe that their happiness and well-being were to be secured by means of institutions rather than by their own conduct. Hence the value of legislation as an agent in human advancement has usually been much over-estimated. To constitute the millionth part of a Legislature, by voting for one or two men once in three or five years, however conscientiously this duty may be performed, can exercise but little active influence upon any man's life and character. Moreover, it is every day becoming more clearly understood, that the function of Government is negative and restrictive, rather than positive and active. . . .

—Samuel Smiles, *Self-Help,* 1882

Document 4

The era of the enlargement of English society dates from the Reform Bill of 1832, and if it has brought with it some contradictions, anomalies, and inconveniences, it has also been instrumental in the accomplishment of great and undoubted good. It has substituted, in a very large degree, the prestige of achievement for the prestige of position. The mere men of fashion, the fops, dandies, and exquisites, the glory of whose life was indolence, and who looked upon any thing in the way of occupation as a disgrace, have gone out of date never to return. . . .

—Thomas Escott, *England: Her People, Polity, and Pursuits,* 1885

Document 5

Image: Gustavé Dore, Newgate Exercise Yard, Newgate Prison

GO ON TO THE NEXT PAGE.

Document 6

Image: Victorian Home Comforts

Document 7

But, it will be instantly admitted, Civilization has increased man's producing power. Five men can produce bread for a thousand. One man can produce cotton cloth for 250 people, woollens for 300, and boots and shoes for 1000. Yet it has been shown throughout the pages of this book that English folk by the millions do not receive enough food, clothes, and boots. Then arises the third and inexorable question: If Civilization has increased the producing power of the average man, why has it not bettered the lot of the average man? There can be one answer only—MISMANAGEMENT.

—Jack London, *The People of the Abyss,* 1903

Document 8

But all the advantages of this [industrial] revolution are monopolized by the capitalist and great landowners. To the proletariat and to the rapidly sinking middle classes, the small tradesmen of the towns and the peasants, it brings an increasing uncertainty of existence, increasing misery, oppression, servitude, degradation, and exploitation. Ever greater grows the mass of the proletariat, ever vaster the army of the unemployed, ever sharper the contrast between oppressors and oppressed, ever fiercer that war of classes between bourgeoisie and proletariat which divides modern society into two hostile camps and is the common characteristic of every industrial country.

—The Erfurt Program, 1891

GO ON TO THE NEXT PAGE.

Document 9

1. A VOTE for every man twenty-one years of age, of sound mind, and not undergoing punishment for crime. 2. THE BAL-LOT .-To protect the elector in the exercise of his vote. 3. NO PROPERTY QUALIFICATION for Members of Parliament-thus enabling the constituencies to return the man of their choice, be he rich or poor. 4. PAYMENT OF MEMBERS, Thus enabling an honest tradesman, working man, or other person, to serve a constituency, when taken from his business to attend the interests of the country. 5. EQUAL CONSTITUENCIES, securing the same amount of representation for the same Num-ber of electors, instead of allowing small constituencies to swamp the votes of large ones. 6. ANNUAL PARLIAMENTS, thus presenting the most effectual check to bribery and intimidation, since though a constituency might be bought once in seven years (even with the ballot), no purse could buy a constituency (under a system of universal suffrage) in each ensuing twelvemonth; and since members, when elected for a year only, would not be able to defy and betray their constituents as now.

—*The Six Points of the People's Charter*, 1838

Document 10

[This] is a statute which is calculated, more than any other of recent times to elevate the masses of the people and is the result of many years agitation by the various religious denominations and political parties in the State. The object which it will accomplish may be stated in a very few words. It will place an elementary school wherever there is a child to be taught, whether of rich or poor parents: and it will compel every parent and guardian of a child to have it taught, at least, the rudi-ments of education, and that without reference to any religious creed or persuasion.

—Preface to *The Elementary Education Act*, 1870

END OF PART A

GO ON TO THE NEXT PAGE.

EUROPEAN HISTORY

SECTION II

Part B

(Suggested writing time—70 minutes)

Percent of Section II score—55

<u>Directions:</u> You are to answer TWO questions, one from each group of three questions below. Make your selections carefully, choosing the questions that you are best prepared to answer thoroughly in the time permitted. You should spend 5 minutes organizing or outlining each answer. In writing your essays, <u>use specific examples to support your answer</u>. Write your answers to the questions on the lined pages of the free-response booklet. If time permits when you finish writing, check your work. Be certain to number your answer as the questions are numbered below.

Group 1:   Choose ONE question from this group. The suggested writing time for this question is 30 minutes.

1.   Describe the ways in which the modern notion of individualism was born on the Italian peninsula during the period from 1450 to 1550.

2.   Analyze the different reactions to the Protestant Reformation in Southern and Northern Europe.

3.   Describe the changing nature of the relationship between the Stuart kings and English Parliament in the period 1600 to 1715.

Group 2:   Choose ONE question from this group. The suggested writing time for this question is 30 minutes.

4.   Analyze the extent to which Napoleon's policies reflected Enlightenment principles.

5.   Analyze the causes of the Russian Revolution.

6.   Analyze the expansion of European power during the imperialist era.

END OF EXAMINATION

AP European
History
Diagnostic Test
Answers and
Explanations

AP EUROPEAN HISTORY DIAGNOSTIC TEST ANSWER KEY

1.	D	41.	A
2.	E	42.	C
3.	C	43.	D
4.	A	44.	C
5.	B	45.	A
6.	A	46.	D
7.	E	47.	B
8.	A	48.	C
9.	C	49.	D
10.	B	50.	D
11.	B	51.	E
12.	D	52.	A
13.	C	53.	B
14.	B	54.	D
15.	D	55.	C
16.	E	56.	C
17.	A	57.	A
18.	D	58.	C
19.	C	59.	D
20.	A	60.	C
21.	E	61.	B
22.	E	62.	A
23.	B	63.	D
24.	C	64	E
25.	D	65.	C
26.	A	66.	C
27.	A	67.	D
28.	E	68.	B
29.	D	69.	C
30.	C	70.	D
31.	E	71.	E
32.	B	72.	C
33.	A	73.	A
34.	D	74.	C
35.	A	75.	B
36.	C	76.	C
37.	A	77.	D
38.	B	78.	B
39.	D	79.	D
40.	D	80.	D

80.	D	In the mid-1970s, the controversial Russian writer Alexander Solzhenitsyn had finally published his masterpiece: a book about the atrocities of life in a Siberian gulag, based on his own experiences as a political prisoner. It wasn't published in the Soviet Union, but the KGB found a copy of it and immediately stripped him of his citizenship. At that point, such a person would normally have been sent to the Siberian gulag, but with the eyes of the world upon him, and considering the subject matter of the book, the Soviet government presumably sensed the immense irony of what they would be doing. Instead, he was merely forced into exile to West Germany, at which point he ultimately travelled to the United States. This showed a strong sense of self-awareness on the part of the Soviet government.

THE DBQ EXPLAINED

The Document-Based Question (DBQ) section begins with a mandatory 15-minute reading period. During these 15 minutes, you'll want to (1) come up with some information not included in the given documents (your outside knowledge) to include in your essay, (2) get an overview of what each document means and the point of view of each author, (3) decide what opinion you are going to argue, and (4) write an outline of your essay.

The DBQ in Practice Test 1 concerns the issue of human rights during the French Revolution. You should be prepared to discuss how the French Revolution advanced the cause of human rights and also explain the ways that some individuals wanted a more narrow definition of who should be eligible to enjoy these rights. You will need to know something about human rights in France prior to the outbreak of the Revolution in 1789 and also know how the concept of human rights changed over the course of the Revolution.

The first thing you want to do, BEFORE YOU LOOK AT THE DOCUMENTS, is to brainstorm for a minute or two. Try to list everything you know (from class or leisure reading or informational television programs) about the issue of human rights in France both prior to the French Revolution and after. This list will serve as your reference to the outside information you must provide to earn a top grade.

Next, read over the documents. As you read them, take notes in the margins and underline those passages that you are certain you are going to use in your essay. Make note of the opinions and position of the document's author. If a document helps you remember a piece of outside information, add that information to your brainstorming list. If you cannot make sense of a document or it argues strongly against your position, relax! You do not need to mention every document to score well on the DBQ.

Here is what you might assess in the time you have to look over the documents.

The Documents

Document 1

This excerpt from a letter by Florence Nightingale (considered by many to be the founder of modern nursing) shows that she was instrumental in the planning of a new hospital. She mentions that it is the best thing that she's done, and she also notes her special concern for the ladies near the end. This can be connected to the rise of feminism.

Document 2

This testimony from a working-class woman is a sobering look at exactly how harsh daily life was for a person born in the lower levels of nineteenth-century society after the start of the Industrial Revolution. Most interestingly, she refers to her two children "who are too young to work," as though that were their sole purpose. She also refers to working with six other women and six boys or girls in a very wet pit, which demonstrates the stark divide between the lives of middle- and lower-class women and children.

Document 3

Samuel Smiles points out that happiness comes from one's own conduct, that government intrusion is largely negative, and that voting will have little influence upon one's life. It would be easy to use this source to indicate the perspective of the conservatives in nineteenth-century British society who opposed egalitarianism. However, it could be argued that Smiles, and others like him, also probably never worked in a rainy pit for twelve hours a day (Document 2).

Document 4

In this document, Escott announces that since the Reform Bill of 1832, which enfranchised most of the male members of English society, meritocracy has been on the rise. He also gleefully notes (using words such as *dandies* and *fops*) that the effete men of the upper classes, the ones living on inherited wealth, are going to become extinct, unless they become productive and contribute to society in some meaningful way. He appears quite optimistic for the life of the average person.

Document 5

Newgate Prison was one of the most infamous prisons in English history. It features extensively in the work of Charles Dickens, as well as many other works of literature. This illustration, by Gustave Doré, depicts just how dark and miserable it was for the mass of people who found themselves inside the English penitentiary system during this century. This document would also be a good way to mention the debtors' prisons that were so popular during this century—if you couldn't pay your bills, you were thrown behind bars, which wasn't an improvement in your quality of life.

Document 6

In contrast with Document 2, this illustration of Victorian home comforts paints a familiar picture of an ideal family: a mother ensconced safely inside the house, dressed in purest white, her three children snuggled nicely up against her. This is the *private* sphere. Standing in the doorway is a pair of men, one of whom is presumably her husband, dressed in finery, returning home from the *public* sphere. It would be worth pointing out that these people's lives seem a world away from the life of the working class (Document 2, Document 4).

Document 7

Jack London, an American, asks an important question about the British society. Why is it that, despite the massive growth of the economy during the Industrial Revolution, living conditions are so bad for so many people? He blames mismanagement of resources—a society allocating too much of its wealth to the upper tier and too little to the lower tiers.

Document 8

While the Erfurt School was based in Germany, its ideas are directly applicable to England at that time. Similar to the ideas of Document 7, the Erfurt School points out that all of society is divided into those who benefit from ownership of capital (*bourgeoisie*) and those who do not (proletariat). If that sounds familiar to you, it should; these were precisely the ideas that Karl Marx promoted in his book *The Communist Manifesto*. It would be excellent to connect that text with this document as an example of where the social and economic inequalities of nineteenth-century England inevitably led.

Document 9

The People's Charter was a manifesto written by a group of middle-class men (skilled artisans at first) who demanded better representation from the political system. It was part of the Chartist movement. The document reveals that the Chartists demanded payment for members of Parliament (nobles had never thought to pay politicians, since they were holders of inherited wealth), no property requirement (since land-owning was part of the nobility), protected voting rights, annual Parliaments, and so on. This is pretty much the definition of egalitarianism at this time.

Document 10

The Elementary Education Act of 1870 was the single biggest piece of education legislation in English history. It introduced mandatory public education for all children everywhere, which represented a massive turn in attitudes. Remember, just forty years earlier (Document 2), children had been working in factories. Interestingly, the document notes that "it will compel every parent" to educate their child, which implies that many parents didn't see the point of education yet. In that case, it seems that the Parliament was more progressive than the people.

Comments on Essay Organization

It would quite easy to show either side of this argument—that life got either better or worse for English citizens through the nineteenth century. The most shrewd choice, however, might be to straddle the topic, maintaining that life became easier in some areas, for some people, and more difficult in other areas, for other people. In fact, choosing such a "fifty-fifty" type of thesis is usually preferable, because

- It lends itself more easily to sophisticated thoughts.
- It allows you to point out contradictions (a very good thing).
- It lets you use virtually all the documents.

Another common theme to these documents is the effect of social class and gender upon one's life. Given that, it would be logical to use a thesis like this:

Throughout the Industrial Revolution and the Victorian era, the fortune of an individual depended largely upon the social class and gender to which he or she was born.

Your mileage may vary, of course, but this option would allow a lot of flexibility in your analysis. As for organization, feel free to group your essay in any of the following ways:

    Education (Documents 2, 10)
    Public works (Documents 1, 5)
    Gender (Documents 1, 2, 6)
    Political representation (Documents 3, 7, 8, 9)
    Economics (Documents 7, 8)
    Social Class (Documents 4, 6, 7, 8, 10)

Another method of organization that seems to work for many students—and you may have heard this before—is to use the acronym PERSIA.

> *Politics*
> *Economics*
> *Religion*
> *Social*
> *Intellectual*
> *Artistic*

Whatever you choose, know that there are a number of ways to cut up this cake. Don't forget to acknowledge the bias in at least three different documents.

Furthermore, one of the easiest (and necessary) ways to improve your score is to include outside information not found in the documents. Nineteenth-century England is rife with specific people, places, and events that could be worked into this essay. Here is a list, in no particular order, of such examples.

- The lives of the peasantry in eighteenth-century England were ruled largely by their attachment to the land, by the sun, by the seasons. This ended with the enclosure movement and the rise of the cottage industry, and then transformed utterly with the Second Industrial Revolution. Though technically outside the scope of this essay, these changes could be used in the introduction as background.
- The literary works of Charles Dickens, such as *Great Expectations* and *Oliver Twist*, which illustrate the inhumanity of urban living conditions
- The technological advancements that made the Second Industrial Revolution possible, such as the Bessemer process
- The invention of the railroad system, which slowly became used not only for transporting coal but also for transporting humans more efficiently
- The Midlothian Campaign, in which Benjamin Disraeli and William Gladstone, candidates for prime minister, fought for popular votes. It was the first ever political campaign, and it was largely waged from the back of trains.
- Philosophers who attempted to wrestle with this question, such as Jeremy Bentham and John Stuart Mill (*On Liberty*). Also, Karl Marx (*The Communist Manifesto*) lived in London for part of his life.
- Emily Pankhurst, the most prominent leader of the feminist suffrage movement, which was born in the nineteenth century but didn't flower until the early twentieth century
- Other political events within and following the Chartist Movement that gradually enlarged the enfranchised voters. These include the Petition of 1842, the General Strike, the Reform Act of 1867 (under Disraeli's conservative government), and the Ballot Act of 1872 (which gave the secret ballot).
- The harsh life experienced by those unlucky enough to be sent to the workhouses, which attempted to give accommodation and employment to those who couldn't support themselves

The Free-Response Essay Questions Explained

Question 1

1. Describe the ways in which the modern notion of individualism was born on the Italian peninsula during the period from 1450 to 1550.

Essay Notes

If you would like to discuss the ways via the popular literature, you can bring up these examples.

- *Oration on the Dignity of Man*, by Pico della Mirandola. It's the clearest manifesto of the Italian Renaissance.
- Lorenzo Valla, the father of modern textual criticism. Never before had an individual felt quite so free to individually verify or reject tradition. He exposed the Donation of Constantine (which gave the papacy much of its power) as a forgery. He attacked the Catholic Church's 1500-year-old tradition of scholastic-Aristotlean thought from a linguistic point of view. He even compared different translations of the New Testament, laying the groundwork for later Biblical criticism.
- Castiglione's *The Courtier* was a handbook containing advice to those men who wished to "polish" themselves for success in courtly life. (Sample advice: "Don't clean your teeth with your finger in public.")
- *The Prince*, by Niccolò Machiavelli. Morality aside, it could be seen as a textbook promoting individual political success.

If you would like to discuss the ways via visual arts, you can bring up these examples.

- Background, perspective, and proportion were incorporated into European paintings for the first time. Because they were drawn from an individual's point of view, these works attained a measure of realism that had been missing in the flat fields and cookie-cutter figures of medieval art. Brunelleschi, for example, used perspective beautifully in his Baptistry in Florence.
- The *David*, by Michelangelo. All fig leaf jokes aside, it stands as an example of the most careful attention to anatomical detail that the art world had ever seen, and continues to do so today.
- Artists began signing their own work.
- The communal-based guild system died a slow death, replaced by a more entrepreneurial system of taking commissions for money (or what today we would call hustling for grants).
- *Vitruvian Man,* by Leonardo da Vinci, was a reworking of an older sketch by an architect Vitruvius that purported to use geometry to analyze the individual human body.

If you would like to discuss the ways via the popular literature, you can discuss the *studia humanitatis*, which was a new learning curriculum that tossed overboard the old medieval religious system. The new system focused on history, grammar, rhetoric, logic, mathematics, natural philosophy, and classical literature. It created graduates who were better prepared to argue their point of view in public, a very individualistic goal.

Question 2

2. Analyze the different reactions to the Protestant Reformation in Southern and Northern Europe.

Essay Notes

The reactions in Southern Europe are best exemplified by the following:

- The Council of Trent (1545–1563) was supposed to be a long look into Catholic dogma by its leadership. While it did ultimately end the sale of indulgences, it did nothing to change the portions of the Catholic theology that were being challenged by the Protestants. These elements included the power of the priests (Luther had proposed a "priesthood of all believers") and the papacy as the ultimate moral authority. Protestants had been turning to the Bible for that authority, partly because Gutenberg's printing press was making books more widely available.
- The founding of the Society of Jesus, a.k.a. the Jesuits. Ignatius Loyola, Francis Xavier, and other young Spanish men formed this order of priests dedicated to near-military discipline for the spreading of Catholic theology. Pope Paul III legitimatized them, and their influence was strongest in Spain, Portugal, Italy, and the New World (though they did prevent Poland and Lithuania from going totally Protestant). Other religious orders were also founded, such as the Capuchins.
- The Inquisition, though it had always existed in the Catholic Church, was used to punish those who had been found guilty of Protestant heresy. It was a Catholic institution, administered by the Congregation of the Doctrine of the Faith, which was composed of church leaders. It also oversaw the local inquisitions, which were much more numerous in the South than in the North.
- While the Inquisition took on special significance in Spain, with the horrendous *autos-da-fé* (public burning) and the forced conversions of Jews and Muslims, this did *not* occur in reaction to the Protestant Reformation and occurred independent of the Catholic Church. Emphasis on this aspect of the Inquisition wouldn't support the question.

The reactions in Northern Europe are best exemplified by the following:

- The Dutch Revolt occurred in 1566 when Protestant forces, led by William of Orange, rose up against the Catholic Spanish monarchical forces that controlled the country thanks to the crafty marriages that made up the Habsburg empire. The Spanish King Phillip II initially suppressed the rebellion, but after many decades the northern part of the country eventually became the independent Netherlands, which was solidly Protestant.
- The Peace of Augsburg settled the question of how principalities in southern Germany (also known inaccurately as the Holy Roman Empire, since they were neither holy nor Roman nor an empire) would decide upon the question of this new Lutheranism spreading amongst the peasants. Their decision: Each prince would decide for his own territory, and no principality could interfere with another's decision. They essentially rolled out the red carpet for Protestantism, since the people had turned *en masse* away from Catholicism.
- Following that, the Thirty Years' War was initially fueled by conflict between the Calvinist League of Evangelical Union and its counterpart, the Catholic League. It also took place in the Holy Roman Empire.

- In France, the French Protestants were known as Hugenots. Though formally recognized by the Catholic crown, they were subject to periodic attacks, the worst of which was the St. Bartholomew's Day Massacre, in which thousands of Hugenots were slaughtered by Catholics in Paris. Following that, King Henry IV issued the Edict of Nantes, which supposedly gave them full equality in the eyes of the law, but they once again saw this protection eroded under King Louis XIV, and eventually most Hugenots fled to the countryside or emigrated to the New World.
- There was backlash from mainstream Protestants against extremist groups. The Anabaptists, for example, fled to the New World and eventually became the Amish. And in England, the Puritans felt that the Church of England—Protestant, established by Henry VIII so he could get a divorce—hadn't gone far enough. Teaming with the Scottish Presbyterians, this led to the English Civil War, during which Europe's first Protestant, Oliver Cromwell, took the "throne" (but refused to call it that).

Question 3

3. Describe the changing nature of the relationship between the Stuart kings and English Parliament in the period 1600 to 1715.

Essay Notes

The big story of the era, of course, is how the Stuart monarchs grappled with the rise of Parliament. It wasn't easy, but over 115 years, power shifted from the monarchy to Parliament, and the king became seen not as divinely ordained, but as subject to a popular constitution.

An essay on this subject should address some of the following specific points:

- **Queen Elizabeth**, the last Tudor regent, started the process by dying childless. Having executed the Catholic Mary, Queen of Scots (a "frenemy" whom Elizabeth had been protecting from angry Scots despite Mary's plotting against her), Elizabeth recognized Mary's son, James, as her heir. Unlike his mother, James was raised a Protestant, and while he was known as James VI in Scotland, when he assumed the English throne he was known as...
- **James I**. As the first Stuart, and the personal symbol of the new supposed political union between England and Scotland, he suffered from a somewhat inflated sense of himself. He had also been reading a lot of French philosophy about royal absolutism and the divine right of kings, which he took to heart. His relationship with Parliament was almost entirely one-sided, with James assuming total powers and mocking the institution. However, Parliament held one card: the power of the purse. It controlled spending, and whenever James needed more money to run his side of government, he was forced to ask Parliament for money, a scenario that occurred often.
- **Charles I**, his son, exacerbated these same problems by making a series of stupid military blunders that forced him to ask for even more money than his father had. He had committed himself to a war with Spain—which was still embarrassed by the destruction of their Armada decades earlier—but lost a couple of expensive battles. He tried to force wealthy nobles to give him a loan and then threw several members of Parliament into prison when they wouldn't comply, all of which resulted in his being forced to sign the **Petition of Rights**, outlawing such tyrannical measures. Eventually, after having the Speaker of the House literally held down in his chair, Charles I dissolved Parliament for eleven years (a period known as the Personal Rule of Charles) and ruled England as a tyrant, raising money by extending a "ship money" tax even to people who didn't live near ships or

the ocean. When he finally called Parliament back into session, in 1640, it lasted only three weeks (the **Short Parliament**). Charles called the next session later that same year to pay what amounted to blackmail; the Scots had destroyed his own ragtag army and were now demanding money for their "assistance" in (read: occupation of) northern England. This Parliament lasted twenty years (the **Long Parliament**), and it marked the end of the monarchy. It impeached and executed Charles's two chief ministers, abolished the king's special prerogative courts, supported the Grand Remonstrance (a list of complaints), and demanded that the royal ministers be people that Parliament could trust. Charles I found all of this untenable. He attempted to arrest five leading members of Parliament, but they slipped away. All of this culminated in…

- **The English Civil War**. The Royalists versus the Parliamentarians. It lasted for several years, and Charles I was eventually taken captive by the Scots and "sold" to the Parliamentarians for 100,000 pounds. Back in England, he secretly negotiated with the Scots to support his Royalists in another battle (the Second English Civil War), but upon the Scots' loss in 1649, he was captured and executed by Parliamentarian forces.

- **Oliver Cromwell** wasn't a king, but it would be worth mentioning his eleven-year interregnum as a good counterexample of the difficulty of working with Parliament. Known as the Lord Protector of the United Commonwealth, this Puritan ruler eventually gave up cooperating with Parliament, and instead relied upon several military generals.

- When Cromwell died, the political crisis was acute enough that the surviving son of the executed Stuart king, **Charles II**, was invited to rule. His tensions with Parliament mostly centered upon religious issues, primarily the Clarendon Code, a pro-Anglican set of laws that he signed despite his desire for religious tolerance.

- His younger brother, **James II**, had a much rougher time during his short reign. A strong Catholic, he was determined to make the kingdom legally safe for Catholics by issuing the Declaration of Indulgence, which resulted in strong opposition from Anglican-dominated Parliament. The English elites invited **Mary**, James II's daughter, along with her husband **William of Orange,** to invade England and depose her own father in what has become known as the **Glorious Revolution**.

- The final piece of the puzzle came with the establishment of the Bill of Rights (limiting many royal prerogative rights), the Act of Toleration (a compromise bill regarding the rights of Catholics versus Protestants), the Mutiny Act (which brought the army under Parliamentary control), the Act of Settlement (which prevented the Stuarts from ever regaining the throne), and the Act of Union (which officially unified England and Scotland, creating Great Britain).

Question 4

4. Analyze the extent to which Napoleon's policies reflected Enlightenment principles.

Essay Notes

Given that the Enlightenment thinkers valued logic and reason, Napoleon stands as both an enlightened ruler and an imperialistic tyrant. An essay on this subject could either be one-sided or a mixture of both positions. In any case, it should touch on some or all of the following ideas:

- Agree: Napoleon was "enlightened."
  o In ending feudalism completely, Napoleon went a step beyond what enlightened despots such as Catherine the Great and Frederick the Great had attempted to do. Within the military, he promoted officers based on their performance, not their class of birth. This is **meritocracy** in action for the first time, and it reflects his own humble birth on the distant island of Corsica, far from the salons of Paris.

o He safeguarded all forms of private property, an idea lifted directly from John Locke.

o He upheld equality before the law, regardless of social class.

o He supported scientific research.

o He supported religious toleration (though many Enlightenment thinkers doubted the necessity of any religion whatsoever).

o Many of these advances were enshrined in the **Napoleonic Code**, which was at that time the most progressive legal document in history.

- Disagree: Napoleon was an imperialist tyrant.

o He named himself "**consul for life**" and eventually emperor, mocking the notion of representative democracy.

o He declared Catholicism the official religion of France, restoring ecclesiastical influence in the country through the **Concordat of 1801**.

o He censored and controlled the press and personally regulated the public school system.

o He suppressed political enemies through the use of spies and surprise arrests.

o His equality before the law extended only to men, who had extensive rights over their wives and children.

o Despite his supposed meritocracy, he also employed nepotism, choosing blood relatives to head up many satellite kingdoms. He appointed his brother Louis to rule the Netherlands, his brother Jérôme to rule Westphalia (a region in Germany), his brother Joseph to rule Spain, his stepson Eugène to rule the Kingdom of Italy, and his brother-in-law Joachim Murat to rule the Kingdom of Naples.

o He reinstituted slavery in Haiti.

o His series of wars killed about one in five Frenchmen, showing a massive disregard for the lives of his citizenry.

Question 5

5. Analyze the causes of the Russian Revolution.

Essay Notes

An essay on this subject should touch on some or all of the following:

- For two hundred years, the **Romanov dynasty** had been oppressing the lower classes in various ways. While it's true that the reforms of Alexander II had brought the emancipation of the serfs, that emancipation also imposed harsh economic conditions on the peasants and did not satisfy their need for farmland. Instead, they were drawn by industrial jobs into urban centers. For the first time, the peasantry was within close living quarters of each other (as opposed to being spread out in the hinterlands), where this exploited working class was a receptive audience for radical ideas. Anger and resentment spread quickly.

- Western technology had been adopted by Russian elites for over 100 years, which brought all sorts of Western ideas about humanitarianism. This led to a portion of the intelligentsia to grow politically radical, especially in universities. **Anarchism**, for example, flourished, with **Mikhail Bakunin** being its most famous proponent.

- Russian Orthodox Christianity had been static for centuries, and its ignorant clergy often persecuted religious dissenters. Anti-Semitism had been growing for decades, particularly with the **pogroms** of Nicholas II and the publication of the **Protocols of the Elders of Zion**, a fake document purportedly showing the Jewish desire to achieve world domination. This caused many Jews to radicalize, demanding the establishment of a homeland where they could be free from such persecution.
- Rumors circulated that Tsarina Alexandra, who was German by birth, was cooperating with the Germans while Tsar Nicolas II was guiding the mobilization on the Eastern Front. Rumors also said that she had turned over day-to-day running of the country to **Rasputin**, her corrupted but hypnotic lover. Also, the Imperial Army's losses against Germany made the tsar, who took personal responsibility for the outcome of the war, appear weak. Most importantly, the war took millions of men from the fields, which resulted in reduced crop yields and widespread hunger, causing further unrest in the cities.

Question 6

6. Analyze the expansion of European power during the imperialist era.

Essay Notes

Any essay worth its salt will begin with **King Leopold II of Belgium**, who established the giant colony of the Belgian Congo for his personal gain. He forced the natives to extract sap from rubber trees, cutting off the hands of those who didn't meet their quotas. Millions lost their lives. After an international outcry, he reluctantly turned over control of the enterprise to his own government.

- **Social Darwinism** was the intellectual idea in vogue, with the implication (sometimes not so subtle) that Africans were no better than children and that Europeans were responsible for civilizing them. This was exemplified in the poem "The White Man's Burden" by Rudyard Kipling.
- At the **Berlin Conference of 1885**, the European attendees resolved to address this responsibility by treating the natives with care, a decision that was not necessarily followed. They also determined that to possess a piece of African territory, a colonial power needed to actually place people there to claim it.
- For well over a century, Britain had been economically tied to India through the British East India Company, but as the nineteenth century wore on, the English established political dominance as well. Following the **Sepoy Rebellion** in 1857, colonial control became more centralized, with many more independent states falling under their control. To facilitate their access to India, England established a protectorate over the **Suez Canal**, which had been built by the French, who in return received a guarantee of zero British intervention in French colonies in North Africa. Thus, the longstanding and unchallenged French influence in Algeria, Tunisia, Morocco, and other areas.
- In China, Britain insisted on trading opium (derived from Kashmir through India) to the Chinese in exchange for silk and tea. Upset by the opium dens that littered the port cities, the Han dynasty attempted to stop the trade. Thus ensued the **Opium Wars**, which ended with the utter defeat of the Chinese. At the **Treaty of Nanking**, the British guaranteed the continued trade of opium— and also seized the island of Hong Kong as a colony. (It was returned to Chinese sovereignty in 1997.)
- Similar to the British experience in India, the Dutch first expanded into present-day **Indonesia** through the United East India Company, extracting rubber and spices. Their hold upon this archipelago was much more tenuous, however, owing to the geographic isolation of many of the outer islands.

- The English and the Russians competed for control of **Afghanistan**, owing to its important traditional position as "the crossroads of Asia."
- As a result of its victory in **the Spanish-American War**, the United States took possession of Guam, Puerto Rico, and the Philippines.
- Imitating the imperialistic fad, Japan fought Russia over Manchuria and Korea. The resulting **Russo-Japanese War** saw an unexpected Japanese victory, and the subsequent Japanese control of Korea for the next thirty-five years.

Part II
About the
AP European
History
Exam

THE STRUCTURE OF THE AP EUROPEAN HISTORY EXAM

The AP European History Exam consists of three sections. First, you will fill out several forms; this takes 10–15 minutes. Then, you will complete an 80-question multiple-choice section, for which you are given 55 minutes. Afterward, you will be given a break of approximately 10 minutes. This break is the only one you get during the test. Then there is the Document-Based Question (DBQ) section, which consists of a mandatory 15-minute reading period, followed by a 45-minute writing period. Finally, there are two free-response essay questions. You have 70 minutes to complete both. We will discuss each of these sections in detail in the following chapters.

To do	Time
Fill out forms	10–15 minutes
80-question multiple-choice section	55 minutes
Break	10 minutes
Document-Based Question (DBQ) reading period	15 minutes
Document-Based Question (DBQ) writing period	45 minutes
Two free-response essay questions	70 minutes

HOW THE AP EUROPEAN HISTORY EXAM IS SCORED

How the Multiple-Choice Section Is Scored

The Multiple-Choice section of the AP European History Exam consists of 80 questions and you have 55 minutes to complete this section. This section is called Section I. You receive one point for each question you answer correctly. You receive no points for a question that you leave blank or answer incorrectly. So if you are completely unsure of a question, guess! However it is always best to use process of elimination (more on that later) to narrow down your choices and make an educated guess. This section accounts for 50% for your total grade on the AP European History Exam.

How the Essay Section is Scored

Section II, the Essay Section of the AP European History Exam (or as they call it the free-response section), includes two types of essay questions: Document-Based Questions (DBQ) and thematic questions. In your AP European History Exam you'll encounter one DBQ and two thematic questions (chosen by you from an assortment of six different possible questions). We'll go into more detail about these question types later in the book. As far as scoring, these essays are read and graded by AP Readers and within this section, the DBQ essay is weighted 45 percent and the two thematic essays together are weighted 55 percent. The full essay section accounts for 50 percent of your final AP European History Exam grade (and the Multiple-Choice section accounts for the other half, as we discussed above).

How the DBQ Is Scored

The College Board uses a "core-scoring method" that is graded on a 1–9 scale. This means that for each DBQ, you can earn up to six points by performing what the graders consider basic tasks, such as using the majority of documents or displaying a point of view or bias in at least three of the documents. In addition, you can earn up to three more points in what they call the "expanded core," by excelling in more difficult areas. To earn any points from the expanded core, students must earn all six points in the basic core.

The following chart should make this scoring system somewhat more understandable.

Basic Core Points

You may earn a total of six points by earning one point in each of the following areas:

Core Skill	Points
1) Provides a clearly stated and appropriate thesis that addresses all parts of the question. **This thesis should not merely be a restating of the question.**	1
2) Discusses a majority of the documents individually and specifically	1
3) Demonstrates an understanding of the basic meaning of the documents (you may misinterpret no more than one document)	1
4) Supports thesis with an appropriate interpretation of the majority of the documents	1
5) Shows point of view or bias in at least three documents	1
6) Analyzes documents by organizing them into at least three appropriate groups	1

Expanded Core Points

If you earn a 6 on the Basic Core, you can then earn up to *three* additional points by displaying some of the following skills:

> 7) Having a clear, analytical, and comprehensive thesis
>
> 8) Using every document or almost every document
>
> 9) Skillfully using documents as evidence
>
> 10) Displaying an understanding of the nuances within the documents
>
> 11) Discussing bias or point of view in at least four documents
>
> 12) Analyzing documents by creating additional groupings or using some other advanced method
>
> 13) Incorporating outside historical knowledge in the essay
>
> 14) Addressing all aspects of the question thoroughly

What About My Final Score?

Your score on the computer-scored multiple-choice questions is combined with the AP readers' scores on the free-response questions and then the weighted raw scores are summed to give a composite score. The composite score is then converted to a number grade on the AP's special 5-point scale:

AP Grade	Qualification
5	Extremely well qualified
4	Well qualified
3	Qualified
3	Possibly qualified
1	No recommendation

AP Exam grades of 5 are equivalent to A grades in the corresponding college course. AP Exam grades of 4 are equivalent to grades of A–, B+, and B in college, and AP Exam grades of 3 are equivalent to grades of B–, C+, and C in college.

OVERVIEW OF CONTENT TOPICS

The College Board provides a breakdown of the exam's questions by era and by general subject matter. This breakdown will not appear in your test booklet. It comes from the preparatory material the College Board publishes. Here it is:

Breakdown by Era

	Percent of Questions	Number of Questions
1450 to 1815	50	40
1815 to 1900	25	20
1900 to present	25	20

Breakdown by General Subject

	Percent of Questions	Number of Questions
Political and diplomatic themes	30–35	24–28
Cultural and intellectual themes	30–35	24–28
Social and economic themes	30–35	24–28

As you can see, the test seeks to achieve a measure of balance between the period from the High Renaissance to Napoleon and the period after 1815. Also, note that equal emphasis is placed on political/diplomatic history, cultural and intellectual questions, and social and economic themes. Remember this as you study.

HOW AP EXAMS ARE USED

Different colleges use AP Exams in different ways, so it is important that you go to a particular college's web site to determine how it uses AP Exams. The three items below represent the main ways in which AP Exam scores can be used:

- **College Credit.** Some colleges will give you college credit if you score well on an AP Exam. These credits count towards your graduation requirements, meaning that you can take fewer courses while in college. Given the cost of college, this could be quite a benefit, indeed.

- **Satisfy Requirements.** Some colleges will allow you to "place out" of certain requirements if you do well on an AP Exam, even if they do not give you actual college credits. For example, you might not need to take an introductory-level course, or perhaps you might not need to take a class in a certain discipline at all.

- **Admissions Plus.** Even if your AP Exam will not result in college credit or even allow you to place out of certain courses, most colleges will respect your decision to push yourself by taking an AP Course or even an AP Exam outside of a course. A high score on an AP Exam shows mastery of more difficult content than is taught in many high school courses, and colleges may take that into account during the admissions process.

OTHER RESOURCES

There are many resources available to help you improve your score on the AP European History Exam, not the least of which are your teachers. If you are taking an AP class, you may be able to get extra attention from your teacher, such as obtaining feedback on your essays. If you are not in an AP course, reach out to a teacher who teaches European History, and ask if the teacher will review your essays or otherwise help you with content.

Another wonderful resource is **AP Central**, the official site of the AP Exams. The scope of the information at this site is quite broad and includes the following items:

- Course Description, which includes details on what content is covered and sample questions
- Full-length practice test
- Essay prompts from previous years
- AP European History Exam tips

The AP Central home page address is **http://apcentral.collegeboard.com**.

The AP European History Exam Course home page address is **http://apcentral. collegeboard.com/apc/public/courses/teachers_corner/2122.html**.

Finally, **The Princeton Review** offers tutoring for the AP European History Exam. Our expert instructors can help you refine your strategic approach and add to your content knowledge. For more information, call 1-800-2REVIEW.

DESIGNING YOUR STUDY PLAN

As part of the Introduction, you identified some areas of potential improvement. Let's now delve further into your performance on Test 1, with the goal of developing a study plan appropriate to your needs and time commitment.

Read the answers and explanations associated with the Multiple-Choice questions (starting at page 31). After you have done so, think about the following items:

- Review the Overview of Content Topics on page 59 and, next to each one, indicate your rank of the topic as follows: "1" means "I need a lot of work on this," "2" means "I need to beef up my knowledge," and "3" means "I know this topic well."

- How many days/weeks/months away is your AP European History Exam?

- What time of day is your best, most focused study time?

- How much time per day/week/month will you devote to preparing for your AP European History Exam?

- When will you do this preparation? (Be as specific as possible: Mondays and Wednesdays from 3 to 4 P.M., for example)

- What are your overall goals in using this book?

DID YOU HEAR ABOUT TEST CHANGES?

The College Board recently announced that the AP European History Course and Exam will be changing soon. The redesigned course begins in fall 2015 followed by the revised AP European History Exam in May 2016.

The new test gives AP classes flexibility to choose topics to cover in depth, rather than racing through 500 plus years of history. The redesign will emphasize a deeper understanding of European history topics using 9 historical thinking skills. In addition, the multiple-choice questions will go from having 5 possible answer choices to 4 possible answer choices.

The new AP European History exam will consist of four parts:

- 55 multiple-choice questions (55 minutes, 40% of score)

- 4 short answer questions (45 minutes, 20% of score)

- 1 document-based question (60 minutes, 25% of score)

- 1 long essay question (35 minutes, 15% of score)

This book is a preparation guide for the May 2015 AP European History Exam. Visit the AP Central section of the College Board's website (**APcentral.college-board.com**) for updates about the changing AP European History course and exam.

Part III
Test-Taking Strategies for the AP European History Exam

Chapter 1
How to Approach
Multiple-Choice
Questions

HOW TO APPROACH MULTIPLE-CHOICE QUESTIONS

The Basics

The directions for the multiple-choice section of the AP European History Exam are pretty simple. They read as follows:

Directions: Each of the questions or incomplete statements below is followed by five suggested answers or completions. Select the one that is best in each case, and then fill in the corresponding oval on the answer sheet.

In short, you are being asked to do what you have done on lots of other multiple-choice exams. Pick the right answer and then fill in the appropriate bubble on a separate answer sheet. You will *not* be given credit for answers you record in your test booklet (e.g., by circling them) but not on your answer sheet. The section consists of 80 questions. You will be given 55 minutes to work on the section.

The College Board provides a breakdown of the exam's questions by era and by general subject matter. This breakdown will *not* appear in your test booklet. It comes from the preparatory material the College Board publishes. We glanced at this earlier in the book, but let's give it another look now:

Breakdown by Era

	Percent of Questions	Number of Questions
1450 to 1815	50	40
1815 to 1900	25	20
1900 to present	25	20

Breakdown by General Subject

	Percent of Questions	Number of Questions
Political and diplomatic themes	30–35	24–28
Cultural and intellectual themes	30–35	24–28
Social and economic themes	30–35	24–28

Types of Questions

The majority of questions on the multiple-choice section of the test are similar to this:

3. The Dreyfus Affair had political repercussions that lasted well into the twentieth century because

    (A) it helped deepen the religious and political conflicts that plagued the Third Republic

    (B) it created a consensus in French politics which eventually led to a strengthening of the Third Republic

    (C) it reminded people of the German threat

    (D) it ultimately helped the French army get ready for the First World War

    (E) it led to a fundamental overhaul of the French political system

Answers to sample questions appear near the end of this chapter, just before the Summary.

Sometimes, the College Board makes the questions a little trickier. One way it does this is by phrasing a question so that four answers are correct and one is incorrect. We call these questions "NOT/EXCEPT" questions because they usually contain one of those words (in capital letters, so they're harder to miss). Look at the following example:

6. All of the following led to the Russian Revolution of 1917 EXCEPT

    (A) the outbreak of World War I

    (B) the failure of autocratic government

    (C) growing disenchantment of the intellectual class

    (D) decline in the rate of industrialization in the decade leading up to 1917

    (E) the failure of the 1905 revolution to bring about genuine political reform

Once or twice during the multiple-choice section, you will be asked to interpret an illustration—often a map, political cartoon, painting, or poster. These questions are usually easy. The key is *not* to read too much between the lines.

Here is an example:

Source: Daily Mail

45. The political cartoon above implies that

    (A) Hitler broke his promise not to destroy the German Communist Party

    (B) Hitler betrayed his 1939 nonaggression pact with Stalin

    (C) Stalin was warned by the Western Allies that Hitler was dangerous

    (D) a nonaggression pact with Germany was fraught with problems

    (E) Hitler and Stalin deserved one another

Finally, one or two questions on the test will ask you to interpret a graph or chart. Again, these are usually very straightforward, and the most important thing for you to do is *not* over-interpret the data. The correct answer will be indisputably supported by the information in the chart.

Here's an example:

Rate of Industrial Production in Great Britain
(percentage increase per decade)

1800 to 1810	22.9
1810 to 1820	38.6
1830 to 1840	47.2
1840 to 1850	37.4
1850 to 1860	39.3
1860 to 1870	27.8
1870 to 1880	33.2
1880 to 1890	17.4
1890 to 1900	17.9

13. Which of the following conclusions can be drawn from the information presented in the chart above?

(A) The drop in industrial production in the 1860s was due to the American Civil War.

(B) The rate of industrial production remained steady throughout the century.

(C) Great Britain's industrial production remained higher than the rest of Europe's.

(D) By the last decades of the century, the rate of industrial production was in an irreversible decline.

(E) The period between 1830 and 1860 witnessed the greatest increase in industrial production.

No Military History and No Trivial Pursuit

Here's some good news. The AP European History Exam doesn't ask specifically about military history. You will *never* see a question on the AP exam like the one below:

16. During the First World War, the Battle of Passchendaele

(A) was a British defeat due to the weakening of their right flank at a critical time

(B) ended with a German counterattack and breakthrough of the British lines

(C) was a British defeat due to insufficient artillery support

(D) witnessed the last attempt by the British to blast their way through the German lines without the element of surprise

(E) was postponed for four weeks due to the inclement weather

Although the British assault on German positions at the Battle of Passchendaele serves as an important example of the foolhardiness of Britain's military leadership, you won't be asked about it on the test. The AP European History Exam does not ask about military strategy per se. When it asks about war, the questions concern the political or social implications of a war or the introduction of new technology rather than strategic questions. The correct answer, by the way, is (D).

Also, AP European History questions never test rote memorization *only*. You have to know your facts to do well on this test; the questions, however, always ask for information in the context of larger historical trends. Therefore, you will *never* see a question like this one:

21. The treaty that marked the end of the Thirty Years' War was called the

    (A) Peace of Ghent
    (B) Peace of Versailles
    (C) Peace of Paris
    (D) Peace of Westphalia
    (E) Peace of Augsburg

Chronological Order and the Order of Difficulty

Here's some more good news: The folks who write the AP European History Exam organize the multiple-choice section in a predictable way. Questions will be organized in groups of approximately four to seven. Each group of questions will be presented in roughly chronological order. For example, the first question in a group may ask about the Renaissance and Reformation; the second, about the Industrial Revolution and its effect on society; the third, about the French Revolution and Napoleon; and so on. You will notice a sharp break in chronology when you move from one group of questions to another. When you see a question about the Brezhnev Doctrine followed by a question on Renaissance humanism, you will know that you have moved on to a new grouping.

Remember that easy questions have easy answers. Do not choose an obscure or trivial answer for an easy question. Remember also that all questions are worth an equal amount toward your final score. Therefore, it is important that you go slowly enough in the beginning so that you do not make careless mistakes on the easier questions. The points you lose early in the test will be much harder to make up later when the questions get more difficult.

Ask yourself how you can use this information to your advantage as you look at the following three questions (the answer choices have been omitted purposely):

17. The Prussian victory over Austria in 1866 helped pave the way for

18. The Paris Commune came in the wake of the collapse of

19. By the end of the nineteenth century, British politics were dominated by

Here's what you may have figured out: Because the test goes in order of difficulty, and because these are questions 17, 18, and 19 out of 80, these three questions are relatively easy. When you actually answer these questions, this information should give you confidence. Second, from reading the first and third questions, you should have realized that the Paris Commune took place some time between 1866 and the end of the nineteenth century. If you had forgotten about the Paris Commune, this information should help you find the correct answer, or at least eliminate a few incorrect answers. Now let's look at those three questions *with* the answer choices:

17. The Prussian victory over Austria in 1866 led to

   (A) the reentry of Great Britain into European affairs to check Prussian expansion
   (B) Prussian domination over the Northern German states
   (C) an alliance between France and Austria
   (D) Serbian attacks on Austria
   (E) the loss of Alsace and Lorraine

18. The rise of the Paris Commune was the result of

   (A) the fall of the Orleans monarchy in 1848
   (B) political disagreements that arose following the collapse of the French Second Empire
   (C) a large influx of unemployed agricultural workers into the capital
   (D) anger and fear following the outbreak of a massive cholera epidemic in the city
   (E) the collapse of the Paris stock exchange

19. By the end of the nineteenth century, British politics were dominated by

   (A) the Liberal and Conservative parties
   (B) extraparliamentary pressure groups
   (C) a series of coalition governments
   (D) the Conservative and Labour parties
   (E) political infighting within the House of Lords

Here's How to Crack It

Because you know that these are relatively easy questions, you can eliminate any answers that would require you to know something trivial. Furthermore, the correct answers will affirm a basic principle of European history during the era in question, and the incorrect answers should contain information that clearly identifies them as incorrect.

Consider **question 17**. We know that one of the main themes in nineteenth-century European history is the development of nation-states in Italy and Germany. The last stage of German unification was the Franco-Prussian War of 1870, at which time France was defeated, in part because it was diplomatically isolated and therefore had to face Prussia alone. That would eliminate choices (A) and (C) as well as (E), because the loss of Alsace and Lorraine followed the French defeat. Choice (D) would also not be the likely answer because it does not address this larger theme of German unification. The correct answer is (B).

Now, let's look at **question 18**. The chronological order of the questions reveals that the Paris Commune occurred sometime between 1866 and the end of the nineteenth century. Therefore, we can easily eliminate (A) because it occurred prior to the period in question. To successfully answer this question, you need to be aware of one of the most critical events that took place in France during this period—the rise of the French Third Republic following the collapse of the Second Empire of Napoleon III after the Franco-Prussian War of 1870. This Republic, you may recall, was beset with a host of problems including, in its earliest days, a radical revolution in the streets of Paris following the Franco-Prussian War. Therefore, we should choose (B).

Question 19 asks about the state of British politics in the late-Victorian period. One of the things you should be aware of concerning this time period is that British politics were remarkably stable. You can eliminate (B) because, although there were extraparliamentary groups at work during this time, such as organizations to bring about women's suffrage, there is no indication that they dominated British politics. Answer (C) implies that British politics rested on a precarious balance of power among assorted political parties, something that was simply not the case. Choice (E) also implies a measure of instability, while (D) is not correct because the Labour party did not emerge as a major player in British politics until the twentieth century. The correct choice is (A).

The Big Picture

In the explanations for questions 17–19 above, we hinted at one of the most important characteristics of AP European History multiple-choice questions. The questions and answers are designed to illustrate **basic principles** of European history. Multiple-choice questions will NOT ask about exceptions to historical trends; the test ignores these, because the test writers are trying to determine whether you have mastered the important generalizations that can be drawn from history. They do not want to know whether you have memorized your textbook (they already know that you haven't).

Therefore, you should always keep the **big picture** in mind as you take this exam. Even if you cannot remember the specific event or concept being tested, you should be able to answer the question by remembering the general social and political trends of the era.

Let's look at this illustrative example:

68. In his *Institutes of the Christian Religion,* Calvin argued that from the beginning of time, God

  (A) allowed humans to select their own path to salvation, provided that it included some degree of faith
  (B) knew few would be granted salvation unless they performed charitable works
  (C) selected those who would be saved and those who would be condemned, and that human actions play no role in this
  (D) operated as the divine creator but played no real role in the daily workings of this world
  (E) had prevailed upon the Catholic Church to do his heavenly bidding here on Earth

Here's How to Crack It

The first thing you should notice is that this is question number 68, so it's pretty difficult. At first glance, this question appears to assume that you have read Calvin's *Institutes*, something I doubt you got around to doing. (You probably didn't even read the SparkNotes). The question, however, is not really that tricky. What it is really asking you is whether you understand the fundamentals of John Calvin's theology. Calvin believed God selected only a very few individuals to be saved. Nothing these individuals did affected their own ultimate salvation, because to imply they had a role in it would mean that God's authority was not total, something Calvin did not accept. Choices (A) and (B) are therefore incorrect, as they both imply some measure of human free will. Choice (D) could not be correct; it represents the Deist point of view dating from the eighteenth-century Enlightenment and bears little resemblance to what a sixteenth-century theologian like Calvin would have believed. (E) is clearly incorrect; Calvin was a Protestant and therefore rejected the teachings of the Catholic Church. The correct answer is (C), which illustrates a "big picture" principle, the primacy for Protestants of faith over works.

Process of Elimination and Guessing

There will be times, however, when you can eliminate one or more clearly wrong answers and still have more than one reasonable answer choice left over. You may not be able to decide which one is right. When this happens, you should guess. Does this advice take you by surprise? Lots of students think that they should never guess on an exam. But even the College Board will tell you that's not true. As we mentioned earlier, AP exams, as of May 2011, will no longer have any sort of "guessing penalty" for every incorrect answer. Instead, students will be assessed only on the total number of correct questions. A lot of AP materials, even those you receive in your AP class, may not include this information. It is really important to remember that if you are running out of time, you need to fill in all the bubbles before the time for the multiple-choice section is up. Even if you don't plan to spend a lot of time on every question, and even if you have no idea what the correct answer is, you need to fill something in. We don't recommend random guessing as an overall strategy, but taking smart guesses at the right time can substantially increase your raw score on the multiple-choice section of the test.

Let's see when guessing can help you. There are five answer choices for each multiple-choice question. If you were able to eliminate just one wrong answer for each question on the entire multiple-choice section, random odds say you would get one-fourth of the questions correct. That's about 7.5 questions—round up to 18 questions or points. Even if you get rid of just one wrong answer from each question throughout the test, you begin to gain points. What does that mean for you when you take the test? It means you should take your best guess as long as you can eliminate even one answer choice.

However, you will rarely be faced with a question for which you can't eliminate at least one of the answer choices. In many cases, you will be able to eliminate two or even three incorrect answers. Whenever you get this far but can go no further, you *must* guess from among the remaining answer choices.

If it seems that we are focusing more on eliminating incorrect answers than on finding the correct answers, it's because this is the most efficient way to take a multiple-choice exam. Use **Process of Elimination** to whittle down the answer choices to one on all but the easiest questions (on easy questions, the correct answer will be obvious), because incorrect answers are much easier to identify than the correct one. When you look for the correct answer among the answer choices, you have a tendency to try to justify how each answer *might* be correct. You'll adopt a forgiving attitude in a situation in which tough assertiveness is rewarded. Eliminate incorrect answers. Terminate them with extreme prejudice. If you have done your job well, only the correct answer will be left standing at the end.

This all probably sounds pretty aggressive to you. It is. The fact is, aggressiveness pays on this test. Sift through the answer choices, toss incorrect answers into the bin, guess without remorse, and prowl the test searching for questions you can answer—all with the tenacity and ruthlessness of a shark. Okay, maybe that overstates the case a *little*, but you get the point. Guess if you don't know the answer but can eliminate at least one answer choice.

Common Sense Can Help

Sometimes, an answer on the multiple-choice section contradicts common sense. Eliminate those answers. Common sense works on the AP European History Exam. Which of the answer choices to the question below don't make sense?

---

26. During the period when England was a republic (1649–1660), which of the following applied to Ireland?

    (A) Ireland became primarily Protestant.
    (B) Ireland won its independence.
    (C) Ireland obtained extensive military assistance from the French.
    (D) An army led by Cromwell invaded Ireland and solidified English control.
    (E) Ireland underwent a brief but glorious cultural renaissance.

Here's How to Crack It

Common sense should allow you to eliminate answer choice (A) immediately, since you are probably aware that the whole of Ireland has never been primarily Protestant. (B) can be eliminated because independence only came for the Republic of Ireland in the early twentieth century. If (C) actually occurred, then perhaps (B) would have taken place, but that was not what happened. Also, while there is a wonderful Irish literary tradition, there was no "renaissance" during the Cromwellian wars. That leaves (D) as the only correct answer.

Context Clues

Some questions contain context clues or vocabulary words that will either lead you to the correct answer or at least help you eliminate an incorrect answer. Look at the following question.

60. In his *Economic Consequences of the Peace* (1919), John Maynard Keynes

    (A) supported the reparations payments by the Germans as a necessary evil
    (B) argued that the reparations amount was too low to seriously compromise the German economy
    (C) charged that by punishing the Germans with a large reparations bill, the entire European economy was threatened
    (D) urged that the issue of reparations be postponed for a decade so that the postwar economies could adjust to peace
    (E) argued that reparations should be tied to a more stable currency like that of the United States

Here's How to Crack It

Again, you are dealing with a book and an author that you might be less than familiar with, but don't panic—the question itself contains a major clue. The word "consequences" in the title of Keynes's work provides you with the hint that Keynes was possibly critical of the reparations component of the Treaty of Versailles. This bit of information allows you to eliminate (A), (B), (D), and (E), because these answers indicate at least some level of support by Keynes for reparations. The one that stands out from the others is choice (C); it alone seems to be critical of the very concept of German reparations.

DRILL

Here is a group of five questions that could have come from the multiple-choice section of the AP European History Exam. As you work through them, try to apply everything you have learned in this chapter. Use the chronological ordering of the questions to eliminate impossible answers. Keep the big picture in mind as you consider the answer choices. Use Process of Elimination. If you can get rid of one or more answer choices and go no further, guess and move on. Use common sense and context clues. The answers and explanations of how to attack these questions follow the drill. Good luck!

33. Fascism emerged triumphant in Italy in 1922 following

   (A) an armed coup
   (B) a political compromise worked out by the Italian monarch authorizing the Fascists to form a government
   (C) a civil war involving Communists and Fascists
   (D) the assistance of German Fascists
   (E) the emergence of Mussolini as sole leader of the Fascist party following an internal party struggle for power

34. During the Spanish Civil War, the British and French governments

   (A) encouraged the Soviet Union to come to the aid of the Spanish Republic
   (B) refused to offer assistance to the Spanish Republic
   (C) encouraged the League of Nations to intervene to stop the fighting
   (D) waited to see what position the United States would take
   (E) discreetly organized volunteers to go to Spain to aid the Republic

35. The Great Purges eliminated from the Soviet Union

   (A) the Romanovs
   (B) the kulaks
   (C) the Old Bolsheviks
   (D) the intelligentsia
   (E) the Russian Orthodox Church

36. The Truman Doctrine emerged in response to the

   (A) building of the Berlin Wall
   (B) Korean War
   (C) death of Joseph Stalin
   (D) Berlin blockade
   (E) Greek Civil War

37. At the Council of Trent (1545–1563), the Catholic Church

   (A) agreed to work with Protestant theologians to work for an acceptable compromise
   (B) accepted Protestant positions on most issues but still refused to allow for clerical marriage
   (C) decided to wait to formulate a position on most of the issues addressed by the Protestants
   (D) rejected Protestant positions on the sacraments, the giving of wine to the laity during communion, and clerical marriage
   (E) placed certain constraints on the papacy to limit its ability to implement reforms

Here's How to Crack It

The five questions in the drill are of medium difficulty. On average, between 50 and 70 percent of those taking the test will get each one right. As we discuss how to take your best guess on the previous questions, it should go without saying that, if you know the correct answer to the question, you should simply select it and move on. Also, chronological order should have told you that the drill began in the middle of one grouping of questions and that question 37 started a new grouping.

Question 33 has a "big picture" idea that is critical to your understanding of twentieth-century European history. Fascists in both Italy and Germany came to power not through the violent seizure of power but through the democratic process, though once in power, they destroyed all traces of democracy. With this in mind, you can instantly eliminate choices (A) and (C). Choice (D) can also be eliminated because the question provides you with a hint that makes that choice clearly incorrect when it states the year was 1922. Fascism became a significant presence in German political life only following the Depression in 1929, while Hitler became German Chancellor in 1933. Since Mussolini was the founder and undisputed leader of the Fascist Party of Italy, choice (E) is rather unlikely, which leads us to the correct answer, (B).

Question 34 also has one of those "big picture" ideas, this time on the issue of appeasement, the attempt by Britain and France to give in to German demands to avoid war. (E) might have led to a provoking of Hitler, who was openly supporting Franco and the rebels, so it must be wrong; the volunteers from the European democracies and the United States who fought in Spain in support of the Republic did so without any support from their governments. The United States was in isolationist mode at this time, so there was no need to wait for what the Americans would do, because there was never any doubt that they would do nothing. Therefore, (D) is incorrect. By 1936, the year of the start of the Spanish Civil War, the League of Nations had shown itself to be a paper tiger, so (C) is unlikely. It would take a real stretch of the imagination to think that Britain and France, two nations that greatly mistrusted the intentions of the Soviet Union, would encourage the latter's participation in the Spanish Civil War. Therefore, choice (A) is not correct. This leaves us with (B), a tragic mistake by the French and British, though quite in keeping with their desire for appeasement.

Question 35 can be answered by thinking in terms of the chronology of the four questions in this group. Question 33 deals with 1922 and question 34 with 1936. Question 36 can take place no earlier than 1945, because that marks the first year of the presidency of Harry Truman, and in fact, the Truman Doctrine was announced in 1947. This means that question 35 takes place roughly between 1936 and 1945. With this in mind, you can eliminate (A) and (E), because both the old aristocracy and the established Church were immediate targets following the Bolshevik Revolution in 1917. You may not have recalled that the collectivization of Soviet agriculture, which led to the mass destruction of the kulaks (wealthy peasants), took place between 1929 and 1933, though if you didn't, at least you could have made an educated guess between this choice and the correct one, (C).

Question 36 requires you to think which provocation led President Truman to state that the United States would come to the aid of nations being subverted either internally or externally by Communists. The death of Stalin was not exactly an act of provocation, so choice (C) is out, and the Berlin Wall was built in 1961, some time after the Truman presidency. You are then left with three events that are close in date and are thematically linked. Although you might want to guess at this point, you may recall that events in Greece were pivotal in shaping an American response to what they saw as the subverting of legitimate regimes in Eastern Europe, and that the Berlin airlift and the entry of the United States into the Korean conflict were examples of the United States carrying out the ideas contained in the Truman Doctrine. The correct answer is therefore (E).

Question 37 jumps back in time several centuries. You have moved up to a slightly more difficult set of questions. Again, think "big picture." What was the Catholic response to the Protestant Reformation? Did the Catholics decide to accept Protestant demands on certain key religious tenets? Certainly not. Therefore, the answer that captures the correct Catholic response can only be choice (D).

Finally, here are the answers to the questions that appear in the first part of this chapter. 3: (A); 6: (D); 45: (B); 13: (E); 16: (D); 21: (D).

Summary

o   Familiarize yourself with the different types of
    questions that will appear on the multiple-choice
    section. Be aware that you will see almost an even
    split between questions on political and diplo-
    matic history, cultural and intellectual trends, and
    social and economic themes. Tailor your studies
    accordingly.

o   Look for "big picture" answers. Correct answers
    on the multiple-choice section confirm important
    trends in European history. The test will not ask
    you about weird exceptions that contradict those
    trends. It also will not ask you about military his-
    tory. You will not be required to perform miracu-
    lous feats of memorization; however, you must be
    thoroughly familiar with all the basics of European
    history. There are a lot of them!

o   Use the chronological ordering of questions to
    figure out about which time period you are being
    asked. Be aware that the questions are presented in
    groups of four to seven, that each group maintains
    chronological order, and that each group is a little
    more difficult than the one that precedes it.

o   Use Process of Elimination on all but the easiest
    questions. Once you have worked on a question,
    eliminated some answers, and convinced yourself
    that you cannot eliminate any other incorrect an-
    swers, you should guess and move on to the next
    question.

o   Use common sense. Look for context clues.

Chapter 2
How to
Approach Essays

HOW TO APPROACH ESSAYS

There are two types of essay questions on the AP European History Exam. The first is the Document-Based Question (DBQ), which requires you to answer a question based on ten to twelve primary-source documents and whatever outside knowledge you have about the subject. The second is the free-response question, which is more like a typical essay question on a history exam. For the free-response section, you are given six questions, three about the period from the Renaissance to the Napoleonic era and three about the period following it. You are required to answer two of these essay questions, one from each group. We will discuss each of these question types in greater detail in the next two chapters. First, let's talk about the basics of writing a successful AP essay.

What Are the AP Essay Graders Looking For?

In conversations with those who grade AP European History Exams, it is clear that what they want above all else is for you to address the question. In some of your classes, you may have gotten into the habit of throwing everything but the kitchen sink into an essay without truly addressing the question at hand. Do not try to fudge your way through the essay. The graders are all experts in history, and you will not be able to fool them into thinking you know more than you actually do.

It is also very important to focus on the phrasing of the question. Some students are so anxious to get going that they start writing as soon as they know the general subject of the question, and many of these students lose points because their essays do not answer the question being asked. Take, for example, an essay question that asks you to discuss the effects of fascism on the daily life of the average German in the 1930s. If you are an overanxious test taker, you might start rattling off everything you know about German fascism—the reasons for its electoral success in the years leading up to 1933, the personality cult around Adolf Hitler, the Holocaust, and so on. No matter how well this essay is written, you will lose points for one simple reason—not answering the question!

Second, a good essay does more than rattle off facts. Just as the multiple-choice questions seek to draw out certain general principles or the "big picture" of European history, the essay questions seek to do the same. The readers are looking to see that you understand some of the fundamental issues in European history and that you can successfully discuss this material in a coherent manner.

If all this sounds intimidating, read on! There are a few simple things you can do to improve your grade on the AP essays.

Reasons to Be Cheerful

AP graders know that you are given only 15 minutes to prepare and 45 minutes to write about the DBQ and only 70 minutes to write both of your free-response questions. They also know that is not enough time to cover the subject matter tested by the question. The fact is, many very long books have been written about any one subject that you might be asked about on the DBQ and the free-response questions.

The College Board's *AP European History Course Description* (which can be downloaded from the College Board's web site) advises students to write an essay that has a well-developed thesis, provides support for the thesis with specific examples, addresses all parts of the question, and is generally well organized. Therefore, expressing good ideas and presenting valid evidence in support of those ideas are important. Making sure you mention every single relevant piece of historical information is not so important.

Also, you should remember that graders are not given a lot of time to read your essays. When they gather to read the exams, the graders go through more than 100 per day. No one could possibly give detailed attention to all points in your essay when he or she is reading at such a fast clip. What he or she can see in such a brief reading is whether you have something intelligent to say and whether you have the ability to say it well. Also, as I know from my own career as a professor, when you read many bad essays (and there will be quite a few even among AP students), you tend to give those that are not completely awful more credit than they possibly deserve. Just hope that the essay being read before your own was written by someone who didn't buy this book and was therefore completely unprepared.

Things That Make Any Essay Better

There are two essential components to writing a successful timed essay. First, plan what you are going to write before you start writing! Second, use a number of tried-and-true writing techniques that will make your essay appear well-organized, well-thought-out, and well-written. This section is about those techniques.

Before You Start Writing

Read the question carefully. Underline key words and circle dates. Then, brainstorm for one or two minutes. Write down everything that comes to mind in your test booklet. (There is room in the margins and at the top and bottom of the pages.) Look at your notes and consider the results of your brainstorming session as you decide what point you will argue in your essay; that argument is going to be your thesis. Tailor your argument to your information, but by no means choose an argument that you know is wrong or with which you disagree. If you do either of these things, your essay will be awful. Finally, sort the results of your brainstorm.

Some of what you wrote down will be "big picture" conclusions, some will be historical facts that can be used as evidence to support your conclusions, and some will be garbage.

Next, make an outline. You should plan to write five paragraphs for each of the three essay questions, and plan to go into special detail in each of the paragraphs on the DBQ. (Remember: You will have the documents and your outside knowledge to discuss on the DBQ. Plus, you will have more time.) Your first paragraph should contain your thesis statement, in which you directly answer the question in just a few sentences. Your second, third, and fourth paragraphs should each contain one argument (for a total of three) that supports that statement, along with historical evidence to support those arguments. The fifth paragraph should contain your conclusion and reiterate your answer to the question.

Before you start to write your outline, you will have to decide what type of argument you are going to make. Here are some of the classics.

1. Make Three Good Points

This is the simplest strategy. Look at the results of your brainstorming session, and pick the three best points supporting your position. Make each of these points the subject of one paragraph. Make the weakest of the three points the subject of the second paragraph, and save the strongest point for the fourth paragraph. If your three points are interrelated and there is a natural sequence to arguing them, then by all means use that sequence, but otherwise, try to save your strongest point for last. Begin each paragraph by stating one of your three points, and then spend the rest of the paragraph supporting it. Use specific, supporting examples whenever possible. Your first paragraph should state what you intend to argue. Your final paragraph should explain why you have proven what you set out to prove.

2. Make a Chronological Argument

Many questions lend themselves to a chronological treatment. Questions about the development of a political, social, or economic trend can hardly be answered any other way. When you make a chronological argument, look for important transitions and use them to start new paragraphs. A five-paragraph essay about the events leading up to the French Revolution, for example, might start with an introductory discussion of France and the role of royal absolutism. This is also where you should state your thesis. The second paragraph might then discuss the economic crisis that led to the calling of the Estates General. The third paragraph could deal with concern among members of the third estate that their interests might not be represented at Versailles, despite the vital economic role they played in eighteenth-century France. The fourth paragraph could be concerned with the events leading up to and including the King's agreement to meet the three estates as a National Assembly. Your conclusion in this type of essay should restate the essay question and answer it. For example, if the question asks whether the French Revolution was inevitable, you should answer "yes" or "no" in this paragraph.

3. Identify Similarities and Differences

Some questions, particularly on the free-response section, ask you to compare events, issues, and/or policies. Very often, the way the question is phrased will suggest the best organization for your essay. Take, for example, a question asking you to compare the impact of three events and issues on the decision to execute the English monarch Charles I in 1649. This question pretty much requires you to start by setting the historical scene prior to the three events/issues you are about to discuss. Continue by devoting one paragraph to each of the three, and conclude by comparing and contrasting the relative importance of each. Again, be sure to answer the question in your final paragraph.

Other questions will provide options. If you are asked to compare Italian and Northern humanism during the Renaissance, you might open with a thesis stating the essential similarity or difference between the two. Then, you could devote one paragraph each to a summary of certain trends and authors, while in the fourth paragraph you could point out the major similarities and differences between Italian and Northern humanism. In the final paragraph, you could draw your conclusion (e.g., "their similarities were more significant than their differences," or vice versa).

Or, using another angle altogether, you might start with a thesis, then discuss in the body of your essay three pertinent philosophical, religious, or political issues, then discuss how Italian humanists dealt with such questions, then move on to the Northern humanists, and wrap up with an overview of your argument for your conclusion.

4. Use the Straw Dog Argument

In this essay-writing technique, choose a couple of arguments that someone taking the position opposite yours would take. State their arguments, and then tear them down. Remember that proving your opposition wrong does not mean that you have proved you are correct; that is why you should choose only a few opposing arguments to refute. Summarize your opponent's arguments in paragraph two, dismiss them in paragraph three, and use paragraph four to make the argument for your side. Or, use one paragraph each to summarize and dismiss each of your opponent's arguments, and then make the case for your side in your concluding paragraph. Acknowledging both sides of an argument, even when you choose one over the other, is a good indicator that you understand that historical issues are complex and can be interpreted in more than one way, something teachers and graders like to see.

Conclusion

No matter which format you choose, remember to organize your essay so that the first paragraph addresses the question and states how you are going to answer it. (That is your thesis.) The second, third, and fourth paragraphs should each be organized around a single argument that supports your thesis, and each of these arguments must be supported by historical evidence. Your final paragraph ties the essay up into a nice, neat package. Your concluding paragraph should also answer the question. And remember to stay positive!

As You Are Writing, Observe the Following Guidelines

- **Keep sentences as simple as possible.** Long sentences get convoluted very quickly and will give your graders a headache, putting them in a bad mood.
- **Throw in a few big words.** But don't overdo it, because it will look like you are showing off. Remember that good writing does not have to be complicated; some great ideas can be stated simply. NEVER use a word if you are unsure of its meaning or proper usage. A malapropism (misuse of a word) might give your graders a good laugh, but it will not earn you any points, and it will probably cost you.
- **Write clearly and neatly.** As long as we are discussing your graders' moods, here is an easy way to put them in good ones. Graders look at a lot of chicken scratch; it strains their eyes and makes them grumpy. Neatly written essays make them happy. When you cross out, do it neatly. If you are making any major edits—if you want to insert a paragraph in the middle of your essay, for example—make sure you indicate these changes clearly.
- **Define your terms.** Most questions require you to use terms that mean different things to different people. One person's "liberal" is another person's "conservative," and yet another person's "extremist." What one person considers "expansionism," another might call "colonialism" or "imperialism." The folks who grade the test want to know what you think these terms mean. When you use them, define them. Take particular care to define any such terms that appear in the question. Almost all official College Board materials emphasize this point, so do not forget it. Be sure to define any term that you suspect can be defined in more than one way.
- **Use transition words to show where you are going.** When continuing an idea, use words such as *furthermore*, *also*, and *in addition*. When changing the flow of thought, use words such as *however* and *yet*. Transition words make your essay easier to understand by clarifying your intentions. Better yet, they indicate to the graders that you know how to make a coherent, persuasive argument.

- **Use structural indicators to organize your paragraphs.** Another way to clarify your intentions is to organize your essay around structural indicators. For example, if you are making a number of related points, number them ("First…Second…And last…"). If you are writing a compare/contrast essay, use the indicators "on the one hand" and "on the other hand."
- **Stick to your outline.** Unless you get an absolutely brilliant idea while you are writing, do not deviate from your outline. If you do, you will risk winding up with an incoherent essay.
- **Try to prove one "big picture" idea per paragraph.** Keep it simple. Each paragraph should make one point and then substantiate that point with historical evidence.
- **Back up your ideas with examples.** Yes, we have said it already, but it bears repeating: Do not just throw ideas out there and hope that you are right (unless you are absolutely desperate). You will score big points if you substantiate your claims with facts.
- **Try to fill the essay form.** An overly short essay will hurt you more than one that is overly long.
- **Make sure your first and last paragraphs directly address the question.** Nothing will cost you points faster than if the graders decide you did not answer the question. It is always a safe move to start your final paragraph by answering the question. If you have written a good essay, that answer will serve as a legitimate conclusion.
- **Always place every essay into a historical context.** For example, if you are given an essay asking you to compare and contrast Newton's and Einstein's ideas on the universe, don't make it an essay on science. Instead, show how each of these men was a product of his respective time period, and show how their ideas influenced their contemporaries as well as future generations.

Summary

o   Read questions carefully. Be sure you are answering the question that is asked. You must answer the question in order to get full credit.

o   Do not start writing until you have brainstormed, chosen a thesis, and written an outline.

o   Follow your outline. Stick to one important idea per paragraph. Support your ideas with historical evidence.

o   Write clearly and neatly. Do not write in long, overly complex sentences. Toss in a couple of "big" words you know you will not misuse. When in doubt, stick to simple syntax and vocabulary.

o   Use transition words to indicate continuity of thought and changes in the direction of your argument.

o   Provide a strong historical context. You may be faced with questions focusing on science, economics, philosophy, literature and art, religion, and other disciplines. Always remember this is a history exam.

o   Remember also that this is a European history exam (not an American history exam). So, for example, if you get a question on technological changes in the nineteenth century, you should focus on Marconi, Siemens, or Bessemer, not on Edison or Bell. Similarly, on Cold War questions, don't avoid the United States, but have your answer reflect Europe's situation as much as possible.

o   Study the question. Make sure you understand what it is asking you to write about. Address all parts of the questions. If it asks for "social, political, and economic changes," make sure you discuss all three. If you cannot address the whole question, either choose another question or fake it. If you don't know anything about the social impact, then try to use logic—how would something like this affect society?

o   Try for at least two or three concrete facts to support each of your themes or assertions.

CRACKING THE DOCUMENT-BASED QUESTION (DBQ)

What Is the DBQ?

DBQ stands for "Document-Based Question." The DBQ is an essay question that requires you to interpret *primary-source* documents. (There are typically ten to twelve documents in a DBQ.) These documents will include many, if not all, of the following: newspaper articles and editorials, letters, diaries, speeches, excerpts from legislation, political cartoons, charts, and graphs. The documents will *not* include excerpts from current textbooks. Occasionally, one or two of the documents will be taken from something "classic" that you may have seen previously, but generally, the documents will be new to you. However, they will discuss events and ideas with which you should be familiar. All the documents will pertain to a single subject. The average document is about six lines long, although occasionally you will see something longer.

The 45-minute DBQ is the second part of the AP European History Exam; it is administered immediately after the 10-minute break that follows the multiple-choice section. At the beginning of the DBQ, you will be handed a green booklet in which the essay question and documents are printed, as well as a separate form on which to write your essay. The DBQ session begins with a 15-minute mandatory reading period, during which you are allowed to read the documents and take notes in the DBQ booklet. You may not start recording your essay on the essay form until the 45-minute writing period begins. However, if you finish taking notes and outlining your essay before the reading period is over, you should write a first draft of your opening paragraph in your DBQ booklet; then, when the writing period begins, you can transcribe it into your essay booklet and continue.

To give you an idea of what you can expect on your DBQ, let's look at what appeared on a previous test. The question asked students to describe and analyze problems in the relationship between the English and Irish in the period from 1800 to 1916. The documents included excerpts from the following:

- A quote from English Prime Minister William Pitt, the creator of the Act of Union of 1801, in which he states that "Ireland must be governed in the English interest"
- A parliamentary speech by a Protestant Irish leader dating from 1805 demanding the continuation of exclusive Protestant political rights within the United Kingdom
- A poem written in 1842 by an Irish Nationalist that speaks of the commonality of interests between Irish Protestants and Catholics
- An article in the English Conservative Party newspaper from 1848 that claims that anything good in Ireland is due to the influence of England, while the Irish have only themselves to blame for all their problems

- A declaration of principles from 1879 by the National Land League that states that the "land of Ireland belongs to the people of Ireland."
- A piece of writing from 1900 by Maud Gonne, founder of the Daughters of Ireland, in which she declares that her organization wants to help establish Irish independence in part through a revival of indigenous Irish culture
- A map showing the distribution in 1901 of Protestants and Roman Catholics in the Irish population
- A 1907 speech by a Nationalist politician stating that in the long run, the Protestants cannot expect more than the rights enjoyed by minorities in other countries
- An impassioned speech from a 1911 rally in which Edward Carson, the leader of the Ulster Unionists, warns that, should Home Rule be granted, Protestants must seize the reigns of power in Ulster
- A proclamation issued during the Easter Rebellion of 1916 declaring the establishment of an independent Irish republic

As you can see, a typical DBQ may contain documents you have seen prior to the exam. (The proclamation from the Easter Rebellion is often quoted in textbooks.) However, the DBQ also includes documents you certainly have not seen before. Each of the documents, though, represents a political position you have studied. Although you may not know much about the authors of these documents, with the exception of William Pitt the Younger, the tensions between England and Ireland might be familiar to you. In other words, you will not be starting from square one, even when the documents are new to you. Also, the writers of the AP European History Exam provide a paragraph summary of the historical background of the question being asked, which may also provide you with much needed information.

Is There a "Right" Answer to Each DBQ?

No. DBQs are worded in such a way that you can argue any number of positions. In the previous example, the documents provide evidence for various issues that stand at the heart of the Irish-English conflict, such as religious bigotry and questions concerning Home Rule. As long as you support your argument with evidence, you can argue whatever thesis you want.

Graders are supposed to take into account the strength of your argument and the evidence you offer in support of it. In other words, if you forget to mention a good, illustrative historical event but manage to back your point up in some other way, you will not be penalized.

However, the best DBQ responses will contain relevant *outside information*. You will notice that your DBQ contains a phrase that looks something like the following:

Using the Documents AND Your Knowledge of the Subject…

"Your knowledge of the subject" is the outside information. It includes historical facts and ideas that are relevant to the question but that are not mentioned in the DBQ documents. For example, in the England and Ireland DBQ described above, any information offered about the writers' backgrounds would count as outside information, as would information concerning, for example, Charles Stuart Parnell and the Land League. Some students make the mistake of throwing everything they know about a subject into their essays, whether or not it pertains to the question. That type of information receives partial credit at best.

HOW IS THE DBQ SCORED?

The College Board uses a "core-scoring method" that is graded on a 1–9 scale. This means that for each DBQ, you can earn up to six points by performing what the graders consider basic tasks, such as using the majority of documents or displaying a point of view or bias in at least three of the documents. In addition, you can earn up to three more points in what they call the "expanded core," by excelling in more difficult areas. To earn any points from the expanded core, students must earn all six points in the basic core.

The following chart might make this scoring system somewhat more comprehensible.

Basic Core Points

At the start of the book, we shared a scoring rubric for how these point breakdowns work. Let's review that here and then go a bit deeper.

Core Skill	Points
1) Provides a clearly stated and appropriate thesis that addresses all parts of the question. **This thesis should not merely be a restating of the question.**	1
2) Discusses a majority of the documents individually and specifically	1
3) Demonstrates an understanding of the basic meaning of the documents (you may misinterpret no more than one document)	1
4) Supports thesis with an appropriate interpretation of the majority of the documents	1
5) Shows point of view or bias in at least three documents	1
6) Analyzes documents by organizing them into at least three appropriate groups	1

Expanded Core Points

If you earn a 6 on the Basic Core, you can then earn up to *three* additional points by displaying some of the following skills:

7) Having a clear, analytical, and comprehensive thesis

8) Using every document or almost every document

9) Skillfully using documents as evidence

10) Displaying an understanding of the nuances within the documents

11) Discussing bias or point of view in at least four documents

12) Analyzing documents by creating additional groupings or using some other advanced method

13) Incorporating outside historical knowledge in the essay

14) Addressing all aspects of the question thoroughly

Getting the Points

Here are concrete ways to earn the points for each of the skills.

The Basic Core 6 Points

Skill 1

Study the question carefully; make sure you are writing about what the question is actually asking. Misinterpreting the question is the most common mistake students make and results in a zero on the essay. Also, be careful to provide a thesis that is not a regurgitation of the exam question. Failure to come up with your own thesis will also result in a zero.

Skill 2

Try to use every document either explicitly or implicitly.

Skill 3

Show your reader that you understand the basic meaning of the documents. This doesn't mean that there won't possibly be a number of ways of interpreting the document, but make it clear that you understand the connection of your document to the topic at hand.

Skill 4

Write each of your body paragraphs about one of your document groups. Start off with a topic sentence, and write an analysis of the information drawn from the documents in that group. Use quotes or examples to support your analysis. Just quoting for the sake of quoting is a common error among students. Do not assume that quotations can simply stand on their own without any elaboration. Be sure to show the graders that you understand what the quotation means and use the quote in a manner that furthers your argument.

Skill 5

The documents may not be fact; they may be **opinions**. Write the essay in such a way that this is made clear to the reader.

1) Make a big effort to find point of view, and keep in mind that *tone* can also present a point of view: e.g., outrage, contempt, or concern. Before you read the document, look at who the author is and when he or she made this statement. Why did the author have this particular point of view? What about the author's background or the time, place, or historical circumstance that shaped the writer's outlook on life? Is there an ulterior motive behind the statements made? Do not hesitate to use logic. For example, if the DBQ is about the various views on German unification in the 1860s, why would a German poet, the Italian Foreign Minister, and Otto von Bismarck support unification, while an ethnically French citizen of Alsace-Lorraine, a French socialist politician, and Napoleon III all oppose it?

2) Demonstrate that you are aware that certain documents are more credible than others. A document giving statistics from a government census, for example, is considered more credible than claims made by an editorialist for a party newspaper.

Skill 6

Have three or more groupings. A group cannot contain just one document, and it's safest to use more than two (in case one is used incorrectly). It is fine to use a document more than once.

How to group will vary according to the question. Some DBQs, for example, may ask you to show how various segments of society view a particular issue; some will ask how views on a particular issue have changed over time. Find the documents that have similar points of view and write about those views; in other words, pro versus con, German versus French, liberal versus conservative, nineteenth century versus twentieth century.

You may group according to the reasons and motives behind the arguments. Your groups might be, for example, individuals influenced by nationalist idealism, individuals representing the power politics of the era, and groups representing the internationalism promoted by Karl Marx.

The Additional 3 Points

Skills 8, 10, 11, and 12 ask you simply to take the Basic Core skills even further. Skills 7, 9, and 13 are discussed below.

Skill 7

The thesis is not simply restating the question. It must also answer the question and indicate the various groupings into which the essay is divided.

Skill 9

Use attribution as much as possible. Attribution means that you give credit to the authors of the statements used. It is also useful to cite the document you are quoting. For example, you might write "British Prime Minister William Gladstone stated in his address to Parliament 'blah-blah-blah' (Document 8)." (Citing the document is not mandatory, but it makes it easier for the reader to see which documents you used.) Never write an essay that says, "In document 8, such-and-such is said, which is contradicted by document 13." Your essay is not about the documents; it is about the opinions of the people quoted in the documents.

Skill 13

The AP European History Exam does not *require* students to bring in outside information. However, if it is possible to bring in any outside information, such as comments about the time period your essay addresses, or historical events that may have been affected by the issue being discussed, this could show a greater historical understanding and give you an extra point in the expanded core. But don't get too wrapped up in earning additional points; the focus of your essay should be on completing the tasks required in the basic core.

GETTING STARTED ON THE DBQ: READ THE QUESTION

Start by reading the question. This direction may seem obvious, but it really is not, given how many students write essays on subjects that are only marginally related to the question being asked. Students miss the question because they get anxious during the exam. They panic. They think they are going too slowly. In an effort to speed up, they read half the question, say to themselves, "A-ha! I know what they're going to ask!" and stop reading. Do NOT make this mistake! The question is probably the shortest thing you have to read on the DBQ. Take your time; savor it. Explore its nuances. Essays that address the question fully earn huge bonuses; those essays that ignore parts of the question are doomed to a grade of 5 or lower.

Here's a sample question:

1. "Analyze and discuss why the year 1848 brought about an explosion of revolutionary activity throughout Europe."

As you look over the question, you should ask yourself two questions.

- Do I have an opinion about this subject?
- What must I discuss in order to write a successful essay?

Of the two questions, the second is much more important. You can construct a position later, after you have gathered the information you want to include in your essay. First, you need to figure out what issues you must address and what data you will use in your discussion.

To begin, you might want to break down the question in a variety of ways. Perhaps focus first on economic issues, such as the economic downturn of the 1840s, a decade that some referred to as the "hungry forties." Then move on to critical political issues such as a backlash against the repressive nature of politics in the decades after 1848 or the role of nationalism in the revolutions of 1848. Others might find it more useful to discuss events in 1848 on a nation-by-nation basis, beginning with the collapse of the Orleans monarchy in France and moving on to the revolutionary movements in places such as the German states, the Austrian Empire, Italy, and so on. Finally, you must include a discussion of the given documents and your outside knowledge in the essay.

However you decide to approach the question, it is essential that you take your time. Read carefully to make sure that you understand what issues must be addressed in your essay. Then, determine how to organize the information you plan to collect from the documents and from memory for inclusion in the essay.

Organizing Your Essay: Use Grids and Columns

Many DBQs ask you to draw comparisons. For those questions, you can always organize your thoughts about a DBQ in a grid. Drawing a grid helps in seeing all sides of an argument, which is important because DBQ graders will reward you for acknowledging arguments other than your own.

For the DBQ question on the revolutions of 1848 (on the previous page), you may find it useful to create a grid like the one shown below. Such a grid will allow you to see the complexity of the events of 1848 and how economics, domestic politics, and nationalism all played a role in fanning the flames of revolution across Europe.

	Economics	Politics	Nationalism
France			
Prussia			
Austria			
Italian States			

As you remember appropriate outside information and as you read the documents, take notes in the appropriate boxes. When it comes time to write your essay, you will find it easier to compare and contrast because your information will already be organized in a way that makes similarities and differences more obvious.

If you cannot draw a grid for a question, you can instead set up column headings. Because every DBQ can be argued from at least two different positions, you can always set up two (or more) columns, designating one for each position. Consider the DBQ about Ireland, which we discussed at the beginning of the chapter. You could create one column, entitled "England," where you can provide examples of English justification for holding onto Ireland. A second column, labeled "Unionist," will give the Unionist argument for remaining part of the United Kingdom, and a third, labeled "Nationalist," can provide their argument for creating an independent Irish state, free from British domination. You might even want a fourth column, for information that you know belongs in your essay but that you cannot yet classify (give that the title "To be classified").

Good essays do not just flow out of your pen by accident. They happen when you know what you are going to say *before you start writing*. Although it is difficult (if not impossible) to prepare your entire DBQ essay before you begin writing, given the time constraints, pre-organization and a good outline will get you much closer to that goal.

A Sample Question

Let's take a look at another possible DBQ question.

1. Discuss whether Napoleon was a supporter of the ideas espoused in the eighteenth-century Enlightenment or whether he was an enemy of individual liberty. Answer this question by using BOTH the documents AND your knowledge of the Enlightenment and Napoleonic era.

Your essay will have to show whether you understand certain basic tenets of the Enlightenment and also show your knowledge of the period of Napoleon's domination over France (1799–1815). You will, of course, have to include both analysis of the documents and outside information. Since the question is asking for a basic comparison, you might want to make a simple three-column grid like the one below:

Ideals of Enlightenment	Napoleon pro	Napoleon con

Once you have created your grid, begin organizing information for your essay. At this point, you are probably eager to start reading the documents. Resist the temptation. You have one more important job to do before you start reading.

Gather Outside Information

Most students read the DBQ documents first and *then* try to think of outside information to supplement their essays. This is a mistake. The reason? *The power of suggestion.* Once you have read the documents—a chore that can take from six to eight minutes—those documents will be on your mind. If you read the provided passages and *then* brainstorm outside information, you will invariably think of things you *just* read about, rather than things you *have not* read about.

Plus, reading and processing the documents is a big task. Once you have accomplished that, you will want to get started right away on organizing and writing your essay while the documents are fresh in your mind. So, brainstorm outside information *before* you read the documents.

Here's what you should do. Look at your grid or columns and brainstorm. In a separate blank space in your green booklet (*not* in your grid/columns), write down everything you can think of that relates to the question. Spend just two or three minutes on this task, and then look at what you have written. Enter the useful information into your grid/columns in the appropriate spaces.

Chances are that some of the "outside information" you think of will be mentioned in the documents, which means that it will not be outside information any more. That is no big deal. In fact, you should think of it as something good. If some of what you remembered shows up in the documents, that means you are on the right track toward answering the question!

This is what a brainstorming grid for the Napoleon question might look like.

Ideals of Enlightenment	Napoleon pro	Napoleon con
religious tolerance	• extended religious freedom throughout the empire • concordat	
rational government	• codex Napoleon • increased centralization of government	
equality of individuals	• favored meritocracy	• created imperial title and a new aristocracy • placed relatives on foreign thrones
freedom from repression		• created secret police censorship • jailed and executed political opponents

Read the Documents

After you have gathered outside information to include in your essay, you are ready to read the documents. As you read, keep the following things in mind:

- **The order in which documents appear is almost always helpful.**
  Very often, the documents in the DBQ appear in chronological order. When they do, it often indicates that you are expected to trace the historical development of the DBQ subject. On such questions, you do not have to write an essay that adheres strictly to chronological

order, but chronology should play an important part in the development of your thesis. When the documents appear in an order other than chronological, they are usually organized so that you can easily compare and contrast different viewpoints on a particular event or issue. On these questions, one of your main goals should be to draw those same comparisons.

- **Watch for inconsistencies within and among the documents.** The documents will not necessarily agree with one another. In fact, they are almost certain to present different viewpoints on issues and almost as certain to present conflicting accounts of a historical event. Some documents might even contradict themselves! This is intentional. The exam is testing your ability to recognize these contradictions. You are expected to resolve these conflicts in your essay. To do so, you will have to identify the sources of the documents. (See below.)

- **Identify the sources of the documents.** Why do two accounts of the same event contradict each other? Why do two historians, looking at the same data, come up with dissimilar interpretations of their significance? Is it because the people giving these accounts—the sources of the documents—have different perspectives? Identify the sources and explain why their opinions differ. As you explain these differences, look for the following differences among sources:
  - political ideology
  - class
  - race
  - religion
  - gender

Consider the question on Napoleon. A supporter of the exiled Bourbons would offer a very different point of view on this question than a member of Napoleon's inner circle. The graders will be looking specifically to see if you have tried to explain those differences.

- **Look for evidence that could refute your argument**. Once you have decided what your thesis will be, you will be looking through the documents for evidence to support your argument. Not all the documents will necessarily back you up. Some may appear to contradict your argument. Do not simply ignore those documents! As you read them, try to figure out how you might incorporate them into your argument.

Again, let's consider the Napoleon DBQ. Suppose you argue that Napoleon was a supporter of the ideals of the Enlightenment. Now suppose that one of the documents presents evidence that Napoleon kidnapped a Bourbon prince living in exile in one of the German states and then had him killed. You might be tempted to pretend that the document does not exist. However, you will be better off if you incorporate the document into your essay. By doing this you are acknowledging that this historical issue, like all historical issues, is complex. This acknowledgment is good. AP essay graders are instructed to look for evidence that you understand that history has no simple answers and to reward you for it.

As you read the documents, be aware that each one holds a few morsels of information for your essay. Do not fixate on any one document, but at the same time, do not ignore any. Also, as you read the documents, take note of any "outside information" that the document reminds you of and enter it into your grid/columns.

DRILL

Below is a "mini-DBQ" (it has only four documents, instead of the usual ten to twelve). Read through the documents, taking notes in the margins and blank spaces.

———————————◯———————————

1. Discuss the roles of women in the religious conflicts of the sixteenth century.

Document A

> Source: a printed pamphlet addressed to Katherine von Bora, the wife of Martin Luther
>
> Woe to you, poor fallen woman, not only because you have passed from light to darkness, from the cloistered holy religion into a damnable shameful life, but also that you have gone from the grace to the disfavor of God, in that you have left the cloister in lay clothes and have gone to Wittenberg like a chorus girl. You are said to have lived with Luther in sin.

Document B

> Source: Letter written in 1523 by Argula von Grumbach, the daughter of a Bavarian noble, to the faculty of the University of Ingolstadt after they had forced a young member of the teaching staff to recant his belief in Luther's theology
>
> What have Luther and Melanchthon taught save the Word of God? You have condemned them. You have not refuted them. Where do you read in the Bible that Christ, the apostles, and the prophets imprisoned, banished, burned, or murdered anyone? You tell us that we must obey the magistrates. Correct. But neither the pope, nor the Kaiser, nor the princes have any authority over the Word of God.

Document C

Source: Examination of Elizabeth Dirks before a Catholic court in 1549 on the charge of being an Anabaptist

Examiner: We understand that you are a teacher and have led many astray. We want to know who your friends are.

Elizabeth: I am commanded to love the Lord my God and honor my parents. Therefore I will not tell you who my parents are. That I suffer for Christ is damaging to my friends.

Examiner: What do you believe about the baptism of children, seeing that you have had yourself baptized again?

Elizabeth: No my Lords, I have not had myself baptized again. I have been baptized once on my faith, because it is written, "Baptism belongs to believers."

Document D

Source: *The Way of Perfection* by St. Teresa of Avila (1515–1582), a prominent Catholic reformer and author of spiritual books

At about this time there came to my notice the harm and havoc that were being wrought in France by these Lutherans and the way in which their unhappy sect was increasing. I felt that I would have laid down a thousand lives to save a single one of all the souls that were being lost there. And, seeing that I was a woman, and a sinner, I determined to do the little that was in me—namely, to follow the evangelical counsels as perfectly as I could, and to see that these few nuns who are here should do the same.

Here's How to Crack It

The writers of the exam have provided you with four different examples of the ways in which women participated in the religious disputes of the sixteenth century. **Document A** may initially look somewhat confusing until you take a moment to think about the source: It is a pamphlet addressed to the wife of Martin Luther. If you forgot about the story of Katherine von Bora and her marriage to Luther, you're in luck, since the document provides you with some background. You should be aware, however, that the position taken in the pamphlet is entirely hostile to both Katherine and Martin Luther. Therefore, it does not take much of a leap of faith to conclude that the document was written by a Catholic who was horrified by Katherine's leaving the cloistered life and by her marriage to Luther.

Document B reveals another side of the participation of women in the religious debates of the Reformation. It is from a woman who actively participated in such questions by championing a young Lutheran teacher. The author, Argula von Grumbach, will not be a familiar name to you, but you can see from the document that she was fully aware of the major issues of the conflict, such as Luther's emphasis on the Bible as the sole source of faith and his rejection of papal authority. Challenging the authorities on behalf of this young man is an interesting example of open defiance, something not usually expected from women in the sixteenth century.

Document C is part of a transcript of a trial of a woman who was accused of being an Anabaptist. Don't panic if you have forgotten what the Anabaptists believed in, since the document explains that Anabaptists believed in adult baptism. As the accused woman Elizabeth Dirks says, "Baptism belongs to believers," implying that it's not appropriate for unaware infants. There are other things that you can pull from this document. One of the accusations that the Catholic authorities mentioned is that she was a teacher, albeit one who was leading people astray. Considering that women were rarely literate in this age, her profession is something to be noted, as should her intense loyalty to her friends, whom she refuses to betray by revealing their presence at her rebaptism. She must have been aware that such a refusal would bring her additional torture, the typical means of extracting a confession.

Document D can be compared with Document B, since, once again, a woman actively threw herself into the religious debates of the period. This time, however, our author, St. Teresa of Avila, used her pen not to challenge the Catholic Church but to defend it. She revealed that she found herself as a defender of the Church in response to Lutheranism taking root in France. She also grappled with the question as to how, as a woman, she could best serve her church. She would have liked, if the opportunity arose, to "have laid down a thousand lives to save a single one of all the souls that were being lost there," but since that cheery prospect was not open to her, she had to find some other outlet for her anger. So she organized the nuns who still remained in the monastery and recommitted them to the Catholic Church.

That's it for the documents. Now, formulate a thesis, figure out how and where to fit all your information into your argument, and write an essay. Relax. It is easier than it sounds.

––––––––––––––––––––––

Developing a Thesis

Before you decide on your thesis, GO BACK AND READ THE QUESTION ONE MORE TIME! Make sure that your thesis addresses all the pertinent aspects of the question. Your thesis should not simply restate the prompt; it also has to answer the question. It should include a mention of the groups you have chosen for this question.

For this sample question, your thesis might read as follows: Women played an active role in the religious debates of the sixteenth century, both as supporters of a break with Rome and as defenders of the Catholic Church. You can then bring in the variety of experiences revealed in the four sources above to buttress this thesis.

Before the Writing Period Begins, Create an Outline

At this point, you should still have time left in the mandatory 15-minute reading period. Create an outline with one Roman numeral for each paragraph. Decide on the subject of each paragraph and on what information you will include in each paragraph. Do not rely on your grid/columns if you do not have to. The grid or columns are good for organizing your information but are less efficient for structuring an essay.

If you *still* have time after writing an outline, write a rough draft of your first paragraph in your green booklet, and then transcribe it to your essay form once the writing period starts.

Write Your Essay

The most important advice for writing your exam is to stay confident. Everyone else taking the test, all across the country, is at least as nervous about it as you are.

Summary

o The DBQ consists of an essay question and ten to twelve historical documents. Most likely, you will not have seen most of the documents before, but they will all relate to major historical events and ideas. The DBQ begins with a 15-minute reading period, followed by a 45-minute writing period.

o There is no single "correct" answer to the DBQ. DBQs are framed so that they can be successfully argued from many different viewpoints.

o Read the essay question carefully. Circle and/or underline important words and phrases. Once you understand the question, create a grid or columns in which to organize your notes on the essay.

o Before you start reading the documents, brainstorm about the question. This way you will gather the all-important "outside information" before you submerge yourself in the documents.

o Read the documents. Read them in order, as there is usually a logic to the order in which they are presented. Pay attention to contradictions within and among the documents and also to who is speaking and what sociopolitical tradition he or she represents. If you have decided on a thesis, keep an eye out for information that might refute your thesis, and be prepared to address it in your essay.

o Decide on a thesis; then write an outline for your essay.

o Use sparingly the historical background provided as part of your essay.

o Your introductory paragraph should set the historical scene and include a thesis.

o Try to include as many of the documents as you can in your essay.

o When you write the essay, do not be concerned with literary merit. Be sure your essay is logically organized, easy to understand, and always focused on the thesis.

o   Know the core. Be sure you address each of the six basic criteria.

o   Stay positive. Do not panic. Everyone else is as nervous as you are.

CRACKING THE FREE-RESPONSE QUESTIONS

What Are the Free-Response Questions?

The free-response questions consist of six questions grouped into two sections. The first group of three contains questions covering the period from the Renaissance to the Napoleonic era, and the second group of three covers the period from the end of the Napoleonic era to the present. You are required to answer two of these essay questions, one from each group. These questions are probably very similar to the essays your AP teacher has given you on tests throughout the academic year.

The free-response questions are the final section of the AP European History Exam. This section is administered immediately following the DBQ. (You do not get a break between sections.) You are given 70 minutes to write both free-response essays.

The free-response questions, like the DBQ, have no single "correct" answers. Unlike the DBQ, though, the free-response questions are not accompanied by documents; *everything* you include in your free-response answer will be outside information. Also, because you have less time to plan and write the free-response essays, these essays can be shorter and not as comprehensive as your DBQ essay. A simple, defensible thesis, accompanied by an organized essay discussing as much relevant information as you can remember, should earn a top grade. Most free-response questions ask you to *analyze*, *assess*, or *evaluate* the causes and effects of a historical subject, allowing you to write an essay that is primarily descriptive. Here are two examples:

1. Assess the impact of any THREE of the following on the growth of industrialization in Great Britain in the first half of the nineteenth century:
   Choose three: the rise in population
                         the entrepreneurial ethic
                         plentiful natural resources
                         political and social stability

2. Analyze the ways in which Renaissance humanism affected the concept of the individual.

As you can see, the free-response questions allow you to recite what you have learned in class. The subjects should be familiar; the questions are straightforward.

These essays are graded on a 1–9 scale like the DBQ. The DBQ is worth more on your final grade, however, than each free-response essay. When computing your final score, the College Board multiplies your DBQ score by 4.5 and each of your free-response essays by 2.75. Yes, it's confusing, but don't sweat it. All you need to know is the end result: The DBQ is worth 45 percent of your essay grade, and each free-response question is worth 27.5 percent.

Which Questions to Choose

Choose the questions about which you know the most specific details, NOT the ones that look easiest at first glance. The more you know about the subject, the better your final grade will be.

How to Write the Essays

Since we have covered this information already in the previous two chapters, here are brief directions for how to structure your essay.

- First, read the question and analyze it.
- Second, create a grid or columns and take notes.
- Third, assess your information and devise a thesis.
- Fourth, write a quick outline.
- Finally, write your essay.

If any of these instructions are unclear, reread the previous two chapters.

As best you can, *split your time evenly between the two essays*. Too many students spend most of their time on the first essay and then do not have enough time to write a decent second essay. Both essays are worth the same number of points. Treat them equally. Pace yourself, watch the clock, and make sure you are finishing (or, better yet, have finished) your first essay when 35 minutes have passed. Then move directly on to the next essay.

A Final Note

This section is short, not because the free-response questions are unimportant, but because we have already discussed in previous chapters what you need to know to write successful AP essays. The free-response questions are worth more than one-quarter of your grade; they are VERY important. Many students are tempted to ease up when they finish the DBQ because it is so challenging. Do not make that mistake. Reach down for that last bit of energy like a long-distance runner coming into the home stretch. When you reach the free-response questions, you have only a little more than one hour to go. *Then*, you can take it easy.

Summary

o The free-response section consists of two groups of three questions. You must answer one question from each of the groups. The first group covers the period up to the end of the Napoleonic era, and the second group covers the post-1815 period.

o Choose the questions about which you know the most specific details, not the ones that look easiest.

o Study each question carefully. Make sure you are answering the question exactly. If you misinterpret a question and write about something other than what the prompt asks, you will receive a 0 for that question.

o Circle all key words. Consider the dates given; they are clues to what you are to write about. If, for example, a question asks, "How did the nature of the Soviet regime change after 1924?", the question is in fact asking you to show the differences between the leadership and policies of Lenin and Stalin.

o Do not ignore any part of the question. If a question asks you to "Compare and contrast the different personalities and leadership styles of Charles V, Holy Roman Emperor, and his son Philip II, King of Spain, and how these influenced the methods they used to counter the Protestant movement," be sure to address *personalities*, *leadership styles*, and *the ways these influenced policy toward the Reformation*. If you find yourself in a situation in which you do not know enough to answer a part of the question, do not ignore that part. Use the historical knowledge you have, combined with logic, to guess at the answer.

o Once you understand the question, create a grid or columns in which to organize your notes.

o Decide on a thesis, and then write an outline for your essay.

o Follow your outline. Stick to one important idea per paragraph. Provide concrete examples to support the point you are making. We recommend at least two examples per issue.

○ Stay focused on the question, and don't go off on tangents. Write only about what the question asks, and carefully choose the evidence to support it. You have very little time to throw together these essays. Do not spend time including information that isn't directly relevant.

○ Your introductory paragraph is more than just your thesis. It should also set the historical scene (time, place, historical situation) so that the reader can more clearly understand what your essay is about. In your thesis, do not simply restate the question; be sure to also *answer* the question. The thesis tells the reader what the main points of the essay are.

○ Remember: This is a European history exam. If you write about the Cold War, for example, put as much focus as possible on what the Europeans are doing. If your essay deals with literature, art, philosophy, science, economics, social issues, and so on, place the discussion in the correct historical context.

○ Do not be concerned with literary merit. Be sure your essay is logically organized, easy to understand, and **always focused on the thesis.** Each paragraph should have a topic sentence, and the essay should close with a concluding paragraph.

○ Write clearly and neatly. Do not write in overly complex sentences. Toss in a couple of "big" words that you know you will not misuse. When in doubt, stick to simple syntax and vocabulary.

○ Use transition words to indicate continuity of thought and changes in the direction of your argument.

○ Keep a close watch on the time. Spend approximately 45 minutes writing the DBQ and 30 minutes on each free-response question. This will ensure that you don't suddenly find yourself with 10 minutes left and an entire essay still to write.

○ Stay positive. Do not panic. Everyone else is at least as nervous as you are.

Chapter 3
Using Your Time Effectively to Maximize Points

USING YOUR TIME EFFECTIVELY TO MAXIMIZE POINTS

Very few students stop to think about how to improve their test-taking skills. Most assume that if they study hard, they will test well, and if they do not study, they will do poorly. Most students continue to believe this even after experience teaches them otherwise. Have you ever studied really hard for an exam and then blown it on test day? Have you ever aced an exam for which you thought you weren't well prepared? Most students have had one, if not both, of these experiences. The lesson should be clear: Factors other than your level of preparation influence your final test score. This chapter will provide you with some insights that will help you perform better on the AP European History Exam and on other exams as well.

Pacing and Timing

A big part of scoring well on an exam is working at a consistent pace. The worst mistake made by inexperienced or unsavvy test takers is that they come to a question that stumps them, and rather than just skip it, they panic and stall. Time stands still when you're working on a question you cannot answer, and it is not unusual for students to waste five minutes on a single question (especially a question involving a graph or the word *except*) because they are too stubborn to cut their losses. It is important to be aware of how much time you have spent on a given question and on the section on which you are working. There are several ways to improving your pacing and timing for the test:

- **Know your average pace.** While you prepare for your test, try to gauge how long you take on 5, 10, or 20 questions. Knowing how long you spend on average per question will help you identify how many questions you can answer effectively and how best to pace yourself for the test.

- **Have a watch or clock nearby.** You are permitted to have a watch or clock nearby to help you keep track of time. It is important to remember, however, that constantly checking the clock is in itself a waste of time and can be distracting. Devise a plan. Try checking the clock after every 15 or 30 questions to see if you are keeping the correct pace or whether you need to speed up; this will ensure that you are cognizant of the time but will not permit you to fall into the trap of dwelling on it.

- **Know when to move on.** Since all questions are scored equally, investing appreciable amounts of time on a single question is inefficient and can potentially deprive you of the chance to answer easier questions later on. If you are able to eliminate answer choices, do so; but don't worry about picking a random answer and moving on if you cannot find the correct answer. Remember: Tests are like marathons; you do best when you work through them at a steady pace. You can always come back to a question you don't know. When you do, very often you will find that your previous mental block is gone, and you will wonder why the question perplexed you the first time around (as you gleefully move on to the next question). Even if you still don't know the answer, you will not have wasted valuable time you could have spent on easier questions.

- **Be selective.** You don't have to do any of the questions in a given section in order. If you are stumped by an essay or multiple-choice question, skip it or choose a different one. In the section below, you will see that you may not have to answer every question correctly to achieve your desired score. Select the questions or essays that you can answer and work on them first. This will make you more efficient and give you the greatest chance of getting the most questions correct.

- **Use Process of Elimination on multiple-choice questions.** Many times, one or more answer choices can be eliminated. Every answer choice that can be eliminated increases the odds that you will answer the question correctly. The section on multiple-choice questions will go through strategies to find these incorrect answer choices and increase your odds of getting the question correct.

Remember: When all the questions on a test are of equal value, no one question is that important; your overall goal for pacing is to get the most questions correct. Finally, you should set a realistic goal for your final score. In the next section, we will break down how to achieve your desired score and present ways of pacing yourself to do so.

Getting the Score You Want

Depending on the score you need, it may be in your best interest not to try to work through every question. Check with the schools to which you are applying. Do you need a 3 to earn credit for the test? If you get a raw score of 48 (out of 80) on the multiple-choice section and do as well on the essays, you will get a 3.

Keep in mind that there is no "guessing penalty" for an incorrect multiple-choice answer. Instead, students are assessed only on the total number of correct answers. A lot of AP materials, even those you receive in your AP class, may not include this information. It is really important to remember that if you are running out of time, you should fill in all the bubbles before the time for the multiple-choice section is up. Even if you don't plan to spend a lot of time on every question and even if you have no idea what the correct answer is, you need to fill something in.

Test Anxiety

Everybody experiences anxiety before and during an exam. To a certain extent, test anxiety *can* be helpful. Some people find that they perform more quickly and efficiently under stress. If you have ever pulled an all-nighter to write a paper and ended up doing good work, you know the feeling.

However, *too much stress* is definitely a bad thing. Hyperventilating during the test, for example, almost always leads to a lower score. If you find that you stress out during exams, here are a few preemptive actions you can take.

- **Take a reality check.** Evaluate your situation before the test begins. If you have studied hard, remind yourself that you are well prepared. Remember that many others taking the test are not as well prepared, and (in your classes, at least) you are being graded against them, so you have an advantage. If you didn't study, accept the fact that you will probably not ace the test. Make sure you get to every question you know something about. Don't stress out or fixate on how much you don't know. Your job is to score as high as you can by maximizing the benefits of what you do know. In either scenario, it is best to think of a test as if it were a game. How can you get the most points in the time allotted to you? Always answer questions you can answer easily and quickly before you answer those that will take more time.

- **Try to relax.** Slow, deep breathing works for almost everyone. Close your eyes, take a few slow, deep breaths, and concentrate on nothing but your inhalation and exhalation for a few seconds. This is a basic form of meditation, and it should help you to clear your mind of stress and, as a result, concentrate better on the test. If you have ever taken yoga classes, you probably know some other good relaxation techniques. Use them when you can (obviously, anything that requires leaving your seat and, say, assuming a handstand position won't be allowed by any but the most free-spirited proctors).

- **Eliminate as many surprises as you can.** Make sure you know where the test will be given, when it starts, what type of questions are going to be asked, and how long the test will take. You don't want to be worrying about any of these things on test day or, even worse, after the test has already begun.

The best way to avoid stress is to study both the test material and the test itself. Congratulations! By buying or reading this book, you are taking a major step toward a stress-free AP European History Exam.

REFLECT

Respond to the following questions:

- How long will you spend on multiple-choice questions?

- How will you change your approach to multiple-choice questions?

- What is your multiple-choice guessing strategy?

- How much time will you spend on the DBQ? The first thematic essay? The second thematic essay?

- What will you do before you begin writing an essay?

- How will you change your approach to the essays?

- Will you seek further help outside of this book (such as a teacher, tutor, or AP Central) on how to approach multiple-choice questions, the essay, or a pacing strategy?

Part IV
Drills

Chapter 4
1450–1815: Political and Diplomatic Questions

1450–1815: POLITICAL AND DIPLOMATIC QUESTIONS

Multiple-Choice Questions

1. The new class of families that achieved wealth in Italy in the fifteenth century did so mostly through

   (A) land ownership
   (B) papal favoritism
   (C) court intrigue
   (D) banking
   (E) trade

2. To prepare for careers as public figures, young civic humanists in Renaissance Italy studied the art of rhetoric as written by

   (A) Cicero
   (B) Aristophanes
   (C) St. Augustine
   (D) Petrarch
   (E) Lorenzo Valla

3. The Cathedral of Florence commissioned Michelangelo to sculpt the *David* to

   (A) help Michelangelo survive as an artist
   (B) demonstrate the Medici respect for the classical ideals of the Renaissance
   (C) create totally original subject matter in the city of Florence
   (D) symbolize the resistance of Florentines against dominance by Milan and the papal states
   (E) get rid of a giant block of marble

4. *Utopia*, which imagined a world in which all common property was abolished, was written by

   (A) Jan Hus
   (B) Thomas More
   (C) Desiderus Erasmus
   (D) Karl Marx and Friedrich Engels
   (E) George Orwell

5. Prior to the Renaissance, the political power of the Catholic Church had been damaged by all of the following EXCEPT

(A) the Great Schism
(B) the Black Death
(C) the rise of pietism
(D) Simony
(E) John Eck's debates in Leipzig

6. The Diet of Worms is most notable for

(A) the altering of Catholic theology to please Protestant reformers
(B) Martin Luther defending his theology to the Holy Roman Emperor Charles V
(C) the arrest of Martin Luther afterwards by Prince Frederick, Elector of Saxony
(D) the gathering of Philip Melanchthon, Ulrich Zwingli, and John Calvin to protest Luther's trial
(E) the stubborn resistance of the Holy Roman Emperor to pressure from the Catholic Church regarding Martin Luther

7. In 1534, the Act of Supremacy

(A) acknowledged the King of England as the Supreme Head of the Church of England
(B) announced the end of the Tudor dynasty
(C) was issued by "Bloody Mary" to the Protestant heretics
(D) killed thousands of English Catholics
(E) eased the quick and easy transition from divine monarchy to constitutional monarchy

8. The *hacienda* system was created by the Spanish in the sixteenth century to

(A) turn the Incas against themselves, thus facilitating Pizarro's ambitions
(B) treat the natives humanely and respectfully
(C) exploit the agricultural and mineral riches of the New World
(D) combat the slave trade that had begun in Africa
(E) indulge the Spanish penchant for Moorish architecture

9. During the seventeenth century, the biggest difference between the Stuart dynasty and the Bourbon dynasty was

   (A) the willingness to bend to the will of the people
   (B) the desire to wage war against neighboring countries
   (C) the response to religious uprisings
   (D) the tax burdens placed upon its people
   (E) the hope for a better future for its people

10. The monarchs' growing rate of taxation in the seventeenth century was caused primarily by

   (A) the greed for more land in overseas conquests
   (B) the desire to punish the peasantry
   (C) the rise of permanent mercenary armies
   (D) the nobles who demanded relief from a traditionally heavy tax burden
   (E) the trusted clergy who stole money from royal coffers

11. In France, the office of the *intendent* was created to

   (A) collect taxes on behalf of the monarch
   (B) attack political dissidents
   (C) administer proper medical care
   (D) oversee agricultural yields
   (E) strengthen the power of the nobility

12. Throughout the first half of the sixteenth century, the biggest threat to stability on the Italian peninsula came from

   (A) internal dissent
   (B) Moorish attacks
   (C) Savonarola's assumption of power in Florence
   (D) French and Spanish struggle for domination over the Italian city-states
   (E) Machiavelli's radical and amoral ideas about power

13. Centralization of power on the Spanish peninsula occurred in the late fifteenth century for all of the following reasons EXCEPT

    (A) the marriage of Ferdinand of Aragon and Isabella of Castile
    (B) the establishment of a uniform tax code
    (C) the overthrow of the Moors at Granada
    (D) the expulsion of the Jews
    (E) the launching of Christopher Columbus's expedition to the New World

14. Philip V launched the Spanish Armada against England because

    (A) he had been embarrassed by his loss to the English in the Battle of Lepanto
    (B) England was aiding the Dutch revolt against Habsburg rule
    (C) Spanish power was quickly declining as New World resources were drying up
    (D) he had entered into an alliance with Scotland, which wanted to overthrow its southern neighbor
    (E) the Thirty Years' War had left the English vulnerable to attack

15. The leaders of the German principalities of the Holy Roman Empire avoided centralization under Charles V by

    (A) rejecting the Golden Bull of Charles IV
    (B) holding a special recall election to remove Charles V from the throne
    (C) formally changing the official language of their principalities
    (D) using the Peace of Augsburg as a pretext to proclaim their independence
    (E) outlawing lay piety groups

16. The reasons for the prolonged nature of the Thirty Years' War do NOT include

    (A) Albrecht von Wallenstein's enormous standing army in Bohemia that was in need of a conflict
    (B) the involvement of outsiders, such as the King of Denmark, wanting to protect the interests of Protestants in Germany
    (C) the alteration of the constitution of the Holy Roman Empire as a result of the Palatinate's electoral vote being given to Bavaria
    (D) the success of the Edict of Restitution, which triggered Sweden's entrance into the war
    (E) the arrival of papal troops at the Bavarian front

17. The Second Defenestration of Prague occurred when

(A) the ruler of Czechoslovakia was advised to reduce the tax burden upon the peasants or risk another rebellion
(B) the Catholic advisors to the new king of Bohemia were thrown out of a window by Protestant nobles
(C) the Protestant ruler of Slovenia was thrown out of a window by Catholic nobles
(D) an invading Swedish army systematically raped the female Catholic population of Bavaria two years in a row
(E) the Dutch Revolt spread into central Europe

18. The most violent example of persecution of French Hugenots occurred during

(A) the Siege of Turin
(B) the Peace of Westphalia
(C) the Battle of White Mountain
(D) the St. Bartholomew's Day Massacre
(E) the Battle of Bordeaux

19. The phrase "Paris is worth a Mass" was uttered by

(A) Henry IV, who finally converted to Catholicism to keep peace in Paris
(B) Louis XIV, who forced nobles to turn Catholic
(C) Cardinal Mazarin, who asked the people to accept a Catholic regent
(D) Louis XVI, who was trying to calm the urban masses with religion
(E) Napoleon I, who brought Catholicism into the French state

20. The quotation "I am the state" best represents the political philosophy of

(A) James II of England
(B) Louis XIV of France
(C) Cardinal Richelieu
(D) Gustavus Adolphus of Sweden
(E) Charles V of the Holy Roman Empire

21. The mass production of French porcelain can be traced back to the mercantilist policies of

(A) Adam Smith
(B) Denis Diderot
(C) Jean-Baptiste Colbert
(D) Napoleon I
(E) John Maynard Keynes

22. The Treaty of Utrecht accomplished all of the following EXCEPT

(A) ending the War of Spanish Succession
(B) allowing the same monarch to rule Spain and France
(C) concluding Louis XIV's expansionist policies
(D) installing a Bourbon on the throne of Spain
(E) ceding Gibraltar to the English

23. Elizabeth I's decision to remain the "Virgin Queen" did NOT give her which of the following benefits?

(A) The ability to use marriage as a tool of diplomacy
(B) The status as sole political decision maker in England
(C) The creation of a cult of personality around her virginity
(D) The guarantee of a Protestant successor to her throne
(E) The prevention of foreign aggression upon her land

24. The English Civil War was caused by

(A) Protestants demanding a voice in the government
(B) Parliament's execution of King Charles I
(C) Oliver Cromwell's lust for power
(D) a stalemate between the monarchy and Parliament regarding the appropriation of funds
(E) Thomas Hobbes's urging of violent revolution

25. Oliver Cromwell was confronted with a conflict between two groups of his own supporters called

    (A) Levellers and Diggers
    (B) Independents and Presbyterians
    (C) the House of Lancaster and the House of York
    (D) Conservatives and Liberals
    (E) Jacobins and Girondins

26. Which of the following religious actions of King James II antagonized England the LEAST?

    (A) Demanding a repeal of the Test Act
    (B) Issuing the Declaration of Indulgence
    (C) Imprisoning seven Anglican bishops for refusing to read the new laws allowing more civil rights to Catholics
    (D) Fathering a newborn son while in office
    (E) Quashing a rebellion in Scotland led by the Duke of Argyll

27. Which of the following forced Scotland to give up its Parliament?

    (A) The Bill of Rights
    (B) The Act of Toleration
    (C) The Mutiny Act
    (D) The Act of Settlement
    (E) The Act of Union

28. During the seventeenth century, the most politically decentralized nation in Europe was

    (A) Russia
    (B) France
    (C) Italy
    (D) The Netherlands
    (E) Poland

29. An advocate of *laissez-faire*

    (A) promotes tariffs designed to protect domestic manufacturing

    (B) believes that only natural laws are legitimate

    (C) argues that the government should refrain from trying to regulate the economy

    (D) argues that the government should act as an "invisible" hand to regulate the economy

    (E) insists that a monarch rules by divine command

30. The "general will" of the people granting sovereignty to the ruler is found in the writings of

    (A) Denis Diderot

    (B) Jean-Jacques Rousseau

    (C) Voltaire

    (D) Baron de Montesquieu

    (E) David Hume

31. All of the following rulers could be described as "enlightened despots" EXCEPT

    (A) Elizabeth I of England

    (B) Catherine II of Russia

    (C) Joseph II of Austria

    (D) Frederick the Great of Prussia

    (E) Louis XVI of France

32. The War of the Austrian Succession was NOT caused by

    (A) Charles VI's lack of an heir

    (B) France's breaking of the promise to honor the Pragmatic Sanction

    (C) Prussia's perception of Maria Theresa as unable to hold together the Holy Roman Empire

    (D) the opposition of the Hungarian nobility

    (E) Frederick the Great's seizure of Silesia

33. Poland was eventually "wiped off the map of Europe" in 1795 by

(A) Andrzej Kościuszko's loss to the Russians
(B) three partitions undertaken by Prussia, Russia, and Austria
(C) a ruling class of nobles who betrayed their own people
(D) King Poniatowski's spurning of Catherine the Great's romantic advances
(E) its lack of a written constitution

34. The Seven Years' War did NOT result in

(A) the defeat of the French in North America and the confiscation of their colonies there
(B) a historically unusual alliance between the English and the Prussians
(C) the appearance of victory on the part of Frederick the Great
(D) the shattering of the new Prussian state
(E) the withdrawal of the Russian army by the new Russian tsar, Peter III, due to his admiration for Frederick

35. The first unofficial prime minister of Britain was

(A) Edmund Burke
(B) George Grenville
(C) Benjamin Disraeli
(D) Cecil Rhodes
(E) Robert Walpole

36. The Civil Constitution of the Clergy was significant in the French Revolution because it

(A) subjugated the clergy to the state
(B) forced the priests to behave appropriately
(C) was France's first written constitution
(D) gave religious permission to the *sans-culottes* to destroy their opponents
(E) reaffirmed the place of the Church in the French government

37. All of the following people played important roles in the moderate phase of the French Revolution EXCEPT

    (A) Thomas Jefferson
    (B) Marquis de Lafayette
    (C) Maximilian Robespierre
    (D) Count of Artois
    (E) Marie Antoinette

38. During the French Revolution, "the Mountain" and "the Plain" refer to

    (A) the two groups of men willing to risk their lives for freedom
    (B) the code names used for places where the working-class could find bread
    (C) the adherents of hierarchy versus the adherents of democracy
    (D) the two parts of the seating chart at the National Convention
    (E) the two most infamous types of guillotine

39. The Republic of Virtue was

    (A) an Italian city-state founded by the pope on the principles of Christian behavior
    (B) a French movement dedicated to eradicating all traces of the monarchical regime
    (C) an American term invented by Calvinist Puritans who emigrated to New England
    (D) a Swiss term for an ideal society
    (E) a satirical Irish drinking song

40. The Directory held onto power through its control of

    (A) the military
    (B) the sans-culottes
    (C) the Catholic church
    (D) important tracts of land
    (E) Napoleon Bonaparte

41. The British victory at the Battle of Trafalgar was significant because

  (A) Napoleon's Grand Army was destroyed
  (B) the Continental system was immediately stopped
  (C) the British navy defeated the French and Spanish fleets, becoming the rulers of the ocean
  (D) it marked a new friendship between England and France
  (E) Napoleon was captured and sent to the island of Elba

42. The defeat of Napoleon's Grand Army in Russia primarily demonstrated

  (A) the strength of Russia's ties with the Ottoman Empire
  (B) the danger of insulting the tsar
  (C) the difficulty of fighting the Russian army on its own soil during the winter
  (D) the need for auxiliary troops in extreme climates
  (E) the necessity of good hygiene in the winter

43. The Civil Code of 1804 did NOT

  (A) allow for equal rights between the sexes
  (B) forbid privileges based on birth
  (C) establish the framework for the modern-day French legal system
  (D) make it more difficult for a woman to file for divorce
  (E) allow freedom of religion

Free-Response Questions

44. Compare and contrast the ways in which Peter the Great and Catherine the Great succeeded in establishing a powerful Russia.

_____

_____

_____

_____

_____

_____

_____

_____

_____

_____

_____

_____

_____

_____

_____

_____

_____

_____

_____

_____

_____

_____

_____

_____

_____

_____

_____

_____

_____

45. Discuss the reasons for the changing aims and methods of the French Revolution.

_____

_____

_____

_____

_____

_____

_____

_____

_____

_____

_____

_____

_____

_____

_____

_____

_____

_____

_____

_____

_____

_____

_____

_____

_____

_____

_____

_____

_____

_____

_____

_____

_____

_____

_____

Chapter 5
1450–1815: Political and Diplomatic Answers and Explanations

ANSWER KEY

1.	E	23.	D
2.	A	24.	D
3.	D	25.	B
4.	B	26.	E
5.	E	27.	E
6.	B	28.	D
7.	A	29.	C
8.	C	30.	B
9.	A	31.	A
10.	C	32.	D
11.	A	33.	B
12.	D	34.	D
13.	B	35.	E
14.	B	36.	A
15.	D	37.	C
16.	E	38.	D
17.	B	39.	B
18.	D	40.	A
19.	A	41.	C
20.	B	42.	C
21.	C	43.	A
22.	B		

ANSWERS AND EXPLANATIONS

1. **E** The rise of the merchant class is the great story of the Italian Renaissance. The trading that they initiated with the Arabs, and thus the exposure to Middle Eastern and even Asian goods and ideas, was the impetus behind the Renaissance.

2. **A** Cicero was the classical Roman orator whose most famous work on rhetoric, *De Oratore*, served as the blueprint for successful political speech until the nineteenth century. His influence cannot be underestimated; the rediscovery of his works almost singlehandedly sparked an Italian love affair with public affairs, and even the Renaissance itself.

3. **D** The *David* was intended as a propaganda piece that would inspire the Florentines to remain strong in the face of the powerful neighbor Milan. David, as a historical subject, was seen as an underdog against Goliath. While the Florentines may have respected the rebirth of classicism, that wasn't the primary purpose of commissioning the statue (B), and neither was it the first David in the city (C).

4. **B** Thomas More, the famous English Renaissance humanist, invented the word *utopia* (literally, "without a place") to describe an ideal world. On this imaginary island in the Atlantic, hospitals were free, divorce was permitted, multiple religions were tolerant of one another, toilets were made of gold, and private property was abolished. Marx and Engels probably would have agreed with that last part, but they lived in the nineteenth century. Erasmus was a contemporary of More's, and Orwell was the twentieth-century writer of *1984*, which was a dystopia, or nightmarish imaginary place. Jan Hus was a Reformation figure who was burned at the stake for suggesting that the common people should share the wine at Catholic mass.

5. **E** John Eck was a prominent church theologian who challenged Martin Luther at these debates. However, you more likely got the answer by eliminating the other four—all of which were contributing factors to the weakening of the papacy. The Great Schism split the church for at least seventy years into two, and sometimes three, competing popes. The Black Death killed a third of Europe and severely weakened the existing political systems. Pietism stated that no intermediaries were required between a human being and God, which obviated the need for a priest or a church. Simony was the selling of church offices.

6. **B** Luther was called before the Diet of Worms by Charles V to explain himself. The Holy Roman Emperor had done so at the behest of Catholic authorities, the opposite of (E). No Catholic dogma was altered at any time during the Reformation (A). (C) is wrong because Frederick actually protected Luther after the Diet, and (D) is entirely imagined.

7. **A** The Act of Supremacy was passed by Parliament under Henry VIII, and it represents England's final political and religious break with the Catholic Church, marking the beginning of the English Reformation. The Tudor Dynasty wouldn't end until 1600 (B) and was not issued by Bloody

Mary (C), though she did kill thousands of Protestants. (D) is fiction, and the transition from divine to constitutional monarchy (E) was not quick or easy.

8. **C** The *hacienda* system was essentially a plantation system (reproduced all over today's Latin America), using the local native people as forced labor. Many of those involved in this *encomienda* died from disease, malnutrition, and overwork, forcing the Spanish to begin importing African slaves.

9. **A** The biggest difference between England and France during this period was the Stuarts' painful and slow acceptance of the power of Parliament, turning the throne into a constitutional monarchy. In France, this never happened: The Bourbons, through Louis XIII and Louis XIV, continued to accumulate more and more power. Both were involved in the Thirty Years' War (B), both responded badly to religious uprisings (C), and both placed unfair tax burdens upon the peasantry (D).

10. **C** While warfare had always been in existence, the way in which it was waged changed in the seventeenth century. A nasty cycle began in which standing armies were suddenly necessary, largely to keep order over a peasantry that was overtaxed in order to fund that same standing army. Slowly, the European nation-states were beginning to coalesce into larger bureacracies.

11. **A** The *intendentes* were the roving tax collectors of the Bourbon dynasty. They were sent to the provinces to collect money for the king's treasury in Paris, as well as to mete out justice. They served as the eyes and the ears of the throne. The nobles in these areas naturally resented their presence, but Louis XIV built the Palace at Versailles to distract them from this sneaky usurpation of power.

12. **D** (C) would have been good, except it happened just prior to the sixteenth century. It was the match that lit the fire. After Savonarola's short-lived puritanical rule of Florence ended with his execution, the Italian city-states found themselves in a series of wars of domination involving themselves, France, Spain, and even Switzerland, Scotland, and England. These so-called Italian Wars finally ended in 1559, when Habsburg Spain took over the rule of the region for the next one hundred and fifty years.

13. **B** 1492 was a big year for Spain. A few years earlier, the marriage that united two northern kingdoms had occurred (A). The wars against the Moors (African Muslims who had lived in southern Spain for 800 years) had just culminated in the final *reconquista* of Granada (C). The Jews, who had lived more or less peacefully in those lands for centuries, were booted out by Ferdinand and Isabella (D). And that same year, Columbus set sail from Seville, ushering in the era of Spanish domination of the New World and consolidating governmental power (E).

14. **B** As head of the Habsburg Empire (which ruled both Spain and the Netherlands) Philip spent much time and money trying to impose Catholic Counter-Reformation practices in the Netherlands. That country, however, had turned strongly Protestant, and the resultant revolt drained him of much money over the next decades. Since the Protestant revolt was aided by Elizabeth I of England, he desperately decided to attack England.

15. **D** The Peace of Augsburg was a meeting of several of the leaders of German principalities. They essentially came up with the idea of "he who rules: his religion." This principle of noninterference was cleverly designed to limit the Catholic but powerless monarch from asserting his own power by imposing his religion upon each of the 300 principalities in the Holy Roman Empire. It also signaled to Rome that they would not go to war with each other over religion.

16. **E** The Thirty Years' War was an enormously complex series of events, instigated by the election of a Catholic king in Bohemia. Like a horrific symphony, the conflict moved through three different phases of violence, spurred by mercenary soldiers, outside involvement, and the question of religion. By the end, eight million people were dead, and nothing had essentially changed. They simply reaffirmed the Peace of Augsburg. All of the answer choices are true except for (E), since the papacy was never directly involved.

17. **B** When Ferdinand of Styria was crowned the king of Bohemia, the Protestants were aghast: He was a Catholic. Their resentment and suspicion grew, especially when it became clear that he was intolerant of their newfangled views about religion. At last, things boiled over, and to send a warning to the new king, a group of Protestant nobles threw his advisors out of a third-floor window. (*Defenestration* means throwing out of a window, weirdly enough.) The advisors survived, either due to angelic intervention (the Catholic story) or by falling into a pile of manure (the Protestant story). This event sparked the Thirty Years' War.

18. **D** The St. Bartholomew's Day Massacre occurred when Henry IV of Navarre, who was Calvinist, was to marry the king's sister. This greatly concerned the powerful Catherine De Medici, who urged the king to assassinate a top Hugenot, Coligny, two days after the wedding. When that didn't work, the king ordered a slaughter of 3,000 top Hugenots, an event that spread to the populace. Eventually, between 30,000 and 50,000 French Protestants were killed, and Catholicism had instituted itself as a bloody, persecutorial religion.

19. **A** Henry IV had been flipping back and forth between Calvinism and Catholicism. He pragmatically noted that the people of Paris were Catholic. He also noted that Spain, which had been trying to make inroads in France, was doing so by appealing to the historically Catholic nature of his people. He decided to stay Catholic permanently, making his famous utterance at his conversion.

20. **B** Louis XIV stands as the ultimate example of absolute monarchy. There was no representation, nothing but centralized power in Paris, all of which was controlled, either directly or indirectly, through him. This power was supposedly divinely inspired as well. The only other ruler in Europe who came close to the same level of absolute power was Peter the Great of Russia.

21. **C** As Louis XIV's trusted Minister of Finance (all the ministers were upper middle-class bourgeoisie, incidentally, none from the nobility), Colbert was responsible for figuring out that a trade imbalance was actually good. More exports than imports would create a surplus of cash in the royal treasury, so he embarked upon an ambitious program of domestic production, which led to the production of Louis XIV style glass, tapestry, clothing, and yes, porcelain.

22. **B** The Treaty of Utrecht concluded the belligerent policies of expansion of Louis XIV (which, incidentally, nearly bankrupted France and led to the obscenely high taxation that incited the French Revolution). As the English and the Dutch were allied against Louis for a war that lasted nearly twenty-five years, the peace treaty recognized Louis XIV's grandson Philip V as king of Spain. However, Philip was compelled to renounce for himself and his descendants any right to the French throne, despite some doubts as to the lawfulness of such an act.

23. **D** Biology should give you the answer here. Elizabeth died childless, guaranteeing a very awkward situation in which a Scottish prince named James VI had to be invited to become the king of England. The other answers, however, were all true. Elizabeth used her bachelorette status to negotiate tricky foreign alliances (basically, she flirted with foreign leaders to prevent invasions) and to create an unusual type of support among her people, who wondered if or when they might get a king.

24. **D** After marrying the Catholic sister of the king of France, and then waging expensive wars with Spain and France, King Charles I was not a popular individual. When he provoked a war with Scotland, which then invaded England, he was forced to ask for more money from Parliament, which refused his request—unless he curb his own monarchical powers. This was the root of the English Civil War. Choice (B), the execution of the king, was a result, not a cause.

25. **B** The Presbyterians and Independents disagreed on the amount of dissent that would be allowed in the new English state church that they were planning—Presbyterians favored tolerance for all factions except Catholics, while the Independents promoted zero tolerance for anybody else.   The Levellers and the Diggers (A) were both radical groups inside Cromwell's army, but they weren't at odds with one another. All the other groups were either in the wrong country or the wrong time.

26. **E** Choices (A), (B), (C), and (D) all heightened the alarm that the people and Parliament felt against this new ruler who was openly Catholic—and who was using this issue to slowly bring back a measure of absolute monarchical authority. He repealed anti-Catholic laws, passed new ones allowing tolerance, opposed Protestants with other laws, and worried the people by announcing that his son, who was being raised Catholic, would assume the throne, and not his grown daughter Mary, who was Protestant. (E) is irrelevant, since there was little love between the rebellious Scots and anybody in England.

27. **E** Taken together, these five answers constituted the English response to a century of internal strife and political intrigue. (A), (C), and (D) were naked power grabs by Parliament, designed to limit the power of the monarchy, and didn't concern Scotland. (B) was a compromise bill designed to get the support of non-Anglican Protestants. (E), however, was the legal act that unified England and Scotland—and the latter had to submit to English Parliament by disbanding its own.

28. **D** Russia and France were examples of the opposite—totally centralized power. Though Italy was certainly decentralized, it wasn't yet a nation. And Poland was dominated by a confederation of nobles before succumbing to a Swedish invasion halfway through the century. Only the Netherlands (D) prospered under a minimalist government whose head, the *stadholder* of the House of Orange, was primarily a military officer.

29. **C** The French term *laissez-faire* translates as "leave it alone," which is exactly what it means: Government is urged to let the economy run free (with the important exception of private property rights). It was coined by French finance minister Colbert, though Adam Smith and others popularized it in the eighteenth century.

30. **B** Rousseau stated in *The Social Contract* that "All men are born free, but everywhere they are in chains." Believing that powerless people were largely unable to effect change, he stated that only a large mass of people could create an improvement in their condition—and that the ruler owed his power to that general will. If the ruler ignored this contract, the people had the right to overthrow him. This was the ideological justification for the French Revolution.

31. **A** Though Elizabeth I was by all reports a shrewd leader and quite logical, she died just before the start of the seventeenth century, and thus never got a chance to experience the full flower of the eighteenth-century Enlightenment. The other leaders mentioned in choices (B), (C), and (D) were responsible for freeing the serfs, allowing freedom of speech, and promoting religious toleration—though they were still constrained by the realities of their time.

32. **D** The Hungarian nobility actually rescued Maria Theresa as she struggled to maintain her new position in the face of an aggressive Prussia and France. In return, they asked for, and received, recognition as an independent kingdom. All the other answer choices actually occurred.

33. **B** Slowly, over several decades, the three powerful surrounding countries of Prussia, Russia, and Austria sliced off pieces of Poland, which had no natural barriers to impede invading armies. However, they did defeat the invading armies now and then (A), boast a class of committed nobles (C), and Europe's first written constitution (E). King Poniatowski had even had an affair with Catherine the Great of Russia prior to taking the throne (D).

34. **D** It's not much of an overstatement to say that nothing shattered the Prussian state. Their military was the strongest in Europe, and their spiked helmets became the symbol of fearsome aggression for the next hundred years. Even the Seven Years' War, in which Frederick got himself into a lot of international trouble, didn't prove fatal; neither when the Russian army rolled into Prussia, since it rolled right back out again, nor when the new tsar ordered retreat out of respect for Frederick (E).

35.   E   As Chancellor of the Exchequer in the first half of the eighteenth century, Robert Walpole became the first unofficial prime minister of England, owing to his influence in the Cabinet. Edmund Burke (A) was a conservative Whig and political thinker, but never a prime minister in any way. Both Grenville and Disraeli, (B) and (C), were prime ministers later. Cecil Rhodes (D) was an unrepentant colonialist (Rhodesia, now called Zimbabwe, was named for him), mining magnate (he was the first chairman of De Beers diamond company), and bestower of a scholarship to Oxford University (the Rhodes Scholars).

36.   A   The Civil Constitution of the Clergy greatly limited the power of the Catholic Church in France, mostly by the destruction of the religious orders. Remember that the peasants were rather indiscriminate in who they were revolting against (as long as those people were powerful) and the Church had been very much part of the power structure in this strongly pro-Catholic country.

37.   C   Robesipierre, the chairman of the Committee on Public Safety, turned the French Revolution violent by first purging the National Convention of all Girondins, and then turning his purge to the streets of Paris. The other figures were all involved earlier in the process. Jefferson helped Lafayette, (A) and (B), to write the Declaration of the Rights of Man, the Count of Artois (D) urged Louis XVI to abandon Paris, and Marie Antoinette (E) was alive only through the moderate phase before being beheaded.

38.   D   "The Mountain" refers to the Jacobins, who seated themselves on a raised dais on the left side of the National Convention. On the right sat the conservative Girondins. Incidentally, from this divide comes the present-day division between left-wing and right-wing politics. In between were the representatives who weren't part of either party; they became known as "the Plain." (Today, we call them "swing votes.")

39.   B   The Republic of Virtue was a movement during the violent part of the French Revolution to expunge all remnants of monarchical or Catholic culture from the country. The Cathedral of Notre Dame was renamed the Temple of Reason. The weekly calendar was even changed to ten days per week, and the annual calendar was reworked to begin with Year One. Robespierre himself created the Cult of the Supreme Being.

40.   A   With hundreds of thousands executed or imprisoned as a result of the Reign of Terror, France in 1795 was a place where might made right. Despite its unpopularity in the temporary ruling bodies it had established, the Directory managed to keep control of the military, even assigning a hotshot young general Napoleon Bonaparte to head up its efforts in Italy and elsewhere.

41.   C   The Battle of Trafalgar established England's supremacy on the open seas. Admiral Horatio Nelson engineered victory by ignoring the prevailing military tactic of arranging the ships in a parallel line. Though he died in the battle, his British fleet didn't lose a single ship, whereas the combined Spanish and French lost twenty-two.

42. **C** As Napoleon deployed almost 700,000 troops into Russia, many problems emerged. First, as the winter set in, life became unbearable for the troops on the ground, many of whom died of hypothermia. Second, their supply lines were stretched to nearly 1,000 miles long, and were therefore susceptible to attack. And third, because the retreating Russian army destroyed their own land, French troops began hunting for food at night, and were subsequently captured by Cossacks. The list goes on and on.

43. **A** Better known as the Napoleonic Code, the Civil Code of 1804 was quite democratic in many ways. However, it did assert the power of paternalism, announcing that the male was the head of a household, and was nearly unchallengeable in a court of law.

The Free-Response Essay Questions Explained

Question 44

44. Compare and contrast the ways in which Peter the Great and Catherine the Great succeeded in establishing a powerful Russia.

Essay Notes

While both rulers had the same objective—to modernize Russia—they used different tactics with very different results. Peter the Great was famous for his military and technological advancements:

- He constructed a brand-new capital city, **St. Petersburg**, on the Neva River, which facilitated trade with the outside world. It became the capital very quickly, simply because he settled there. He decorated the city in French and Italian styles.
- A port without any ships is useless, and Peter commissioned **the first Russian navy** to be built. As a young man, he had spent many months working in the shipyards of the Dutch, learning from the master shipbuilders.
- He waged wars against the Swedes for nearly twenty years in **the Great Northern War**. Only after the battle at Poltava did the tide turn in his favor, and Charles XII of Sweden admit defeat. Russia gained Estonia and Latvia, though it had to give up Finland. Nonetheless, it emerged as a new power on the continent.
- Peter may or may not have executed his own son, Alexei. He certainly had his son arrested for refusing to participate in the military. And his son was certainly sentenced to death. But he may have died in prison before it could be carried out.
- Most interestingly, Peter instituted a very unpopular **beard tax**. This was designed to bring Russians into the European style of smooth faces, but he was challenging a long-standing Russian tradition by doing so.

Catherine succeeded in also expanding Russia's power, but she did so through different means, including more land acquisition and artistic matters.

- Like Peter the Great, Catherine spent much time in Western Europe. In fact, she had been born in Prussia, and her father was a German prince.

- Like Peter the Great, she was cruel to those closest to her. She engineered a coup that overthrew her husband, Peter III, and she may have even murdered a close relative, a nephew also named Peter.
- Like Peter the Great, she extended Russian land holdings by absorbing parts of **Poland**. She fought the Ottomans with far more success than he had, however, and successfully got a Russian foothold in the Black Sea by taking over the **Crimean peninsula**.
- Like Peter the Great, she attempted to remake Russia according to less feudal and more rational, scientific methods. One way she did so was her attempt to redo the Russian legal system, the **Nakaz**, using such ideas. She also called the **first legislature**, listening to the problems of the serfs.
- Unlike Peter the Great, she forced the **Russian Orthodox Church** to become part of the national government. All of its property and holdings—including one million serfs—were confiscated.
- Unlike Peter the Great, she created one of the world's most impressive art collections at the Winter Palace in St. Petersburg. She also hosted many of the leading thinkers of the **Enlightenment**, including Diderot, and corresponded with Voltaire. She attempted to revamp some of the educational institutions in Russia as well.

Question 45

45. Discuss the reasons for the changing aims and methods of the French Revolution.

Essay Notes

The *moderate* phase of the Revolution (1789–1791) was motivated by the fact that legislative conflict was still a viable way to resolve France's deep problems. The bourgeoisie attempted to limit the power of the monarchy, aristocracy, and clergy. A good essay will mention terms such as *Ancien Régime*, Three Estates, Estates General, *cahiers* ("complaints"), National Assembly, tennis-court oath, storming of the Bastille, *Declaration of the Rights of Man*, August Decrees, and the March to Versailles.

The *radical* phase (1791–1795) occurred when the politicized urban working class of Paris seized control and attempted to create a more democratic government and a more egalitarian society. The causes of this development include the king's attempt to secretly flee Paris, the outbreak of war with Austria and Prussia, the division of the National Assembly into political factions, and the rise of the *sans-culottes*. As things devolved, the tactics used by these people devolved as well—voting to end the monarchy turned into the execution of King Louis XVI, and the new constitution devolved into the violent Jacobin purges of Girondins. All essays should mention Robespierre, the Committee on Public Safety, and the Reign of Terror.

The *Directory* period (1795–1799) was a reaction to the horrific excesses of the radial phase. After the Thermidorian Reaction had settled, and the remaining Jacobins had been hunted down and killed, power was concentrated in the hands of a conservative five-person board called the Directory. Their methods were simple: to maintain stability by using the military to succeed abroad and to stamp out rebellions at home (both of which were spearheaded by a young upstart named Napoleon Bonaparte). Old-fashioned forms of pompous dress returned into fashion. Other possible terms to be mentioned could include Council of the Ancients, Council of Five Hundred, and Abbé Siéyès (who helped shrink the Directory down to only three men). Also, plebiscites were Napoleon's favorite method of yanking power from the remaining two members of the Directory, as well as naming himself First Consul.

Chapter 6
1450–1815: Cultural and Intellectual Questions

1450–1815: CULTURAL AND INTELLECTUAL QUESTIONS

Multiple-Choice Questions

1. The Grand Tour was

    (A) Henry VIII's review of English monasteries following their dissolution

    (B) Napoleon's parade of triumph celebrating French conquest in North Africa

    (C) an aristocratic rite of passage in which young, educated Englishmen would travel through continental Europe

    (D) the Spanish naval conquest of the new world

    (E) a papal procession to the Holy Land

2. The work of Pico della Mirandola most clearly conveys which of the following themes of the Italian Renaissance?

    (A) Optimism about man's potential for greatness

    (B) Uncompromising realism in art

    (C) A rediscovery of the classical past through Greek and Roman Literature

    (D) Naivety toward modernity

    (E) Disdain for medieval art and philosophy

3. The King James Bible (1611)

    (A) was the first royally sanctioned English translation of the Bible

    (B) was provocatively named after James I in defiance of the King's prohibition on any new Bible translations

    (C) was quickly adopted by Catholic communities in France

    (D) was the first bible translation to not include the Old Testament

    (E) constituted a royal concession to Puritan demands

4. Savanarola's charismatic grip on fifteenth-century Florence indicates that Renaissance culture was in fact

    (A) agnostic, if not atheist

    (B) centered exclusively on the pursuit of artistry and physical beauty

    (C) influenced by theocratic Christianity

    (D) democratic and rational

    (E) influenced by religions other than Christianity

5. Erasmus's *In Praise of Folly* was inspired by

(A) superstition and corruption in the Catholic Church
(B) Sir Thomas More's martyrdom under Henry VIII
(C) Martin Luther's 95 theses
(D) factionalism among European aristocrats
(E) sixteenth-century controversy surrounding German imperial succession

6. Salons were

(A) ad hoc execution committees assembled during the Reign of Terror
(B) small chambers in which detainees of the Inquisition were held
(C) eighteenth-century exhibitions of controversial art
(D) operatic performances
(E) discussion venues often organized by educated women

7. What differentiated the heliocentric models of Kepler and Copernicus?

(A) The size of the sun
(B) Orbital shape
(C) The size of the earth
(D) The number of planets
(E) The position of the sun

8. Leonardo Bruni's *History of the Florentine People* was the first historical work to

(A) employ chapter divisions
(B) divide its subject into three periods: antiquity, medieval, and modern
(C) cite documentary evidence
(D) be published in print
(E) criticize a contemporary government

9. The sentence, "I have always believed, I must imitate antiquity not simply to reproduce it, but in order to produce something new," most closely captures the aims of which of the following groups?

(A) Enlightenment *Philosophies*
(B) Renaissance Humanists
(C) Renaissance Mannerists
(D) Seventeenth-century Empiricists
(E) Nineteenth-century Pre-Raphaelites

10. Deists believed that

(A) the world was created by a God who ceased to influence human history following the act of creation
(B) the sinfulness of man was innate and binding
(C) the Catholic Church retained primacy following the Reformation
(D) God ceased to exist after the French Revolution
(E) there is no deity

11. Enlightenment discourse in England is most often associated with which of the following spaces?

(A) The theater
(B) Buckingham Palace
(C) The coffee house
(D) The Radcliffe Camera, Oxford University
(E) Westminster Cathedral

12. Which of the following individuals attempted to catalog universal knowledge during the Enlightenment?

(A) Denis Diderot
(B) John Locke
(C) Jean-Jacques Rousseau
(D) Voltaire
(E) Conrad Gesner

13. Sir Thomas More's *Utopia*

(A) describes More's journey to the new world
(B) describes an ideal society ruled by a benign monarch
(C) describes a mythical island characterized by learning, peace, and democratic governance
(D) is a morality play about adultery and its consequences
(E) was banned on publication

14. Michelangelo's Statue of David represents

(A) a Greek myth
(B) a Roman myth
(C) Florentine pride, or *campanilismo*
(D) a continuation of medieval sculptural techniques
(E) a figure from the New Testament

15. The crowning of Petrarch as poet laureate in 1341 was meant to reference

(A) Dante's *Sweet New Style* and the rise of Italian poetry
(B) the high status given to poets and literature in Roman antiquity
(C) the papacy of Benedict XII
(D) the end of the plague
(E) the return of Rome to Christianity

16. The Middle Ages were first called "The Dark Ages" by

(A) Coluccio Salutati
(B) Dante
(C) Pico Della Mirandola
(D) Leonardo Da Vinci
(E) Petrarch

17. Rene Descartes is most closely associated with

   (A) radical subjectivism
   (B) humoral theory
   (C) the rationalist credo "I think therefore I am"
   (D) the discovery of differential calculus
   (E) Existentialism

18. Lorenzo Valla's falsification of the *Donation of Constantine* owed itself to

   (A) Valla's uncompromising religious faith
   (B) Humanism's emphasis on the study of language and documentary evidence
   (C) a program of intellectual investigation stimulated by the Catholic Reformation
   (D) the discovery of an ancient scroll inside a Roman crypt
   (E) changing opinions about democracy

19. Which pair of characteristics best describes Baroque art?

   (A) Restrained color and muted light
   (B) Realism and sedate characterization
   (C) Overwhelming emotion and lavish ornament
   (D) Linear perspective and hierarchical scaling
   (E) Geometric forms and primary colors

20. John Locke's *Essay on Human Understanding* concerns

   (A) childhood and the acquisition of knowledge
   (B) the Enlightenment effort to categorize and contain universal knowledge
   (C) a critique of traditional systems of government
   (D) universal human rights
   (E) Locke's literary techniques

21. All of the following individuals have been described as metaphysical poets EXCEPT

  (A) Andrew Marvell
  (B) John Donne
  (C) Henry Vaughan
  (D) George Herbert
  (E) Edmund Spenser

22. The invention of printing occurred in

  (A) sixteenth-century Flanders
  (B) fourteenth-century Germany
  (C) fourteenth-century Italy
  (D) fifteenth-century Germany
  (E) thirteenth-century Iran

23. Which of the following individuals is credited with the discovery of linear perspective?

  (A) Michelangelo
  (B) Giotto
  (C) Filippo Brunelleschi
  (D) Leon Battista Alberti
  (E) Donatello

24. Jacques Louis David's painting *The Death of Marat* depicts

  (A) a writer sympathetic to the Girondin cause who was assassinated by a royalist spy
  (B) a supporter of the *sans-culottes* who was murdered by a Girondin sympathizer
  (C) a symbolic representation of the beheaded monarch, Louis XVI
  (D) a self-portrait in David's classicizing style
  (E) the death of a classical philosopher

25. William Harvey and Andreas Vesalius revolutionized anatomical science by

   (A) describing the human body in astronomical terms
   (B) distributing their discoveries in manuscript
   (C) relying on dissection and observation
   (D) implementing humoral theory in the practice of medicine
   (E) adopting Chinese medicinal practices and treatments

26. Which of the following individuals is traditionally credited with the invention of the experimental method?

   (A) Descartes
   (B) John Locke
   (C) Baruch Spinoza
   (D) Francis Bacon
   (E) Molière

27. Neoclassicism championed

   (A) a return to the Baroque style in music and art
   (B) Greek and Roman art and architecture
   (C) a revolution in artistic expression
   (D) naturalism and childlike experience
   (E) a rejection of architectural heritage

28. Though contemporary with other Enlightenment thinkers, Jean-Jacques Rousseau ran contrary to Enlightenment thought primarily in

   (A) his emphasis on emotion, feeling, and a return to nature
   (B) his support of religious toleration
   (C) his interest in childhood education and developmental psychology
   (D) his critique of political and social traditions
   (E) his belief that all men were born free

29. Mary Wollstonecraft's *Vindication of the Rights of Women* addressed an inconsistency in

   (A) the Enlightenment's support of enfranchisement and equality
   (B) the Catholic Church's stance on women in the church
   (C) the mother's role in childhood education
   (D) the Protestant position on primogeniture
   (E) sixteenth-century education

30. Sixteenth- and seventeenth-century writers and artists were most dependent on which of the following forms of payment?

   (A) Private commissions
   (B) Patronage
   (C) State subsidies
   (D) Royalties
   (E) Donations

31. The concept of *Sprezzatura* was first defined in which of the following works?

   (A) William Shakespeare's *Love's Labour's Lost*
   (B) Ludovico Ariosto's *Orlando Furioso*
   (C) Erasmus's *In Praise of Folly*
   (D) Castiglione's *The Book of the Courtier*
   (E) Boccaccio's *Decameron*

32. Which of the following intellectual systems did Humanism supplant?

   (A) Scholasticism
   (B) Subjectivism
   (C) Neoclassicism
   (D) Existentialism
   (E) Objectivism

33. The Catholic Counter Reformation most closely coincided with which of the following schools of art?

    (A) Early Renaissance
    (B) Baroque
    (C) Neo-Realism
    (D) Expressionism
    (E) Linear Perspectivism

34. The High Renaissance (1490–1520) is most closely associated with which of the following Italian cities?

    (A) Florence
    (B) Venice
    (C) Siena
    (D) Rome
    (E) Perugia

35. All of the following are characteristic to Rembrandt's art EXCEPT

    (A) chiaroscuro
    (B) depictions of Greek and Roman history
    (C) expressive line and brushwork
    (D) portraiture
    (E) etching

36. Sir Isaac Newton's *Principia Mathematica* (1687) demonstrated the validity of

    (A) Galileo's observations of Venus
    (B) Harvey's description of systemic circulation
    (C) Kepler's heliocentric model
    (D) John Locke's idea of the *tabula rasa*
    (E) Catholic cosmogony

37. "All men are born free, but everywhere they are in chains." This sentence best describes the sociopolitical ideology behind which of the following cultural movements?

(A) The Enlightenment
(B) Renaissance Humanism
(C) Calvinism
(D) Nationalism
(E) Italian Nationalism

38. Galileo's telescopic observations of Venus in 1610 demonstrated

(A) that the Ptolemaic system, though largely accurate, required modification
(B) that the Copernican system was inaccurate
(C) that the Ptolemaic system was inaccurate
(D) that telescopes distorted rather than clarified astronomical observations
(E) that Venus was nearer to the sun than was originally believed

39. Machiavelli's *The Prince* advocated which of the following forms of government?

(A) Theocracy
(B) Republicanism
(C) Autocracy
(D) Enlightened Absolutism
(E) Monarchism

40. Donatello's bronze statue of *David* (ca. 1440) was remarkable in that

(A) it was the first unsupported male nude sculpture to be made since antiquity
(B) it was the only nude sculpture to be displayed publicly in the fifteenth century
(C) it remained unknown in the Medici palace until the nineteenth century
(D) it inspired increased appreciation for Medieval statuary in Italy
(E) surpassed Michelangelo's *David* in realism and size

41. All of the following individuals wrote during the "Elizabethan Renaissance" EXCEPT

(A) Ben Jonson
(B) Thomas Hobbes
(C) William Shakespeare
(D) Christopher Marlowe
(E) Sir Philip Sidney

42. Geoffrey Chaucer's *Canterbury Tales* is similar in literary form and structure to

(A) Ludovico Ariosto's *Orlando Furioso*
(B) Boccaccio's *Decameron*
(C) Dante's *Divine Comedy*
(D) Petrarch's *Rime Sparse*
(E) Shakespeare's *Sonnets*

43. The humanist scholar Leonardo Bruni proposed an educational system that

(A) allowed for the participation of women
(B) replaced textbooks with classroom lectures and debate
(C) introduced the modern grading system
(D) laid the groundwork for early childhood education in later centuries
(E) constituted a return to medieval precedent

Free-Response Questions

44. Describe and analyze the conflicting styles of Dutch and Flemish art during the 16th and 17th centuries; what cultural, political, economic, and religious influences gave rise to these differences?

_____

_____

_____

_____

_____

_____

_____

_____

_____

_____

_____

_____

_____

_____

_____

_____

_____

_____

_____

_____

_____

_____

_____

_____

_____

_____

_____

45. Analyze how and to what extent the concepts of childhood and human psychology changed during the Enlightenment.

Chapter 7
1450–1815: Cultural and Intellectual Answers and Explanations

ANSWER KEY

1.	C	23.	C
2.	A	24.	B
3.	E	25.	C
4.	C	26.	D
5.	A	27.	B
6.	E	28.	A
7.	B	29.	A
8.	B	30.	B
9.	B	31.	D
10.	A	32.	A
11.	C	33.	B
12.	A	34.	D
13.	C	35.	B
14.	C	36.	C
15.	B	37.	A
16.	E	38.	C
17.	C	39.	E
18.	B	40.	A
19.	C	41.	B
20.	A	42.	B
21.	E	43.	A
22.	D		

ANSWERS AND EXPLANATIONS

1. **C** The tradition of the Grand Tour prompted young Englishmen to travel and collect antiquities throughout continental Europe. Typically comprising a long voyage through France and Italy, this privilege was restricted to the aristocracy and social elite.

2. **A** Pico Della Mirandola's *Oration on the Dignity of Man,* often referred to as "The Manifesto of the Renaissance," praises the potential in human intellect, creativity, and passion. Pico Della Mirandola believed intellectual achievement and the pursuit of knowledge could lead to communion with God.

3. **E** The King James Bible was first devised at the Hampton Court Conference, called in response to Puritan demands for reform in the Millenary Petition. The King James Bible further distanced Anglicanism from Catholic practice, placating some Puritan concerns.

4. **C** Girolamo Savanarola, a Dominican friar and preacher, was intent on eradicating perceived hedonism in fifteenth-century Florence. Through his orations, he successfully inspired wealthy Florentines to destroy their material possessions (vanities). Florentine receptivity to his message suggests that Renaissance culture was still deeply influenced by Catholic dogma and religious piety.

5. **A** Northern Humanism was often critical of corruption in the Catholic Church. Following in this tradition, Erasmus's satire addresses concerns voiced by learned Catholics (including Thomas More) regarding corruption and duplicity in the papal curia.

6. **E** During the eighteenth century, particularly in France, aristocratic women began to patronize and encourage thinkers, artists, and philosophers. This patronage often took the form of small receptions (known as salons) in which debates, discussions, and readings were staged.

7. **B** Both the Copernican and Keplerian models are heliocentric, placing the sun, and not the earth, at the center of the galaxy. However, Kepler deduced that the orbit of the planets around the sun is elliptical and not, as Copernicus believed, perfectly symmetrical and circular.

8. **B** Bruni was one of many Renaissance thinkers who conceived of the Renaissance as the beginning of a modern era. Bruni facilitated this historical narrative by contrasting contemporary history with the medieval centuries that it succeeded.

9. **B** Renaissance Humanists not only admired classical antiquity, but believed it could provide impetus for innovation and progress. Never content to copy the classical past verbatim, Renaissance Humanists were instead inspired by Greek and Roman art and culture to develop new methods and modes of creative expression. The quote is Coluccio Salutati's (an early Humanist), as translated by Stephen Greenblatt in *The Swerve*.

10.   **A**   The French Revolution and the Enlightenment sought to distance society from religious dogma—the Enlightenment was not atheistic, however. Instead, many Enlightenment thinkers redefined God as an engineer who was content to construct a mechanical universe and leave it to develop and function unimpeded.

11.   **C**   As a conduit for printed news culture, controversial information, and gossip, the eighteenth-century coffee house became an intellectual hub for learned discourse during the English Enlightenment.

12.   **A**   Announced in 1750, Diderot's *Encyclopédie* sought to catalogue universal knowledge—the project ultimately came to define this characteristically Enlightened effort.

13.   **C**   More's *Utopia* describes a journey to a mythical island. The island is governed by a representative democracy and has little to no social discord on account of its exacting societal structure and rules.

14.   **C**   Contemporaries identified the biblical hero David with Florence, a weak outsider under constant threat of destruction by the nearby Goliath, Rome.

15.   **B**   Petrarch was crowned poet laureate in Rome on April 8, 1341. A common practice during the Roman Republic, his crowning was intended to align Renaissance Italy with the revered classical past of Horace, Cicero, and Virgil.

16.   **E**   Petrarch, the "father of humanism," sought to distance his fourteenth-century Italian context from medieval precedent. He therefore described medieval intellectual and artistic culture as dark, barbaric, and uncivilized.

17.   **C**   The philosophical proposition, "I think therefore I am," was introduced by Descartes in his *Discourse on the Method* (1644). Descartes thus argues that by thinking about the self, one proves that the self indeed exists.

18.   **B**   Lorenzo Valla successfully falsified *The Donation of Constantine* by identifying inconsistencies in the language, handwriting, and textual history of the available documentary evidence. *The Donation of Constantine* was a forged imperial decree in which the Roman emperor Constantine supposedly transferred authority over Rome to the Papacy.

19.   **C**   Baroque art, as evidenced in the sculpture of Bernini and the painting of Caravaggio, is characterized by dramatic expression, intense emotion, and ornamentation. Bernini's *Ecstasy of Saint Teresa* (1647), for example, shows Saint Teresa enthroned in gold and enraptured by the presence of the Holy Spirit.

20.   **A**   Published in 1689, Locke's *Essay on Human Understanding* introduced the concept of *tabula rasa*—blank slate—as a theory of developmental psychology. Locke believed that children acquired ideas, knowledge, and concepts through experience. This form of intellectual acquisition and growth extended to the child's morality and personality.

21. E   Edmund Spenser did not write using the metaphysical technique of "conceit." He is most known for his allegorical epic poem *The Fairie Queene,* published in 1590.

22. D   The goldsmith Johann Gutenberg first developed moveable type and employed it in the production of printed works on vellum and paper in fifteenth-century Mainz, Germany (ca. 1454).

23. C   An architect and mathematician famous for the design and engineering of the Florentine *Duomo,* Brunelleschi was the first to formulate the mathematical principles underlying the visual phenomenon of linear perspective.

24. B   Jacques Louis David was an active supporter of the French Revolution. In consequence, David portrays the death of Revolutionary hero Jean-Paul Marat in a sympathetic light. Marat was assassinated by Charlotte Corday, a Girondist, in 1793.

25. C   Harvey and Vesalius were among the first medical practitioners to rely on dissection and observation in formulating their medical theories and models. Harvey was the first to describe the systematic circulation of blood; Vesalius compiled a comprehensive anatomy of the human body, *De humani corporis fabrica* (On the fabric of the human body), in 1543.

26. D   In *The Advancement of Learning* (1605), Francis Bacon devised the experimental method in its modern form, writing: "If a man will begin with certainties, he shall end in doubts; but if he will be content to begin with doubts, he shall end in certainties." This is the philosophical basis of empiricism as well as the modern scientific method.

27. B   Contemporary with the Enlightenment, Neoclassicism returned to the perceived rationality and clarity of the classical past. In this regard, Neoclassicism can be seen as an aesthetic reflection of the Enlightenment's philosophic principles. This "reflection" is evident in the paintings of Jacques Louis David and Palladian architecture, as seen in Thomas Jefferson's Monticello.

28. A   Unlike many Enlightenment thinkers, Rousseau believed that nature, unimpeded, would provide viable solutions to entrenched social problems. In contrast with Locke, Rousseau believed that children were born innately good, for example. Locke, on the other hand, believed children entered the world as "blank slates" and would acquire morality and reason only through experience.

29. A   Though nominally democratic, most Enlightenment political thought did not allow for female involvement in governance. Mary Wollstonecraft identified this hypocrisy and wrote against it in her *Vindication of the Rights of Women,* published in 1792.

30. B   Before the introduction of copyright and efficient methods of production and distribution, artists such as composers, writers, and painters relied almost exclusively on royal or aristocratic patronage. Artists subsisting on patronage would often dedicate their works to their patrons.

31. **D** Castiglione defined *Sprezzatura* in *The Book of the Courtier* as "a certain nonchalance, so as to conceal all art and make whatever one does or says appear to be without effort and almost without any thought about it." This concept reflects Renaissance Humanism's preoccupation with multi-talented individualism; social skill was merely another branch of knowledge to be studied, learned, and perfected.

32. **A** Formalized and consummated by St. Thomas Aquinas, Scholasticism was based on disputation—debates designed to reconcile conflict in Christian patristic literature. Humanism supplanted Scholasticism with an emphasis on documentary study, linguistic expertise, classical literature, and rhetoric.

33. **B** The Counter Reformation (ca. 1540–1650) almost directly coincided with the Baroque. The Catholic Church commissioned late-Renaissance and Baroque artists to adorn churches and sacred spaces, thus aligning the Baroque's visually striking style with the political and theological aims of the Counter-Reformation.

34. **D** While the Renaissance originated in Florence, the High (Late) Renaissance flourished around the papal court in Rome. Michelangelo's *Sistine Chapel* is perhaps the most recognizable product of the High Renaissance, a period effectively terminated by the imperial sack of Rome in 1527.

35. **B** Rembrandt rarely depicted images from Greek and Roman history, preferring biblical scenes, contemporary imagery, and mythology. His secular scenes are particularly striking for their emotional depth and complexity. His painting *The Night Watch* (1642), for instance, depicts a contemporary, military scene and contains a variety of anonymous characters.

36. **C** By applying his mathematical description of gravity to Kepler's heliocentric model of planetary motion, Newton effectively disproved geocentricism (earth-centered galactic models). Kepler's model was thenceforth considered valid and factual on a mathematical basis.

37. **A** This quote from Jean-Jacques Rousseau's *Social Contract* (1754) captures the Enlightenment's belief in inalienable rights and universal enfranchisement under representative forms of government.

38. **C** The geocentric Ptolemaic system placed earth at its center. Therefore, by recording his observations of Venus orbiting the sun and not the earth, Galileo demonstrated that the galaxy is, in fact, heliocentric, disproving the Ptolemaic model of planetary motion.

39. **E** Machiavelli's *The Prince* was dedicated to Lorenzo di Piero de' Medici in an attempt to persuade Lorenzo to lead Florence as a "new prince." Machiavelli therefore advocated for a strong monarchy and not representative forms of government.

40. **A** After the decline of the Roman Empire, the casting techniques necessary to produce a free-standing bronze statue were lost. Donatello's *David* is therefore remarkable in that it reintroduced these methods in a distinctly Renaissance style.

41. **B** All of Thomas Hobbes's works postdated the Elizabethan Renaissance (1558–1603). His *Leviathan,* written during the English Civil War, was published in 1651, nearly half a century after Elizabeth's death in 1603.

42. **B** Chaucer's use of a frame narrative to introduce a sequence of individual tales told by an assorted cast follows the structure and style of Boccaccio's *Decameron*. Chaucer himself admitted Boccaccio's influence.

43. **A** As one of Humanism's leading theorectians, Bruni formulated a comprehensive system of childhood education which allowed for the participation of aristocratic women.

The Free-Response Essay Questions Explained

Question 44

44. Describe and analyze the conflicting styles of Dutch and Flemish art during the 16th and 17th centuries; what cultural, political, economic, and religious influences gave rise to these differences?

Essay Notes

You should begin your essay by providing relevant background information, describing and discussing the political and religious upheavals that affected the Netherlands in the seventeenth century. A discussion concerning the economic, social, and political ramifications of these conflicts should evolve neatly into an analysis of their manifestation in art. Essentially, Dutch art depicted the secular, wealthy world of the Protestant north (still life, portraiture, and religious domestic scenes); Flemish art, in contrast, often depicted traditional religious subjects in the characteristically Catholic style of Italian Mannerism and the Baroque. Key Dutch artists include Rembrandt and Jan Vermeer; and perhaps *the* key Flemish artist is Peter Paul Rubens. Key terms to use are The Dutch Golden Age, The Thirty Years' War (The Dutch War of Independence), The Eighty Years' War, The Seventeen Provinces, Phillip II, The Habsburg Crown/Monarchy, The Dutch East India Company, and the Amsterdam Stock Exchange.

- Following the success of the Protestant Reformation, conflicting states allied to the Catholic or Protestant cause attempted to gain political and religious control in contested areas. The wars which resulted (The Dutch Revolt, The Thirty Years' War, and the Eighty Years' War) saw the eventual division of Catholics and Protestants on geographical lines. The Thirty Years' War began as a religious conflict, but would eventually determine the borders, nations, and powers of Europe in its (roughly) modern shape and form.

- The Habsburg Monarchy maintained control of the Netherlands during the sixteenth century. Seventeen provinces comprising the Northern Netherlands revolted against the Habsburg (and Catholic) Phillip II of Spain in 1568, beginning The Dutch War of Independence (The Eighty Years' War). These 17 northern provinces (consolidated in 1579 under the Treaty of Utrecht) eventually established a Republic under William of Orange. The cultural differences of the Northern and Southern Netherlands were the result of this political, religious, and geographical division. The northern Dutch Republic was only recognized as an independent state following the signing of the Peace of Munster in 1648, terminating the Eighty Years' War.

- As trade and European finance became increasingly centered on the Dutch Republic (specifically Amsterdam), a middle class with substantial discretionary income arose. These new *burghers* of the Dutch Golden Age were overwhelmingly Protestant. As such, they did not commission artworks in what was then the recognizably Catholic baroque or mannerist styles. In consequence, many Northern Dutch artists began to specialize in still life and representations of domestic scenes rather than their previous stock-in-trade of religious icons, altar pieces, and clerical portraiture. For example, Jan Vermeer demonstrated a masterful control of light and shade in his intimate depictions of Dutch domestic life. Rembrandt, a member of the Protestant reformed church, typically worked in secular portraiture and landscape. He also produced moving, though modest, depictions of biblical characters and scenes. Rembrandt's characteristically mute color palette contrasts with the voluptuousness of Baroque painting.

- Crucially, the Dutch trading empire (facilitated by the Dutch East India Company) and the first stock exchange (founded in Amsterdam in 1602) made the Northern Republic exceedingly wealthy. This wealth allowed artists to continue work while receiving pay from burghers, or urban merchants. Prior to the Protestant Reformation, the Church was the largest and most dependable patron of the arts. Thus, in a way, the Dutch Golden Age introduced a new form of artistic economy—private commission.

- In contrast to his northern contemporaries, Peter Paul Rubens, a Flemish (Catholic) Baroque painter of the sixteenth and seventeenth centuries chose subjects and stylistic renderings that were heavily influenced by the aesthetics of the Catholic Counter Reformation and of the Italian Baroque. Typical features of this style include vibrant color, voluptuous figures, classical themes, and emotional characterization.

Question 45

45. Analyze how and to what extent the concepts of childhood and human psychology changed during the Enlightenment.

Essay Notes

Any analysis of Enlightenment educational theory should invoke John Locke's *Essay Concerning Human Understanding* (1689) and Jean-Jacques Rousseau's *Emile, or A Treatise on Education* (1762). Further, a discussion and comparison of these two works allow for elaboration and cultural analysis. As background, you should note relevant precedents: Childhood during the early modern period (fifteenth–sixteenth centuries) was not viewed as a distinct life phase. Until the seventeenth century, children were viewed as small adults with similar needs and mental processes. Contradicting this view, Locke and Rousseau believed that childhood was a distinct period in human psychological development. Both men consequently periodized human life into four stages: infancy, adolescence, adulthood, and old age. The ultimate goal of both the Lockean and Rousseauian systems of education is the production of a morally upright, reasoning individual, capable of retaining his or her inborn dignity in any sociopolitical station/environment.

Nevertheless, while both address the same topic for similar reasons, Rousseau chose to emphasize the emotional development of the child over intellectual ability and reason. Conversely, Locke, following dominant Enlightenment themes, saw reason as primary in importance. In consequence, Locke viewed a child's emotional development as secondary. Locke's concept of the *tabula rasa* should also be contrasted with Rousseau's idea of innate human goodness.

- John Locke's *Essay Concerning Human Understanding* (1689) introduced the influential concept of *tabula rasa*—the blank slate. Locke believed that children, upon birth, are void of knowledge and ignorant of the Christian ideas of predestination and original sin. Thus, Locke believed, knowledge was gained only via experience—i.e., observation and sensory stimuli. This, rather simplistically, describes Locke's empiricist theory of knowledge as it pertains to psychological development.

- Though similar to Locke in distinguishing childhood from adulthood, Rousseau believed that children were not born void of moral understanding, but were instead brought into the world as morally pure individuals, ignorant of sin yet in full command of an innate human goodness—this idea is summarized in the opening sentence of *Emile*, or *Treatise on Education* (1762): *"Everything is good as it leaves the hands of the Author of things; everything degenerates in the hands of man."*

- Crucially, however, Rousseau did not believe that his contemporaries would be innately good if left to develop outside of society's influence. Social indoctrination, achieved through the guidance of a tutor, was, according to Rousseau, necessary in mitigating the oftentimes destructive selfishness of man in his natural state. Rousseau suggested that the ideal state of man was one of "emotional self-sufficiency." Furthermore, Rousseau questioned empiricist models of epistemology and instead explored the influence of emotion and self reflection on psychological development.

- Both Locke and Rousseau are similar in their emphasis on experience and the sensory exploration of one's surroundings. Both believed that children learned best through direct observation and through a tactile engagement with their environment.

- Finally, you should note that the influence of Locke and Rousseau can be observed in modern systems of education and educational theory.

Chapter 8
1450–1815: Social and Economic Questions

1450–1815: SOCIAL AND ECONOMIC QUESTIONS

Multiple-Choice Questions

1. In the late fifteenth century, European nations began sailing to new regions of the globe including the Americas and the Orient. Which of the following best explains the rationale for the earliest expeditions?

   (A) To find gold and riches to finance their respective nations
   (B) To establish new trading routes with the Orient
   (C) To conquer new lands and expand their respective domains
   (D) To convert and offer salvation to non-Christians in other regions of the world
   (E) To provide better maps for seafaring travel

2. All of the following religious groups were targeted for persecution by the Spanish Inquisition EXCEPT

   (A) Catholics
   (B) Moors
   (C) Jews
   (D) Protestants
   (E) Witches

3. During the late sixteenth century, Spain controlled a vast empire including large regions of Western Europe and the Americas, yet remained financially burdened resulting in increasing inflation. Which of the following best describes why Spain remained tasked with economic problems?

   (A) The Protestant Reformation triggered social unrest in the Northern and Eastern reaches of the empire.
   (B) Barbary pirates were limiting the valuable import of silver and gold from New World territories.
   (C) Spain was involved in costly wars with other European powers to maintain and expand its political and social influence.
   (D) A plague swept through the Iberian Peninsula resulting in the deaths of a large portion of the labor force.
   (E) Spain lacked a consolidated empire on the Iberian peninsula.

4. The Catholic counter-reformation during the sixteenth century was effective in reestablishing control over many regions and peoples that had embraced protestant beliefs. All of the following were largely Catholic by 1600 C.E. EXCEPT

   (A) Spain
   (B) Italy
   (C) Scotland
   (D) France
   (E) Portugal

5. The Elizabethan Age (1558–1603) marked a golden age for the English. Which of the following represents a major event during the age?

(A) England and Scotland were consolidated under a single crown.
(B) The Muscovy Company and British East India Company emerged as global trading powers.
(C) Jamestown and Plymouth colonies were founded in present-day Virginia and Massachusetts.
(D) England became a predominately Catholic country sharing a prolonged peace with Catholic power Spain.
(E) Great Britain was formed.

6. Which of the following was the primary reason for the abrupt increase in prices, known as the Price Revolution, during the sixteenth and seventeenth centuries in Europe?

(A) Population growth
(B) Large influx of precious metals from the New World
(C) Widespread drought and disease
(D) Increases in the cost to maintain agriculture and livestock
(E) Introduction of new crops from the New World

7. During the Golden Age in the Netherlands (during the seventeenth century), Netherlands stood out from the rest of Europe because

(A) it remained almost entirely Catholic during the duration of the century
(B) it was tolerant of religious minority groups such as Jews and Anabaptists
(C) it had established its own currency
(D) it established key trading companies to expand trade with East India
(E) it remained ruled by a monarch

8. Which of the following cities became the center for commerce and banking in Northern Europe during the late sixteenth and early seventeenth centuries?

(A) London
(B) Antwerp
(C) Paris
(D) Amsterdam
(E) Moscow

9. In 1685, Louis XIV revoked the Edict of Nantes. Which of the following religious groups was most affected by this decision?

    (A) Catholics
    (B) Jews
    (C) Huguenots
    (D) Anabaptists
    (E) Moors

10. Following the Glorious Revolution, all of the following were passed to reform the English state and settle political and social unrest EXCEPT

    (A) the Act of Toleration
    (B) the English Bill of Rights
    (C) the Act of Union
    (D) English Test Acts
    (E) the Mutiny Act

11. All of the following are differences between medieval art and Renaissance art EXCEPT

    (A) medieval art was mostly isolated to cathedrals whereas Renaissance art could be found in both religious and public places
    (B) medieval art displayed humans as very flat or stiff in appearance, whereas Renaissance art made humans more realistic and softer in appearance
    (C) religious leaders mostly commissioned medieval art, whereas religious and secular leaders commissioned Renaissance art
    (D) medieval art was generated largely during the Middle Ages, whereas Renaissance art was generated after the start of the Italian Renaissance
    (E) medieval art was almost entirely religious in subject, whereas Renaissance was almost all secular in subject

12. Martin Luther's list of 95 Theses was largely written for which of the following reasons?

    (A) Luther sought to organize the Germanic states into one unified political state.
    (B) Luther protested the use of Catholic indulgences as a means of controlling salvation and availability of the word of God to non-Latin speaking peoples.
    (C) Luther attempted to undermine the power of the Roman Catholic church and that of the pope.
    (D) Luther aimed to consolidate the power of religion and state into a single Saxon state.
    (E) Luther was imprisoned at the time and forced to write them to prevent his execution.

13. Which of the following accurately describes the economic theory of mercantilism?

   (A) Colonialism is essential to the economic competitiveness of a nation.
   (B) National security is linked to control of foreign trade and a favorable trade balance.
   (C) Merchants must form corporations or joint-stock companies to ensure growth and reduce risks.
   (D) Isolationism provides stability by limiting dependency on foreign goods.
   (E) The nation with the largest navy will have the largest economy.

14. The development of the Gutenberg press in the mid-fifteenth century was significant for all of the following reasons EXCEPT

   (A) it constituted the first printing press in the world
   (B) it made books more easy to produce and more affordable to the general European public
   (C) it promoted the printing of texts in languages other than Latin and thus more accessible to the reading public
   (D) it led to increased higher education and literacy across Europe
   (E) it led to increased communication and spread of information across the world

15. Which of the following had the LEAST impact on the increases in population size and life expectancy during the Industrial Revolution?

   (A) An increase in the birth rates across Europe
   (B) A decrease in the death rates across Europe
   (C) Improved hygiene and sanitation
   (D) Increased agricultural production yielding more available food
   (E) Improved safety measures and acceptable hours in the workplace

16. Adam Smith in his *Inquiry into the Nature and Causes of the Wealth of Nations* advocated most closely for which of the following economic systems for prosperity and fairness?

   (A) Capitalism
   (B) Socialism
   (C) Communism
   (D) Marxism
   (E) Oligarchism

17. All of the following contributed to the advent of the French Revolution EXCEPT

   (A) unequal representation by the Third Estate in the Estates General
   (B) financial instability due to costly wars with the English
   (C) inability of Louis XVI to tax the upper class
   (D) lack of support from clergy for the grievances of the Third Estate
   (E) success of the American revolution

18. Marquis de Lafayette wrote the *Declaration of the Rights of Man and Citizen*, which clarified the rights and liberties of French citizens. Which of the following most directly influenced this work?

   (A) *The Magna Carta* (1215)
   (B) The English *Bill of Rights* (1689)
   (C) The American *Declaration of Independence* (1776)
   (D) John Locke's *Essay Concerning Human Understanding* (1689)
   (E) *The Bible* (first century)

19. In 1791, Olympe de Gouges wrote *The Rights of Women* where she argued for woman to enjoy all of the following equal rights as men EXCEPT

   (A) the right to vote and run for political office
   (B) the right to be educated
   (C) the right control and own property
   (D) the right to initiate a divorce
   (E) the right to be born free

20. The Girondins and Jacobins differed in their view of the role of the government in the economy of the state. Which of the following most accurately describes the views of the two factions?

   (A) The Girondins believed that the government must play an active role in the economy to control trade and prevent inflation, whereas the Jacobins believed in the idea of *laissez-faire*.
   (B) The Jacobins believed that the government must play an active role in the economy to control trade and prevent inflation, whereas the Girondins believed in the idea of *laissez-faire*.
   (C) The Girondins and Jacobins both believed in the idea of *laissez-faire*, but the Girondins advocated for establishing an independent government commission to oversee the economy.
   (D) The Girondins and Jacobins both believed in the idea of *laissez-faire*, but the Jacobins advocated for establishing an independent government commission to oversee the economy.
   (E) The Girondins and Jacobins both believed that the government should play an active role, but only when in times of distress.

21. The French Civil Code of 1804, commonly referred to as the Napoleonic Code, was significant because

    (A) it provided a single legal system for the entirety of France
    (B) it established equality of law for all people
    (C) it protected the rights of property holders
    (D) it allowed for freedom of religion
    (E) it provided all of the above

22. In 1781, Joseph II of Austria issued the first of a series of Edicts of Toleration which granted freedom of worship to all of the following religious minorities EXCEPT

    (A) Lutherans
    (B) Jews
    (C) Calvinists
    (D) Greek Orthodox
    (E) Catholics

23. Sir Thomas More's *Utopia* painted a picture of a society that had which of the following unique properties?

    (A) No religion
    (B) No private property
    (C) No king
    (D) No slaves
    (E) None of the above

24. All of the following were significant writers and playrights during the Elizabethian Renaissance EXCEPT

    (A) Geoffrey Chaucer
    (B) Christopher Marlowe
    (C) William Shakespeare
    (D) Ben Jonson
    (E) Thomas Dekker

25. Which of the following became the focus of the majority of printings by the Gutenburg press shortly after its production?

   (A) Laws and decrees
   (B) Deeds and landowner agreements
   (C) Religious texts
   (D) Literary texts
   (E) Newspapers

26. Leonardo da Vinci is considered the archetype of a Renaissance man. All of the following constitute hobbies and professions of Leonardo da Vinci EXCEPT

   (A) scientist
   (B) inventor
   (C) architect
   (D) politician
   (E) painter

27. Anabaptists believed which of the following religious practices was most effective for the clearing of one's sins?

   (A) Baptism at birth
   (B) Baptism as adults
   (C) Baptism as both infants and adults
   (D) Baptism at marriage
   (E) No baptism throughout life

28. What was the Society of Jesus?

   (A) A separate religion
   (B) An order of the Catholic church
   (C) A secret political organization
   (D) A conservative cult-like society
   (E) An agrarian society founded in the New World based on the literal interpretation of the Bible

29. Which of the following most accurately describes fifteenth- and sixteenth-century Spanish *haciendas*?

(A) A system of forced labor
(B) Plantations
(C) Urban houses
(D) Shared food made available to the public
(E) Wagons or carts used for trade

30. The success of the Spanish in conquering large portions of the New World was largely due to which of the following factors?

(A) Superior technology
(B) Availability of horses
(C) Greater wealth
(D) Resistance to infectious diseases
(E) Religious tolerance

31. All of the following were Italian explorers EXCEPT

(A) Amerigo Vespucci
(B) Marco Polo
(C) Christopher Columbus
(D) Vasco da Gama
(E) Giovanni da Verrazzano

32. Facing conflict over Calvinist and Catholic religious factions, which of the following French kings declared "Paris is worth a Mass" and issued the Edict of Nantes?

(A) Louis XIII
(B) Henry IV
(C) Louis XIV
(D) Charles IX
(E) Louis XVI

33. The Act in Restraint of Appeals enacted by English parliament in 1533 was significant for England because it

   (A) declared that the king has authority over spiritual matters within the state rather than the pope
   (B) declared that parliament has authority over spiritual matters within the state rather than the pope
   (C) declared that the Archbishop of Canterbury has authority over spiritual matters within the state rather than the pope
   (D) declared that the pope has authority over spiritual matters within the English state
   (E) declared that England would be open to religious tolerance and that there would be no official state religion

34. Which of the following best describes why Mary I of England was better known as "Bloody Mary"?

   (A) Mary had her cousin Mary Queen of Scots executed for treason against the crown.
   (B) Mary had her sister Elizabeth executed to retain control of the English throne.
   (C) Mary was Catholic and had several hundred Protestants burnt at the stake for heresy.
   (D) Mary was Protestant and had several hundred Catholics burnt at the stake for heresy.
   (E) Mary fought valiantly alongside her forces in the wars over Normandy against the French

35. The Medici family of Florence became very wealthy through which of the following trades?

   (A) Politics
   (B) Banking
   (C) Law
   (D) Medicine
   (E) Farming

36. Which of the following best describes the Catholic view of transubstantiation?

   (A) Humans had free will over their salvation based on their own decisions and actions.
   (B) God has already chosen the fate of humans at birth and only a selected few may be saved.
   (C) The bread and wine consumed during Communion could be transformed into the embodiment of Christ only through an ordained priest.
   (D) The bread and wine consumed during Communion already represents the embodiment of Christ and would not require an ordained priest.
   (E) The holy trinity represents the three stages that the soul must pass through following death.

37. The principle of primogeniture stated which of the following?

(A) The wealthiest son would inherit the bulk of the estate to ensure that the family's wealth remained intact.

(B) The oldest son would inherit the bulk of the estate to ensure that the family's wealth remained intact.

(C) The youngest son would inherit the bulk of the estate to ensure that the family's wealth remained intact.

(D) The most politically successful son would inherit the bulk of the estate to ensure that the family's wealth remained intact.

(E) The eldest daughter would inherit the bulk of the estate if she was born first to ensure that the family's wealth remained intact.

38. Which of the following best describes the three-field system of agriculture?

(A) Three fields were planted with the same crop to prevent a loss of resources from the soil.

(B) Three fields were planted with three different crops and altered between years to prevent a loss of resources from the soil.

(C) Two fields were planted with crops and one field left vacant and the crops rotated between years to prevent a loss of resources from the soil.

(D) One field was planted with crops while two fields were left vacant and the crops rotated between years to prevent a loss of resources from the soil.

(E) Every other year, all three fields would be left vacant to replenish the soil.

39. What role did a woman play in the control and possession of her dowry?

(A) Once a dowry was given, a woman never had control or possession of her dowry.

(B) Once a dowry was given, a woman would only be able to decide the fate of her dowry upon her death.

(C) A woman had the ability to choose who would receive her dowry and what would be done with it upon her death.

(D) A woman had the ability to choose who would receive her dowry, manage its possessions during her life and decide what would be done with it upon her death.

(E) Women had no control or possession of their dowry.

Luther at the Diet of Worms
(1877) by Anton von Werner

Ortellius Map (1590)

40. The image above depicts Martin Luther's speech at the Diet of Worms. The Diet of Worms was convened to ask Luther to do which of the following?

(A) Reform the Catholic Church within the realm of the Holy Roman Empire

(B) Defend Jon Hus who was on trial for heresy

(C) Oversee the crowning of Charles V as ruler over the Holy Roman Empire

(D) Rewrite his 95 Theses for a hastened execution

(E) Recant his teachings in opposition to the Catholic Church

41. The image above depicts the Ortellius, the sole ship of Magellan's fleet to complete the circumnavigation of the world. Magellan's trip was significant not only because it successfully showed the world was round, but also because

(A) it laid claim to much of the unexplored world for Spain

(B) it showed that European craftsmanship could permit long-distance travel

(C) it provided the path of the Northwest Passage to Asia

(D) it expanded Catholicism to new parts of the world

(E) it demonstrated that the New World was not part of Asia

Execution of Mary Queen of Scots
(1617) by Unknown Artist

Un matin devant la porte du Louvre
(1880) by Édouard Debat-Ponsan

42. Mary Queen of Scots was executed in 1587. Which of the following best explains why Mary was imprisoned and executed?

(A) Mary was executed because she was an ardent Catholic and Elizabeth sought to fortify England's position as a Protestant kingdom.

(B) Mary was executed because she was an ardent Protestant and Elizabeth sought to fortify England's position as a Catholic kingdom.

(C) Elizabeth thought that executing Mary would gain her support from Scottish leaders who sought the throne.

(D) Mary remained heir to the English throne and plotted with Spain against the English throne.

(E) Mary was conspiring with the Hapsburgs to overthrow the English throne.

43. The image above depicts the aftermath of the St. Bartholomew's Day Massacre. Which of the following accurately describes the events of the massacre?

(A) It was a bloody event between loyalists to King Louis XIV and Cardinal Richelieu, where thousands of loyalists were killed in Paris.

(B) It was a bloody event between loyalists to King Louis XIV and Cardinal Richelieu, where thousands of supporters of Richelieu were killed in Paris.

(C) It was a bloody event between Catholics and French Huguenots, where thousands of Catholics were killed in Paris.

(D) It was a bloody event between loyalists to Catholics and French Huguenots, where thousands of Huguenots were killed in Paris.

(E) It was a bloody event between Catholics and Jews, where thousands of Jews were killed in Paris.

Free-Response Questions

44. Describe and analyze the events that led to the onset of the French Revolution.

_____
_____
_____
_____
_____
_____
_____
_____
_____
_____
_____
_____
_____
_____
_____
_____
_____
_____
_____
_____
_____
_____
_____
_____
_____
_____
_____
_____
_____
_____

45. Analyze and discuss the works of THREE Renaissance artists. Include in your discussion particular emphasis on how these artists differed from the works of the Middle Ages.

_____

_____

_____

_____

_____

_____

_____

_____

_____

_____

_____

_____

_____

_____

_____

_____

_____

_____

_____

_____

_____

_____

_____

_____

_____

_____

_____

_____

_____

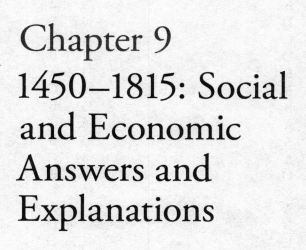

Chapter 9
1450–1815: Social
and Economic
Answers and
Explanations

ANSWER KEY

1.	B	23.	B
2.	A	24.	A
3.	C	25.	C
4.	C	26.	D
5.	B	27.	B
6.	A	28.	B
7.	B	29.	B
8.	D	30.	D
9.	C	31.	D
10.	D	32.	B
11.	E	33.	A
12.	B	34.	C
13.	B	35.	B
14.	A	36.	C
15.	A	37.	B
16.	A	38.	C
17.	D	39.	B
18.	C	40.	E
19.	A	41.	E
20.	B	42.	D
21.	E	43.	D
22.	E		

ANSWERS AND EXPLANATIONS

1. **B** The first voyages by the Spanish (in 1492) and Portuguese (in 1488) were organized to find new efficient trading routes to Asia. It was later discovered that vast stretches of land and wealth were available and capable of being attained (A) and (C). The goal of converting natives did not become a focus of nearly all sailing expeditions (D), although it certainly became a part of European conquests. Although cartography (E) was growing as a trade, this was not the primary focus of sea voyages at the time.

2. **A** Ferdinand and Isabella were ardent Catholics and formed the Spanish Inquisition to create a unified Spanish religious state. Initially, Spanish Moors (B), Muslims from North Africa living in Spain, and Jews (C) were targeted for persecution and expulsion. Though, not the primary target, witches (E), members of the occult and mysticism, were also targeted by the Inquisition. However, Protestants (D) quickly became the primary target with the advent of the Protestant Reformation.

3. **C** During the late sixteenth century, Spain was involved in ongoing wars with the Dutch, English, and French which exhausted much of the gold and silver recovered from the New World. Although the Protestant Reformation (A) did trigger social unrest, it does not directly explain the financial downturn of Spain. Barbary pirates (B) were actively involved in attacking shipping lanes within the Mediterranean; however they played a minor role in affecting the import of silver and gold from the New World. A major plague (D) struck Spain at the end of the sixteenth century (1596–1602) killing up to 10% of the Spanish labor force. However by this time, the ongoing wars continued to absorb most of the Spanish wealth. The Spanish empire remained consolidated and strong (E) on the Iberian peninsula during this time.

4. **C** Scotland during the Protestant reformation embraced the ideology of John Knox and Calvinism. Spain (A), Italy (B), France (D) as well as Portugal (E) and southern Germany remained largely catholic during this time.

5. **B** The Muscovy Company monopolized trading routes with northwestern regions of Russia and the British East India Company controlled trade with large regions of the Indian subcontinent. Both of these companies emerged as trading powers during the Elizabethan Age. England and Scotland would be consolidated under a single crown (A) with the death of Elizabeth in 1603 and the reign of James I. During the reign of James I, the colonies at Jamestown (1607) and Plymouth Bay (1620) were founded (C). Elizabeth was protestant (D) and the country had tense relations with Spain during her reign including the assault of the Spanish Armada (1588). Great Britain (E) would not be formed until the Treaty of Union (1707).

6. **A** The significant increase in prices across Europe was due to a major boost in population. Although there was a large increase in influx of gold and silver from the New World (B), this had limited impact in comparison to the pressure that population growth had on basic commodities. Droughts

and disease (C) continued to impact the European populations; however these events were not constant and did not contribute to long-term increases in prices. There were not significant changes in the methods or technology to maintain agriculture or livestock (D) during this period. Although new crops did come in from the New World (E), these did not increase local prices.

7. **B** During the Golden Age, the Netherlands showed high tolerance for religious minorities in the predominantly Calvinist population including Jews (fleeing from the Spanish Inquisition), Anabaptists and Catholics. The Netherlands remained mostly Protestant (Calvinist) during the Golden Age, making (A) incorrect. Many European nations issued their own currency (C) and the English were also quite active with the British East India Company (D). Many nations were ruled by monarchs (E) at the time.

8. **D** Following the sacking of Antwerp during the Dutch War for Independence, Amsterdam became the established center for commerce and banking. The Bank of Amsterdam founded at the beginning of the seventeenth century also played a major role in shaping the city as a major financial and commercial center in Europe.

9. **C** The Edict of Nantes provided French Huguenots rights and privileges in France. Louis XIV wanted a united religious state and revoked the Edict to eliminate Calvinism in France. As a result of the revocation, Huguenot schools and churches were destroyed, their civil rights were removed, and many fled France for England and the Netherlands.

10. **D** The English Test Acts (1678) were meant to prevent Catholics from serving in any civil or military office. These acts were passed prior to the Glorious Revolution. The Act of Toleration (1689), the English Bill of Rights (1689), the Act of Union (1707), and The Mutiny Act (1689) were all passed following the overthrow of James to resolve political and social unrest in England.

11. **E** Renaissance art still maintained a heavy influence from the Church despite more secular art being generated. Humanism during the Renaissance had a major impact on the development of art. Medieval art was practically all religious in subject having been commissioned almost solely by the Church and appeared flat and stiff in appearance. The Renaissance saw realism and humanism enter art. Both secular and religious leaders commissioned Renaissance art and the subjects were quite broad compared to medieval art.

12. **B** Martin Luther contested the power of the Catholic Church obtained through the selling of indulgences to lessen the time of purgatory. He viewed this as an abuse of the power of the Church to maintain power and raise money. He maintained that the way to salvation was through grace rather than indulgences. Another critique of the Church was that the word of God and the lessons of God were available only in Latin. Consequently, he was instrumental in translating the first German bible.

13. **B**   Mercantilism emerged during the Age of Exploration. Essentially, the theory stipulates that countries should trade with foreign powers, but not import more than they export (trade deficit) as this would build a dependency and confer weakness. Colonialism (A) was a critical step for European countries to avoid a trade deficit; however it is an application of mercantilism rather than explanation of it. Corporations or joint-stock companies (C) provided stability to merchants during this time, but this did not explain the economic system of mercantilism. Isolationism (D) would limit or prohibit trade with foreign nations. Though having a large and dominant navy certainly aided mercantilism at the time (E), it was not the defining characteristic of the theory.

14. **A**   The moveable type printing press was actually invented by the Song dynasty in China in the eleventh century in China. However, Europe did not develop and use a printing press until Johannes Gutenberg's invention in the mid-fifteenth century. The development of the press led to increased book production (B), printing of texts in local vernaculars (C), increased literacy and education (D) in Europe, and increased communication and spread of knowledge (E).

15. **A**   The birth rates in Europe did not increase substantially during the Industrial Revolution. Increases in population and life expectancy were mostly due to people living longer (B) rather than the birth of more people. The primary reason for people living longer was improved hygiene and sanitation in the work place and in medical practice (C) and increased food production due to the agricultural revolution (D). Improvements (E) during the middle and end of the Industrial Revolution in the workplace were very important for improved life.

16. **A**   Adam Smith suggested that economic prosperity and fairness was linked to economic systems that permit private means of production and open free markets or capitalism. Socialism and communism originated from the economic systems described by Karl Marx and others that viewed that privatization failed to protect the workers and resulted inequality in the workplace.

17. **D**   A large contingent of lower clergyman and clergy from simple parishes sympathized with the views of the Third Estate and joined them during the early days of the revolution. The primary catalysts for the French Revolution were unequal representation among the three estates (A), the financial dilemma due to costly wars with the English (B), inability of the French monarch to effectively tax nobles (C), and the knowledge of the success of the American revolution against the British crown (E).

18. **C**   The French *Declaration of the Rights of Man and Citizen* was directly inspired by the language of the American *Declaration of Independence*. In fact, Thomas Jefferson aided Lafayette in the writing of the declaration. Although the English *Magna Carta* (A), *Bill of Rights* (B), and John Locke's *Essay* (D) share some of the same principles, the French declaration combined the new philosophical views and arguments of the Enlightenment with the founding principles described in the American declaration. The Bible (E) had little impact on the French work.

19. **A**   De Gouges did not argue for full political equality for woman in her work. However, her demand for equal education (B), rights to own and control property (C), to initiate divorce (D), and the acknowledgement that women (just as men) are born free (E) did inspire later woman's rights activists.

20. **B**   The Jacobins believed that the government must play an active role in the economy to control trade and prevent inflation. The Girondins, who were much more conservative, feared of giving the government too much authority and believed in the idea of *laissez-faire* or no government involvement leaving the economy to local autonomy.

21. **E**   The Napoleonic code was significant because it provided a single legal system for all of France (A), equality under law (B), protected the rights of landowners (C), and freedom of religion (D).

22. **E**   Catholics constituted the religious majority of eighteenth-century Austria and were not the target of Joseph II's Edicts of Toleration.

23. **B**   Thomas More's *Utopia* exhibited a society where all wealth and property were common (no private property) to mitigate political and economic injustices. His island did have slaves (D), a king (C) and religion (A) which were common among the nations of Europe at the time.

24. **A**   Geoffrey Chaucer (1343–1400), the writer of *The Canterbury Tales*, lived and wrote his famous work during the fifteenth century. Chrisopher Marlowe, Ben Jonson, William Shakespeare, and Thomas Dekker were well-known writers and playwrights during the Elizabethan era.

25. **C**   The Gutenberg press revolutionized the availability and awareness of the Bible during the fifteenth century. Prior to its production, monks produced all religious texts by hand. Although civil documents such as laws, decrees, and deeds were printed, most remained written and signed during the earliest years of the press. Literary texts (D) and newspapers (E) would not see an appreciable increase until later when literacy began to increase among the general population.

26. **D**   Leonardo da Vinci was involved in nearly every trade, practice, or profession associated with the Italian Renaissance including being a scientist (A), architect (B), inventor (C), and painter (E). However, he remained outside of the political sphere, never holding a public office.

27. **B**   Anabaptists believed that since infants were unaware of the significance nor able to make the decision for themselves, their baptisms were nullified and had no meaning. Anabaptists advocated for baptism as adults, a practice later referred to as rebaptism (though it constituted the first and only baptism of Anabaptists).

28. **B**   The Society of Jesus (or Jesuits) were a teaching order of the Catholic Church which played a critical role as missionaries for the church in its early days.

29. **B**   *Haciendas* were plantations established to exploit the agricultural and earthly benefits of the land. *Encomienda* describes the forced labor system, which was largely responsible for the success of the *haciendas*.

30. **D** Infectious diseases were responsible for reducing the population of the New World by as much as 90% over the fifteenth and sixteenth centuries. Diseases such as smallpox played a critical role in permitting the Spanish to conquer great civilizations such as the Aztecs and Incas.

31. **D** Vasco da Gama was a Portuguese explorer who was responsible for finding shipping routes by sea to India. Amerigo Vespucci (A), Marco Polo (B), Christopher Columbus (C), and Giovanni da Verrazzano (E) were all Italian explorers, though their explorations were largely funded by other nations or states.

32. **B** Henry IV faced ongoing political and military struggles with Spain, which sought to weaken the French state and convert permanently to Catholicism. In the midst of the Calvinist and Catholic religious factions, Henry ultimately opted for Catholicism declaring that "Paris is worth a Mass." However, to mitigate religious strife in France, he also issued the Edict of Nantes, which provided religious freedom of worship to the Huguenots.

33. **A** The Act in Restraint of Appeals (1533) provided Henry VIII with justification to nullify his marriage to Catherine in order to marry Anne Boleyn by making him the head authority on spiritual cases with the realm.

34. **C** Mary Tudor (Mary I) was an ardent Catholic who was married to Philip II of Spain and faced religious strife as a result of Henry VIII's formation of the Church of England and the English Reformation. To gain favor with the pope, Mary had several hundred Protestants burnt at the stake for heresy, thus giving her the title of "Bloody Mary." Note: Mary did not have her cousin Mary Queen of Scots (A) executed (her sister Elizabeth did) nor did she have her sister executed (B), though it was certainly considered.

35. **B** The Medici family gained their wealth through banking. Later Medicis would play a major role in politics for the region; however the initial wealth of the family came from controlling banking in Florence during the rise of the Renaissance.

36. **C** The Roman Catholic church viewed transubstantiation as the transformation of bread and wine during the Eucharist (Communion) into the body and blood of Christ by God through the medium of an ordained priest. Martin Luther claimed that Christ already was embodied in the bread and wine of the Eucharist and did not require an ordained priest (D). Choices (A) and (B) describe opposing views on free will and predestination. Choice (E) does not describe Christian doctrine.

37. **B** Upon the passing of a family patriarch, the majority of the wealth and possessions would be passed to the first-born son. Often this created feuds for possessions due to differences in status, wealth, or position.

38. **C** In the three-field system of agriculture, two fields were planted with crops and one field was left vacant and the crops rotated between years to prevent a loss of resources from the soil. This process resulted in an increase in production because it helped the fields retain nutrients creating a much more bountiful harvest during growing seasons.

39. **B** Dowries were provided by the father of the woman to be married and their fate was only to be decided by the woman upon her death. During her lifetime, the power and possessions of the dowry remained in the management and control of her husband.

40. **E** During the Diet of Worms, Charles V asked Luther, "Do you or do you not repudiate your books and the errors they contain?" The focus of the Diet was to put Luther on trial for his teachings in opposition to the Catholic Church. They specifically wanted him to recant his teachings. Luther did not recant and was banished from the realm (however he did remain in the Empire under protection by the Elector of Saxony).

41. **E** The circumnavigation of the world by Magellan's crew in 1519 demonstrated conclusively that the land thought to be the Far East identified by Columbus was in fact, an entirely new continent. Spain already had a footing in much of the New World by this time (A). Ships were already traveling great distances (B). The Northwest Passage (C) was never identified. The aim of the exploration was not to convert (D) the world (although later trips appeared so).

42. **D** Mary Queen of Scots was heir to the English throne during the reign of Elizabeth I. As monarch of Scotland, Elizabeth kept Mary alive to suppress any chance for a rebellion. However, when Elizabeth learned of plots with Spain and that her son was being raised Protestant, Elizabeth had Mary executed.

43. **D** St. Bartholomew's Day Massacre was a wave of directed violence against French Huguenots to fortify the French position of Catholicism in Paris. During the massacre, Admiral Coligny and nearly 3,000 people were estimated to have been killed by the wave of violence often attributed to the will of Catherine de Medici and her son King Charles IX.

The Free-Response Essay Questions Explained

Question 44

44. Describe and analyze the events that led to the onset of the French Revolution.

Essay Notes

For the first part of your essay, you should outline the events prior to the reign of Louis XVI, which led to a decline in the wealth and stability of France. Key points of discussion include the following concepts:

- France was enveloped in several wars in the years preceding the French Revolution including (but not limited to) the Thirty Years' War (1618–1648), War of Spanish Succession (1701–1714), War of Austrian Succession (1740–1748), Seven Years' War (1756–1763). These wars were costly and put stress on the French finances and particularly burdened the peasentry whom had to pay taxes to support the King's war efforts and glory seeking.
- Louis XIV (1638–1715) declared "L'état, c'est moi" or "I am the state" and viewed the title of king having been provided by the divine right of God. He felt that there was no political or religious authority which could impinge upon his right to rule. To control the aristocracy, Louis XIV spent great wealth building and maintaining Versailles. Doing so consumed a large amount of French wealth.
- Louis XV continued to put massive wealth into luxuries (including expanding and maintaining Versailles) and ongoing wars. The revenue of the state was far exceeded by the accruing debt. In 1745, he created a tax on all classes to address budget issues; however the revenue generated failed to overcome the increasing budget deficit. These poor economic policies and increased taxes angered all classes and financially burdened the French state.

For the second part of your essay, you need to explain how social, political, and economic issues in France led directly to the French Revolution. Key points of discussion include the following concepts:

- *Social*: The French population by the late eighteenth century was among the largest in Europe (second only to Russia) and the population of Paris was among the largest of European cities. Subsequently, there was a high demand for resources which manifested in famine and food shortages, rising inflation, and resentment towards the aristocracy and bourgeoisie. In addition to lack of resources, the lowest class were burdened with high taxes and poor representation in political decisions, creating anger and resentment towards the king and the wealthy, who lived in luxury and showed disregard for the whims of the poor. Lastly, the poor had a particular issue with Louis's wife Marie Antoinette, who was Austrian and cared not for, nor was aware of, the issues with the poor, and their apparent impotency. Rising fear of Louis XVI seizing the lowest class by force created a widespread panic or Great Fear.
- *Political:* When the financial situation became extremely bad in the 1780s, Louis called an Assembly of Notables to see whether he could institute a land tax to raise revenue. The nobles refused and Louis XVI looked to the Estates General for a solution. The Estates General utilized equal votes for the Three Estates (First Estate—clergy, Second Estate—nobility, Third Estate—commons) despite greater than 95% of the population falling into the Third Estate. This triggered a demand for more fair representation and the king allowed for a doubling of the number of representatives; however the Third Estate still held an equal vote with the other two estates. The inability of the king and aristocracy to compromise led directly to eventual overthrow.

- *Economic:* By the reign of Louis XVI, the French state was in high debt, inflation was rampant, taxation heavily burdened all (especially the Third Estate), and the monarchy continued to live in extravagance despite the financial whims of the country. Marie's "let them eat cake" embodies the settlement of the privileged; they neither cared nor were aware of the issues plaguing the poor.

Lastly, you may decide to finish by discussing the specific events comprising the start of the Revolution including the following:

- *Issues of the Estates General*: The lack of representation and unfair taxation causes friction between the Third Estate and the King. This builds frustration and triggers the Great Fear among the poor.
- *Tennis Court Oath*: Demanding of the Third Estate for a constitution built upon solid foundations.
- Storming of the Bastille: The lowest class seize the fortress prison as an outward sign of standing up to the absolute despotism of the monarchy and the aristocracy.

Question 45

45. Analyze and discuss the works of THREE Italian Renaissance artists. Include in your discussion particular emphasis on how these artists differed from the works of the Middle Ages.

Essay Notes

For your essay, you should begin by describing the works of three Renaissance artists. Below are potential artist options and some of their more famous works. For your chosen works, briefly describe the scene and explain how it embodies the spirit of the Renaissance and differs from Medieval art.

- **Leonardo da Vinci**: *Mona Lisa, Annunciation, Baptism of Christ, Virgin on the Rocks, The Last Summer*
- **Raphael:** The *School of Athens, The Adoration of the Magi, Madonna with the Child*
- **Michelangelo:** *David, Pietà, The Last Judgement* and scenes from Genesis (in the Sistine Chapel)
- **Titian:** *The Woman at the Mirror, Assumption, Danae, The Rape of Europa*
- **Donatello:** *David, Statue of St. George, St. John the Evangelist*

For the second part of the essay, you should describe key differences between Medieval art and Italian Renaissance art including:

- Medieval art was mostly centered on the themes of the Church, whereas humanist philosophy during the Renaissance re-evaluated the classics and themes of a more secular nature. One clear example was the diminished use of haloes in Renaissance art compared to that of Medieval art. Several of the works listed above focus on these themes such as *The Rape of Europa* and *The School of Athens*.
- Medieval art also tended to use less natural depictions of humans and used proportion and size to represent spiritual significance. Renaissance art focused more on natural appearance and proportions. Nearly all of the works above support this point.
- Medieval art also failed to adequately use contrasts in color and tone to provide three dimensions to images. The use of *chiaroscuro* or contrasting colors of light and dark by Renaissance arts made images appear more realistic and alive. Nearly all of the works above support this point.

Chapter 10
1815–1900: Political and Diplomatic Questions

1815–1900: POLITICAL AND DIPLOMATIC QUESTIONS

Multiple-Choice Questions

1. Following the defeat of Napoleon at Waterloo, which of the following ascended to the French throne during the restoration?

    (A) Louis XIV
    (B) Louis XV
    (C) Louis XVI
    (D) Louis XVIII
    (E) Charles X

2. Which of the following shared political views that were most similar to those of Jeremy Bentham?

    (A) Thomas Malthus
    (B) Adam Smith
    (C) John Stuart Mill
    (D) David Ricardo
    (E) Joseph de Maistre

3. The Franco-Prussian war (1870) was significant for all of the following reasons EXCEPT

    (A) it established France as the leading power in Central Europe
    (B) it established Prussia as the leading power in Central Europe
    (C) it helped consolidate and unify the Germanic states into a single empire
    (D) it demonstrated the superiority of Prussian training and leadership
    (E) it provided Prussia with the Alsace-Lorraine region along the French border

4. What were the Carbonari?

    (A) Secret nationalist societies that opposed monarchial policies and rule in Italy
    (B) Military conscripts used by Italian monarchs to limit political uprisings during the nineteenth century
    (C) Socio-economic laws which provided justification for economic inequality in several Italian cities
    (D) Loyalists that provided financial support to King Ferdinand of Naples
    (E) None of the above

5. What triggered the Decembrist Revolt in Russia in 1825?

   (A) Costs associated with the Napoleonic wars and excess spending during the reign of Alexander I triggered an economic collapse.
   (B) Confusion surrounded the succession of the throne following the death of Alexander I.
   (C) Wealthy nobles were dissatisfied with the recent abolition of serfdom in Russia.
   (D) Russia's population growth could not be sustained by its agricultural production.
   (E) Widespread acceptance of nihilism led to public discontent with the political policies of Alexander I.

6. Following the Peterloo Massacre in 1819, English Parliament passed the Six Acts that did which of the following?

   (A) Provided universal male suffrage
   (B) Ensured annual parliaments
   (C) Banned demonstrations and imposed censorship
   (D) Legalized unions in the workplace
   (E) Imposed new taxation on wealthy landowners to replenish British coffers emptied during the Napoleonic wars

7. Lord Tennyson's famous poem, *The Charge of the Light Brigade,* describes an engagement in which of the following wars?

   (A) The Boer Wars
   (B) The Crimean Wars
   (C) The Franco-Prussian War
   (D) Napoleonic Wars
   (E) American War of 1812

8. Which of the following became the first and only president of the brief French Second Republic after the election of 1848?

   (A) Louis XVIII
   (B) Napoleon III
   (C) Charles X
   (D) Adolphe Thiers
   (E) Louis-Philippe I

"Germany is not looking to Prussia's liberalism but to her power…it is not by speeches and majority resolutions that the great questions of the time will be decided—that was the mistake of 1848 and 1849—but by iron and blood."

9. Which of the following is famous for delivering the speech of which an excerpt is shown above?

(A) Napoleon I
(B) Otto von Bismarck
(C) William I
(D) Wilhelm II
(E) Karl Marx

10. Which of the following was the main focus of the Berlin Conference (1884–1885)?

(A) Reorganization of German power following the unification of the German states
(B) Regulation and moral justification of imperialism on the African continent
(C) Formation of a political alliance between Germany and Austria-Hungary
(D) The nature of socialism and Marxism in Central Europe
(E) Control and freedom of travel in the Suez Canal

11. All of the following were goals of the Chartism movement in Britain EXCEPT

(A) universal male suffrage
(B) secret ballots
(C) five-year parliaments
(D) equal electoral districts
(E) abolition of property requirements for members of Parliament

12. Which of the following was true of the Congress of Vienna (1815)?

(A) It punished France greatly for Napoleon's military aggression.
(B) Only two of Europe's most powerful nations attended.
(C) It destabilized Europe.
(D) It provided Napoleon with amnesty.
(E) Its goal was to prevent future revolutions.

13. Which of the following wrote the work, *Reflections on the Revolution in France* (1790), which is credited with the start of modern conservatism and became quite popular during the Restoration period?

(A) Joseph de Maistre
(B) Edmund Burke
(C) Adam Smith
(D) John Stuart Mill
(E) Jeremy Bentham

14. All of the following contributed to Napoleon's cheap sale of the Louisiana territories to the United States EXCEPT

(A) he needed money to finance his wars on Europe.
(B) losses in colonial battles drove Napoleon to abandon his efforts to rebuild New France.
(C) he was angered by Spanish reluctance to transfer the territory back to France and knew that sale of the territory to the United States would anger them.
(D) he knew that the Louisiana territory would be indefensible due to Britain's control of the seas.
(E) none of the above

15. The result of which of the following ultimately convinced Napoleon not to invade England?

(A) The Battle of Ulm
(B) The Battle of Trafalgar
(C) The Treaty of Amiens
(D) The Treaty of Tilsit
(E) The Battle of Jena

16. The Civil Code of 1804 was also known by what other name?

(A) The Six Acts
(B) The Continental System
(C) The Napoleonic Code
(D) The Declaration of the Rights of Man
(E) The July Ordinances

17 In John Stuart Mill's *On Liberty*, what was Mill's leading concern of liberty as it relates to democracy?

(A) Too much liberty can result in radicalism and revolutions.

(B) The democratic majority could deny liberty to the minority.

(C) Constraints must be placed on monarchies to ensure democratic representation.

(D) Democratic systems of government fail to provide basic liberties to the people.

(E) Democracies fail to provide the stability that a monarch may provide.

18. The July Revolution of 1830 began in which of the following?

(A) Prussia
(B) Great Britain
(C) Russia
(D) Spain
(E) France

19. What was the French Restoration?

(A) Reconstruction of Paris and France following the Napoleonic Wars

(B) A sociopolitical plan to provide the lowest class with more political influence

(C) Return of the Bourbons to the throne following the defeat of Napoleon

(D) Implementation of a revised Declaration of the Rights of Man

(E) Formation of the French Second Republic and implementation of democracy

20. Approximately what percentage of men in Great Britain could vote following the passing of the Great Reform Bill (1832)?

(A) 20%
(B) 40%
(C) 50%
(D) 90%
(E) 100%

21. For many years during the eighteenth century, France faced religious intolerance and persecution. Catholic hostilities became more profound during the revolution. How did Napoleon address religion as leader of France?

   (A) He declared Catholicism the official state religion and exiled French Protestants and Jews to Spain to ensure religious uniformity.
   (B) He had himself crowned emperor by the Pope as a symbol of his and France's commitment to the Catholic Church.
   (C) He formed a special committee comprised of Catholic, Protestant, and Jewish religious leaders to approve state religious decrees.
   (D) He created a concordat with the Pope that would formally declare that Catholicism was the religion of the majority without establishing the faith as the official state religion to ensure religious tolerance.
   (E) He ignored the religious situation in France and focused his efforts on defining and expanding his rule to maintain political and religious stability.

22. Which of the following best describes a Junker within Prussia during the nineteenth century?

   (A) A military conscript
   (B) A wealthy landowner or noble
   (C) A cart or wagon used for trade
   (D) A small town, village, or hamlet
   (E) A serf

23. Which of the following decisions would trigger the fall of the French during the end of the Napoleonic wars?

   (A) Napoleon's decision to invade Britain
   (B) Napoleon's decision to invade Prussia
   (C) Napoleon's decision to invade Russia
   (D) Napoleon's passing of the Treaty of Tilsit
   (E) Napoleon's defeat at the Battle of Trafalgar

24. Following the overthrow of Napoleon, which of the following monarchs ascended to the throne of Spain?

   (A) Ferdinand VII
   (B) Joseph I
   (C) Charles X
   (D) Charles IV
   (E) John VI

25. The Congress of Vienna (1815) was formed to help bring peace following which of the following wars?

(A) Crimean War
(B) Boer War
(C) Napoleonic Wars
(D) Franco-Prussian War
(E) The French Revolution

27. During the nineteenth century, which of the following was considered "the Sick Man of Europe"?

(A) Austria
(B) Prussia
(C) Russia
(D) Ottoman Empire
(E) Spain

26. Which of the following factions did not fight for Greek independence during the 1820s?

(A) Great Britain
(B) Turkey
(C) Russia
(D) France
(E) Revolutionaries of the First Hellenic Republic

28. Which of the following led the famous 1,000 "red shirts" and conquered the Kingdom of the Two Sicilies?

(A) Giuseppe Garibaldi
(B) Count Camillo di Cavour
(C) Giuseppe Mazzini
(D) Benito Mussolini
(E) Victor Emmanuel

29. In 1861, who was declared the first king of Italy following unification of nearly the entire Italian peninsula?

    (A) Benito Mussolini
    (B) Victor Emmanuel
    (C) Giuseppe Garibaldi
    (D) Count Camillo di Cavour
    (E) Giuseppe Mazzini

30. Unification of the entire Italian Peninsula required acquiring the final state of Rome. Which of the following accurately describes how Rome was ultimately acquired?

    (A) The French withdrew troops following the Franco-Prussian war.
    (B) The Prussians withdrew troops following the Franco-Prussian war.
    (C) The Austrians withdrew troops following the Franco-Prussian war.
    (D) The Spanish withdrew troops following the Franco-Prussian war.
    (E) The Serbians withdrew troops following the Franco-Prussian war.

31. All of the following fought together during the Crimean War EXCEPT

    (A) France
    (B) Ottoman Empire
    (C) Great Britain
    (D) Kingdom of Sardinia / Italy
    (E) Russia

32. Who was appointed emperor of the German Empire in 1871?

    (A) Otto von Bismarck
    (B) Wilhelm I
    (C) Wilhelm II
    (D) Frederick II
    (E) Frederick III

33. What triggered the end of the brief French Second Empire?

   (A) The June Days conflict
   (B) The Franco-Prussian War
   (C) The Crimean War
   (D) Rise of the Paris Commune
   (E) Election of Louis Napoleon as president

34. How did the influence of the monarchy in British politics change during the reign of Queen Victoria?

   (A) The influence of the monarchy was strengthened by Victoria's ability to play a role in the selection of prime ministers throughout her reign.
   (B) The influence of the monarchy was weakened by Victoria's ability to play a role in the selection of prime ministers throughout her reign.
   (C) The influence of the monarchy was weakened by Victoria's inability to play a role in the selection of prime ministers throughout her reign.
   (D) The influence of the monarchy was strengthened due to increased diplomatic ties between Victoria and other monarchs of Europe.
   (E) The influence of the monarchy was weakened due to increased diplomatic ties between Victoria and other monarchs of Europe.

35. By 1850, serfdom had been abolished in all of the following EXCEPT

   (A) England
   (B) Prussia
   (C) Austria
   (D) Russia
   (E) Scotland

36. The British Empire during the reign of Queen Victoria was immense. All of the following were parts of the British Empire during her reign EXCEPT

   (A) India
   (B) Australia
   (C) New Zealand
   (D) Indochina
   (E) South Africa

Napoleon su son lit de mort
by Horace Vernet (1826)

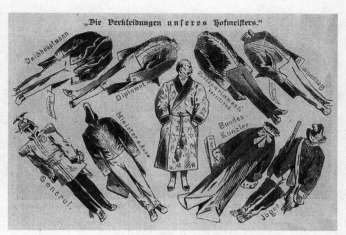

Die Verkleidungen unseres Hofmeisters
by Wilhelm Scholz (1867)

37. The image above depicts an artist's rendition of Napoleon on his deathbed wearing a crown reminiscent of the leaders of Roman Empire. All of the following represent similarities between Napoleon's French Empire and the Roman Empire EXCEPT

   (A) both were ruled by emperors
   (B) both controlled much of Europe at their peak
   (C) both ultimately fell due to inability to control their vast territories
   (D) both relied on the power of a strong military
   (E) both were ultimately absorbed by conquering peoples

38. The image is a political cartoon that depicts the many roles and titles of which one of the following men?

   (A) Otto von Bismarck
   (B) Frederick William IV
   (C) Klemens von Metternich
   (D) William I
   (E) William II

Charge of the Light Brigade
by Richard Caton Woodville (1894)

39. The painting above depicts the charge of the Light Brigade.
Where did this attack take place?

(A) France
(B) Turkey
(C) Russia
(D) England
(E) Prussia

*Sultan of the Ottoman Empire, Abdulmecid I;
Queen of United Kingdom and Ireland, Victoria;
and President of France,
Napoleon III* by Unknown

40. The image above depicts several critical European leaders
during the nineteenth century. What likely brought them
together for this meeting?

(A) Franco-Prussian War
(B) Crimean War
(C) Congress of Vienna
(D) The Austro-Prussian War
(E) Congress of Berlin

Illustrierte Zeitung (1848)

41. What event is depicted in the cartoon above?

   (A) Political unrest in Paris
   (B) Plebiscite vote during the rule of Napoleon
   (C) French presidential election of 1848
   (D) June Days event
   (E) Conscription in Paris for the Franco-Prussian war

42. The Communist Manifesto (shown above) is one of the most influential political texts in history. Which of the following people was an author of this text?

   (A) Louis Blanc
   (B) Adam Smith
   (C) John Stuart Mill
   (D) Karl Marx
   (D) Joseph de Maistre

The Coronation of Napoleon
by Jacques-Louis David (1804)

43. The famous painting above depicts the coronation of
Napoleon as emperor of the French Empire. According
to historical accounts, rather than having the Pope crown
him, he crowned himself. What was the significance of this
move?

(A) To show the Pope that he controlled the church
(B) To show that he made himself ruler, not God or through
his birthright
(C) To demonstrate that France controlled the Papal
States
(D) To undervalue the tradition of French monarchy
(E) To ensure that the religious minorities would not
revolt

Free-Response Questions

44. Describe and analyze the rise and fall of Napoleon's French Empire.

45. The creation of the German Empire following the Franco-Prussian War had a profound impact on the future of Europe. Describe and analyze how the formation of the German Empire changed the dynamics of Europe.

Chapter 11
1815–1900: Political and Diplomatic Answers and Explanations

ANSWER KEY

1.	D	23.	C
2.	C	24.	A
3.	A	25.	C
4.	A	26.	B
5.	B	27.	D
6.	C	28.	A
7.	B	29.	B
8.	B	30.	A
9.	B	31.	E
10.	B	32.	B
11.	C	33.	B
12.	E	34.	C
13.	B	35.	D
14.	E	36.	D
15.	B	37.	E
16.	C	38.	A
17.	B	39.	C
18.	E	40.	B
19.	C	41.	C
20.	A	42.	D
21.	D	43.	B
22.	B		

ANSWERS AND EXPLANATIONS

1. **D**   Louis XVIII was the younger brother of Louis XVI and ascended to the throne during the French restoration following the demise of Napoleon at Waterloo. Louis XIV (A), Louis XV (B), and Louis XVI (C) all ruled France prior to the rise of Napoleon. Charles X (E), the younger brother of Louis XVI and Louis XVIII, would succeed Louis XVIII after his death in 1824.

2. **C**   John Stuart Mill was a disciple of Bentham's and shared many of his utilitarian views regarding the role of government to provide the "greatest happiness for the greatest number." Thomas Malthus (A), Adam Smith (B), and David Ricardo (D) all published famous works focusing on economic theory rather political. De Maistre (E) was conservative and felt that the monarchies should have absolute control and resist any forms of political reform.

3. **A**   France was quickly defeated by Prussia during the Franco-Prussian War. The war established Prussia as a power in Central Europe (B) and consolidated Germany into a large unified state (C) with a superior military strength (D) and newly acquired territories on the French border (E).

4. **A**   Carbonari (or charcoal burners) were secret nationalist groups, which were unhappy with the political and social policies on the Italian peninsula in the nineteenth century.

5. **B**   Following the death of Alexander I in 1825, Constantine, the older of his surviving brothers, decided not to take the throne, which made Nicholas I the new king. A group of military officers felt that Constantine was unjustly removed from the succession and staged the December revolt. Although the Napoleonic wars did apply some economic pressure (A), Russia emerged as a European power following Napoleon's defeat and did not suffer an economic collapse or inadequacy of agricultural production (D). Serfdom (C) was not abolished in Russia until 1861. Nihilism (E) became a more common philosophical doctrine during the later half of the nineteenth century.

6. **C**   The Six Acts were a repressive set of legislation, which labeled any effort for radical reform as a treasonable conspiracy. Among the acts were banning of demonstrations and increased censorship. The Peterloo Massacre occurred during a demonstration requesting universal male suffrage and annual parliaments.

7. **B**   Tennyson's poem describes a cavalry charge during the Crimean Wars (1854–1856). The Crimean Wars were marked by military blunders and incompetence of nearly all participating nations. This poem captures what has become the most famous of them.

8. **B**   Louis Napoleon, nephew of Napoleon Bonaparte, was elected president of the Second Republic in 1848. Shortly after, he organized a *coup d'état* and took the throne in 1852 as Napoleon III with the title of Emperor of the French. Louis XVIII (A) ruled from 1814 to 1824, immediately following the fall of Napoleon Bonaparte except for a brief period in 1815. Charles X (C) was Louis XVIII's successor ruling from 1824 to 1830. Adolphe Thiers (D) was the first president of the Third Republic ruling France from 1871 to 1873. Louis-Philippe I (E) ruled from 1830 to 1848.

9. **B** Bismarck delivered his famous "Iron and Blood" speech to the Prussian parliamentary budget commission asking for additional military funding. Though he did not receive his requested funds, he raised them through taxes anyway. Napoleon I (A) was the ruler of France and had died well before this speech was made. William I (C) was the Prussian king at the time of the speech. Wilhelm II (D) became the emperor of Germany during the later rule of Bismarck. Karl Marx (E) did not play a major role in military.

10. **B** The Berlin Conference focused on control of the Congo and involved discussing regulation of European colonization of the African continent. From this conference, it was decided that Europeans had a moral obligation to care for the African people.

11. **C** One of the key points of the People's Charter of 1838 was that they wanted annual parliaments to limit the power and influence of long duration parliaments. This remains the only act that wasn't eventually passed.

12. **E** The primary goal of the Congress of Vienna was to bring peace and stability to Europe by preventing future revolutions or wars. France was not punished severely for its aggression (A), all of Europe's most powerful nations attended (B), it provided stability to Europe (C), and declared Napoleon an outlaw (D).

13. **B** Edmund Burke wrote *Reflections on the Revolution in France* in which he attacked the principle of the rights of man and natural law as being dangerous to natural order and placed emphasis on the rights of those in positions of authority.

14. **E** Napoleon's losses in his conquests and reducing coffers pushed him to drop his efforts to reform New France and focus his military and financial powers to the war in Europe. All of the reasons mentioned supported Napoleon's decision.

15. **B** The Battle of Trafalgar represented a key battle of the war over naval superiority. Despite heavy losses, the British destroyed the French fleet ensuring naval supremacy throughout the war and afterwards. Without control of the seas, Napoleon was forced to abandon his plans for a conquest of England. The Battles of Ulm (A) and Jena (E) were both military victories for France over Austria and the Prussians, respectively. The Treaties of Amiens (C) and Tilsit (D) were with the British and Prussians and had no impact on his decision to invade England.

16. **C** The Civil Code of 1804 was also called the Napoleonic Code. Napoleon set out to reform the French legal system and as leader formed a unified code for all of France. This document provides the legal framework of the system still used today.

17. **B** Mill's chief concern regarding democracies and liberty was that the democratic majority with voting power and control would be able to deny liberties to the minority.

18. **E** The July Revolution (also sometimes referred to as the French Revolution of 1830) saw the overthrow of Charles X in favor of his cousin, Louis-Philippe. This revolution triggered smaller revolutions all throughout Europe. Coincidentally, Louis-Philippe would also be overthrown 18 years later.

19. **C** The French Restoration marked the return of the Bourbon monarchy to the throne of France following the defeat of Napoleon. Although it would not last long, it was widely supported by the other nations of Europe and did offer a brief peace following the Napoleonic wars.

20. **A** Following the passing of the Great Reform Bill, men who had become wealthy as a result of industrialization could now vote. However, the bill remained very restrictive on membership of the voting electorate. It did represent though a step towards political reform.

21. **D** Napoleon knew that religion could trigger another revolt or potentially re-ignite the revolution. His view on religion was to ensure religious tolerance while pleasing the Catholic majority through the creation of a concordat with the Pope. He declared France to be majority Catholic and outlined the church's position on selecting clergy and acquisition of lands. He did not, however, make Catholicism the official state religion in order to ensure formal tolerance of Protestants and Jews.

22. **B** Prussian Junkers were wealthy nobles that owned land. They maintained much of their aristocratic power and control by holding land and controlling serfdom. Baron von Stein and Count von Hardenberg sought to end the Junker monopoly on ownership of land and serfdom and did so by reorganizing the Prussian military to remove incompetent Junker leaders and aimed to encourage peasants to fight for the state.

23. **C** Prior to his invasion of Russia, Napoleon's army had defeated most of Europe. His decision to invade Russia was based on the knowledge that they had a weakened military and remained the only major force that could resist his newly formed empire. He invaded Russia; however the Russians retreated rather than attacked. Napoleon pursued them deep within the nation; however he ultimately decided to retreat and would lose the majority of his troops to Russian attacks and the brutal winter. Napoleon's weakened force and a new coalition of Britain, Prussia, Austria, and Great Britain triggered his demise.

24. **A** A revolt broke out in 1807 in Spain over the incompetence of King Charles IV; his son Ferdinand VII, then ascended to the throne. Napoleon took the political unrest as an opportunity to seize control of Spain and placed his elder brother (Joseph I) on the throne. Following the overthrow of Napoleon, Ferdinand VII was reestablished as king of Spain.

25. **C** The Congress of Vienna was assembled in 1814 by the four great powers (Great Britain, Austria, Prussia, and Russia) to bring peace and stability to Europe following the Napoleonic Wars. Though successful in many respects, it failed to address several issues related to nationalist fervor and resulted in formal alliances during the nineteenth century, which would ultimately lead to subsequent wars.

26. **B** In the 1820s, Great Britain, Russia, and France allied with the Greek revolutionaries (who called themselves the First Hellenic Republic) to gain independence from the Ottoman Empire (which was based in Turkey). In 1832, Greece gained its independence and formed a monarchy.

27. **D** The Ottoman Empire was in decline and faced multiple revolts and breakaway regions during the nineteenth century. Referred to as "the Sick Man of Europe," the Ottomans saw Greece and the Serbians gain independence. Stability of the state continued to decline throughout the century as Ottoman leaders were unable to keep the various ethnic groups united.

28. **A** Following encouragement from Cavour, Giuseppe Garibaldi took an army of 1,000 "red shirts" and conquered the Kingdom of the Two Sicilies. This victory would ultimately have implications for the unification of much of the Italian peninsula by the 1860s.

29. **B** Victor Emmanuel, King of Piedmont-Sardinia, was able to gain control of all of the papal states (except Rome and Venetia) and unite them as an Italian state. On March 17, 1861, he was declared King of Italy.

30. **A** Following the start of the Franco-Prussian war, the Italians were able to gain control of Rome uniting the Italian peninsula after the French troops withdrew in 1870. Rome was made the new capital of Italy the following year.

31. **E** The Crimean War was fought over rights to the holy land and the decline of the Ottoman Empire. Initially, the war was fought between the Ottoman Empire and Russia. However, Great Britain, France, and the Kingdom of Sardinia (Italians) joined with the Ottomans to defeat the Russians.

32. **B** After the success of Otto von Bismarck during the Franco-Prussian war, the German states were unified and the king of Prussia, Wilhelm I, was declared emperor of the German empire in 1871 in Versailles.

33. **B** Military blunders by Napoleon III and his eventual capture during the Franco-Prussian War resulted in the end of the French Second Empire in 1870. This would give rise to the Third Republic.

34. **C** Throughout Victoria's long reign, she oversaw a continual deterioration of the influence and power of the monarchy. One leading reason for this was that Victoria had little role in the selection of the British prime minister. This decline led ultimately to the current role of the British monarch today.

35. **D** Serfdom was abolished in Russia in 1861 by Alexander II. By 1850, nearly all of Europe had abolished serfdom. Serfdom was obsolete in England by the sixteenth century and was abolished in Scotland (1747), Austria (last in 1848), and Prussia (1807).

36. **D** After the Franco-Prussian war, there was a renewed effort of imperialism and formation of colonies. The British Empire would include India, Australia, New Zealand, and South Africa among many other nations. Indochina, however, would remain in French control until their fight for independence in the mid-twentieth century.

37. **E** Following Napoleon's demise, France was not absorbed by the allied opposition. Rather, it was felt that peace would be best achieved if Europe were returned to much of the geographic organization it had prior to the Napoleonic wars.

38. **A** Otto von Bismarck played many roles in Prussia and the later German Empire including general, minister, diplomat, and soldier.

39. **C** The charge of the Light Brigade occurred during the Crimean War in Crimea, which was part of Russia (modern Ukraine). The charge was immortalized by Alford Lord Tennyson's famous poem and this painting and became the symbol of the Crimean War.

40. **B** Pictured are the Sultan of the Ottoman Empire, Abdulmecid I; the Queen of Great Britain, Victoria; and the President of France, Napoleon III. These three leaders allied together during the Crimean War against the Russians.

41. **C** This cartoon depicts the presidential election of 1848. Multiple elements of the cartoon state Louis Napoleon, who would ultimately win the election and become the first president of the French Second Republic.

42. **D** The Communist Manifesto written by Karl Marx and Friedrich Engels in 1848 outlined the basic statement of principles surrounding their newly organized Communist League. This text and later works by Marx formed the basis of Marxism and the rise of socialism.

43. **B** Napoleon's self-crowning was symbolic of his own hand in making him emperor of the state. Traditionally, the Pope would crown the monarch. However, he wanted it clear that he was responsible and not God or some other birthright, for his ascension to power.

The Free-Response Essay Questions Explained

Question 44

44. Describe and analyze the rise and fall of Napoleon's French Empire.

Essay Notes

For the first half of your essay, you should outline the events, which led to the rise of Napoleon as leader of the French people. There are several main points, which could be addressed including the following:

- France had just gone through a bloody revolution and was politically unstable. Napoleon Bonaparte was appointed by the formed government (called the Directory) to put down a rebellion, which he did swiftly and successfully. He quickly grew in power due to several military victories which rallied the people around him.

- He overthrew the Directory in a *coup d'état* when it had become unstable and staged a plebiscite (a vote of the people) to approve a new constitution, which would have him as First Consul.
- Using his seat of power, he provided amnesty for the revolution and made several social reforms, which gained the favor of the people including creating a concordat with the Pope to ensure religious tolerance of Protestants and Jews and establishing the Civil Code (or Napoleonic Code) as a uniform legal system.
- He made sure that any political enemies were unable to unseat him or reduce his power or influence.

For the second half of your essay, you need to explain how his war played a role in the strength and fall of his empire:

- He took advantage of political and social unrest in other nations of Europe as a means of declaring war and expanding French territory. Among his successful conquests were nearly the entirety of the Iberian peninsula (Spain and Portugal), Austria (by means of the Battle of Ulm), Prussia (Battle of Jena), and much of Eastern Europe.
- His plans to invade England however were unsuccessful. He fought the British at the naval Battle of Trafalgar. The English victory in this battle ensured that the British, rather than the French, would maintain naval supremacy in Europe.
- His plans to restore the New France colony failed after disease destroyed a contingent of his forces in the Caribbean and he decided to focus his efforts more on Europe. He ultimately sold the Louisiana territory to the United States for approximately $11 million for money for the war.
- The conquest of Spain and its subsequent maintenance required a large troop presence and continued to apply pressure throughout the war.
- His primary downfall came with his decision to invade Russia. He took his Grand Army and invaded. However, the Russians simply retreated deeper into their vast country and destroyed Moscow. Needing supplies and sensing that he would be unable to take Russia, he retreated in the middle of the Russian winter. This resulted in heavy losses among his men.
- The wars caused European states to ally against him and he was finally defeated in 1814. Despite a short 100-day return to power, he was unable to reestablish himself, was defeated at the Battle of Waterloo, and was exiled to St. Helena.

Question 45

45. The creation of the German Empire following the Franco-Prussian war had a profound impact on the future of Europe. Describe and analyze how the formation of the German Empire changed the dynamics of Europe.

Essay Notes

There are many ways to tackle this essay; you may want to structure your essay around paragraphs focusing on the key changes to Europe and how they manifested themselves in the future of the continent. Here are some key examples:

- By winning the war and forming the German Empire, the Prussians greatly expanded their territory and political influence in Central Europe.
- The victory of the Prussians in the Franco-Prussian War represented a profound change in the military strength of nations in Europe. Prior to the war, France was believed by many to have the finest army in the world. However, the Prussians defeated them soundly in battle. Following the war, Europe recognized the German Empire as a formidable military power and regional superpower in Central Europe.

- In order to maintain strength of resources and power with the newly created German Empire, the power nations of Europe increased their imperialist policies and created new colonies. This would lead to nearly the complete European colonization of the African continent by the start of World War I.
- The newly acquired German territories of Alsace and Lorraine (which were taken from France) caused much resentment between the French and Germans. In addition, the French were forced to pay a huge indemnity to Germany for starting the war. This resentment and bitter dislike between France and Germany would re-emerge in World War I, the Treaty of Versailles, and World War II.

Chapter 12
1815–1900: Cultural and Intellectual Questions

1815–1900: CULTURAL AND INTELLECTUAL QUESTIONS

Multiple-Choice Questions

1. The efforts of the Chartists can be best described as

   (A) ultimately successful through successful revolution against Parliament
   (B) immediate failures, but most of the Chartists' demands were gradually met over the course of the century
   (C) extremely modest and limited in scope and inherently conservative in intent
   (D) radically socialist and violent
   (E) representing the interests of the landed elites.

Source: http://en.wikipedia.org

2. Charles Darwin's theory of natural selection could be said to have drawn most inspiration from which of the following thinkers?

   (A) Thomas Malthus
   (B) John Maynard Keynes
   (C) John Stuart Mill
   (D) Adam Smith
   (E) Jeremy Bentham

3. The painting above is representative of which school of art?

   (A) Impressionism
   (B) Romanticism
   (C) Cubism
   (D) Realism
   (E) Post-Modernism

4. Which demographic best describes the majority of textile mill laborers at the turn of the nineteenth century?

   (A) Females
   (B) Skilled artisans
   (C) Young children
   (D) Unskilled males
   (E) The elderly

5. The Alfred Dreyfus Affair was significant for all the following reasons EXCEPT

   (A) it showed how deeply engrained anti-Semitism still was in the minds of the French.
   (B) it demonstrated the justice of the French legal system by acquitting Dreyfus of charges against him.
   (C) it revealed the paranoia in the Third Republic towards another war with Germany.
   (D) it was a strong impetus for the development of Zionism.
   (E) it demonstrated the power of the press for inflaming the French public's opinion.

6. David Ricardo's "Iron Law of Wages" most directly argued that

   (A) higher wages earned by workers would transmit into smaller family sizes
   (B) higher wages earned by workers in a country would demonstrate its superiority to the world
   (C) higher wages earned by workers would transmit into larger family sizes
   (D) the only way a firm would remain competitive in a perfectly competitive market would be to pay its workers as little as possible
   (E) social status directly corresponds to one's wage with higher wages commanding higher stations.

7. The *Kleindeutsch* solution preferred by the Frankfurt Assembly

   (A) would have included Austria as well as the German states
   (B) was not ratified by all the German states present at the assembly and therefore was not proposed
   (C) offered the crown of all of Germany to the liberal emperor of Austria
   (D) was rejected by the King of Prussia
   (E) attempted to integrate all the German states into a customs union

8. Nationalist revolts occurred in all of the following regions in 1848 EXCEPT

(A) Poland
(B) Hungary
(C) Italy
(D) Scotland
(E) Germany

9. Marxism differed from earlier Socialist theory in that

(A) Marxism sought to carry out political reform through constitutional means
(B) Marxism tried to elevate the worker socially and economically to be the equal of master artisans
(C) Marxism espoused the complete dissolution of private property altogether
(D) Marxism espoused revolutionary class struggle as the main vehicle of effecting political change
(E) Marxism was not founded upon historical economic theory.

10. The "New Imperialism" differed from previous methods of empire building in all the following ways EXCEPT

(A) it involved European powers making invasive treaties with respect to the governance of subject countries
(B) it involved the complete depopulation of subject areas and resettlement with national immigrants strictly for the sake of cultural homogeneity
(C) it involved private investments in subject countries
(D) it penetrated further into previously unconquerable continents, such as Africa and Asia, than was possible for Europeans to do before
(E) it was aided philosophically by the application of scientific theories justifying imperialism

11. Nineteenth-century Liberalism espoused

(A) the obligations of all citizens towards the state
(B) the divine right of monarchs to rule their kingdoms and subjects as personal fiefdoms
(C) few, if any, government restrictions on commerce
(D) few government restrictions on the rights of citizens to assemble, but complete suppression of all non-conforming religions within the state.
(E) complete lack of centralized government apparatuses

12. Over the first half of the nineteenth century, the participation of children in the English workforce

   (A) increased as economic conditions for male wage-earners worsened

   (B) lessened as Parliament bowed to pressure from the working classes to ameliorate working conditions for children

   (C) remained constant as women took up more unskilled factory jobs from men who were drafted to fight in the Napoleonic Wars

   (D) increased as economic growth propelled by industrialization created a great demand for any sort of labor

   (E) did not exist, since children were never a part of the English workforce in the nineteenth century

Source: http://historyrhymes.files.wordpress.com/2010/02/765px-maerz1848_berlin.jpg

13. The image depicted above most directly corresponds with

   (A) nationalism
   (B) anarchism
   (C) monarchism
   (D) democracy
   (E) urbanization

14. Upon the publication of *On the Origin of Species*,

    (A) most people were won over by the concise and accurate scientific arguments Darwin proposed

    (B) Darwin was widely ignored as his ideas were not sensational

    (C) the theories of Natural Selection Darwin proposed would be retooled into many other philosophies

    (D) most people were not won over immediately, but by the turn of the nineteenth century, almost every Englishman had been convinced of the veracity of the theory of evolution

    (E) the church's centrality to British society had been vindicated, as stalwart religionists won many people back to the fold in reaction to Darwin's proposals

15. Throughout the later half of the nineteenth century, European states can be said to have

    (A) generally de-emphasized public education as lawmakers were primarily concerned with having as much cheap labor as possible to sustain economic growth in the face of economic depression

    (B) gradually expanded the scope and scale of their public education systems as they viewed literacy and basic arithmetic as vital skills for their citizenry

    (C) left their educational systems alone as reforms in the eighteenth century had already laid the groundwork for universal public education systems

    (D) supported parochial education systems chiefly as a philosophical bulwark against anti-governmental secular ideas

    (E) universally mandated pro-nationalist educational regimes in public education in order to impress upon their citizens the importance of revanchism

16. The Roman Catholic Relief Act passed by Parliament

    (A) was inspired by liberal Irishmen who wished to impose Catholicism on the entirety of the United Kingdom

    (B) permitted the practice of Catholic rites in the United Kingdom for the first time since the Glorious Revolution

    (C) was liberal in spirit, but conservative in intent.

    (D) was passed under the liberal Prime Minister William Gladstone who empathized with the Irish Catholics' plight

    (E) secured overwhelming support for the Tory regime of Wellington

17. Which of the following is best described as representing conservative values?

    (A) The Chartist movement

    (B) The Triple Alliance

    (C) The Congress of Vienna

    (D) The Peace of Westphalia

    (E) The Paris Commune

18. The status of European Jews over the course of the nineteenth century can be said to have

(A) gradually improved across the whole of Europe to the point of equality with Christian citizens

(B) gradually improved across Europe on account of new liberal laws, with the exception of Russia where Jews were treated harshly

(C) become superior to that of Christians on account of overwhelming Jewish financial support for the explosive growth of industries across the continent.

(D) gradually improved across the whole of Europe, but political rights and offices remained closed to Jewish citizens.

(E) had improved greatly in the wake of the Congress of Vienna, but were greatly rescinded following the revolutions of 1848.

"When Zarathustra was alone, however, he said to his heart: "Could it be possible! This old saint in the forest hath not yet heard of it, that God is dead!"

19. Who, among the following authors, wrote the above quotation?

(A) Charles Dickens
(B) Sigmund Freud
(C) Otto von Bismarck
(D) Friedrich Neitzche
(E) Rudyard Kipling

20. Bismarck's *Kulturkampf*

(A) was inspired by Bismarck's desire to make Protestantism the only religion practiced in Germany

(B) led to a lengthy and protracted political struggle between Bismarck and the Catholic church in which Bismarck managed to triumph, but only at the cost of alienating many Catholics in Germany

(C) was the name Bismarck gave for his wars of German unification

(D) was undertaken to promote good relations with Sweden and Great Britain

(E) came very close to causing war with Catholic Austria-Hungary

21. The relationship between European nation-states and organized religion throughout the later half of the nineteenth century could be best described as one of

(A) suspicion, in that liberal values that permeated the governments of many nation-states, as well as greater reliance on rationalism threatened the usual functions of organized religion in many states, whereas nation-states were concerned about the powers of international churches to subvert their own national identities and autonomy

(B) churches hostile to the nation-states, in that liberal values that permeated the governments of many nation-states, as well as greater reliance on rationalism threatened the usual functions of organized religion in many states, whereas nation-states saw organized religion as a valuable unifying force

(C) cooperation, in that conservative values that permeated the governments of many nation-states, as well as a general religious revival across Europe buttressed the usual functions of organized religion in many states, whereas nation-states saw organized religion as a valuable unifying force

(D) animosity, in that organized religion attempted to inspire the citizenry to overthrow the strong centralized governments of the nation-states and re-impose the centrality of old feudal arrangements, whereas nation-states were concerned about the powers of international churches to subvert their own national identities and autonomy

(E) ambivalence, in that neither organized religion nor nation-states tended to act against or in cooperation with one another

22. The development of Realism was inspired as a reaction against which school of art?

(A) Romanticism
(B) Impressionism
(C) Naturalism
(D) Modernism
(E) Darwinism

"I contend that we are the first race in the world, and that the more of the world we inhabit the better it is for the human race...If there be a God, I think that what he would like me to do is paint as much of the map of Africa British Red as possible..."

23. Cecil Rhodes's quote above most directly supports which of the following philosophies?

(A) Manifest Destiny
(B) Social Darwinism
(C) Monarchism
(D) Romanticism
(E) Socialism

24. Which of the following was NOT a major problem suffered by industrial cities in the nineteenth century?

    (A) Disease and poor sanitation
    (B) Growing crime and local political corruption
    (C) A failure to attract labor from the countryside
    (D) Dangerous and congested slums
    (E) Social unrest

25. The Greek Revolution of 1821 particularly appealed to European adherents of which school of thought?

    (A) Romanticism
    (B) Feudalism
    (C) Asceticism
    (D) Realism
    (E) Social Darwinism

26. The Decembrist Revolt was inspired chiefly by

    (A) reactionary sentiments of the Russian army generals, who were alarmed at the Tsar's planned liberal constitution
    (B) nationalist fury from some inhabitants of Poland
    (C) clamors for social justice from disaffected urban industrial workers
    (D) liberal outrage from the Russian Duma which the Tsar had ordered to be dissolved
    (E) liberal thoughts taken up by Russian soldiers who occupied France following the Napoleonic Wars

27. The Irish Potato Famine revealed

    (A) how successful contemporary British interventionist economic policy was by sustaining large numbers of impoverished farmers in workhouses
    (B) the consequences of British liberal economic reluctance to provide aid to starving workers
    (C) the strength of Catholic charity and social support systems to feed and sustain the impoverished
    (D) the aggression of Protestant inhabitants of Ireland towards rebellious Catholics
    (E) the effective failure of Irish Home Rule on account of its inability to mitigate the crisis

28. Which of the following painters could best be considered an Impressionist?

(A) Van Dyck
(B) Eugène Delacroix
(C) Titian
(D) Eduard Manet
(E) Francisco Goya

29. The expansion of the British electorate throughout the nineteenth and early twentieth centuries is best described as a process in which

(A) voting restrictions based on wealth were gradually relaxed by successive acts, though universal male suffrage was never achieved
(B) voting restrictions based on wealth were gradually strengthened as the power of the urban bourgeoisie and aristocracy exerted their influence, precluding the poor from politics
(C) voting restrictions based on wealth were gradually relaxed by successive acts and redistricting moved power away from traditional locales in the rural areas and towards burgeoning industrial towns
(D) voting restrictions based on wealth were gradually relaxed by successive acts, but Catholics and Jews were forbidden from participating at all in politics
(E) voting rights were rescinded by a resurgent absolutist faction in the House of Lords

30. Women's suffrage movements in Britain and the Continent differed in that

(A) British suffragettes failed to gain any significant sympathy from the rest of society, while suffragettes on the Continent easily gained public support for the right to vote
(B) British suffragettes were deeply divided over the use of violence in protesting, while Continental suffragettes had no such qualms
(C) British suffragettes were generally supported by conservatives, but Continental suffragettes relied on the support of socialists
(D) British suffragettes utilized peaceful and more radical tactics and were ultimately successful, whereas Continental suffragettes failed to gain any support since they were connected with Socialists and other undesirable political parties
(E) British suffragettes worked closely with their American counterparts to achieve suffrage, but Continental suffragettes mainly lobbied through religious officials to gain sympathy for their cause

31. The Papacy's reactions to the revolts of 1848 can most appropriately be described as

(A) reactionary, in that they inspired the Catholic church to actively work against liberal revolutions that threatened its existence
(B) conciliatory, in that in the aftermath of the revolts, the Church used its higher moral station to champion the cause of the revolutions
(C) conservative, in that the Catholic church sought only to preserve its independence as a state and worked to ameliorate the conditions that caused the revolts in the first place
(D) liberal, since the doctrine of papal infallibility promulgated before the revolts allowed open criticism of the pope and his actions
(E) socialistic, as the pope's departure from any temporal power immediately following the revolts led to the creation of the Roman Republic as a socialist workers' paradise

32. Which of the following best describes the impact of the industrial revolution on the social status of women in the nineteenth century?

   (A) It improved many women's prospects for wage labor, though they were often paid far less than their male counterparts.
   (B) It guaranteed access to all levels of education but still precluded women from the workforce.
   (C) It lowered the standing of all women considerably as their primary function as keepers of the household could now be much more easily done by machines.
   (D) It guaranteed women access to the workforce but precluded them from any education as industry needed a cheap, uneducated workforce.
   (E) It inspired most males of the age to think of women as their equals in every way as both worked equally menial jobs in the factories.

33. Which event most directly led to the freeing of the Russian serfs?

   (A) Russian victory in the Napoleonic Wars
   (B) Russian victory in the Russo-Turkish War of 1877
   (C) Russian defeat in World War I
   (D) Russian defeat in the Crimean War
   (E) Russian defeat in the Russo-Japanese War

34. Which of the following did NOT contribute to the rise of an effective middle class in many European countries throughout the nineteenth century?

   (A) Improved access to all levels of education
   (B) Improved standards of living caused by the technological advances of the Industrial Revolution
   (C) Strengthened feudal arrangements, which had been largely ignored in the years before the Napoleonic Wars
   (D) The rise of wage labor throughout Europe whereby certain members of society managed to improve their economic standing through their work in the factories
   (E) A powerful and conscious effort on the part of certain members of society to improve their standings by any means possible

35. Which of the following technologies was a part of the Second Industrial Revolution?

   (A) Textile manufacturing machinery
   (B) The steam engine
   (C) The cotton gin
   (D) The seed drill
   (E) Steel

36. Which of the following feminists embarked on a decidedly aggressive strategy to achieve suffrage in Britain?

    (A) Harriet Taylor
    (B) Millicent Fawcett
    (C) Hubertine Auclert
    (D) Emmeline Pankhurst
    (E) Marie Mauguet

37. Which of the following best characterizes the nature of population growth in Europe during the nineteenth century?

    (A) It was wracked by major wars that precipitated a demographic collapse.
    (B) It was aided by the implementation of more advanced medicines and sanitation that allowed people to live longer.
    (C) The pollution caused by industrialization forced death rates to climb just as quickly as population growth.
    (D) It slowed down across all of Europe as labor moved from the countryside to the cities, leaving less agricultural land cultivated to feed the population at large.
    (E) It increased as the increased prosperity in Europe inspired larger family sizes.

38. Which of the following best characterizes Zionism?

    (A) A response to the pressures of nineteenth-century bigotry by seeking a Jewish homeland in Poland
    (B) A radical movement headed by Theodore Herzl to bring down the French Third Republic for its crimes in the Dreyfus Affair
    (C) A Jewish adaptation of nineteenth-century nationalism
    (D) The European interest in carving up the Ottoman Empire, with special regard to its Mesopotamian provinces
    (E) The gradual process of Jewish enfranchisement in Germany over the course of the nineteenth century

39. The Young Turks of the Ottoman Empire

    (A) found traditional Muslim practices to be much stronger than secular European beliefs
    (B) successfully instituted a strong policy of industrialization and militarization that revitalized the Ottoman Empire
    (C) found the Ottoman Empire's strongest asset was the multitude of nationalities it contained as subjects
    (D) thought that the Ottoman Empire's natural ally was Russia
    (E) were inspired to bring reform to the Ottoman empire through the same belief in nationalism that was so strong in Europe

40. Which of the following nations implemented the first major national social welfare reforms?

    (A) France
    (B) Germany
    (C) Austria-Hungary
    (D) Sweden
    (E) The United Kingdom

41. Trade Unions in the later half of the nineteenth century

    (A) tended to have few members
    (B) were generally unable to enforce their demands through strikes
    (C) desired a return to the old guild systems that were in place prior to industrialization
    (D) supported conservative parties in their respective countries
    (E) represented only master craftsmen rather than collectives of industrial labor

42. Which of the following did NOT contribute to the rising prestige of science in the nineteenth century?

    (A) The increased literacy at large of the population
    (B) The impressive advancements made by scientific discoveries over the course of the century
    (C) The applicability of scientific thought to contemporary philosophical discourse
    (D) Widespread conservative thought across Europe
    (E) The growth of secular ideas about government

43. The Cult of Domesticity

    (A) suggested European women adopt subject colonial children to be reared in the Western tradition
    (B) was primarily oriented towards middle-class women
    (C) allowed for women to pursue their own independent lives outside of traditional family structures
    (D) excluded women from the management of the household as their only responsibility was to rear children
    (E) limited men's importance within the family structure at home as equal to women's

Free-Response Questions

44. The year 1848, called "The Year of Revolutions" by contemporary observers, saw civil unrest spread across the whole of Europe. Compare and contrast the social and intellectual causes and results for the revolt in France to that in Hungary.

_____

_____

_____

_____

_____

_____

_____

_____

_____

_____

_____

_____

_____

_____

_____

_____

_____

_____

_____

_____

_____

_____

_____

_____

_____

_____

_____

45. It can be said that during the nineteenth century, organized religion in Europe was never more vulnerable but yet never stronger. In an essay, evaluate the previous statement using specific historical events, scientific and philosophical developments, and social changes.

_____

_____

_____

_____

_____

_____

_____

_____

_____

_____

_____

_____

_____

_____

_____

_____

_____

_____

_____

_____

_____

_____

_____

_____

_____

_____

_____

_____

Chapter 13
1815–1900: Cultural and Intellectual Answers and Explanations

ANSWER KEY

1.	B	23.	B
2.	A	24.	C
3.	D	25.	A
4.	A	26.	E
5.	B	27.	B
6.	C	28.	D
7.	D	29.	C
8.	D	30.	D
9.	D	31.	A
10.	B	32.	A
11.	C	33.	D
12.	B	34.	C
13.	A	35.	E
14.	C	36.	D
15.	B	37.	B
16.	C	38.	C
17.	C	39.	E
18.	B	40.	B
19.	D	41.	A
20.	B	42.	D
21.	A	43.	B
22.	A		

ANSWERS AND EXPLANATIONS

1. **B** The Chartists tried in vain to ram through a charter of six main political reforms in the United Kingdom, though five of these six were eventually granted by Parliament as the nineteenth century continued. They did not seek to use violent revolution against the government, nor were these calls for reform modest, so eliminate (A), (C), and (D). Finally, the Chartists represented the new urban industrial workingmen so their efforts absolutely did not represent the interests of the landed elites. (E) can safely be eliminated as well.

2. **A** Remember that Charles Darwin's theory of natural selection states that certain alleles become expressed in a population by virtue of the reproduction of the members of that society. It would stand to reason that if members of that society were to die out on account of starvation, then they could not reproduce and spread their genes. Malthus's theories about humanity outstripping its available resources leading to the eventual starvation of many people would most directly fit this description, making the answer (A). Keynes was a leading twentieth-century British economist, so he is not in the correct time period, thus eliminating (B). Mill's hallmark achievement was expounding what would eventually become Classical Liberalism, and has very little to do with natural selection, so you can eliminate (C). Adam Smith was a prominent Scottish economist whose claim to fame was writing *The Wealth of Nations*, which had more to do with limiting government involvement in economics than population management, and leads you to eliminate (D). Finally, Jeremy Bentham was John Stuart Mill's teacher and early proponent of Utilitarianism, though he is certainly a more obscure name than the other four in the list. When in doubt, go with your gut and choose a name you're more familiar with! Remember, on the AP Exam, there's no such thing as a guessing penalty!

3. **D** When you are confronted with picture questions on the AP Exam, remember that the answers of the question must be directly supported by the picture. In this case, we have an accurate and somewhat somber depiction of peasants picking grain from the ground with their bare hands. This allows us to eliminate Romanticism, (B), Cubism, (C), and Post-Modernism, (E), for their hallmark fanciful and inaccurate portrayals of things. Impressionist pieces tended to include action and movement in them and often hosted vibrant and colorful depictions of real life. This painting with its almost grim depiction of a harvest does not fit that description, so eliminate (A) as well.

4. **A** Read the question carefully, as it specifies that the time period in question is the very beginning of the 1800s and also specifies textile mills. The mills at the turn of the century were the origin of the first industrial revolution and saw the beginnings of mechanization of labor. We can eliminate (B) right away then. Young children and males were certainly fixtures of labor, but the original labor source for the mills of the early 1800s was largely women—children and males were typically involved in mining or agriculture, so eliminate (C) and (D). Finally, the elderly should not appear as an enticing answer as you should not remember much from your AP European History class in which the elderly and factory labor were in the same sentence. Eliminate (E).

5. **B** The Dreyfus Affair caused a very contentious debate in France surrounding the actually trumped-up charges of treason against a Jewish French artillery officer from Alsace-Lorraine who was accused of giving sensitive defense information to the Germans, so eliminate (A) and (C). The affair was fanned into the public consciousness by a sensationalist press, so eliminate (E). Finally, the affair convinced many Jews across Europe that the recent improvements in their public standing could easily be completely reversed and that security would come only from the establishment of a Jewish state in the homeland, so eliminate (D).

6. **C** David Ricardo was an economist at around the same time as Thomas Malthus was writing down his theories on unsustainable population growth. The "Iron Law of Wages" argued that the more wages a worker earns, the more children the family unit would produce, and that process would carry on to eventually depress wages through plentiful labor. You can eliminate (A) because it is the exact opposite process, and (B), (D), and (E) as they do not pertain to family size at all.

7. **D** The *Kleindeutsch* solution referred to the unification of German states with the exception of Austria whose disparate nationalities were seen as incompatible with a united Germany. You can eliminate (A) immediately from that. (B) is not accurate either, because the *kleindeutsch* solution is exactly what was proposed at the Frankfurt Assembly. (C) can be eliminated either because you know that the Frankfurt Assembly offered the crown to Prussia, or because the emperor of Austria is never liberal in the nineteenth century, lest his empire fall apart. (E) refers to the *zollverein* customs union that came out of the end of the Napoleonic wars and is not related to what the question is asking for.

8. **D** This question leads you perfectly with "nationalist revolts" and the year 1848. Even if you did not remember the significance of the year of revolutions (1848), you can use your knowledge of nationalist hotspots in Europe to determine that Scotland, in the United Kingdom, never used nationalism as a rallying cry to split from the United Kingdom. Meanwhile, Italy and Germany saw many revolts to try to forge nation-states in these areas, and Poland and Hungary saw huge rebellions against Russia and Austria respectively to gain independence in 1848.

9. **D** Marxism arose from the fertile philosophical fields of Utopian Socialism in which workers were brought together in tight-knit communities to bring themselves up by the bootstraps and gain important skills and enrich the community instead of the individual. But Marx's view of Socialism differed from these "utopian" views in that he earnestly believed in class struggle and an inevitable revolution that would take place in Europe. With this, we can eliminate (A) and (B), as those belonged more to Utopian Socialist programs. You should rememebr that the *Communist Manifesto* of Marx and Engels explains the historical precedents for such class struggle, so (E) can be eliminated, but it does not call for the complete abolition of private property, so (C) can be eliminated too. The answer is (D).

10. **B** Be careful about EXCEPT questions and remember you are looking for the answer that does not work! The New Imperialism refers to the unique brand of late nineteenth-century imperialism which saw European empires expand in regions of the world previously unconquered, allowing

you to eliminate (D). Often European countries would make treaties with target nations and offer private investments into these areas to gain control over the governments of subject countries, allowing you to eliminate (A) and (C). Finally, Darwinism was applied to international relations to justify the conquest of weaker states, allowing you to eliminate (E).

11.   **C**   Nineteenth-century Liberalism, or Classical Liberalism, espoused a maximization of the rights of the individual with respect to the state. As such, Liberalism would hardly argue that all citizens had many obligations to their states, nor would it support the principle of divine right to rule that was so popular with absolutists from the 1600s, allowing you to eliminate (A) and (B). From here if you are confused, remember to eliminate answers that are definitely partially wrong because that makes them entirely wrong—Liberals didn't want to completely undo government like anarchists did, thus allowing you to eliminate (E), nor did they believe that the state had any right to suppress the practice of different religions in a state, allowing you to eliminate (D). (C), although it argues the least, in this case is not wrong, and therefore is the best answer.

12.   **B**   The question asks about the participation rate of children in the English workforce during the nineteenth century so that should remind you that children were important cogs of the early industrial workforce, but they gradually were phased out as concerns about their well-being forced better working conditions on child labor. You can eliminate (A) and (D) as they suggest the opposite of what actually happened, and (E) because you know children were a part of the English workforce! If you think (C) is tantalizing, remember that the question asks about the whole nineteenth century, not just the first couple of decades, and so we need an answer that says the participation rate went down.

13.   **A**   Occasionally the AP Exam will present you with a picture and ask you to interpret themes from it. In this case, we can see a rendition of a German revolt from 1848 with the famous federal colors of Germany flying proudly as the rebels' flags. Once you identify that, compare the answers to what you remember about 1848—specifically the year of nationalist revolutions. (B) makes no sense since the rebels are inspired by nationalism to create a unified nation-state under one government. While they did offer the crown of Germany to the Prussian king, these rebels are still liberals and not trying to assert the primacy of the monarchy, eliminating (B) and (C). The rebels were also inspired by democracy, but there is nothing overtly democratic happening in the picture either, so you can safely eliminate (D). Urbanization or the expansion of cities over the countryside with respect to their population certainly aided the revolutions of 1848, but this too is not the focus of the nationalist rebels portrayed, so eliminate (E) as well.

14.   **C**   You should remember that Darwin's theories about Natural Selection were not immediately accepted, nor would they be widely accepted by society at large for quite some time after *On the Origin of Species* was published. As a result, we can eliminate (A) immediately. Darwin's ideas were not ignored, however, as you probably remember the cartoons of Darwin's bearded head atop the body of a chimpanzee, so eliminate (B) too. Answer choice (D) sounds appealing, but be

careful of extreme language such as the phrase "almost every Englishman" and especially look at the timeframe for the answer—the turn of the century. It took much longer to convince almost everyone, if that was even possible, so eliminate (D). Finally while Darwin's theories were divisive, they also did not herald the dawn of religious resurgence in the United Kingdom, so eliminate (E) as well. The only answer left is (C).

15. **B** A quick scan across all the answers reveals that the question is asking about educational developments in nation-states during the later nineteenth century. You should remember that as the nineteenth century continued, the role of the nation in its citizens' lives increased and an extremely important way in which the state invaded the lives of private citizens was through the expansion of primary education for all citizens. This means you can eliminate (C) as educational systems absolutely expanded from how they were in the 1700s, accessible really to only the elites. Nation-states also had huge internal debates about the role of church and education in an era of increasing secularization, so you can eliminate (D). As for (E), not every country pursued revanchist—or revenge seeking—ideas, though nationalism was important to nineteenth-century society, so you can eliminate that answer. Finally, lawmakers saw that education was critical to give citizens the competitive advantages necessary to be good workers in an increasingly complicated industrial world, so having completely uneducated workers would be a disadvantage, such as what Russia and Austria had to tolerate, so (A) is not right.

16. **C** The Roman Catholic Relief Act was passed under the post-Napoleonic ministry of the Duke of Wellington and permitted Catholics to enjoy many civil privileges, such as the franchise, that they had previously been denied, though only wealthy Irish Catholics were permitted these privileges. As such, you can eliminate (D) as Gladstone came much later than Wellington. Catholic rites were not outright banned in the United Kingdom in the Napoleonic era, though they certainly weren't emphasized, so that means that (B) can't be right either. (A) makes little sense as liberals would philosophically never seek to impose their religion onto the state at large, so you can safely eliminate (A). Finally, while the bill did enfranchise wealthy Catholics, it divided the conservative (Tory) party of Wellington, and ended up causing more political fallout than could be healed nationally with this incipient reconciliation, so you can eliminate (E). The law certainly was liberal as it expanded the franchise, but was conservative as it preserved public order, so the answer is (C).

17. **C** We are looking for which important political development in this list that is most representative of conservative values. Remember that conservatism seeks to preserve the way things are, and therefore resists change. The Chartists sought to make all sorts of political reforms to the British electorate, so that's not conservative and you can eliminate (A). The Triple Alliance is the alliance of Germany, Austria-Hungary, and Italy in the years before World War I—more of a defensive alliance to outmuscle the Franco-Russian alliance than one that preserved the way Europe was, so you can eliminate (B). The Congress of Vienna was Prince Metternich's brainchild that guaranteed conservative anti-nationalist policies across the European continent to ensure that the Napoleonic wars would never erupt and threaten Austria and the other absolute monarchies of Europe again,

which is absolutely conservative in nature. The peace of Westphalia was the treaty that ended the Thirty Years' War and settled the question of the sovereignty of rulers more than it preserved the status quo, so eliminate (D). Finally the Paris Commune was the intriguing socialist experiment that arose in the ashes of the Second French Empire after the Franco Prussian War and absolutely stood contrary to the more conservative countryside of France—eliminate (E).

18. **B** European Jews gained many important legal protections and were enfranchised throughout much of Europe, save Russia, where pogroms against the Jews, particularly in Poland, bucked the trend that was occurring across the rest of the continent. With such knowledge you can eliminate (E) because it says that rights were rescinded after the revolutions of 1848. (A) is an appealing answer as well, but it leaves out the important distinction about Russia that (B) contains, so (A) must be eliminated as well. (C) should not resonate as many important capitalists and politicians in the nineteenth century were Christians. (D) is left as a convincing answer, but remember that Benjamin Disraeli was at one point Jewish and he ended up being an important prime minister of Britain, so (D) cannot be right.

19. **D** Neitzche's counter-cultural assertion that *Gott ist tot!* (God is dead!) in *Thus Spake Zarathustra* is probably his most well-known quotation and speaks to the extent to which secular society had broken the bonds imposed on it by religious mores. If you can't remember such specific quotations, look at the nature of the quote. It's clearly not from realistic literature of the kind Dickens would write (*A Tale of Two Cities*), nor is it a psychological piece of the sort Freud would have written, nor was Bismarck an atheist, so that allows you to eliminate (A), (B), and (C). Kipling was a British author from India whose experiences influenced him to write about Imperial adventures, like *The Jungle Book*, so eliminate (E).

20. **B** Bismarck's *Kulturkampf* refers to his strife with the Catholic church in which Bismarck managed to remove Catholic prelates who might have been against Protestant Prussian primacy throughout newly formed Germany, though it came at the cost of alienating many of the Catholics in the country. Bismarck was not trying to eradicate Catholicism in Germany, so you can eliminate (A), and you might remember that there are three separate wars for German Unification that all have distinct names, so you can eliminate (C). (D) is incorrect as religion was far less important for diplomatic relations in the nineteenth century than it had been two centuries before, and by the same token would not have caused a war with Austria-Hungary at this time either, so you can eliminate (E) as well.

21. **A** Sometimes the AP Exam will feature questions with lengthy answer choices, but good use of Process of Elimination can help speed things up if you compare the answers to each other. The question is asking about the relationship of nation-states to organized religion, like the Catholic Church, in the nineteenth century. It certainly wasn't 100% friendly, nor was it 100% hostile either, so eliminate answers that aren't in the middle. (B) and (D) can be safely eliminated then, with (E) joining those answers, as you should remember that there was actually some concern about the role of religion in terms of the state. On a closer reading, (C) ends up being wrong as

well, as the political winds of Europe in the nineteenth century tended more towards liberal, secularized values than conservative and religious ones.

22. **A** Realism as a form of art seeks to portray the world exactly as it is, and was developed as a response to the fanciful nature of the Romantic movement. If you forgot what Realism was, you can use chronology to help you out on this question: Realism came before Impressionism, Naturalism, and Modernism, so those three cannot be what Realism was devised as a reaction to, and Darwinism is more of a scientific or philosophical belief than a form of art.

23. **B** This question is nice as it gives the source of the quotation provided. When you see Cecil Rhodes, you should immediately think of an imperialist and a Social Darwinist. Of these, (B) fits the bill perfectly, allowing you to eliminate (C), (D), and (E) easily and safely. Manifest Destiny applies to the expansion of the United States across the North American continent and not to British colonialism, so (A) can be eliminated as well. The quote definitely supports Social Darwinism as it equates the size of the British Empire to the potential benefits that it could confer upon the world at large, a very Social Darwinist opinion to have.

24. **C** Nineteenth-century cities grew massively on account of the Industrial Revolution, reaching populations never before seen and consequently dealt with problems caused by overpopulation. Look through the list and find which problems could be caused by overpopulation—(A), (D), and (E) certainly could be, and can be eliminated safely. Political corruption caused by the growth of the franchise in European countries certainly plagued nineteenth-century cities as well, so (B) can be eliminated too, leaving (C) as the only answer that makes no sense.

25. **A** This question asks you to understand the philosophical schools listed and compare those to your knowledge of the Greek Revolution of 1821. Remember that Greece, the birthplace of Western Democracy, was revolting against the Ottoman Empire in the 1820s, so a school of thought that advocated adventurism would most likely match best. Romanticism certainly fits the bill. Feudalism and Asceticism are holdovers from the Middle Ages and definitely not right with respect to the timeframe of the question. Realism seeks to understand and portray the world as it is, so the mystique of adventure does not permeate Realist art and thought. Darwinism hadn't come into being in 1820 (Darwin published *On the Origin of Species* around 1860) so that answer can't be right either.

26. **E** The Decembrists were young Russian officers who had been inspired by the liberal ideas that the French Revolution fought to impose across Europe. If you didn't remember that, look at the answers themselves. A Russian Tsar would never, save Alexander II, promulgate anything liberal, no less a constitution, so (A) can't be right. The other three answers require specific knowledge about the names of social movements in Russia—The Poles revolted in 1848 but that is usually lumped in with the other 1848 movements, disaffected urban workers tended to favor socialism, and the Duma was created by Nicholas II following Russia's defeat in the Russo-Japanese War; none of those things have anything to do with the Decembrists, so you can eliminate (B), (C), and (D).

27. **B** The Potato Famine inspired much Irish fury against the British government because of a perceived lack of will to directly aid the starving Irish, but that lack of will could just as easily be attached to British adherence to liberal free-market economic policies that were against heavy intervention in this serious issue. Therefore (A) is not a correct answer choice. We know that the Famine left many dead, so any sort of local support clearly did not work very well, allowing (C) to be eliminated easily. Remember that an important theme of the period is the gradual de-emphasis on religious differences so that the famine was not worsened by religious bigotry as (D) suggests. Finally, the Irish had not yet achieved Home Rule, so (E) makes no sense as well.

28. **D** This question is a simple matter of knowing which artists created what styles of art. Van Dyck and Titian painted in the sixteenth century and tended to paint portraits for the rulers of European kingdoms, not something that is around the time of the Impressionist movement (1870s–1880s). Goya and Delacroix painted in the Romantic style (Remember *Liberty Leading the People*?), leaving Manet as the only remaining answer.

29. **C** The expansion of the franchise in the United Kingdom over the period is one in which wealth qualifications were lowered and the centers of voting were moved to the industrial urban centers instead of the countryside. Compare this process to the answer choices present. (A) is incorrect as universal male suffrage is indeed granted in the United Kingdom. (B) and (E) are also incorrect as the voting rights were not made more stringent. (D) sounds appealing until you read the part about Catholics and Jews, something that absolutely goes against the liberal spirit of the nineteenth century.

30. **D** The principal difference between British suffragettes and Continental suffragettes is that the Contintental suffragettes tended to attach themselves to radical thinkers as their task was much more difficult than it was for their British counterparts. This allows you to eliminate (A) and (E) right off the bat. It is true that there was some discussion in Britain about the place of radical protest, but Continental suffragettes had the exact same discussion, so (B) is not correct either. (C) does not make any sense because conservatives were largely against expanding the franchise to include women. That leaves (D) as the only good answer.

31. **A** The Papacy following the revolts of 1848 lost control of Rome to a new Roman Republic that was ultimately put down by the forces of Austria, and then protected until 1871 by France. The Pope, now on his guard against liberal agitators, took pains to try to roll back the cause of the revolutionaries. You can eliminate (B), (D), and (E) through that understanding alone. (C) ends up being a poor answer choice as well because the church sought more than to preserve its independence and the Pope did not try to rectify the grievances that the nationalist rebels of 1848 had when they revolted, but rather cracked down even harder on them.

32. **A** This is yet another question regarding which you must pay close attention to the complete answer choices to ensure you get it correct. Women certainly gained the ability to work in the factory system for wages, and their wages tended to be much lower than their male equivalents. (B) is incorrect as while women had access to many more educational opportunities, they were not at all

entirely blocked from joining the workforce. (C) makes little sense as an answer in that the only women who stood to benefit from home appliances were the elites whose station was never guaranteed by their working responsibilities. (D) is the opposite answer of (B), but it is still wrong as women gained educational opportunities throughout the nineteenth century. (E) also is incorrect because men did not universally find women their equals; even men in favor of women's suffrage tended to regard them as physically inferior to and weaker than men.

33. **D** This is a straight cause-and-effect question, though a scan of the answer choices with some logic can help make your odds better to guess with if you're not certain about the answer. First of all, Russia would see the need to free the serfs only if it saw in some dramatic fashion that it was socially quite backwards to the rest of Europe, which would mean it needs to lose a war to inspire such a dramatic change. You can eliminate (A) and (B) from that. Remember that Alexander II came to power after Nicholas I was discredited from his defeat in the Crimean War and Alexander's first major decision was the emancipation of the serfs in 1861. Both (C) and (E) occurred in the early 1900s, and are too late for the timeframe of this question.

34. **C** This is a NOT question so we are looking for the answer that doesn't fit with the theme of the rise of the middle class. The middle class grew as industrialization provided the dramatic rise in the quality of living for Europeans and as prosperity grew, so did educational opportunities and technological advances to make life easier, so (A) and (B) are safely eliminated. The factory system commoditized labor systematically and allowed enterprising people to try to climb the rungs of the social ladder, so (D) and (E) are safe to eliminate as well. The only thing here that didn't contribute to the rise of a middle class is the strengthening of feudal arrangements, which did not occur in the nineteenth century, save places like Russia where feudalism limped on until the second half of the century.

35. **E** Remember that the Second Industrial Revolution saw the rise of the steel, chemical, and electric industries, so (E) is obviously the right answer. If you remember the chronology of inventions, the seed drill allowed for more efficient agricultural practices, and textile manufacture was the first industry to be revolutionized by industrialization. The cotton gin was invented to increase the efficiency of cotton gathering after harvest and the steam engine was invented to provide a power source independent of running water. All these were basic inventions of the First Industrial Revolution and would set the groundwork for the second.

36. **D** Another memorization question, this one asks you to associate strategy with suffragette. If you see "aggressive strategy" with regards to women's suffrage in Britain, you should immediately think of Pankhurst. Taylor was the wife of John Stuart Mill, who was important for laying some of the philosophical groundwork for the suffrage movement, so (A) is not correct. Fawcett was the leader of the moderate coalition of suffrage societies and thought that decency and respectability were the keys to the franchise; neither of these should speak to you about aggressive tactics. Both Auclert and Mauguet are French and therefore do not apply to this question.

37. **B** Remember that the nineteenth century witnesses the beginning of the demographic transition in Europe in which the birth rate remains high, but the death rate begins to drop as more food and greater technologies prevent people from dying young of now preventable causes. No incredibly destructive wars like the Thirty Years' War were fought, save the Napoleonic Wars, though these still did not kill off one-third of Germany, so you can safely eliminate (A). While industrialization carried with it the risk of pollution and disease, the death rate lowered, so (C) cannot be right either. (D) is incorrect as food production greatly benefited from new advanced technologies so that surplus labor moved without much incident into the cities. (E) directly borrows Ricardo's "Iron Law of Wages"—a law that ended up being broken as wealthier families tended to have fewer children, not more.

38. **C** Zionism is another name for Jewish nationalism with the intent to seek a permanent Jewish homeland in the land of Israel. Go through the answers to eliminate partially incorrect responses. (A) is true up until it suggests the new Jewish homeland is to be placed in Poland, which renders the whole answer false. (B) brings in the creator of Zionism, Herzl, but Zionism has little to do with bringing down the French Third Republic, so you can eliminate (B). While it is true that Zionism would eventually create the modern state of Israel, Europeans at the time called the planning for the carveup of the Ottoman Empire "The Eastern Question," not Zionism, so (D) is incorrect. Finally it is true that Jews were granted more political rights in Germany as the century progressed, but Zionism is not the name of that process, so (E) is wrong as well.

39. **E** The young Turks were a group of Western-trained Turks from the Ottoman Empire who saw how much the crumbling Ottoman state was at a disadvantage with respect to the European powers and sought to reverse this decline through secular Turkish nationalism. Eliminate (A) right off the bat, as it is not true based on this definition of the Young Turks. Their attempts to strengthen the Ottoman Empire were only partially successful in that they bought the empire a few more years to survive until the end of World War I, so (B) is also false. Nationalism in a strict nineteenth-century sense would have seen the multitude of cultures in the Ottoman Empire as a source of weakness, not strength, so eliminate (C). Finally, the Ottomans had been seriously afraid of Russian moves to annex Constantinople, and saw Russia as anything but a natural ally so (D) is wrong as well.

40. **B** Another question involving memorization of political history with a social spin, it is important to remember that Bismarck's political genius stretched beyond diplomacy and statecraft and into even breaking down rival political coalitions at their core. He promulgated the first national welfare policies even though he was a conservative so as to head the rising socialist party off at the pass and guarantee loyal popular support for his style of government. Germany's welfare system became the envy of Europe and was copied by the other European states as a result. If you are unsure about this question, eliminate (C), as Austria-Hungary would never have done anything as progressive as national social welfare reforms, and take a guess.

41.   **A**   This is a tricky question and requires special attention to the answer choices. While unions had made themselves relevant in European politics, their numbers were not a very significant proportion of the total labor force of their countries. That said, they did employ strikes to great effect in order to improve wages for their members, so eliminate (B). They did not, of course, seek to return to the old medieval styles of production, nor were their allies in government the conservative parties, so eliminate (C) and (D) as well. Finally, while early trade unions tended to focus on skilled industrial labor, by the end of the century unions were accepting collections of unskilled labor to further strengthen their bargaining positions, so (E) does not work either.

42.   **D**   We are looking for which of the answers does NOT contribute to science's prestige, so think critically and find the answers that do support the increase of science's prestige. A more literate population would have greater appreciation for scientific advancements and the logical implementation of the scientific method, so (A) can safely be eliminated. The advancements science itself made in the nineteenth century were bewildering and rapid to contemporary observers and left a great impression on humanity as a whole, so (B) can be eliminated as well. In fact, science had become so legitimate a way to view the workings of the world that it was used to bolster philosophical opinions about the way the world worked—for instance, Social Darwinism applied Darwin's principals of natural selection to international diplomacy—so (C) can be eliminated too. The nineteenth century saw more of a rise of secular and liberal thought than conservative opinions and those conservative opinions would most likely be against the new developments of science, so (D) is probably the answer. In fact, we find the growth of secular ideas about government, divorcing the state from organized religion, is the answer choice for (E) and that definitely happened in our time period. Eliminate (E) too.

43.   **B**   Remember that the Cult of Domesticity was the solidification of "separate spheres" for women and men in which middle-class women were totally devoted to the maintenance of the household and rearing of children and contemporary social customs strongly reinforced the ideal of the at-home mother of the family. (C) therefore is incorrect because women were not allowed to pursue their own independent lives apart from the household, and (E) is incorrect as well as men were still considered to be social superiors to women even in the household. While women were expected to rear children well, (D) suggests that they were not even responsible for the management of the household, which is also incorrect. Finally, (A) has nothing to do with the question and can be safely eliminated.

The Free-Response Essay Questions Explained

Question 44

44. The year 1848, called "The Year of Revolutions" by contemporary observers, saw civil unrest spread across the whole of Europe. Compare and contrast the social and intellectual causes and results for the revolt in France to that in Hungary.

Essay Notes

A good essay would draw from the knowledge that the 1848 revolution in France brought down Louis-Philippe and instituted a democratic government headed by Louis Napoleon, soon to be Napoleon III. As such the revolts in France were inspired more by the opportunity to overthrow the monarchy and a desire to enfranchise the population at large. In addition, the revolts were definitely inspired by economic depression and a desire to ameliorate the conditions of the urban poor. While this revolution was successful in its aims, the national assembly it created through universal suffrage turned out to be more conservative in nature thanks to the more conservative nature of the rest of France.

The Hungarian Revolution of 1848 was caused more by nationalist fervor and desire for independence rather than a reduction of aristocratic privilege. In fact, Hungarian liberals who revolted did so with the support of Hungarian aristocrats and together the two groups attempted to impose "Magyarization" on the disparate populations of the eastern portions of the Austrian Empire. This revolt to make Hungary a separate domain, one with a liberal constitution that nevertheless sought to oppress neighboring peoples with nationalistic fervor, was eventually put down by Austrian forces who were working desperately to roll back the clock of Nationalism.

Question 45

45. It can be said that during the nineteenth century, organized religion in Europe was never more vulnerable but yet never stronger. In an essay, evaluate the previous statement using specific historical events, scientific and philosophical developments, and social changes.

Essay Notes

A good essay about this prompt would focus on the impact of important shifts in the European intellectual culture from new scientific developments in the nineteenth century as well as political events.

It would be most gainful to start by mentioning the longevity of Enlightenment ideals following the defeat of Napoleon, as these ideals would lay the groundwork for the liberal and secularizing movements that would come across Europe. The increased prosperity Europe enjoyed on account of the Industrial Revolution led to the gradual expansion of educational opportunities to all, and with a newly literate public came a population more willing to challenge time-held ideals. These ideals would come into full force especially during the Liberal Revolts of 1848 in which the Pope was essentially ejected from Rome and a new republican government was established there. When these Italian nationalists were defeated, like the majority of the rebels of 1848, the Papacy struck back with a vengeance, tightening its grip on its temporal powers and setting the church squarely against the liberal and scientific ideas that had earlier overthrown its rule in Rome. The Pope declared a doctrine of Papal Infallibility, which meant that the pope was the absolute authority on matters of dogma and faith. Such moves by the church are clearly signs that the church still had great vitality and power, as they were extreme reactions to the questions of the age.

A good essay would absolutely have to mention the impact Darwin's theory of natural selection had on the European intellectual climate. While it is important to note that Darwin's theory grew in rough soil all across Europe, the principle of evolution that it was based on was largely unquestioned in European scientific circles. To this end, Darwin's theory struck a massive blow to a religious community not seen since the days of Copernicus, namely that a literal interpretation of the Bible was not accurate. Nonetheless, that Darwin's theory of natural selection was so heavily lampooned by the population at large indicates that traditional beliefs about the origin of man still remained strong.

Finally a good essay would focus on the secularizing movements in the nation-states forged throughout the nineteenth century. Germany's *Kulturkampf* demonstrated how much disunity still existed in the country, while France's Dreyfus Affair underscored the depths of anti-Semitism and religious bigotry that still permeated society. The vast expansion of the cities and the awful conditions of the urban poor allowed churches to organize relief programs unlike the world had previously seen, but these were simply too few for the population they tried to service. Church missionary groups were strong parts of European colonialism, as they proselytized with great fervor in the new acquisitions of the European empires. While these efforts were waged with full force, the intellectual challenges that society had initially posed to religious dogma meant that many people in Europe itself saw secular life as more appealing than a religiously centered lifestyle.

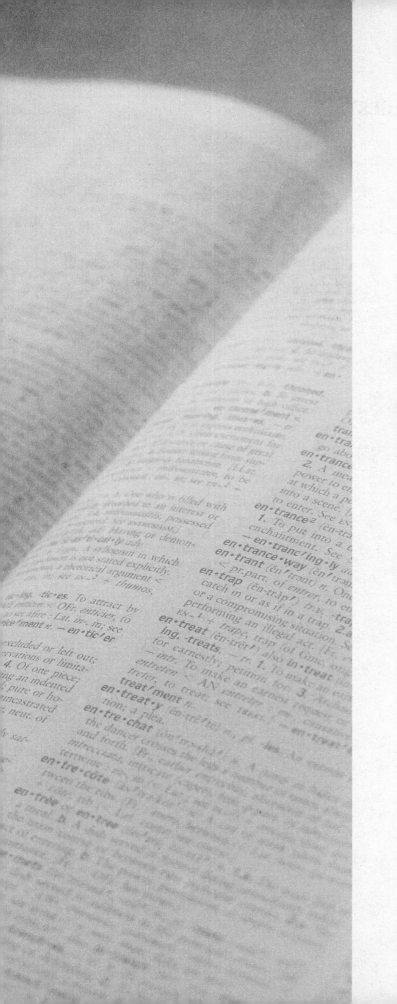

Chapter 14
1815–1900: Social and Economic Questions

1815–1900: SOCIAL AND ECONOMIC QUESTIONS

Multiple-Choice Questions

1. In the period after the Napoleonic Wars, nationalism felt by the common people was most closely tied to a

   (A) pro-capitalism stance
   (B) pro-conservatism stance
   (C) pro-liberalism stance
   (D) pro-authoritarianism stance
   (E) pro-anarchy stance

2. The economic policy of laissez-faire

   (A) was correct in predicting that foreign trade would be detrimental to the countries that participated in it
   (B) suggested that individual businesses should set their own prices and production levels
   (C) directly contributed to an increase in wages for factory workers
   (D) supported Jeremy Bentham's view that government should intervene and help factory workers achieve economic justice
   (E) became obsolete with the rise of neo-liberal economic policies

3. Socialist Henri de Saint-Simon argued that society needed to be organized scientifically, with the leaders of society being

   (A) the proletariat
   (B) the aristocracy
   (C) intellectuals
   (D) the monarchy
   (E) women

4. The 1830 rebellion of army divisions and the middle class in Spain was caused by

   (A) a desire to fight against the rebellions in South Africa that went ignored by the Spanish monarchy
   (B) dissatisfaction with the constitution drawn up by the Cortez
   (C) the dissolution of the liberal constitution by King Ferdinand
   (D) unhappiness with the King's refusal to allow outside assistance from the other countries in Europe
   (E) the French refusal to give Andalucía back to Spain

5. Which of the following was an immediate result of the Peterloo Massacre?

   (A) The Combination Acts were repealed.
   (B) Universal male suffrage was achieved.
   (C) Slavery was banned in the British Empire.
   (D) British Parliament passed the "Six Acts," banning public demonstrations.
   (E) Workhouses for the poor were shut down by Parliament.

6. The construction of workhouses in 1834

   (A) demonstrated Parliament's growing sympathy for the poor
   (B) sought to move members of the working class into Britain's financially stable middle class
   (C) was meant to keep the impoverished from seeking assistance by creating purposely dismal working conditions
   (D) ushered in the Second Industrial Revolution
   (E) eliminated the ghettos in sparsely populated electoral districts

7. Which of the following was effective at helping the poor in Great Britian?

   (A) The Corn Laws
   (B) The Poor Law of 1834
   (C) The Six Acts
   (D) The Factory Act of 1833
   (E) The Combination Acts

8. Which of the following groups was not positively affected by the reforms put into place in the 1820s and 1830s in Great Britian?

   (A) Catholics
   (B) Those who became rich from industrialization
   (C) Workers in poor conditions
   (D) Women in the aristocracy
   (E) Slaves

9. Which country's people experienced the worst living conditions during the "Hungry Forties"?

(A) Great Britain
(B) France
(C) Ireland
(D) Germany
(E) Italy

10. In 1848, a group of students and workers captured Vienna for five months in hopes of obtaining

(A) permanent freedom from a state of monarchy
(B) freedom of the press and the end of censorship
(C) equal voting rights for women
(D) a stop to Europe's attempts to colonize Asia and Africa
(E) the expulsion of Catholics from the city

11. The abolition of the French national workshops occurred because of

(A) the conservative assembly voted into office by republicans in the French countryside
(B) the working class protests during the "June Days"
(C) the establishment of Emperor Napoleon III as dictator of France
(D) the successful efforts of the liberal majority in Paris
(E) a decreased need for jobs after a steep drop in the unemployment rate

12. The Parisian "June Days" indicated that

(A) the working class was satisfied with the results of the assembly election held two months prior
(B) there was a clear divide between the political ideology of people living in the city and those living in the countryside
(C) the French were unanimously supportive of Emperor Napoleon III
(D) the national workshops did little actually to help the impoverished
(E) the government was not strong enough to withstand a revolt

13. Chartism is based on the idea that

 (A) change can be achieved only through violent conflict
 (B) changes in the ruling-class dominated infrastructure would not help the working class
 (C) suffrage is the universal right of adult-male citizens only
 (D) aristocrats were the rightful rulers of the new technologically progressive Europe
 (E) problems in the working class could be corrected by changes in the political organization of the country

14. The People's Charter of 1838 requested all of the following EXCEPT

 (A) universal male suffrage
 (B) abolition of property requirements for Members of Parliament
 (C) the secret ballot
 (D) increased control for factory owners to determine worker wages
 (E) annual parliaments with yearly elections

15. Which of the following was true of England during the Industrial Revolution?

 (A) Religious intolerance allowed for government to have more control over who was involved in the British economy.
 (B) A higher death rate allowed for a smaller number of both factory workers and consumers.
 (C) The island of Great Britain was separated from other countries by water, and relied mainly on domestic production and consumption.
 (D) Banks were mainly localized, which allowed for smaller communities to flourish at the expense of the larger nation.
 (E) Small-scale farmers were pushed into urban areas and became a low-paid workforce for factories.

16. Which of the following was NOT a result of labor-saving devices in the field of cloth production in the late eighteenth century?

 (A) An increase in cloth supply
 (B) A strong price advantage for factory producers over their competition
 (C) Increased cotton imports from colonized nations
 (D) The end of the factory system in England
 (E) Increased reliance on slave labor

17. A result of the destruction of the putting-out (or domestic) system was

    (A) better working conditions for women and children
    (B) family members no longer working in the same location as each other
    (C) lower mortality rates for people living in the city through the elimination of cholera in the general population
    (D) more raw materials being delivered directly to people's homes
    (E) a majority of parents calling for restrictions of working hours for children

18. A Luddite, a term coined by laborers in during industrialization in the nineteenth century, is

    (A) a person who refuses to accept new technologies
    (B) a worker who opposes unions
    (C) aristocrats who fought against the unfair treatment of factory laborers
    (D) a Catholic who rejects the Vatican as the leader of the Church
    (E) a laborer who felt complacent with the wages and working conditions of the time

19. During industrialization, working-class laborers

    (A) embraced new technology that would make their lives easier
    (B) generally continued living as they had before the Industrial Revolution
    (C) created unions and cooperative societies to provide benefits for their members
    (D) were more concerned with religious values than improving working conditions
    (E) were unable to provide assistance to other laborers until the government ban on unions was lifted in 1824

20. A controversy over which nation would control access to the religious sites sacred to Christians in Jerusalem led to

    (A) the uprising of the proletariat in the streets of Paris
    (B) the start of the Crimean War
    (C) the invention of the steam engine
    (D) the conquering of Lombardy and Venetia by the Italians
    (E) the strengthening of the Ottoman Empire

21. Prussia took the lead on German unification for all of the following reasons EXCEPT

(A) Prussia had economic preeminence over other German states
(B) Prussia remained a primarily agricultural state
(C) Prussia was a primarily German state
(D) Prussia had a modernized army
(E) Prussia secured an alliance with Italy

22. During the first ten years of Emperor Napoleon III's reign

(A) aqueducts were built to bring clean water into Paris
(B) the number of Parisian slums tripled
(C) poorly built sewage systems led to an increase in cholera outbreaks
(D) censorship grew increasingly strict
(E) Paris remained a medieval city in a progressively more and more modern world

23. Otto von Bismarck did NOT

(A) establish old age pensions and social benefits for all Germans
(B) called for a ban on Socialist's right to assemble
(C) succeed in reducing public appeal of the socialist party
(D) achieve power by manipulating the press and the moncarchy
(E) deliver the "Blood and Iron" speech

24. In the mid-nineteenth century, the majority of the common people in France

(A) had forgotten the hardships of the French Revolution
(B) shifted their mindsets to become ideologically unified throughout the country
(C) no longer relied on public demonstrations and protests thanks to the "liberal empire" of Napoleon III
(D) supported France's involvement in the Crimean Wars
(E) voted to put Napoleon III in power as a dictator for ten years

25. Serfs freed by Alexander II

   (A) received fertile lands and experienced improved lives
   (B) benefited from Alexander II's radical changes to the Russian constitution
   (C) were eligible to become members of the Russian parliament
   (D) had to buy their freedom with fifty years of payments
   (E) were devastated by the assassination of the liberal Alexander II

26. Which of the following would the average European have access to before the beginning of the nineteenth century?

   (A) Airplanes
   (B) Anesthesia
   (C) Television
   (D) Automobiles
   (E) X-ray scans

27. Social Darwinist Herbert Spencer would most agree that

   (A) charitable acts should be administered to the poor and needy
   (B) all people are equal regardless of their religion
   (C) people from Europe are superior to people from Asia
   (D) colonialism is unjust
   (E) nations and states go through periods of growth and decline, but no one nation is naturally superior to another

28. Which of the following was NOT a reason for the decline of the French Aristocracy?

   (A) The concept of meritocracy eliminated privileges based on birth alone.
   (B) Refrigerated railcars led to more food imports from the United States, Argentina, and Australia.
   (C) Military positions required competitive exams.
   (D) Women were experiencing heightened access to previously unobtainable rights, like employment in professional occupations.
   (E) A wealthier, larger middle class formed after the Revolution.

29. The late 1800s were unique for the class system because

   (A) the aristocracy was larger than ever before
   (B) the middle class were relatively poor
   (C) the working class finally achieved the level of wealth they desired
   (D) the middle class was larger than ever before
   (E) the aristocracy held more power than it ever had before

30. Generally, the middle class during the Second Industrial Revolution

   (A) had fresh running water and central heat
   (B) had at least one servant
   (C) worked as skilled laborers and craftsmen
   (D) worked in newly wealthy occupations, such as engineers and doctors
   (E) took vacations and tourist expeditions

31. A result of the Second Industrial Revolution was

   (A) an increase in church attendance from laborers
   (B) drastic improvements in the quality of workplace conditions
   (C) more free time for workers, who attended dance halls and other events
   (D) an increase of women in high-paying, specialized professions
   (E) a shift in the working class from pro-socialist to pro-capitalist

32. One area where anarchy was heavily supported by laborers and factory workers was

   (A) the French countryside
   (B) populated cities in England, such as London
   (C) the divided regions of Germany
   (D) the Jewish sections of Russia
   (E) the Spanish province of Andalusia

33. To the poor and working class, belief in organized religion

(A) was of little use to them, as clergymen believed that God would care for the needy and offered no charity
(B) was widespread and higher than ever
(C) was exaggerated by fabricated "miracles" put on by the Catholic Church, such as a peasant girl seeing the Virgin Mary in Lourdes
(D) was not considered important
(E) was essential to differentiating themselves from the aristocrats

34. Which of the following is true of the public opinion of the Jewish minority in the nineteenth century?

(A) The economic depression of 1873 benefited the Jewish people, as anti-Semitism was in decline during this time.
(B) According to a commonly held belief spawned by Social Darwinism, Jews were equal to all other races.
(C) Jews were seen as responsible for positive economic trends, such as the creation of the department store.
(D) Russian monarchs used the Jewish people as a scapegoat as a means of redirecting public anger towards them.
(E) Countries attempted to entice Jewish people to move into their countries to bolster the skilled worker population.

35. The Cult of Domesticity

(A) was abolished when men began taking jobs in more skilled professions
(B) had no effect on women who were in the work force
(C) was universally supported by all women
(D) encouraged women to be more aggressive in pursuing their desired lives and passions
(E) put into place a system where women were required to maintain the home and raise children

36. Which of the following women would support the Cult of Domesticity?

(A) Frances Power Cobbe
(B) Emmeline Pankhurst
(C) Maria Montessori
(D) Josephine Butler
(E) Mary Mayson Beeton

37. The difference between suffragists and suffragettes is that

   (A) suffragists are men and suffragettes are women
   (B) suffragists support the Cult of Domesticity, while suffragettes do not
   (C) suffragists rely on peaceful methods of protest, while suffragettes were often violent
   (D) suffragists supported the voting rights of all people, while suffragettes fought only for women's voting right
   (E) suffragists has no effect on woman's suffrage, while suffragettes achieved voting rights for women

38. Feminists at the end of the nineteenth century

   (A) had no foothold in conservative countries such as Greece
   (B) sought the right to divorce and own property
   (C) were unified in their belief that attaining suffrage was their main purpose
   (D) had the benefit of never being arrested or beaten for their protests because of their gender
   (E) were generally from lower-income families

39. Which of the following writings gave a realistic look at the lives of the working class?

   (A) *Hard Times* by Charles Dickens
   (B) *Indiana* by Amandine-Aurore Dupin (aka Geroge Sand)
   (C) *The Life of Jesus Critically Examined* by David Friedrich Strauss
   (D) *Evolutionary Socialism* by Edward Bernstein
   (E) *What Is Property?* by Joseph Proudhon

40. Which of the following colonized nations was an economic success during the period of new imperialism?

   (A) India
   (B) China
   (C) Indonesia
   (D) Belgian Congo
   (E) Brazil

41. Social imperialists viewed colonization as

   (A) unfair to the original inhabitants of the countries being colonized
   (B) a cure of overpopulation
   (C) a way to spread feminism to places all over the world
   (D) a risky endeavor that may result in war
   (E) a threat to nationalism

42. When Great Britain established an "informal empire" in China, it

   (A) attempted to colonize it, but failed
   (B) shared rule of China with Germany
   (C) created an alliance with China without resorting to violent colonialism
   (D) had significant economic power over China, but no political or territorial control
   (E) colonized China in secret without telling any of the other countries in Europe

43. Regarding imperialism, the working class

   (A) displayed their support by publishing pro-colonization articles in newspapers
   (B) hoped that better working conditions would be available in the colonized nations
   (C) were completely against it
   (D) supported the movement more only after the Boer War
   (E) had very little interest in such affairs

Free-Response Questions

44. Identify and describe the factors that explain why Great Britain led the Industrial Revolution in 1750, while countries like France fell behind.

_____

_____

_____

_____

_____

_____

_____

_____

_____

_____

_____

_____

_____

_____

_____

_____

_____

_____

_____

_____

_____

_____

_____

_____

_____

_____

45. Describe the Cult of Domesticity and explain the ways in which the creation of the Cult of Domesticity sparked the feminist movement in Europe. Mention the key figures in this movement.

_____

_____

_____

_____

_____

_____

_____

_____

_____

_____

_____

_____

_____

_____

_____

_____

_____

_____

_____

_____

_____

_____

_____

_____

_____

_____

_____

_____

Chapter 15
1815–1900: Social and Economic Answers and Explanations

ANSWER KEY

1.	C	23.	C
2.	B	24.	E
3.	C	25.	D
4.	C	26.	B
5.	D	27.	C
6.	C	28.	D
7.	D	29.	D
8.	D	30.	C
9.	C	31.	C
10.	B	32.	E
11.	A	33.	D
12.	B	34.	D
13.	E	35.	E
14.	D	36.	E
15.	E	37.	C
16.	D	38.	B
17.	B	39.	A
18.	A	40.	A
19.	C	41.	B
20.	B	42.	D
21.	B	43.	E
22.	A		

ANSWERS AND EXPLANATIONS

1. **C** While capitalism helped the nation's economy, it hurt the "common people," and they mostly opposed it. Authoritarianism by definition is meant to control the general population, so that did little to inspire the working class, and anarchy was undesirable because of its impracticality. Conservative philosophy was favored by the elite. The "common people" were rallied behind a pro-liberalism stance because they sought better lives and working conditions. A unified country, they believed, could bring them the social benefits they desired.

2. **B** Laissez-faire is a hands-off approach to economy that leaves everything in the hands of the private sector, sharing much in common with more modern neo-liberal policies. Its implementation directly led to a decrease in wages and conditions for the working class. Mercantilism and utilitarianism, though very different from each other, both involve government intervention.

3. **C** Henri de Saint-Simon was an aristocrat who believed in a society similar to Plato's call for a "philosopher king." In order to eradicate poverty, the intellectuals needed to take leading roles so they could structure a fairer and more efficient society. He advocated for the basis of government to be formed around science rather than religion. Though he is remembered for his ideas, he had very little influence during his life.

4. **C** Soldiers were already being sent to quell the rebellions in South Africa, and the king was allowing outside aid from other European countries. The people had no problem with Cortez; they were happy with the liberal constitution. What caused unrest was King Ferdinand's continual disregard for the liberal constitution established by Cortez.

5. **D** The Peterloo Massacre occurred in response to a large public protest in Manchester, England. The people demanded a reform of Parliamentary representation because of recent repressive laws such as the Combination Acts. In response, the government passed the repressive "Six Acts," which, among other things, banned public demonstrations entirely. Five years later, they achieved their original goal when the Combination Acts were repealed.

6. **C** The workhouses, though they provided work for the impoverished and unemployed, were established in order to *not* provide adequate assistance to the poor. The workhouses had horrible conditions and provided very little pay, providing absolutely no upward mobility on purpose. The goal was to discourage the poor from even seeking public assistance.

7. **D** In the early days of industrialization, there was little protection for factory workers, including children who often worked extremely long hours. The Corn Laws, the Poor Law of 1834, the Six Acts, and the Combination Acts all had negative effects on the nation's poor. However, the Factory Act of 1833 was a step in the right direction, as it shortened the number of hours children could work and required regular factory inspections.

8. **D** Due to a number of incidents of growing popular unrest, the British government passed a number of popular reforms that eased the discontent of the common people. Factory workers and the lower class experienced minor relief, slavery was on the way out, and Catholics were gaining political traction. However, women, even those in the aristocracy, were still unable to vote or hold office.

9. **C** Though the "Hungry Forties" (also known as the "European Potato Failure") affected most of Western Europe, the affects were most harshly felt in Ireland. In fact, a common misconception is that it occurred only in Ireland. The potato was a key part of the Irish diet, and thus they had the largest number of affected crops, leading to the most deaths.

10. **B** The group that captured Vienna in 1848 sought public control of the press and a total end to censorship. Though there were other pressing concerns the people had with the government, most of them came up later on. The rebellion became violent, and in the end it was unsuccessful.

11. **A** The French national workshops, though they paid very little and had bad conditions, were the only means of employment for a large number of people. The newly elected conservative assembly, voted into office largely by aristocrats who did not live in the cities, chose to close them in order to save money. This was a blow to the agenda of the liberals and it resulted in the protests that took place during "June Days."

12. **B** The "June Days" took place after the closing of the French National Workshops, which was seen as the last straw for the impoverished working class. The divide between the rich living in the countryside and the poor urban factory workers had been increasing, and it reached critical mass with the "June Days." Though the national workshops did little to actually help the impoverished, they were an important source of sustenance for many.

13. **E** Chartists did not call for violent action—they were content with protest and petition as means to achieve change. They believed that change needed to occur within the ruling class in order for the working class to get a better shake. Many Chartists also supported female suffrage, and they in general believed in universal rights for people. Therefore, they called for changes in the political structure in order to solve the problems of the working class.

14. **D** The People's Charter of 1838 called for a number of changes to benefit the working class. Therefore, it contained no provisions to benefit factory owners. It was formulated by six members of Parliament as well as six working-class advocates. It was not formally passed, but represented a clear set of goals for the working class.

15. **E** Religious tolerance was growing at the time, meaning all religions could contribute to the economy. A number of sweeping social transformations were happening at the time due to the new economic structures. The economy was booming, but one of the many side effects was that many small-scale farmers were forced into urban areas in order to join the low-paid factory workforce.

16. **D** The devices that revolutionized the production of cloths and textiles in the early days of industrialization had a number of positive and negative effects, perhaps most notably marking the beginning of the factory system in England.

17. **B** The domestic system was a system in which raw materials were provided to rural producers and then finished products were returned to the merchants. Factories were far more efficient and cost effective, but it meant that families were no longer working together under their own roof. Instead, they were pushed into urban areas for low-wage factory jobs.

18. **A** Luddites refused to accept or utilize new technology. This movement began as a rejection of the new factory systems, which were replacing artisans with unskilled low-wage factory workers. It was one of the many factions that organized in order to express discontent with the state of the working class in nineteenth-century England.

19. **C** In the early days of industrialization, workers' rights were largely nonexistent. Since factories were so new, there were very few laws to protect those who worked in them. As a response, the working class unionized, creating groups to rally for their interests. Labor unions are still important today, and many workers receive benefits for membership.

20. **B** At the time of the Crimean War, Jerusalem was controlled by the Ottoman Empire and conflicts arose regarding Christian rights within the Holy Land. There were numerous other causes, but the spark was the disputes over Jerusalem.

21. **B** Prussia did take the lead on German unification for a number of reasons, but they modernized very rapidly and were not much of an agricultural state. Under Otto Von Bismarck, Prussia aimed to achieve German unification by strengthening their military and revolutionizing their cities. Bismarck's famous "blood and iron" speech outlined his goals.

22. **A** During the reign of Napoleon III, Paris was going through a number of reforms. The slums were torn down in the *Haussman Plan*, which sought to renovate and rejuvenate Paris. Censorship began to loosen as the city modernized, and the implementation of sewer systems reduced cholera almost entirely. Among the new renovations were aqueducts, used to bring clean water into the city.

23. **C** Though Von Bismarck did everything he could to reduce the popularity of the socialist party, he was unsuccessful. Public appeal of socialism only increased during his tenure. His beliefs were more conservative, subscribing to his own *Realpolitik*.

24. **E** In the mid 1800s, France was still recovering from the aftermath of the French Revolution, and the public was still divided ideologically. Protests were still prevalent as a form of expression, even moreso after the population elected Napoleon III as a dictator on the promise of a "liberal empire." A more liberal government meant less censorship and oppression, meaning people could express themselves more freely. Though Napoleon III passed a number of popular reforms, the people still had plenty to complain about.

25. **D** The serfs that were freed by Alexander II were freed only to an extent—in reality it was more like indentured servitude. They had to buy their freedom with fifty years of payments. Alexander II was an emperor, meaning he had strong authority and Russia did not have a parliament or constitution. Though he did not truly free the serfs, he was later dubbed "Alexander the Liberator" for taking the first step.

26. **B** Anesthesia was readily available starting in 1846; all the other choices were not widespread until the twentieth century. Though many civilizations had been using plant mixtures to achieve a similar effect for centuries, it was not until then that anesthesia as we know it today was developed. The discovery of morphine and the development of the hypodermic needle revolutionized medicine and laid the foundation for the modern pharmaceutical industry.

27. **C** Herbert Spencer was one of the early proponents of Social Darwinism, which aimed to apply Darwin's theories on evolution to human society. Therefore, he believed that those with more money and power than others had those things because they were inherently superior (survival of the fittest). He did not believe in aid for the poor—he thought that governments should let them die. Europe, he believed, was inherently superior to Asia because of its economic superiority.

28. **D** After the initial French Revolution, the French aristocracy began to decline dramatically. They were afforded less privileges than ever before, and their influence dwindled as the middle class grew stronger. However, the fact that women began to gain more social and political clout in France during this time period has little to do with the decline of the elite.

29. **D** Up until the nineteenth century, the class gap was extremely wide. As the working class slowly gained more rights and influence, the middle class began to make up a larger part of the economy. The class system had never been so evenly spread.

30. **C** The new, larger middle class found roles as skilled laborers and craftsmen during the Second Industrial Revolution. The unskilled factory workers still worked for low wages, but there was an increased market for artisanal goods. The middle class was by no means wealthy, but they were afforded more opportunities to make a better living.

31. **C** By the time of the Second Industrial Revolution, workers had gained a bit more influence but they still had a long way to go. The workplace conditions did not improve much and women still did not have the same opportunities as men. However, their hours were fairer, so they were able to have more free time for leisure.

32. **E** Though anarchy had small followings across the globe, during the nineteenth century there was a surge in "peasant anarchism" in Andalusia, most notably during the reign of Queen Isabella II.

33. **D** During the First and Second Industrial Revolutions, most working class people did not consider religion important. They had many things to worry about—among them, the day-to-day struggles of being overworked and underpaid. During this time period, religion was more unpopular than ever and many considered it a waste of time.

34. **D** Anti-Semitism seemed to be on the rise during the nineteenth century. Social Darwinism, which was gaining traction, viewed Jewish people as an inferior race. Many national governments publicly stated their distaste for the Jewish people, including the Russian government who used them as a scapegoat for the problems plaguing Russia. It often took violent turns in the form of pogroms, violent riots aimed at Jewish communities in Russia.

35. **E** The Cult of Domesticity gained popularity among housewives during the nineteenth century. It encouraged women to be submissive to their husbands, to do things like cook meals and clean. It was less popular among women in the workforce (though they were still expected to care for children, etc), and it was outright rejected by feminists. Nonetheless, its influence was very widespread and tons of women purchased how-to books on the subject.

36. **E** Mary Mayson Beeton was a strong proponent of the Cult of Domesticity, becoming very popular and well known through her own *Book of Household Management,* released in 1861. The book contained recipes, as well as advice on things like fashion and childcare. It was wildly popular after its release, though it had plenty of detractors.

37. **C** Both suffragists and suffragettes supported voting rights, but suffragettes were known to be more militant in their support for the cause and more focused on women's suffrage. *Suffragist* is a broader term that could apply to any group advocating for voting rights—including male suffrage activists or less radical groups.

38. **B** Though the Cult of Domesticity popularized a more submissive role for women, it also sparked smaller feminist movements. They lacked a coherent "movement," and disagreed on whether suffrage was the most important thing to focus on. Many prominent feminists were wealthy—and largely they were interested in gaining the right to divorce and own property.

39. **A** Charles Dickens's *Hard Times* offered an accurate portrayal of working-class life. Released in the mid-nineteenth century, Dickens took aim at the conditions of the workhouses and the Utilitarian philosophy of Jeremy Bentham. Utilitarianism calls for the "greatest good for the greatest number," but that often meant leaving the poorest to fend for themselves.

40. **A** Many colonies during the period of new imperialism were not profitable for the empires that conquered them. However, India was considered Britain's "jewel of the crown" for its economic importance.

41. **B** Social imperialists viewed colonization as a cure to overpopulation. Social imperialism hoped to improve nationalism through foreign exploits. It was about keeping a socialist façade to maintain stability while practicing imperialism.

42. **D** Britain's "informal empire" in China was quite literal in its name. Though they held no political or territorial control, they had significant control over China's economy. Therefore, they were able to exert their power over China indirectly, rather than through formal means in a traditional colony.

43.   E   Imperialism was of little concern to the working class, even moreso during the rapid industrializa-
          tion of the nineteenth century. People were worried about issues more close to home: working con-
          ditions, wages, the right to vote. The foreign exploits of the government had little tangible effect
          on the lives of the working class, so most of them did not pay attention to it.

The Free-Response Essay Questions Explained

Question 44

44.   Identify and describe the factors that explain why Great Britain led the Industrial Revolution in 1750, while countries like
      France fell behind.

Essay Notes

A good essay will touch upon the following points:

- Britain's expanding population meant more low-wage workers for the factories, as well as more
  consumers. This can largely be attributed to an improved degree of diet and hygiene, making their
  death rate significantly lower than other countries at the time. Comparatively, France's population
  growth stalled.
- Following the Glorious Revolution of 1688, Britain enjoyed both political stability and an increased
  degree of religious toleration, creating an environment that was conducive to economic investment
  and growth. France had been continuing down a path of political turmoil and unrest, marked by
  continuous uprisings and shifts in power.
- There was an increased availability of coal and iron, which were necessary in the early stages of
  industrialization. Additionally, Britain was the first nation to establish a national railroad that
  transported both people and goods across the country rapidly.
- Largely due to the successes of the early agricultural revolution, Britain's unprecedented system
  of farming helped create a surplus of capital. In conjunction with the establishment of The Bank
  of England in 1694, Britain was able to invest in a wide variety of new industries. France had no
  centralized banking structure.
- Forcibly moving people from rural areas to cities through the Enclosure Act meant that more
  people were living in urban areas than ever before. While this provided an even larger workforce,
  the conditions for the working poor degraded rapidly. Rural farmers in France were not forced to
  do the same, and stayed working on the land.
- Note, however, that France dominated the luxury market, and had some economic growth.

Question 45

45. Describe the Cult of Domesticity and explain the ways in which the creation of the Cult of Domesticity sparked the feminist movement in Europe . Mention the key figures in this movement.

Essay Notes

A good essay will touch upon the following points:

- Mary Mayson Beeton: Wrote *Book of Household Management,* a book that became immensely popular in Great Britain. It provided tips for women to better run their households. This supported the Cult of Domesticity, which separated men and women into two different spheres, with men acting as the breadwinners and women acting as the homemakers in a time when the idea of "home" was essential to a happy family.
- The Cult of Domesticity was mostly fulfilled by middle- and upper-class families. Poorer mothers often had to work multiple jobs and did not have time to be homemakers. Nevertheless, they were expected to adhere to these standards as well. The Cult of Domesticity demonstrated a concerted effort to keep women in the house, encouraging submissiveness as a desirable trait.
- Occupations for women (teacher, nurse, secretary) were generally a majority female, and thus could have lower salaries than male-majority jobs.
- This further marginalization of women encouraged them to seek education and attempt to gain more political and social clout
- Josephine Butler: Early feminist figure who helped found the Ladies' National Association in 1869, an all-female group that fought against legislation that discriminated against women.
- Frances Power Cobbe: One of the first female journalists, demonstrating the ability of women to subvert the Cult of Domesticity, later became an active campaigner against medical vivisection.
- Maria Montessori: famous educator and physician,
- Increased birth control and better occupational opportunities helped women fight the Cult of Domesticity.
- Suffragists and suffragettes fought for the female voting right.

Chapter 16
1900–Present:
Political and
Diplomatic
Questions

Multiple-Choice Questions

1900–PRESENT: POLITICAL AND DIPLOMATIC QUESTIONS

Multiple-Choice Questions

1. Democracy lasted in Spain

   (A) only from 1931 to 1936 and then after 1975.
   (B) in the period following World War I, for a brief period after the Spanish Civil War, and following Franco's death in 1975.
   (C) only after Franco's death.
   (D) since the 1990s.
   (E) Never. There is still a monarchy in Spain.

2. The Wannsee Conference

   (A) established the details of the Nuremberg laws including forcing Jews to wear yellow Stars of David saying "Jude."
   (B) was a meeting of Hitler and top S.S. and S.A. strategists to decide what to do next following the Battle of Britain.
   (C) was Germany's answer to the Yalta and Potsdam conference to decide how to respond to the Allied Powers' treaty offerings.
   (D) finalized the details set forth at Yalta and Potsdam, and arranged for systematic freeing and rehabilitation of concentration camp prisoners.
   (E) was a gathering of Nazi leaders in 1942 organized to systematize the extermination of the Jews in Europe as part of Hitler's "Final Solution" since only one million Jews had been killed up to that point.

3. Which of the following is TRUE about the Bolsheviks?

   (A) They supported the Provisional Government.
   (B) They believed, as Marx had stated, that Russia had to proceed through the proven historical stages before achieving the ideal socialist society.
   (C) Of all the Marxist socialist groups, they were considered quite moderate.
   (D) They were not in favor of peace with Germany in 1917 and against the Treaty of Brest-Litovsk.
   (E) Following the ideas of Lenin, they believed that they could seize power on behalf of the working classes.

4. The division of Germany into four zones following the end of World War II

   (A) gave the Allies the opportunity to oversee development of the new political institutions but ultimately left governance to the Germans.
   (B) turned into four different political parties for the newly reconstructed German government.
   (C) enabled the Allies to develop "de-Nazification" processes, but to do so, they had to break up the large industrial cartels.
   (D) was the first stage that displayed the former Allies' mutual dislike and distrust.
   (E) displayed seamless cooperation between the United States, Britain, and France until the Cold War started.

5. Which of the following events did NOT pertain to the establishment of the state of Israel?

(A) The United Nations agreed on a partition of Palestine, granting one state as a Jewish homeland and another as an Arab-Palestinian homeland.

(B) In 1945, the number of Jews outnumbered the number of Arabs in Palestine, following an influx of Jewish settlers in the 1920s and 1930s.

(C) Immediately following the establishment of the State of Israel on May 14, 1948, its Arab neighbors responded with military force.

(D) The British, who had occupied Palestine, had decided to withdraw its forces and decolonize the area.

(E) The six million Jews killed in the Holocaust led to vocal demands for a Jewish state.

6. "Peace in our time" refers to what failed foreign policy strategy?

(A) The League of Nations
(B) German reparations
(C) The Munich Appeasement
(D) Isolationism
(E) The Entente Cordiale

7. All of the following are TRUE about the League of Nations EXCEPT

(A) the formation of the League was outlined in Woodrow Wilson's Fourteen Points.

(B) the League retained power, albeit, ineffectual, until the establishment of the United Nations as its successor.

(C) the League's biggest "victory" was its ability to effectively impose sanctions against Italy when Italy invaded Ethiopia in 1935.

(D) the League was designed to settle disputes between nations including border issues.

(E) Germany had joined the League of Nations by 1925.

8. Although democracy was thriving in Czechoslovakia in the years following World War I, some might argue it was destined to become a player in the origins of World War II because of

(A) its strong liberal tradition and large middle class.
(B) the ethnic and racial composition of the Sudetenland.
(C) differences between the Czechs and the Slovaks.
(D) President Edvard Beneš' ineffective leadership style.
(E) its proximity to Germany.

9. The purpose of paramilitary groups like the Free Corps was to

   (A) provide political stability to fragile republic
   (B) support the work of various social and educational movements
   (C) help put down rebellions by violent left-wing factions in Germany during the Weimar years since the army was ineffectual and almost nonexistent
   (D) enforce the sentences of local magistrates hampered by the ineffective justice system
   (E) restore order amidst the postwar chaos

10. The Anschluss was

    (A) a collective security agreement between Germany and the Austro-Hungarian Empire that led Germany into World War I
    (B) the Prussian area of Poland that Germany lost in the Treaty of Versailles
    (C) a conference in which Germany, France, Great Britain, and Italy agreed that Alsace-Lorraine should be returned to Germany
    (D) Hitler's stated dream in the initial pages of *Mein Kampf*, in which Austria would become part of a larger German Reich
    (E) the annexation of the Germany section of Czechoslovakia

11. The Battle of Britain in World War II ended

    (A) soon after Hermann Goring, in charge of the German Luftwaffe, directed his forces to attack British cities rather than military targets, giving the RAF time to recover and fight back
    (B) because the German forces had broken the British code and discovered they had radar to detect attacks, so they turned their attention to the East
    (C) because the next step for Germany was a land invasion, and the German army was not yet prepared for that step
    (D) when the Germans realized the British Spitfires and Hurricanes were better than their own Messerschmitts and they abandoned air attacks until they could build better aircraft
    (E) when Hitler discovered he had to go bail out the Italians who were in trouble in Greece

12. Which of the following is FALSE about the Basque Separatist (ETA) movement in Spain?

    (A) They have been known to hide out in France with the French Basque population.
    (B) From its beginnings in the late 1950s, the movement has always been about gaining independence from Spain.
    (C) They have waged periodic terror campaigns across Spain, including bombings and assassinations.
    (D) Because Spain recognized "autonomous communities" in 1978 in its Constitution, popular support for the movement waned.
    (E) They have announced cease-fires in their terror campaigns.

13. The French tried desperately to hold on to its colony in Algeria because

   (A) France was smarting from the loss of its colony in Indonesia
   (B) the French army—with all its prestige—didn't want to waste its time fighting a battle it knew it wouldn't win
   (C) the French had ruled in Algeria since 1830 and more than one million native French people lived there
   (D) Algeria was filled with rich natural resources that if lost, would destroy the French economy
   (E) the French had lost Tunisia and Morocco, so they had to draw the line somewhere

14. Which of the following statements was true of trench warfare in World War I?

   (A) Trenches protected soldiers from all kinds of fire—soldiers were wounded or killed only if they went above ground out of the trench.
   (B) Despite the severe difficulties of trench living, most suffered shellshock from wounds, not from the trench experience.
   (C) Surprisingly, trenches could be kept reasonably hygienic despite the continual presence of rats and corpses.
   (D) Trenches began as a rapidly dug series of ditches but evolved into a highly complex network of underground tunnels with fortifications.
   (E) Bayonets were the most effective weapon in trench warfare because it required soldiers to emerge from the trenches and engage face-to-face.

15. The Weimar Republic might have been less fragile if

   (A) Germany had more control over its iron and coal regions
   (B) the army had been better able to control left- and right-wing rebellions
   (C) inflation had been better controlled
   (D) Germany had stayed on the gold standard
   (E) the Constitution had not given the president powers to dissolve the Reichstag and call for new elections

16. English Prime Minister Margaret Thatcher was known for all of the following EXCEPT

   (A) her successful stewardship of Great Britain and its army during the crisis in the Falkland Islands
   (B) a temporary détente in relations between Britain and Northern Ireland
   (C) her hostility towards working for greater pan-European cooperation
   (D) her inability to garner support even among members of her own party
   (E) her economic policies that encouraged austere cuts in both taxes as well as public spending

17. The dismantling of the British empire following World War II

   (A) furthered weakened the British economy at a point when it could ill-afford to suffer more
   (B) was totally a British movement as most colonies were quite satisfied with conditions, especially after the upheavals of World War II
   (C) involved a gradual series of withdrawals from its colonies in Asia and Africa, although British settlers in Rhodesia formed their own government in the colony in 1965, which lasted 15 years until the Africans won control over the land and renamed it Zimbabwe
   (D) was something Winston Churchill wholeheartedly believed in as he thought decolonization would paradoxically strengthen Great Britain's power in the world in the long run
   (E) was mostly peaceful in the Middle East, except for a few skirmishes here and there

18. Which of the following is true of both the Yalta and Potsdam Conferences?

   (A) Anticipating a positive outcome to the war, representatives from the United States, Great Britain, France, and the Soviet Union were in attendance at both, even though the Yalta conference occurred before the end of the war while France was still occupied by the Germans.
   (B) The Allies could not reach final decisions about what to do about the Eastern European countries, leaving the door open for the Soviets to incorporate them into their Union.
   (C) The Allies discussed plans for settlements regarding Japanese reparations payments and territorial issues but nothing ever came to fruition following the atomic bomb blasts.
   (D) At Yalta, the Soviets asked for more control in Western Europe, in the form of some of the Allies' colonial holdings, for their assistance during the war, but the other three powers decided at Potsdam to reward the Soviets with additional reparations payments instead.
   (E) The four powers—the United States, Great Britain, France, and the Soviet Union—battled over the issue of reparations, finally settling on a plan that each country would collect in its own zone, and the Soviets would receive 25 percent of what the other three collected.

19. Unlike many of the former Eastern Bloc nations, Romania's transformation to republic

   (A) started slowly with labor and social movements, only later turning to republican elections

   (B) was quite violent, culminating in the executions of the dictator Nicolae Ceaușescu and his wife, Elena, following their desperate attempts to stay in power

   (C) was triggered primarily by the ethnic Hungarians living in Romania who believed wholeheartedly in the democratic cause

   (D) was fomented primarily by a coup within the government itself, since Ceaușescu's own assistants wanted him out of power

   (E) started with a ban on religious propaganda

20. The Schlieffen Plan was

   (A) a German military strategy involving plans to quickly defeat the East to avoid a two-front war

   (B) a German military strategy involving a rapid advance through Northern France that succeeded in the first year of World War I

   (C) a failed attempt to blockade British shipping in World War II

   (D) a German military strategy to enter France via Norway, the Netherlands, Denmark, and Belgium in World War II to avoid the mistakes of World War I

   (E) a strategy that Bismarck's men developed for future German wars that Kaiser Wilhelm decided to invoke in the later stages of World War I

21. When the German Chancellor Heinrich Bruning called for new parliamentary elections in 1930

   (A) the Nazis received more votes than in the last election, but there was still a chance for the republic to hold on with a stronger leader

   (B) the Communists gained as many seats in the Reichstag as the Nazis, so there might have been a possibility for a very different outcome had the Weimar Republic had a different Constitution and different leaders

   (C) the moderate parties in the center were the only ones to have lost, but it mattered very little since they had very little power anyway because they were not unified and strong to begin with

   (D) instead of finding increased support for his austere economic policies, he found that the rival Communists and Nazis emerged as the big winners

   (E) the Weimar coalition essentially collapsed and the Third Reich essentially began, although it would still be another three years before Hitler would officially assume power

22. The British solution to battles between Hindus and Muslims in India was

   (A) to imprison Gandhi and Nehru for their work towards Indian independence

   (B) to create the Congress Party to assess and resolve all differences between warring factions

   (C) to grant independence to the entire region to allow the former colonials to work it out for themselves

   (D) to create the formation of two independent states, India and Pakistan, with the former Hindu and the latter Muslim. Pakistan would be divided into East and West on either side of India.

   (E) to create a third party group, consisting mostly of neutral Sikhs, to work with the battling parties

23. All of the following are TRUE about Article 231 in the final version of the Treaty of Versailles EXCEPT

    (A) its one concession to Germany was to give Germany and France a 25-75 share of economic control over the coal and iron mines of the Saar border region for 15 years
    (B) it forced Germany and its Allies to accept full responsibility for the war
    (C) the region of Alsace-Lorraine returned to French control
    (D) Germany could no longer staff an army of more than 100,000 men
    (E) French troops occupied a "demilitarized" zone on the western bank of the Rhine and a strip on the right bank

24. The Maginot Line

    (A) successfully blocked the Germans for a while in 1940, forcing them to shift their strategy to the Battle of Britain and attack by air
    (B) was where the French soldiers holed up in damp bunkers battling the Germans in a land war to keep them out of Paris
    (C) was a strategy that would have worked for France if only Belgium and the Netherlands had coordinated their forces a little better
    (D) was France's deluded idea of military strategy, assuming that a second world war would again involve stagnant trenches
    (E) was held valiantly by French troops for weeks, exhausting the Germans, before it finally collapsed in early June of 1940

25. Poland became independent

    (A) by decision at Locarno, making it one of the last territorial dispositions of the first war
    (B) in spite of the fact that it quickly became a dictatorship and potential threat to European stability
    (C) and integrated into its border territories that were primarily only ethnically Polish
    (D) by virtue of one of other treaties signed during the Paris Peace Conferences following World War I
    (E) by agreement during the Potsdam Conference following World War II in which the Soviets allowed Poland to be independent, although they chose to have a Communist regime

26. Glasnost and perestroika

    (A) were the words that Mikhail Gorbachev used to subtly signal people that he was thinking of leaving the Communist party
    (B) was the economic restructuring said to have caused the accident at Chernobyl in 1986
    (C) were the hallmarks of Mikhail Gorbachev's principles for running the Soviet Union in an era of change
    (D) led to renewed discussions with foreign leaders to put an immediate end to Cold War politics
    (E) motivated those involved in the Soviet coup and eventually brought Communism to an end in Russia

27. All of the following are TRUE about the Berlin Wall
EXCEPT

   (A) it began initially as a barbed wire barrier but quickly
       became concretized
   (B) the wall blocked access only to the Soviet zone, which
       was already heavily guarded, while the other three
       zones remained free. Consequently, the Western
       Allies were not too worried about its presence.
   (C) its fall in 1989 marked the beginning of the movement
       for German reunification
   (D) it was constructed by the Soviets in 1961 to stem the
       tide of Communists fleeing to the West
   (E) despite the wall's presence, the Soviets and East
       Germans need not have feared because only about
       15,000 people tried to flee in 1961

29. Russian WWII POWs

   (A) mostly defected to the United States after the war,
       having been traumatized by their experiences
   (B) primarily died in German concentration camps and
       were among those shot quickly just before the camps
       were liberated
   (C) returned home to find a much more tightly controlled
       USSR with the Cold War starting, and found it
       difficult to adjust to the restrictive atmosphere
   (D) were welcomed home as heroes at first, but then many
       committed suicide because the transition to civilian
       life was too difficult
   (E) were not welcome in their home country as they were
       seen as having failed in their duty to the Soviet
       Union or were possibly spies for the West

28. "Star Wars" referred to

   (A) Gorbachev's response to Reagan's reluctance to
       include certain provisions in their nuclear weapons
       negotiations
   (B) a strategic American defense initiative that was
       the stumbling block in nuclear weapon treaty
       negotiations between the United States and the
       Soviet Union in the 1980s
   (C) the arms race between the United States and the Soviet
       Union that the entire world knew could no longer
       continue if the world had a hope of surviving
   (D) the exchange of boycotts of United States and Soviet-
       based Olympics—the United States boycotting
       the Moscow Olympics in 1980 and the Soviets
       boycotting the Los Angeles Olympics in 1984
   (E) Gorbachev's highly publicized visits to the United
       States in 1987, in which he charmed world leaders
       and won tremendous popular support

30. Russia's October Manifesto

   (A) was actually written by Lenin and Trotsky, based on
       Marxist principles, for a new form of government
   (B) established a constitutional monarchy in Russia with a
       Duma, a national parliament, the first of its kind in
       Russia
   (C) gave the workers temporary control of the government
       until a new structure could be put in place
   (D) was the beginning of the Bolshevik Revolution in
       Russia
   (E) began with the overthrow of Tsar Nicholas II and his
       family and ended with the Bolshevik Revolution

31. All of the following have been put forth as arguments for the rise of the Nazi Party in Germany EXCEPT

   (A) very high inflation because of World War I reparations payments
   (B) disgust over the extreme decadence of Berlin culture during the Weimar years
   (C) the Dolchstosslegenda (stab-in-the-back legend) in which many Germans believed they lost World War I because members of various "hated" groups such as Jews and Communists had betrayed them
   (D) threats from extreme leftists groups
   (E) the instability of the Weimar government as a whole

32. Military strategists say that one of the biggest keys to the success of the Normandy invasion

   (A) was the sheer number of the Allied forces involved in the attack—2,000,000 soldiers, 12,000 planes, and 5,000 vessels
   (B) was the ability of Allied soldiers to secure a beachhead to allow the bulk of their soldiers to reach land quickly
   (C) was the fact that planning for the attack began early—at the Teheran conference in October 1943
   (D) was Hitler's confidence in newly developed weapons that would keep the Allies at bay
   (E) was the timing the invasion after a huge gale over the English Channel

33. The Solidarity movement

   (A) joined together groups in Poland that previously had no connections
   (B) was a legal movement according to Polish law, but the rebellions still resulted in many arrests
   (C) caused the Soviet-backed government to respond with the kind of glasnost and perestroika that were now commonplace in Russian governance
   (D) ultimately led to multiparty elections in Poland that resulted in the defeat of all the Communist candidates
   (E) was originally started by Lech Walesa, but others came to the forefront after he was imprisoned

34. The "White" Forces in Russia

   (A) supported Russian nationalists causes, including a return to "Russia for Russians"
   (B) were united primarily by calls for racial and ethnic purity
   (C) were secretly working with the Nazis in the 1930s to create a German-Russian alliance should another war break out
   (D) challenged the Communist rule following the revolution, and consisted of loosely united groups of monarchists and republicans
   (E) were in league with the groups calling for a return to the monarchy and looking for possible survivors of the Tsar's family

35. "Crimes against humanity" was the new legal concept invoked at

   (A) the trial for the Romanian dictator Nicolae Ceauşescu and his wife, Elena
   (B) crimes by the Khmer Rouge in Cambodia
   (C) the Nuremberg Trials, in which many Nazi officials, mostly minor, judges, and military industrialists were tried
   (D) the trial of Adolf Eichmann in Jerusalem for his crimes during the Nazi era
   (E) the war crimes trials for Slobodan Milosevic for genocide in Bosnia

36. The fall of the Soviet Union may be attributed to

   (A) Ronald Reagan's famous quote "Mr. Gorbachev, tear down this wall"
   (B) terrorism by Chechen rebels
   (C) Gorbachev's appointment of hardline politicians to the government, who decided that the leader's policies were not in the best interest of the Soviet Union and staged a coup while Gorbachev was on vacation
   (D) growing grassroots movements within the Soviet Union pushing for greater freedoms, following the models of Solidarity in Poland and collapse of the Berlin Wall in Germany
   (E) the inability of free-market reforms in Russia to work in the former Communist economy, resulting in tremendous economic disparity and poverty

37. Which technical innovations did the Germans introduce to warfare in World War I?

   (A) New arms including Lewis guns and Browning automatic rifles
   (B) Machine guns mounted on motorcycle sidecars
   (C) Disabling gases including tear gas
   (D) Poisonous gases including chlorine and mustard gas
   (E) New warships such as the Q-ships

38. George Kennan's Long Telegram

   (A) expressed the view that although the Soviets believed wholeheartedly in the Communist ideals, there was room for peaceful co-existence of the two superpowers in the post–World War II world
   (B) showed that the answer to Communism was to expose people to the ideas of Communism and let them come to their own conclusions, knowing that Capitalism would show itself to be the superior way of life and in keeping with American values
   (C) expressed the view that the Soviet Union did not see or want to ever peacefully coexist with the capitalist world
   (D) corresponded with the European values expressed in the principles establishing NATO, and formed the basis for greater United States–European cooperation against the Soviets
   (E) stated that propaganda would be useless in the face of all the sophisticated Soviet brainwashing tools already developed

39. The movement known as "Home Rule" was

(A)   when Nationalist forces in Ireland began to demand full independence from Britain
(B)   Algeria's demand for independence from France
(C)   India's plea for freedom from British colonization
(D)   a congress of African nations, who came together to declare their autonomy from their European colonizers
(E)   a march staged by British women on the Home Front demanding more rights, including the right to vote

40. The creation of the European Union is an eventual outgrowth of

(A)   a desire for a larger pool of labor to meet the changing needs of Europe's job market.
(B)   the growing feeling following World War II that greater cooperation was needed between all the European countries in order to prevent any one country—such as Germany or the Soviet Union—of gaining too much power and starting another world war.
(C)   a need to improve communication, trade, and relations between European countries after centuries of intercontinental wars.
(D)   a desire to increase and ease intercontinental tourism and travel.
(E)   a desire to promote education and economic exchange between countries in order to support collective growth and stay competitive as a world power with the United States and the USSR.

41. Ethnic cleansing

(A)   was another phrase Hitler used for the "Final Solution"
(B)   was a plan to prevent murdering undesirables by relocating them
(C)   took place only in a few selected regions during the Bosnian Civil War
(D)   was Yugoslavian President Slobodan Milosevic's policy to have Bosnian Serbs "removed" by killing Muslims and ethnic Bosnians from regions controlled by the Serbs
(E)   was supported by the Serbian civilian populace as a "necessary evil" in order to create a "New World Order" for the Bosnian Serbs

Free-Response Questions

42. Albert Einstein wrote, "I know not with what weapons World War III will be fought, but World War IV will be fought with sticks and stones." Using at least two examples from twentieth-century European and world political history, explain what Einstein means and whether or not you agree with his statement.

_____

_____

_____

_____

_____

_____

_____

_____

_____

_____

_____

_____

_____

_____

_____

_____

_____

_____

_____

_____

_____

_____

_____

_____

_____

_____

_____

_____

_____

_____

43. Margaret Atwood wrote, "War is what happens when language fails." Using at least two examples, describe examples of instances of how conflicts arose out of a failure of diplomacy and negotiation.

_____
_____
_____
_____
_____
_____
_____
_____
_____
_____
_____
_____
_____
_____
_____
_____
_____
_____
_____
_____
_____
_____
_____
_____
_____
_____
_____
_____
_____

Chapter 17
1900–Present:
Political and
Diplomatic
Answers and
Explanations

ANSWER KEY

1.	A	23.	A
2.	E	24.	D
3.	E	25.	D
4.	D	26.	C
5.	B	27.	E
6.	C	28.	B
7.	C	29.	E
8.	B	30.	B
9.	C	31.	B
10.	D	32.	B
11.	A	33.	D
12.	B	34.	D
13.	C	35.	C
14.	D	36.	C
15.	E	37.	D
16.	B	38.	C
17.	C	39.	A
18.	E	40.	B
19.	B	41.	D
20.	B		
21.	D		
22.	D		

ANSWERS AND EXPLANATIONS

1. **A** Following the abdication of King Alfonso XIII in 1931, a coalition of republicans and moderate Socialists governed Spain, establishing the Second Spanish Republic in April of that year, with Manuel Azana in power. Strikes, land seizures, attacks on the church, and taxes drove the wealthy and the churchmen farther to the right. Azana was out by 1933, and the next two years saw increasing social and political violence. By 1935, those on the left joined together to create the Popular Front to defend the republic against the right wing factions but by 1936, the right wing nationalists, organized behind their general, Francisco Franco, Civil War was inevitable. Democracy was restored only after Franco's death in 1975.

2. **E** Because only one million Jews had been killed up through 1941, mostly with machine guns or with carbon monoxide poisoning, a group of top Nazi officials gathered in Wannsee, a suburb of Berlin, in early 1942 for a conference to organize a more systematic way to enact Hitler's "Final Solution." This conference, actually said to be only about 90 minutes long, came to be known as the Wannsee Conference. The plans outlined exactly how Jews would be rounded up and then exterminated.

3. **E** The Bolsheviks were the most extreme of the Russian socialists, and believed, as Lenin did, that a small group of dedicated professional followers could seize power on behalf of the working classes. This differed from the Mensheviks, who insisted Russia had to follow through Marx's proven historical stages before it could achieve the ideal socialist society. The Mensheviks supported the Provisional Government, since they felt it was in keeping with following the historical progression—that a bourgeois revolution must come before the socialist revolution. Germany signed the Treaty of Brest-Litovsk with the Bolsheviks so the Bolsheviks supported both.

4. **D** The Yalta and Potsdam Conferences arranged for the division of postwar Germany into four zones, one governed by each of the Allies. However, the Allies' mistrust of one another was already growing. Lack of cooperation and coordination between the zones did not help, and the lack of an actual peace treaty with Germany left many issues in question including zone governance following the Allies' departure. By 1949, the Soviet-occupied zone became the German Democratic Republic, under Communist rule, while the American, British, and French zones became the Federal Republic of Germany. The city of Berlin was equally split into West and East, Democratic and Communist.

5. **B** In 1945, three years before the State of Israel was established as part of the United Nations' partition of Palestine—which was also supposed to include a second Arab-Palestinian state—the number of Jews was actually smaller than the number of Arabs in Palestine, with approximately one-third of the population there Jewish. However, by 1948, the demographics changed dramatically, shifting to an almost 5:1 ratio of Jews to Arabs in Israel.

6. **C** "Peace in our time" was British Prime Minister Neville Chamberlain's famous declaration following his visit to Munich in September 1938 where he and Prime Minister Edouard Daladier of France ceded to Hitler the Sudetenland—the German area of Czechoslovakia, in return for which Hitler promised he would make no more territorial demands in Europe. Obviously, the annexation of the Sudetenland did not appease Hitler, and war began less than one year later with the invasion of Poland. The League of Nations was not involved in the Munich conferences, nor did the conferences have anything to do directly with German reparations payments. Isolationism was an American foreign policy strategy to try to stay out of European conflicts, and the Entente Cordiale was an agreement between Britain and France prior to World War I.

7. **C** The League of Nations, Woodrow Wilson's dream plan for international cooperation as outlined in his Fourteen Points, was doomed from the start by the American government's refusal to join. While the League did indeed remain in power, such as it was, until the establishment of the United Nations as its successor in 1947, its ability to act effectively was constantly thwarted. Its failure to effectively impose sanctions against Italy when that country invaded Ethiopia in 1935 is a prime example. Not only were the sanctions limited and included many exceptions, but also the United States chose to ignore the sanctions and increase exports to Italy. In the meantime, Britain and France did little to support Ethiopia against Italy either, such as blocking Italy's access to the Suez Canal.

8. **B** Only Czechoslovakia seemed to thrive as a democracy in Eastern Europe during the interwar period when all the other newly created states were experiencing right-wing, nationalist, and fascist sentiment, probably due to the poor economic conditions following the war. In Czechoslovakia, including the highly industrialized area of Bohemia, the economy was strong enough to maintain political stability and parliamentary rule. Even President Edvard Beneš had sufficient support. Thus, it became clear that the greatest threat to the state would be from Germany because of the German population in the Sudetenland, the northern section of Czechoslovakia, should Hitler choose to fire up nationalistic fervor, which he did.

9. **C** In the early years of the Weimar Republic, the German army, weakened by the Treaty of Versailles, had no strength to deal with the threats to the republic, which at that time were coming mostly from far left groups. Friedrich Ebert, the first President of the Weimar Republic and a social moderate, gave approval for the creation of the Free Corps, a voluntary paramilitary group, many of whose members supported far-right causes. The Free Corps helped to stop rebellions by these left-wing groups in the early postwar years. However, in 1920, some Free Corps members became involved in an attempt to overthrow the state—the Kapp Putsch—but a workers' general strike ended the attempt.

10. **D** In 1924, long before he became Chancellor, Hitler published *Mein Kampf*, in which he outlined his plans for his dream of a larger German Reich. From the opening, Hitler, who was born in Vienna, spoke of one day reuniting his birth home of Austria with Germany. In 1938, when Germany invaded Austria and annexed it—the Anschluss—that dream was fulfilled. Hitler paraded through the country feted by jubilant crowds wherever he went.

11.   **A**   The Battle of Britain, which began in the summer of 1940 when the German Luftwaffe began its air assault over England, concluded by the end of September 1940. Hermann Goring, leading the Luftwaffe, decided to end the effective raids against British military targets and chose instead to attack British cities. While the Blitz created tremendous devastation in English cities, it gave the Royal Air Force much needed time to recover and fight back. In addition, the Brits had developed radar and could detect oncoming German attacks.

12.   **B**   The Basque Separatist (ETA) movement in Spain, long associated with terror campaigns throughout Spain, started out in the late 1950s as a group that promoted traditional Basque culture. From there, it evolved into a paramilitary group with a stated goal of gaining independence from Spain. However, the Basque Country in northern Spain is itself one of Spain's seventeen autonomous communities within the government's national structure, causing popular support for a "separatist" movement to wane.

13.   **C**   The French tried desperately to hold on to its colony in Algeria. They had already lost their colony in Indochina (Vietnam), where the country wound up divided into North and South, with the North under Communist rule. However, the French had ruled Algeria since 1830, and more than one million native French people lived there. It was a question of prestige for France, having nothing to do with the army or natural resources. The French also did not have colonial holdings in Tunisia or Morocco.

14.   **D**   Trench warfare in World War I began as a series of rapidly dug ditches to protect against enemy shellfire, but as the war endured, the front lines did not change much and the ditches evolved into a highly complex network of underground tunnels with fortifications. However, soldiers had to share these tunnels with rats, incredibly poor sanitary conditions, and the constant noise of artillery. Within the trenches they were safe from gunfire but not from bombs, hand grenades, and flying shrapnel. Those that were not wounded in the trench still wound up suffering from varying levels of shellshock, a condition that was not very well understood in those days.

15.   **E**   Some might argue that the Treaty of Versailles doomed the Weimar Republic from the start with Article 231's requirements that Germany accept all responsibility for the war, pay exorbitant reparations payments, and dismantle most of its army. The government began with a country impoverished, with a fragile morale, and rebellions brewing on both the far left and far right from which it could not protect its own citizens. Thus, issues of inflation and the gold standard would have had little influence in any case. A stronger army may have helped with symptoms of the rebellions but not the causes, while more control over the coal and iron region may have helped to strengthen the economy but not enough to make up for the Great Depression and reparations payments. However, in the Weimar Constitution, the German president had the power to dissolve the Reichstag and call for new elections. When Heinrich Bruning did this in 1930 in an attempt to get more support for conservative financial legislation, he wound up with a Reichstag with many more Nazis, thus paving the way for Hitler's arrival.

16. **B** Margaret Thatcher was known as "The Iron Lady" for many reasons, among them her refusal to negotiate or compromise her values. Consequently, the idea of a temporary détente in relations between Britain and Northern Ireland during her rule would be almost unthinkable. She did not want to work towards greater European cooperation and had difficulty winning support from members of her own party. Her economic policies were austere, demanding cuts in taxes and public spending. However, she was famous for successfully guiding Britain and its army through the Falklands crisis in 1982.

17. **C** While Great Britain had wanted to keep its empire following World War II, its dependence on U.S. loans and the self-deterministic needs of the British colonies forced Britain's hand. In 1947, India declared its independence, which began Britain's withdrawal from Asia. The British soon announced they were also withdrawing from Palestine. By the 1950s, it was clear Britain would also have to start letting go of their African holdings as well. However, British settlers in Rhodesia formed their own government in the colony in 1965, which lasted 15 years until the Africans won control over their land and renamed it Zimbabwe. Winston Churchill did not believe in the process, nor was it entirely peaceful, as there were wars fought in Asia, the Middle East, and Africa. The British were also highly reluctant to decolonize, not because of the effects on the economy from colonial holdings, but imperial pride.

18. **E** At the Yalta Conference, in February 1945, the Allies began to debate the future of Germany, both in terms of postwar governance and the issue of reparations. At Yalta, the Allies agreed to a temporary division of Germany into four zones, each ruled by one of the Allied powers, although they could not settle on the reparations payments. At Potsdam, in July 1945, the four countries settled on a plan in which each country would collect payments in its own zone, and the Soviets would receive 25 percent of what the other three collected. There were no discussions about other Eastern Europe territories or settlements with Japan as the war with Japan was still raging in the Pacific. While it was true that French representatives were in attendance, the more important fact was the issue of reparations.

19. **B** While countries such as Bulgaria and Albania had fairly bloodless transitions from communist to democratic forms of government, Romania's transformation was very violent starting when the dictator Nicolae Ceauşescu tried to remove ethnic Hungarians from the town of Timisoara in Transylvania. The ensuing riot resulted in the death of children. As discontent spread, poverty and starvation spread as well as the news of the changes in the other Eastern European countries. Ceauşescu ordered his troops to fire on protestors and hundreds more died. Finally Ceauşescu and his wife were captured and sentenced to death.

20. **B** The Schlieffen Plan—Germany's military strategy in the early weeks of World War I—relied on a rapid advance through Belgium and Northern France that would allow the Germans to quickly defeat both countries. The Germans assumed that France would fall within six weeks, allowing the German army to proceed to Russia. However, Russia's invasion of Belgium violated the neutrality agreement established in 1830 when the country was founded, thus bringing Britain into the war

on the side of the French and Russians. Americans also expressed outrage at this violation of Belgian neutrality.

21. **D** When German Chancellor Heinrich Bruning called for new Reichstag elections in 1930, he had hoped to find more support for the austere economic policies he had proposed that he thought would help pull Germany out of the Depression and out of its economic crisis. Instead, he found himself in a deeper political crisis because the rival Communists and Nazis emerged as the big winners in the election. The Nazis went from 12 seats to 102 seats. Bruning still governed by presidential decree for another two years before he was replaced by Franz von Papen in the spring of 1932. However, by November, the Nazis had 196 seats in the Reichstag so President Paul von Hindenburg selected Hitler as Chancellor in January 1933.

22. **D** When India declared its independence in 1947, there was bitter fighting between Hindus and Muslims. The British solution to the crisis was the creation of two states, India and Pakistan, the former Hindu and the latter Muslim. Pakistan, however, was divided into East and West Pakistan on either side of India. The problem with this solution was that Muslims and Hindus did live together in both territories so drawing accurate boundary lines was nearly impossible. After the two states became fully independent in August 1947, the fighting between the two drove many Muslims out of India, and many Hindus and Sikhs out of Pakistan.

23. **A** Article 231 did not make concessions to Germany. The portion that discusses control over the coal and iron mines of Saar border region actually states that Germany was to cede control of the region to France for fifteen years as compensation for all the destruction Germany caused in the French coalmines. After fifteen years, the Article stated that the sovereignty would be decided by plebiscite. However, by that time, Hitler had taken over as Chancellor in Germany.

24. **D** The French drew the Maginot Line during the interwar period as a series of what they believed to be impenetrable defenses for their army in case of another trench war. The Maginot Line, however, did not extend to Belgium, so the Germans simply went around it and circled the French army. The British, who were at Dunkirk to support the Belgians and French, retreated to their ships when they saw the impending fall of France.

25. **D** Among the treaties signed at the Paris Peace Conferences in 1919 were several that significantly reshaped the map of Europe in the wake of the dismantling of the Austro-Hungarian Empire. One such treaty granted independence to Poland for the first time since the eighteenth century when the Polish commonwealth had been partitioned between Prussia, Russia, and Austria. In addition, the Paris Peace Conferences created the Baltic states of Lithuania, Latvia, Estonia, and Finland from the Russian Empire, Hungary and Romania from the Austro-Hungarian Empire, and the new country of Czechoslovakia, which combined the land of the Czechs and the Slovaks, as well as a number of Germans.

26. **C**   Glasnost (openness in government with a greater freedom of expression) and perestroika (the restructuring of the Soviet system to make it more efficient and more responsive to the needs of the populace) constituted the hallmarks of Mikhail Gorbachev's policy for governing the Soviet Union. The first Soviet leader since Lenin with a university degree, he wanted to repair the social and economic damage of the Stalin era, but still believed he could do it through Communism, with proper economic planning and support.

27. **E**   The construction of an actual Berlin Wall, as opposed to a checkpoint gate, was designed to stem the enormous tide of refugees fleeing from East to West. By mid-1961, some estimates say that East Germany had lost more than 2.5 million of its population at the end of World War II when the Soviet occupation began, most of them younger people who would have been part of the country's workforce. The wall literally went up overnight—the night of August 12-13, 1961—when East Berliners awoke to being fully cut off from life and people and even their jobs in West Berlin.

28. **B**   "Star Wars" (Strategic Defense Initiative) was the nickname for the United States' planned space-based missile-defense shield. The USSR and some U.S. allies protested the plan, which then proved to be a stumbling block in arms-limitation negotiations between Reagan and Gorbachev. Reagan refused to include "Star Wars" in any arms negotiations, while Gorbachev would not sign a treaty without its inclusion.

29. **E**   Soviet Order No. 270, issued in 1941 while the Soviets were battling the Germans, basically said that any soldier who surrendered or had to remove his insignia—for instance, if captured as a prisoner of war—was to be branded a traitor. Hence, any Soviet POWs returning home from World War II were not welcomed home, often even by their families, many of whom would have rather seen them die as heroes than return in disgrace, possibly as a traitor or spy for the West.

30. **B**   Tsar Nicholas's October Manifesto of 1905 created a constitutional monarchy in Russia by establishing a Duma, a national representative assembly, to be chosen by universal male suffrage, which was the first of its kind in Russia. The October Manifesto also promised freedom of the press. However, these reforms were not universally welcome, as some nobles and state officials felt the changes made Russia too much like the West. The Manifesto had nothing to do with Marxism or socialism, nor did it significantly change the condition of the workers in Russia. The Manifesto did not, however, in itself, give rise to the conditions that brought on the Bolshevik Revolution twelve years later—those conditions were already in place and dissent was growing.

31. **B**   Cabaret culture in Berlin was infamous around the world for its decadence, drawing huge crowds and many imitators. However, the rise of the Nazi Party in Germany had much more to do with the social and political factors in Germany than cultural factors. The high inflation, the threats from the far left groups, including high numbers of Communists in the Reichstag itself, and the instability of the Weimar government as a whole all played a role. In addition, the Nazi Party was able to play upon social factors such as Germany's low morale following World War I, including the Dolchstosslegenda—the stab-in-the-back legend—in which it was the fault of the non-Aryan races that Germany lost the war.

32. **B** Planning for the enormous Normandy invasion, a.k.a. D-Day, began at the Teheran Conference in 1943. The strategy involved an initial 150,000 troops attacking the English Channel beaches of western France, since the Germans believed the Allies would land somewhere farther northeast near Calais, where the crossing from England was closer. Behind the initial troops would be 500,000 more, as well as four million tons of support material and parachutists dropping behind enemy lines. Key to the success of this plan, however, was taking and securing a beachhead in the first few hours of the attack in order for the bulk of the troops to get ashore quickly, or else, the sheer numbers of soldiers or equipment or time spent planning the attack would be meaningless.

33. **D** Solidarity was an illegal organization of trade unions Lech Walesa founded in 1980 following years of economic stagnation and unrest in Poland. With ten million members, Solidarity and Walesa helped mobilize opposition to the Communist government. Despite the imposition of martial law, Solidarity persisted in its fight, with the support of the Catholic Church and the new Polish pope John Paul II behind them. Eventually, the Polish government invited Solidarity into negotiations, to which Solidarity agreed in exchange for formal political recognition as a legitimate representative of the people. The ensuing negotiations led to elections, and victory for the Solidarity candidates, effectively ending the Communist regime.

34. **D** The "White" Forces was the name loosely given to all those anti-Communist factions in Russia, including the monarchists as well as the republicans, who were still battling the Communists in the years following the Bolshevik Revolution in 1917. These forces also received a modicum of support from Britain and the United States, who were technically there only to protect Allied supplies that had been sent during World War I.

35. **C** The charge "crimes against humanity" was brought against the defendants tried at the Nuremberg Trials, which began in November 1945. These trials, which lasted through October 1946, sought justice for those maimed and killed in the Holocaust. Military commanders, judges, and industrial magnates were all brought to trial, the highest official being Hermann Goring, who then committed suicide by poison in his jail cell before his sentence of death by hanging could be carried out. In late 1946, responsibility for the adjudication of other Nazi officials was transferred to the German government, who soon let the process die out.

36. **C** With the fall of Communism in many of the Eastern bloc countries, Gorbachev still wanted to find a way to make Communism work in this new era. However, he was concerned that his reforms might lead to the same in the Soviet Union. As a result, he appointed several hard-line government officials, including Boris Yeltsin, and cracked down on some of the nationalist movements in the Baltics. This strategy, however, ultimately failed. In August 1991, a group of hardliners imprisoned Gorbachev in his Crimean vacation home and set up an "Emergency Committee" to take control of the Soviet government. Although the coup fell apart, Yeltsin then, as head of the Russian Parliament suspended the Communist Party and initiated a market economy in Russia, and by December, Gorbachev resigned.

37. **D** While both sides engaged in war with chemical weaponry, especially with the use of tear gas, the Germans introduced the usage of the more poisonous gases such as chlorine and mustard to the battlefield. After several German attacks featuring chlorine gas, the French responded with attacks using phosgene gas. The Germans also used a chlorine-phosgene combination as well as mustard gas. The Canadian Automobile Machine Gun Brigade introduced the machine gun mounted on motorcycle sidecars to the battles in World War I. Lewis guns were American-made and favored by British troops. The Americans brought Browning automatic rifles with them when they joined the battle in 1918. Q-ships were British attack ships disguised as civilian ships.

38. **C** The document that George Kennan, an official in the U.S. State Department, wrote that came to be known as the Long Telegram expressed his view that the Soviet Union did not seek or want peaceful co-existence with the United States and the capitalist world. He said that the Soviets viewed the capitalists as an ideological enemy and that the only route for the United States would be a policy of "containment" of the Soviet Union's expansionist tendencies. Kennan also continued to write about this policy in the journal *Foreign Affairs* using the pseudonym "X."

39. **A** The Home Rule movement was about Nationalist forces in Ireland who began to demand full independence from Britain. Although the issue first arose in earnest in the nineteenth century, Britain had to deal with a Home Rule Bill for Ireland at the same time as it was discussing the growing Serbian crisis as the Archduke had recently been assassinated in Sarajevo.

40. **B** With the continuing instability in the political situation throughout Europe, particularly in Eastern Europe, many leaders had the growing feeling that the only way to prevent another world war, or to prevent any one country from gaining too much power, was to improve cooperation and communication between all the European countries—establishing a European Community. The European Union evolved out of this European Community, first formed in 1967, and its various successors. In its current form, as the European Union (EU), it also shares a common market and common currency.

41. **D** Ethnic cleansing was the phrase President Slobodan Milosevic of Yugoslavia and Bosnian Serbs used when they spoke about "removing," usually by killing, Muslims and ethnic Bosnians from regions controlled by Bosnian Serbs during the civil war that broke out in the area in the 1990s. While ethnic cleansing is considered to be as systematic as Hitler made his "Final Solution," it was never a phrase Hitler used, nor was ethnic cleansing regarded as a "necessary evil." In 1999, Milosevic was indicted by the United Nations' International Criminal Tribunal for crimes against humanity. The charge of genocide was added soon afterwards.

The Free-Response Essay Questions Explained

Question 42

42. Albert Einstein wrote, "I know not with what weapons World War III will be fought, but World War IV will be fought with sticks and stones." Using at least two examples from twentieth-century European and world political history, explain what Einstein means and whether or not you agree with his statement.

Essay Notes

Mentioning any two of these will get you a higher score:

- Lethal poison gas of WWI
- Nuclear weapons of WWII and Cold War
- New technology of computer viruses and/or destruction of satellite technology that could knock out all business and financial systems
- Terrorist activity and mass bombing/mass suicide bombing.

Question 43

43. Margaret Atwood wrote, "War is what happens when language fails." Using at least two examples, describe examples of instances of how conflicts arose out of a failure of diplomacy and negotiation.

Essay Notes

Mentioning any two of these will get you a higher score:

- Munich Appeasement
- Cold War
- The failure of the League of Nations/Treaty of Versailles as one of the causes of World War II
- Battles over reparations payments as a cause of World War II
- Failed pre-World War I alliances (e.g., Entente Cordiale) or failed pre-World War II alliances (e.g., between Germany and Russia)

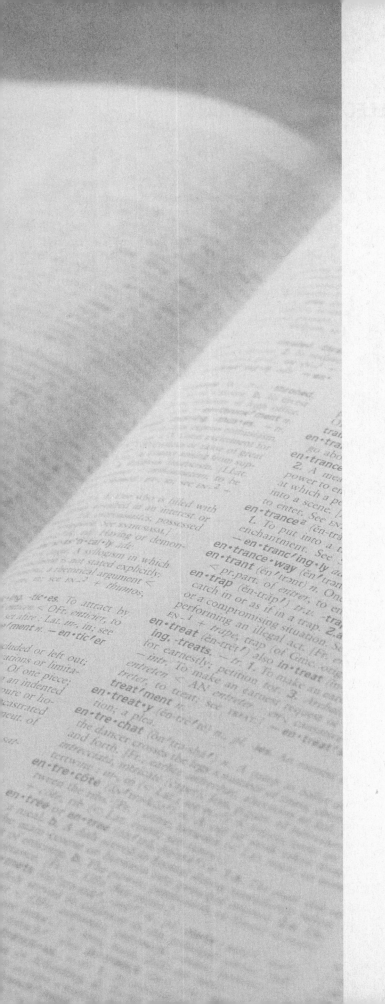

Chapter 18
1900–Present:
Cultural and
Intellectual
Questions

1900–PRESENT: CULTURAL AND INTELLECTUAL QUESTIONS

Multiple-Choice Questions

1. The Lateran Pact, between the Italian government and the Catholic church, was significant because

   (A) the pact enabled the Catholic Church to tacitly comply with Fascist policies
   (B) part of the pact required Mussolini to accept Jesus Christ as his Lord and Savior
   (C) it was the first time the papacy officially recognized the Italian state and resolved long-standing issues between the two
   (D) it enabled Mussolini to get funding for the war effort from the Vatican
   (E) it caused many Catholics in the United States to sympathize with Fascist causes because of the papal support

2. One of the most important points Simone De Beauvoir makes in her groundbreaking book *The Second Sex*

   (A) is that women have certain physical and intellectual characteristics that make them superior to men, and that they need to show it at every given opportunity.
   (B) is that it is the political and social situation and not a woman's body that holds a woman back in the world.
   (C) is that women are trapped in their victimhood and that there really is no exit.
   (D) is that even though there are technically two sexes, the world should really operate according to the principle of there being a single sex.
   (E) is that women's bodies are far superior to men's, but their minds are far inferior, so life with the other sex is always a balancing act.

3. Martin Heidegger said, "If I take death into my life, acknowledge it, and face it squarely, I will free myself from the anxiety of death and the pettiness of life—and only then will I be free to become myself." This quote is an example of which twentieth-century philosophical school?

   (A) The Frankfurt School
   (B) Phenomenology
   (C) Deconstructionism
   (D) Existentialism
   (E) Postmodernism

4. Which of the following is FALSE about the 1968 student uprisings?

   (A) In France, the revolts first expressed opposition to Charles de Gaulle's obsession with foreign policy while University conditions at home were ignored. But then, the rebellions struck at the heart of French power, authority, and established institutions.
   (B) British university students marched in Trafalgar Square, demanding an overhaul of the archaic British educational system.
   (C) German students began with protests against the appearance of the right-wing Shah of Iran, and moved on to more general issues about German institutions themselves.
   (D) The "Prague Spring" saw a brief period of reform in the Communist government in Czechoslovakia.
   (E) Thousands of Italian students in Milan and Trent demonstrated, demanding more control over their institutions and curricula, particularly subjects that felt more "relevant" in a changing world.

5. "Guest workers" refers to

(A) a program for European Union high school students who get to work in another EU country for a summer on an internship, learn the language, and return to their home country with new skills, prior to beginning their university education

(B) an exchange between EU countries for people with differing skills for specific projects requiring those highly specialized—and often highly technical—abilities

(C) unskilled, primarily Turkish and Eastern European, laborers from around the world who came to the United States for jobs

(D) a program many European countries started in order to get cheap labor, fill labor shortages, and rebuild after World War II that has turned into a problem of immigration and citizenship questions, as many have stayed on, had families, but not assimilated into the local culture

(E) immigrants who have come to a particular country specifically for work, but have not yet been granted citizenship

6. The rise of European, as well as American, secular humanism was

(A) based on the idea that humans are innately good

(B) based on the larger idea that belief in a Higher Being—God—was not necessary for living a moral, fulfilled, reasonable life

(C) based on the idea that a human being's nature is shaped by his or her environment

(D) based on the idea that morality develops according to a rational, systematic process

(E) based on the idea that only the individual, by himself or herself, could figure out his or her own moral code

7. The new ecumenical movement in Europe was about

(A) an attempt to bring together religious groups following the religious persecutions in World War II

(B) trying to find ways to create more peace between the warring religious factions in Ireland

(C) creating more dialogues between the leaders of the diverse branches of Protestantism as well as with those of the Roman Catholics and Eastern Orthodox

(D) trying to find ways to increase church attendance in the 1970s and 1980s

(E) an attempt to find ways to get both the Protestant and Catholic churches to allow women to take on more roles in the church hierarchy

8. Which of the following statements is untrue of European anti-Semitism?

(A) The implementation of the Nuremburg Laws in Germany deprived Jews of their rights as citizens.

(B) The establishment of a Jewish homeland in Israel dramatically cut down the amount of anti-Semitism in Europe, although there is still a smattering of it here and there.

(C) Local citizens of many European countries, including the Ukraine and Croatia, assisted in rounding up their Jewish neighbors and marking them for extermination.

(D) The Dreyfus Affair in France gave voice to many of the anti-Semitic rumblings that had been felt in France and continued throughout the twentieth century.

(E) Anti-Semitism was a larger component of Fascism in Germany than it was in Italy.

9. Atonality refers to

   (A) an early twentieth-century art movement where the focus was on sharp angles and decentered images
   (B) a way of composing music after World War I using makeshift instruments that did not create traditional musical "tones"
   (C) a school of music after World War I that focused primarily on rhythmic compositions
   (D) a school of music that includes works by composers such as Alban Berg, Igor Stravinsky, and Sergei Prokofiev that lack the "tonal center" of focusing on a single key—for example, of being composed in the key of C Major or F Minor
   (E) music of the post–World War I era and what has become known as the Second Viennese School in which composers focused on creating sounds particularly jarring to the ear in order to show a musical picture of inner turmoil

10. The rock band U2's song "Sunday Bloody Sunday" commemorates which of the following events?

   (A) A firebombing on the London tube in which many passengers died
   (B) When British soldiers gunned down IRA members in Gibraltar
   (C) When 29 people were killed by a car bomb in Omagh
   (D) When 13 Catholics died after British soldiers fired on civil rights marchers in the Northern Ireland town of Londonderry
   (E) When Protestant gunmen hurled grenades at a Catholic funeral for IRA members

11. The term "British invasion" refers to

   (A) the influx of British cultural trends to America in the 1960s, including the arrival of the miniskirt and television shows such as "Monty Python's Flying Circus"
   (B) the German air attack on Britain in 1940 also known as the "Blitz"
   (C) the British troops that accompanied the American and Canadian forces into Normandy on D-Day
   (D) the arrival of the British rock band The Beatles on the American scene, followed soon after by the Rolling Stones, the Who, and others, ushering in a new era in popular music
   (E) the British counterattack following the "Blitz" on targets in the west of Germany"

12. Picasso painted his famous "Guernica" to commemorate

   (A) the Spain he remembered from his youth before it was divided by the Spanish Civil War
   (B) the glory of the Basque country's marketplaces and people
   (C) the time he spent with his surrealist friends in France, and included a symbol of a minotaur in "Guernica" as a remembrance
   (D) the Nationalists' victory in the Spanish Civil War
   (E) when Germany and Italy bombed a marketplace during the Spanish Civil War, killing hundreds of innocent civilians out shopping

13. The movement in film known as the French New Wave was characterized by

   (A) a rejection of all things American—stars, glamour, high style, linear narrative, happy endings
   (B) homages to Hollywood narrative while deconstructing Hollywood visual style and storytelling
   (C) a re-envisioning of what it means to be French in the postwar era, but without resorting to discourses on politics or social conditions
   (D) a focus on all things French—French stars, French composers, French locales, French traditional family values
   (E) a total rejection of all narrative cinema

14. Postmodernism in European philosophy can be described as

   (A) an attempt to reconstruct the philosophies that the 1968 uprisings had deconstructed
   (B) a handy way to describe the philosophies that came after everything that had been considered "modern," such as existentialism, structuralism, and deconstructionism
   (C) a series of rhetorical strategies that seek to subvert, question, undermine, and destabilize many of the concepts philosophers have spent years, or centuries, taking for granted
   (D) a meaningless term that has been used as a "catch-all" phrase for post-1968 thought
   (E) a socially constructed system in which Western thought has been subverted into nihilism

15. Britain first started broadcasting television

   (A) when the BBC was created in 1922
   (B) in 1955, with the introduction of the ITV network
   (C) when the BBC created its motto, "Nation shall speak peace unto nation"
   (D) in 1936, as a public service with no advertising, since very few people owned a television, although broadcasting was halted during the war years and resumed in 1946
   (E) in 1928, when America started broadcasting from its first mechanical television

16. Werner Heisenberg's Uncertainty Principle in quantum mechanics holds that

   (A) we cannot determine the exact relationships between pairs of variables simultaneously—for example, position and momentum—with any kind of precision
   (B) if we observe the world, we inevitably disturb it in some way, shape, or form
   (C) we cannot be certain of what the next minute will hold for us because no one is a mind reader and can predict the future
   (D) the world is made up of matter that sometimes acts like waves and sometimes acts like particles so you can never be certain whether matter will be acting like waves or particles at a given moment
   (E) we do not really know whether the world is made up of waves or made up of particles so we cannot really be certain of anything without centuries more of research

17. The Mod movement in London in the 1960s

   (A) emphasized health foods, vegetarianism, and all things natural
   (B) lasted into the 1970s, encompassing nearly half a generation of teenagers and young adults
   (C) had very strong gender roles codes—men were very masculine and women were very feminine
   (D) was strongly tied to modernist art, architecture, and design trends
   (E) focused on music and fashion

18. In his Surrealist Manifesto, André Breton defined the eponymous movement as

   (A) completely rooted in waking reality, as opposed to those who those who wanted to create dreamlike worlds
   (B) making connections between ideas that were wholly logical and comprehensible
   (C) taking psychic mechanisms and making them rational and comprehensible to the average viewer
   (D) psychic automatism in its pure state, by which one proposes to express the actual functioning of thought
   (E) finding the psychological disorder in order

19. Thomas Mann's *The Magic Mountain*, Erich Maria Remarque's *All Quiet on the Western Front*, and T. S. Eliot's *The Waste Land* all sent what message about European society in the post–World War I era?

   (A) That Europeans had been to the abyss but were now seeing the joy and magic in life
   (B) That the once civilized world had become overrun with insanity and death
   (C) That the only hope for humankind was in a utopian society of some kind, away from the barbarians who make war
   (D) That the life Europeans had once known was dead, but the new world, which was changing and growing and evolving all the time, offered tremendous hope for the future
   (E) That the answer to society's devastation lies in the creation of great art and poetry

20. The Italian Fascist state differed from the German Fascist state in that

   (A) Italy did not have a charismatic focal leader and Germany did
   (B) Mussolini spent more time making sure all domestic organizations ran like clockwork, whereas Hitler was more concerned with the policing of the country
   (C) Mussolini did not achieve the total revolution and revamping of Italian society many of his followers wanted and instead worked to make peace with already-established groups in Italy, whereas Hitler opted for total racial and national purity in all affairs with no negotiation
   (D) Italy's Fascist party had purged far more enemies of the state than Germany's Fascist party
   (E) Mussolini was much more effective at using the propaganda machine than Hitler was, particularly in the early years, so he was able to build up tremendous support and affection, although Hitler did quickly catch up

21. Which of the following was NOT a reason for the rise of propaganda in World War I?

    (A) The manipulation of public opinion
    (B) The shielding of the public from the full horrors of the war
    (C) The boosting of morale at home and on the frontlines
    (D) The boosting of sagging interest in purchasing new consumer goods during wartime
    (E) Mainting public support for the war

22. Menshevism differed from Bolshevism in all of the following ways EXCEPT

    (A) Menshevism literally means "minority" while Bolshevism literally means "majority"
    (B) the Mensheviks wanted more people involved in party control while the Bolsheviks felt that a smaller elite should control the central party
    (C) Menshevism advocated for cooperation with liberals and other groups while the Bolsheviks thought the way to deal with those who thought differently was to purge them from the party
    (D) Mensheviks believed in a more metaphorical interpretation of Marx, taking only what they needed, while the Bolsheviks believed completely in the literal interpretation of Marxist teachings
    (E) the Mensheviks saw room for reconciliation while the Bolsheviks believed that there could be no compromise in class struggle

23. Aldous Huxley's *Brave New World* and George Orwell's *1984*

    (A) provide the clearest view yet of how modern society is evolving
    (B) present examples of how new technology can be both used and misused
    (C) both show societies that are quite humane overall
    (D) imagine worlds of dictatorships, propaganda, misinformation, war, and the hypnotizing of a passive populace that the authors thought could actually happen in some form in the future if we were not careful
    (E) demonstrate the importance of structure and order in society over anarchy

24. Expressionism in art and film

    (A) arose primarily in Germany and Austria in the early twentieth century, featuring extreme subjective emotions and often displaying harsh, and sometime distorted or contorted, inner truths
    (B) humanized its subjects in profound ways, as it looked for truth and reality
    (C) searched for the objective experience of early twentieth-century reality in postwar Europe
    (D) tried to understand the pain of its subjects but in a way that would make it easier for viewers to grasp without having to experience too much pain themselves
    (E) used either vivid colors, or stark black and whites to show the contrasts between the world of the Impressionists and the new postwar world

25. Freud's *Civilization and its Discontents*

(A) is where Freud, who is by this time suffering from cancer and nearing his own demise, finds strength in religious belief for the first time

(B) says that the key to happiness is simply pursuit of the pleasure principle at all costs

(C) says that in spite of all the frustrations people have with the strictures of authority, love is enough to pull people through this neurosis

(D) is where Freud explains that the concepts of psychoanalysis parallel the development of human evolution

(E) demonstrated the inherent personality traits in humans that would forever doom them in the society

26. The literature of Franz Kafka

(A) was far more dystopian than any of the literature of later writers such as Orwell or Bradbury

(B) provided examples of the kind of unfathomable, unknowable mass bureaucracies created by nineteenth- and twentieth-century industrialization and growth and how impossible it is for a single individual to survive

(C) was rooted in his experiences as a high government official in Prague and the experiences he witnessed from his position of authority

(D) was inspired in part by stint in the armed forces during World War I

(E) was written more in the style of pulp fiction than the more literary style he has come to be known for

27. All of the following were innovations in the early years of the twentieth century EXCEPT

(A) Sigmund Freud's development of psychoanalysis

(B) Marie Curie's discovery of radium

(C) Max Planck's discovery of quantum physics

(D) Charles Darwin's *The Descent of Man*

(E) Henry Ford's Model T automobile

28. Which of the following statements is FALSE about the 1918 flu pandemic?

(A) More U.S. service members fighting in World War I died from the flu in 1918 than from war injuries.

(B) Even previously healthy and non-immuno-compromised people fell victim to the flu.

(C) The second wave of the illness was much deadlier than the first.

(D) Although it was called a "pandemic," the epidemic did not actually reach U.S. soil, confining itself to Europe, Asia, and North Africa, where the fighting was.

(E) What made the virus so deadly was that it would invade the afflicted's lungs, causing pneumonia.

29. Among the major changes in the Catholic Church decided at the Second Vatican Council that met in 1962 to 1965 was

(A) the decision to allow some women to use birth control in life-or-death situations only
(B) the decision to share the Church's wealth with the poor people of the world
(C) the shift from chanting the mass in Latin to chanting it in Italian in Vatican City
(D) the absolution of the Jewish people for the murder of Jesus
(E) the relaxation of its centuries-old condemnations of scientists

30. Science fiction and monster films were very popular during the Cold War era because

(A) after the Second World War, escapist entertainment was highly desirable
(B) the pain and reality of World War II made the idea of exploring worlds of the future a major theme of both business and entertainment activities
(C) the post–World War II beginnings of space explorations brought the ideas of science fiction and the possibilities of monsters "out there" into the zeitgeist so it would be natural for these themes to appear in popular culture
(D) the movies reflected the themes of the fear of invasion of an alien force who threatened to destroy the very fabric of "normal" existence
(E) the appearance of the atomic bomb made the Earth a scarier place to be

31. Which of the following is FALSE about the advances in women's rights and the feminist movements in Europe?

(A) It took until 1977 before French women no longer needed their husbands' permission to work.
(B) Although British women won the right to vote in 1918, it was not until 1944–1948 that the same rights were granted to women in France, Italy, Belgium, and Portugal.
(C) The French government created a Ministry for the Status of Women.
(D) It wasn't until the period of glasnost and perestroika that women in the Eastern bloc and Soviet countries were able to achieve a more equal status with men.
(E) Women in Scandinavian countries fared better in reaching a more equal status than did their counterparts in Southern Europe because of the entrenchment of traditional biases there.

32. "The Troubles" refers to

(A) when Scottish and English settlers first arrived in Ulster hundreds of years ago, setting the scene
(B) the thirty-plus years of sectarian strife in Northern Ireland between the Catholic Irish nationalists and the Loyalist Protestant paramilitaries
(C) the establishment of the Irish Free State in 1922, which was independent but still part of the British Empire
(D) the 1985 Anglo-Irish Agreement, which was an attempt to establish some sort of peace agreement in Northern Ireland
(E) the violence that broke out at the 1968 Civil Rights march in Londonderry

33. Women's suffrage movements in Europe during the World War I period

(A) received a huge boost from the war effort in England as well as in Germany

(B) were rooted in the some of the new writings of psychoanalytic literature

(C) were loud and violent, in order to overshadow the clamor of the war

(D) resulted in immediate universal suffrage for all British women in 1918

(E) were purely about equal pay and power in government in Great Britain and about feminine identity in Germany

34. All of the following are examples of the Americanization of Europe EXCEPT

(A) the arrival of Coca-Cola in the European marketplace in the late 1940s.

(B) the appearance of new "American" words creeping into other languages, such as "le week-end" and "le snack-bar."

(C) the proliferation of large movie studios for filmmaking and cinemas to show these films.

(D) McDonalds' arrival in the 1970s to all the European capitals.

(E) the opening of Euro-Disney in the 1980s in France.

35. Bauhaus style

(A) originated in early twentieth century, featuring little ornamentation and a harmony between design and function

(B) used sharp angles and lots of contrasting colors

(C) was similar to Art Deco style in its elegance, but with cleaner lines and shapes

(D) was a style that clashed against the mass production of art

(E) was more influenced by earlier classical styles than it was by modernism

36. While working in a Swiss patent office, which European physicist came to recognize the insufficiencies of current Newtonian mechanics and worked to overcome the deficiencies in dealing with the relation of space-time continuum?

(A) Werner Heisenberg

(B) Max Planck

(C) Niels Bohr

(D) Albert Einstein

(E) Erwin Schrödinger

37   The importance of the 1929 Alfred Hitchcock film "Blackmail" is

(A)   that it is one of the earliest known works by a major British film director who later became famous for his films in the United States.
(B)   that he made the film with an all-British cast.
(C)   that it was the first successful all-European-made talking picture.
(D)   that the film's climactic scene takes place in the British Museum.
(E)   that it made a significant amount of money for the British Film industry, which desperately needed an influx of cash to help it compete with all the movies coming from Hollywood.

38.   Which of the following statements is TRUE about the Space Race?

(A)   Even though the United States reached the Moon before the Soviets, most people had stopped caring about the space race by that point, having watched so many failed missions in the past.
(B)   Soon after Neil Armstrong and his crew landed on the Moon in 1969, the Soviets put astronauts on the Moon's surface as well.
(C)   All attempts to operate joint United States–Soviet space missions failed miserably due to both language and political obstacles.
(D)   The Soviet Union's successful launch of Sputnik, following its development of an intercontinental ballistic missile, heightened the already inflated tensions of the Cold War.
(E)   The United States was less invested in the Space Race than the Soviets were because the United States knew the Soviets still did not have the technology for an atomic or hydrogen bomb.

39.   The primary significance of the 1972 Munich Olympics was that

(A)   German organizers had worked tirelessly to rid the world of the memory of the previous time the country hosted the Olympic games—during the Nazi era
(B)   German organizers did not take sufficient security measures to protect against all possible attacks
(C)   eleven Israeli athletes and a German police officer lost their lives after being held hostage by Palestinian terrorists
(D)   Olympic competition was suspended for the first time in the history of the games
(E)   Mark Spitz, the American swimmer, won seven gold medals in competitions, a new world record, before the games were suspended

40.   Dolly the Sheep was

(A)   the experimental animal used to test vaccinations for mad cow disease in England
(B)   the first successful example of a mammal cloned from an adult somatic cell
(C)   the mascot for the women suffragists in Britain in the early 1900s and 1910s
(D)   the first mammal recipient of a heart transplant
(E)   the mammal who provided the cells for the first successful mammal cloning experiments in Scotland

Free-Response Questions

41. Salvador Dalí wrote, "Surrealism is destructive, but it destroys only what it considers to be shackles limiting our vision." Without using surrealism, use at least two examples to describe the ways that movements in art, music, theater, film, writing, or philosophy in the early twentieth century sought to "destroy the shackles" and enlarge the vision of the society.

_____

_____

_____

_____

_____

_____

_____

_____

_____

_____

_____

_____

_____

_____

_____

_____

_____

_____

_____

_____

_____

_____

_____

_____

_____

_____

_____

_____

_____

_____

42. John Lennon wrote, "The thing the sixties did was to show us the possibilities and the responsibility that we all had. It wasn't the answer. It just gave us a glimpse of the possibility." Using at least two examples from post–World War II cultural and intellectual history, explain whether you agree or disagree with this statement.

_____

_____

_____

_____

_____

_____

_____

_____

_____

_____

_____

_____

_____

_____

_____

_____

_____

_____

_____

_____

_____

_____

_____

_____

_____

Chapter 19
1900–Present: Cultural and Intellectual Answers and Explanations

ANSWER KEY

1.	C	21.	D
2.	B	22.	D
3.	D	23.	D
4.	B	24.	A
5.	D	25.	E
6.	B	26.	B
7.	C	27.	D
8.	B	28.	D
9.	D	29.	D
10.	D	30.	D
11.	D	31.	D
12.	E	32.	B
13.	B	33.	A
14.	C	34.	C
15.	D	35.	A
16.	A	36.	D
17.	E	37.	C
18.	D	38.	D
19.	B	39.	C
20.	C	40.	B

ANSWERS AND EXPLANATIONS

1. **C** In 1929, Mussolini signed the Lateran Pact with the papacy. This was the first time in history that the papacy had officially recognized the Italian state. In addition, the pact made Vatican City fully independent of Italian rule and the Pope was declared officially "neutral" in all matters of international relations and conflicts unless all parties involved asked for papal mediation. The treaty also resolved long-standing territorial and financial issues between the two parties in order to guarantee their mutual independence.

2. **B** Simone De Beauvoir's *The Second Sex* details the long political and social history of how women have been unjustly subjugated to male authority. She traces the myths society and religion—dominated by patriarchal authority—have created about women in order to maintain their power. She dreams of the day of liberation, not unlike a women's version of the Bolshevik Revolution, when men and women can co-exist as equals, as she states that there are no biological, psychological, intellectual, or spiritual impediments to such a co-existence—only the tales created by the dominant patriarchy.

3. **D** Existentialism, as described by philosophers such as Heidegger and Sartre, examined the nature of Being itself—what does it mean to exist, and thus, what does it mean to cease to exist? Thus, how the knowledge of the certainty of death shapes our life and choices we make was of primary concern. Phenomenology, as described by philosophers such as Husserl, looked at the nature of pure experience. The Frankfurt School, as espoused by philosophers such as Adorno and Habermas, combined such disparate elements as existentialism, Marxism, and intersubjectivity, to understand and critique social development. Deconstructionism, as described by Derrida, sought to find meaning by taking things apart and finding its essential components. Postmodernism is a late twentieth-century philosophical movement, closely associated with people such as Baudrillard, Lyotard, and Jameson, all of whom have questioned what is really "real" in our society of images.

4. **B** The year 1968 saw students mobilize throughout Europe, demanding changes in educational and governmental institutions. However, these uprisings, while pervasive in France, Germany, multiple Italian cities, and even in Prague, despite its Communist government, did not stretch all the way to London's Trafalgar Square. England's youth had already been expressing dissatisfaction with the status quo with the rise of rock music and the Mods and Rockers movements. However, these movements were more cultural than political.

5. **D** The "guest worker" program, which began in the 1960s, was a way for foreigners to come to European countries and provide these countries with cheap labor as Europe's economies were growing as was the need for a larger workforce. While some guest workers worked at skilled jobs, most did unskilled work. What has happened, however, is that many of the guest workers stayed on without applying for citizenship or assimilating into the local culture, creating problems throughout Europe over immigration and citizenship.

6. **B** The rise of European, as well as American, secular humanism was based on the larger idea that belief in a Higher Being was not necessary for living a moral, fulfilled, reasonable life. The first Humanist Manifesto, written and signed in the United States in 1933, speaks of humanism as a religious movement to replace deity-based systems. Later manifestos, however, influenced by World War II and other world events, spoke more philosophically and academically. The Amsterdam Declaration of 2000 outlines principles for the international humanist groups, stressing the importance of ethical, rational action, personal freedom, social responsibility, and human rights, without the dogma of religion.

7. **C** Following the devastation of the world wars, a new ecumenical movement began in Europe to try to create more dialogue between leaders of the diverse branches of Protestantism, as well as with those of the Roman Catholic and Eastern Orthodox Churches. In 1948, the World Council of Churches first met in Amsterdam. The focus of these movements was to try not only to find where the different branches of the religions had commonalities, but also simply to find ways to help people in the wake of the war and postwar destruction.

8. **B** The establishment of a Jewish homeland in the state of Israel did not cut down the amount of anti-Semitism in Europe. Anti-Semitism after the birth of the state of Israel became mired in Israeli-Arab conflicts in the Middle East and question of a Palestinian state. In addition, anti-Semitism in the Soviet Union and Eastern bloc countries also thrived during the Cold War. Fundamentalist groups, from extreme Muslim fundamentalists to Neo-Nazis have also been implicated in various attacks on synagogues and other anti-Semitic acts of violence.

9. **D** Atonal music, as exemplified by such composers as Berg, Schoenberg, and Prokofiev, is music that does not focus on a central key, as in F major. Thus, it is said to lack a tonal center. As a result, it lacks the harmonies and familiar combinations of pitches normally associated with classical music. Some atonal compositions used a twelve-tone technique, in which all twelve notes in the chromatic scales are used as equally as possible, so no one tone becomes the focus. While the Second Viennese School, which included Schoenberg, did compose atonal compositions, there is no direct relation between the music and political and social situation.

10. **D** Among the tremendous amount of bloodshed in violence in Northern Ireland, one incident memorialized in song by the rock band U2 was an incident in January 1972. During a civil rights demonstration in the town of Londonderry in the northwest section of Northern Ireland, thirteen civilians wound up dead, shot by British soldiers. The Omagh bombing was a 1998 event by an Irish Republican Army splinter group who planted a car bomb that killed 29 people. In 1988, British soldiers killed three IRA members in Gibraltar in what was called "Operation Flavius." During the funeral for the three IRA soldiers, a member of the Ulster Defence Association hurled grenades at mourners and fired pistols. There was no specific firebombing on the London tube, but the passengers on the London tube were on constant guard for bomb threats during those years.

11. **D** The "British Invasion" refers to the arrival in America of the Beatles and other British rock bands that followed in their wake, ushering in a new era of popular music and popular culture throughout the world. Beatlemania fully took hold when the Beatles appeared on American television on "The Ed Sullivan Show" in February 1964 in front of 73 million viewers, many of whom were not teenagers or young adults. In music, British bands went on to dominate the Billboard charts for much of the mid-1960s, with the Beatles leading the way until their much publicized breakup in 1970.

12. **E** "Guernica," Picasso's 1937 painting, reflects the artist's horror over the bombing of the marketplace in the city of Guernica by German and Italian planes. The attack killed hundreds of civilians as it was Market Day. Guernica, a village in the Basque country in Northern Spain, was not a military target and the strategy was said to be merely to instill fear amongst those still supporting the republic against Franco and the nationalists.

13. **B** The French New Wave "began" in the late 1950s with the debut films by Francois Truffaut and Jean-Luc Godard, both former film critics at the influential French film magazine Cahiers du Cinema. Their films were, in their own individual ways, homages to traditional Hollywood narrative cinema, while simultaneously new and inventive in terms of their visual style. Both experimented with editing, including discontinuous jump cuts and long takes, as well as trying out different camera techniques, including hand-held cameras, and using different film stocks and exposures to change the lighting effects.

14. **C** Postmodernism, although not a single, cohesive philosophical viewpoint, came to be the umbrella term that represented many of the philosophies that sought to question and destabilize all that we take for granted in modern society as "real." Some academics include under this rubric deconstructionism, structuralism, and post-structuralism, thus combining most of the major philosophical movements of the past fifty years. While some theorists link these schools to the 1968 uprisings, there is no direct causal link between those rebellions and the development of these philosophies. However, both the uprisings and philosophies show that present in cultural zeitgeist was a need to question and deconstruct the basic societal structures—to look beyond appearances to search for the essential truths no matter how buried, disguised, destabilizing, or threatening they may be to the political or social order.

15. **D** Britain started broadcasting television in 1936 through its national station, the BBC, as a public service, free of advertising, eight years after the United States sent out its first television signals. BBC Television did not broadcast during World War II but resumed service after the war in June 1946. The BBC itself was created in 1922, and introduced its motto, "Nation shall speak peace unto nation," in 1927. ITV, Britain's first independent station, began broadcasting in 1955.

16.   **A**   Heisenberg's Uncertainty Principle, among the more famous physics principles known in the lay community, states that there are limits to which we can know for sure the simultaneous measurements of certain pairs of variables, such as position and momentum. The Uncertainty Principle has often been confused with the Observer Effect, which states that by observing something or someone, you necessarily change or influence the event. Mathematically, this means that the results of an experiment will be different when the event is observed from when the event is not observed.

17.   **E**   The Mod movement—short for modern—in Britain in the 1960s centered primarily on music and fashion. Mod bands, such as the Who and the Rolling Stones, incorporated American rhythm and blues styles in their music. Mod fashion featured miniskirts and Mary Quant makeup for women and zoot suits for men. Mod kids often rode around on Vespas and prided themselves on a certain androgynous look, with pixie haircuts quite fashionable for women. As a group, Mods were not concerned with larger trends in art or culture, or health foods, and the movement itself died out by the end of the 1960s. Mods also tended to clash with rival leather-clad youths known as Rockers, who often clashed violently and publicly with Mods.

18.   **D**   André Breton's definition of surrealism—psychic automatism in its pure state—describes surrealism's attempts to create dreamlike worlds with all their seeming incongruities and allow the viewer to find his or her own meanings. Surrealism in art and film tries to make the unconscious conscious, and simply see what emerges in that process. A feeling of being watched may be represented by eyes painted on the walls, or a dripping watch may symbolize time slowing down.

19.   **B**   Thomas Mann's *The Magic Mountain*, written before and after World War I, is set around a sanatorium. Erich Maria Remarque's *All Quiet on the Western Front* is a post–World War I novel describing the stress and fatigue of German soldiers on the frontlines during the war, as Remarque had been. T. S. Eliot's *The Waste Land* begins with the famous line, "April is the cruelest month." All three describe worlds that had once been civilized and were now overrun with insanity and death. Experience has changed the characters—they will never be the same. As Eliot wrote, "I had not thought death had undone so many."

20.   **C**   While the differences between Italian and German fascism can and have comprised entire courses and books, one primary difference was Hitler's focus on total racial and ethnic purity in all affairs with no negotiation with any established institutions. Mussolini was willing to negotiate with the papacy, for example, (e.g., the Lateran Pact) and other established groups in Italian society and build from there. Hitler, however, wanted everyone complete in line with him. Mussolini's additional time in office made no real difference, nor did his level of charisma, as he did have some of his own. Mussolini was also not particularly interested either in domestic policy or propaganda as specific strategies for advancing the fascist state.

21.   **D**   The wartime propaganda machine was primarily concerned with supporting the troops as well as boosting morale on the home front. It was not until after the war was over that propaganda began to be used for such purposes as boosting interest in purchasing new consumer goods—a new concept in the early twentieth century—since that was what the countries needed in order to boost sagging economies following wartime booms.

22.   **D**   The Mensheviks, from the Russian word for "minority," formed when the Russian Social Democratic Labor Party split in 1903, with the Bolsheviks following Lenin. The Mensheviks believed in a much more literal interpretation of Karl Marx's principles, in that there had to be a progression of necessary stages in the process of the socialist revolution. They also believed in making their group open to all, rather than a select, elite few, and advocated for cooperation amongst all liberals, while the Bolsheviks wanted to keep their ranks smaller and purer, as they felt there was no room for compromise in class struggle.

23.   **D**   Huxley's *Brave New World* and Orwell's *1984* both describe "futuristic" worlds in which dictatorships, propaganda, misinformation, war, and the hypnotizing of a passive populace become the norm rather than the exception. In *Brave New World*, society is perfectly ordered—everyone has their caste, their rations of soma to keep them happy, and their recreational sex—that is, until they discover that there is another way of being. In *1984*, society is perpetually at war, and our hero, Winston Smith, works for the Ministry of Truth, since the truth constantly changes. Winston's job is to rewrite past newspaper articles to keep them in line with the current version of the "truth." Neither book was meant to show misuses of technology or structure over anarchy. Rather, both are cautionary tales of a future entirely possible.

24.   **A**   Expressionism in art and film arose primarily in Germany during the period of the first world war as well as the postwar period. Painters such as Max Beckmann and Otto Dix, and filmmakers such as F. W. Murnau, who made "Nosferatu, the Vampire," and Fritz Lang, who directed "Metropolis" portrayed their subjects in high contrast black and white or sharp colors, at distorted angles. The purpose was to display subjective emotions and to get to the often harsh inner truths of their subjects' realities. The expressionists were not looking particularly to humanize their subjects as much as they were trying to get at the essential emotions they were experiencing and explore the deeper, darker recesses of the human soul.

25.   **E**   Freud wrote *Civilization and its Discontents* in 1930, long after he had developed the theory of psychoanalysis and watched it evolve over years of practice. In *Civilization*, he saw that man's instinctual drives—his inherent personality—would doom him in the face of a society that was forcing him to conform to certain ways of being. It deals with some of the paradoxes of living. For example, we live in a civil society to protect ourselves from unhappiness—as one of our basic drives is for pleasure—but this civil society we have created for our protection is one of our greatest sources of unhappiness.

26. **B** The literature of Franz Kafka provided an example of the kind of unfathomable, unknowable mass bureaucracies created by nineteenth- and twentieth-century industrialization. Kafka, who trained as a lawyer, worked for a large insurance company in Prague and had had his share of experience witnessing the smallness of the individual against the system, and much of his literature reflected that. The adjective "Kafka-esque" arose from his writings and has come to describe things labyrinthine, nightmarishly complex, and unknowable.

27. **D** Charles Darwin's *The Descent of Man* was published in 1871, almost 30 years before the turn of the century when these other four innovations came about, although evolution was still very much part of the zeitgeist then as it continues to be to this day. Freud's development of psychoanalysis, Curie's discovery of radium, Planck's discovery of quantum physics, and Ford's Model T radically changed the world at the beginning of the twentieth century and provided a foundation in their respective fields that is arguably still relevant today.

28. **D** An estimated 30 million people or more worldwide died in the 1918 flu pandemic, with approximately one-fifth of the world's population infected with the virus. While theories as to where the flu originated vary from France to the Far East to Kansas, once the disease started spreading, especially among those in close quarters on the battlefields, it reached epidemic proportions quickly. And because of censorship, German, British, French, and American sources contained little coverage of the flu, leaving the bulk of the news to come from Spain, so the disease received the nickname "Spanish flu." However, the United States had just as many cases as European countries, as soldiers would return from the battlefields of Europe with the virus and spread the disease to those at home. Unusual about this strain was that many young healthy adults were infected and died from this strain, and the second wave of the illness proved even deadlier. Most deaths resulted from flu-related pneumonia.

29. **D** When the leaders of the Roman Catholic Church met for the Second Vatican Council from 1962 to 1965, they made a multitude of changes to the beliefs and practices of Catholicism. Among the major changes was to declare the Jewish people free of the responsibility for the death of Jesus Christ as well as to officially condemn anti-Semitism. In addition, they made other changes to practices in an effort to make the Church more accessible to laypeople, including allowing mass to be chanted in the vernacular, rather than in Latin.

30. **D** While the other answers may have a kernel of truth—following the pain of war, escapist entertainment or exploring fantasy worlds may have been desirable, science fiction and monster films became very popular in the 1950s because of their allegorical content. They represented a threat from outside—Soviets disguised as space creatures or blobs or "The Thing From Another World." Those who would try to face the creatures with compassion and understanding often faced ridicule and resistance, not to mention overwhelming opposition. The most popular solution was to send in the army, which inevitably proved useless against these creatures, as did atomic weaponry. One film famously ended with the line, "They're here already! You're next!"

31. **D**   Women's rights gradually improved throughout Europe in the twentieth century, although it was in the Soviet Union and the Eastern Bloc countries where these improvements became visible earliest. In the Soviet Union, for example, approximately 43 percent of the workforce in the 1950s were women. Women in these Eastern bloc countries had more equality earlier than their compatriots in western countries, with many opportunities to work at the same jobs as men. However, women in the workplace were still expected to go home and take care of their families and households as well in addition to their workplace responsibilities.

32. **B**   Although there has been a long history of conflict between England and Ireland, "The Troubles" refers specifically to a thirty-plus year period of sectarian strife in Northern Ireland between the Catholic Irish nationalists and the Loyalist Protestant paramilitaries. More than 3,600 have been killed during these years and countless more injured in these battles. The 1968 Civil Rights March in Londonderry is often cited as the starting point for "The Troubles." The Good Friday Agreement in 1998, which restored self-government to Northern Ireland, seems to have put an end to "The Troubles."

33. **A**   Because the war effort required many women on the home front to take over the work of men while the men were on the frontlines, the women's suffrage movement made great strides in Britain and Germany during the World War I period. The suffrage movements received no boosts from psychoanalytic literature, which concerned itself little with women's issues other than hysteria and penis envy. Some suffragettes were loud and could be violent, but suffragists in general were not. When British women received the right to vote in 1918, that right was not universal—it was only for women ages 30 and older who met minimum property requirements. The right to vote for all women did not come until 1928. There were also no real ideological differences between the British and German suffrage movements—both were simply about the right to vote.

34. **C**   Among the plethora of names credited with the birth of cinema are three Frenchmen—the Lumière Brothers and Georges Méliès. Méliès built the first large film studio in France and helped build the French film industry. Film production thrived as well in Germany, England, and even Japan prior to the Second World War, with no help from Hollywood although American films were exhibited throughout Europe, although the Axis powers banned them during the war in the occupied territories. After the war, film production resumed throughout Europe, with large studios in England, Germany, Italy, France, and Japan, among others. Smaller nations followed.

35. **A**   The school known as Bauhaus integrated crafts, design, and fine arts to create works of art featuring a harmony between design and function, and little ornamentation. The Bauhaus schools originated in Germany during the second decade of the twentieth century, with three actual physical locations—Weimar, Dessau, and Berlin. The original school was founded by Walter Gropius, an architect, with the intent of creating "total" works of art, in which all forms of art could be united, including architecture, graphic design, interior design, and typography.

36   D   Albert Einstein worked in a Swiss patent office while developing his theory of relativity in response to the deficiencies he found in the Newtonian view of the relationship between space and time. The other four, also all physicists, focused on the quantum world. Max Planck, a German physicist, developed the quantum theory itself. Niels Bohr, a Danish physicist, developed the Bohr model of atomic structure, describing the behavior and orbit of atoms, as well as the principle of complementarity—that atoms can sometimes behave like waves and sometimes like particles. Werner Heisenberg, also German, is best known for the Uncertainty Principle, which describes the limit to which we can know for sure certain pairs of variables, such as momentum and position. Erwin Schrödinger, an Austrian physicist, who also studied the quantum world and came up with results that often contradicted the Bohr/Copenhagen school, is best known for his thought experiment "Schrödinger's Cat," in which one must consider how a cat in a box could be dead and alive at the same time, akin to the idea of energy as simultaneously waves and particles.

37.   C   While the United States made news in 1927 with the film "The Jazz Singer," considered the first "talking picture," it took Europe much longer to successfully make a "talkie." A young British director named Alfred Hitchcock, who had made the film "The Lodger" in 1927, a film hailed by British critics, managed to achieve what no other director in Europe could—the first talkie—with his film "Blackmail" in 1929. The film, originally conceived as a silent, was remade with dialogue, although the first ten minutes are still without dialogue.

38.   D   The Soviet Union's successful launch of the first satellite, Sputnik, into space, following that country's development of an intercontinental ballistic missile, served to heighten already inflated tensions in the Cold War. While the United States eventually proved more successful in the Space Race, getting men into space and on the Moon first, to the joy and delight of millions of Americans watching the missions closely on television, those successes were less about beating Russians and more about simply what Americans could do as a superpower.

39.   C   Although all the answers to the above question are true to some extent, the 1972 Summer Olympics in Munich will always be known for the massacre in which eleven Israel athletes and a German police officer lost their lives after being held hostage by Palestinian terrorists. Members of the group Black September snuck into the Olympic Village in the early morning of September 5, 1972, the second week of the Games, ambushing sleeping members of the Israeli team. Two Israeli athletes were killed immediately in the initial battle with the terrorists, but the other nine were taken hostage and eventually killed. Terrorists had been demanding the release of 234 prisoners held in Israeli jails. Five of the eight terrorists were killed in the rescue attempt, and the other three captured. However, those three were released after a Lufthansa plane was hijacked in October 1972.

40.   B   Dolly the Sheep was the first successful example of a mammal cloned from an adult somatic cell. She was cloned at the Roslin Institute of the University of Edinburgh in 1996. She was the product of three mothers, one that provided the egg, another that provided the DNA, and a third that actually carried her to term. Dolly lived for seven years before dying of a progressive lung disease,

although sheep of her type normally live to about eleven or twelve years of age. After Dolly was cloned, scientists were able to clone horses and bulls, but the scientists who cloned Dolly said the technique used to clone her could not be used to clone humans. While England has had episode of mad cow disease, no animals have become famous in the process of testing potential vaccines. Similarly, no animals have become as famous as Dolly in the history of heart transplantation.

The Free-Response Essay Questions Explained

Question 41

41. Salvador Dalí wrote, "Surrealism is destructive, but it destroys only what it considers to be shackles limiting our vision." Without using surrealism, use at least two examples to describe the ways that movements in art, music, theater, film, writing, or philosophy in the early twentieth century sought to "destroy the shackles" and enlarge the vision of the society.

Essay Notes

Mentioning any two of these will get you a higher score:

In Art and Film:
- Expressionism
- Cubism
- Dadaism

In Philosophy:
- Phenomenology
- Existentialism

In Writing:
- Thomas Mann
- Erich Maria Remarque
- T. S. Eliot
- William Butler Yeats
- Members of the Algonquin roundtable

In Music:
- Stravinsky
- Berg
- Schoenberg
- Prokofiev

In Theater:
- Brecht

In Film:
- German expressionists

Question 42

42. John Lennon wrote, "The thing the sixties did was to show us the possibilities and the responsibility that we all had. It wasn't the answer. It just gave us a glimpse of the possibility." Using at least two examples from post–World War II cultural and intellectual history, explain whether you agree or disagree with this statement.

Essay Notes

Mentioning any two of these will get you a higher score:

Art:
- Pop Art
- Conceptual Art
- Digital Art

Philosophy:
- Deconstructionism
- Structuralism
- Postmodernism
- Feminism

Music:
- Rock
- Punk
- New Wave
- Hip Hop

Chapter 20
1900–Present: Social and Economic Questions

1900–PRESENT: SOCIAL AND ECONOMIC QUESTIONS

Multiple-Choice Questions

1. Archaeologist Sir Arthur Evans was instrumental in the excavation and study of which of the following early cultures?

   (A) Egyptians
   (B) Phoenicians
   (C) Minoans
   (D) Lydians
   (E) Spartans

2. Which of the following did NOT contribute to the rapid worldwide spread of the 1918 Spanish flu pandemic, which was responsible for over thirty million deaths?

   (A) It was the first time that Europeans had been exposed to a pandemic influenza virus.
   (B) Trench warfare resulted in close quarters of large populations of men aiding rapid spread.
   (C) Men returned from the war bringing the virus to unexposed populations.
   (D) Increases in transportation technology allowed for rapid transmission over great distances.
   (E) Limited knowledge about viruses and virus infections facilitated the spread of the disease.

3. All of the following played an important role in the start of the Russian Revolution in 1917 EXCEPT

   (A) nationwide food shortages
   (B) incompetence of leaders in the tsarist regime
   (C) significant losses in the war
   (D) lack of political allies
   (E) revolutionary groups

4. Which of the following nations was last to grant women's suffrage?

   (A) England
   (B) France
   (C) Germany
   (D) Ireland
   (E) Spain

5. The Treaty of Versailles signed in 1919 had a devastating effect on postwar Germany including all of the following EXCEPT

(A) payment of war reparations to the Allies
(B) dissolution of the German state
(C) territorial losses
(D) high inflation and economic meltdown
(E) disarmament

6. Which of the following ultimately triggered the downfall of the Weimar Republic?

(A) The rise and growing support for the National Socialist Workers' Party
(B) Financial instability of the Weimar state due to demand for costly war reparations
(C) Rise of political organizations loyal to Italian fascist leader Benito Mussolini
(D) The defeat of Germany during WWII
(E) The rise of Italian fascism in the republic

7. The Great Depression hit hardest in Germany and the United States. Which of the following best explains why Germany was particularly susceptible to the Great Depression?

(A) Germany was still paying war reparations from World War I.
(B) Germany's economic recovery was tied to credit from the United States.
(C) Germany had invested considerably in the American stock market.
(D) Germany was heavily dependent on the Gold Standard.
(E) Germany lacked an economic plan.

8. Which of the following accurately describes John Maynard Keynes's economic view regarding how best to deal with the depression?

(A) Governments should increase deficit spending temporarily providing people with jobs and money to spur growth in the private sector.
(B) Governments should rein in their spending and reduce their military costs in order to balance budgets.
(C) Governments should increase tariffs on foreign goods to protect domestic manufacturing.
(D) Governments should discontinue social support programs to redirect funds to the economy.
(E) Governments should start wars to spur war time production and manufacturing.

9. Approximately what percent of the German population was unemployed during the Great Depression?

(A) 5%
(B) 10%
(C) 35%
(D) 50%
(E) 90%

10. Which of the following groups was the chief target of Hitler's "Night of the Long Knives"?

(A) Jewish community
(B) The Nazis
(C) The Sturmabteilung (S.A.)
(D) The Roma community
(E) Homosexuals

11. Which of the following people primarily led the Bolshevik party?

(A) Vladimir Lenin
(B) Karl Marx
(C) Nicholas II
(D) Gregory Rasputin
(E) Leon Trotsky

12. The Treaty of Versailles was meant to

(A) settle territorial borders and establish financial reparations at the end of World War I
(B) settle territorial borders and establish financial reparations at the end of World War II
(C) settle territorial borders and establish financial reparations at the end of the Korean War
(D) establish the United Nations as a platform for resolving international disputes
(E) establish an international platform to prevent the proliferation of infectious diseases following the outbreak of the Spanish flu

13. The Marshall Plan was meant to

    (A) settle territorial borders at the end of World War I
    (B) establish war reparations at the end of World War II
    (C) help rebuild Europe at the end of World War I
    (D) help rebuild Europe at the end of World War II
    (E) none of the above

14. Which of the following effectively removed the Russians from World War I allowing them to focus on domestic issues related to the revolution?

    (A) Treaty of Versailles
    (B) Treaty of Brest-Litovsk
    (C) Execution of the Romanov family
    (D) High inflation and food shortages triggering unrest and desertion among the Russian military ranks
    (E) The German conquest of Moscow in 1917 leading to the fall of the Russian empire

15. Hitler's "Final Solution" targeted all of the following groups EXCEPT

    (A) Roma (Gypsies)
    (B) Homosexuals
    (C) Aryans
    (D) Jews
    (E) Jehovah's witnesses

16. Dr. Josef Mengele became known during World War II because of which of the following?

    (A) He helped run a French resistance movement in collaboration with the Catholic Church.
    (B) He made critical decisions on the fate of captured Jews at Auschwitz and ran brutal unscientific human experiments.
    (C) He formed the International Red Cross following the downfall of World War II.
    (D) He was instrumental in the German development of the V2 rocket and later helped the Americans in establishing their space program during the space race.
    (E) None of the above

17. To Germans, which of the following years is known as "Zero Hour"?

   (A) 1881
   (B) 1918
   (C) 1939
   (D) 1945
   (E) 1990

18. American President Roosevelt and British Prime Minister Churchill put forward the Atlantic Charter, which would trigger the establishment of which of the following after the war?

   (A) Monroe Doctrine
   (B) Marshall Plan
   (C) United Nations
   (D) NATO
   (E) OPEC

"There are now two great nations in the world, which starting from different points, seem to be advancing toward the same goal: the Russians and the Anglo-Americans... Each seems called by some secret design of Providence one day to hold in its hands the destines of half the world."

19. The quote above by Alexis de Tocqueville was written in 1835; however, it has often be quoted in reference to which of the following?

   (A) World War I
   (B) World War II
   (C) Cold War
   (D) Vietnam War
   (E) War in Afghanistan

"[Our policy is] to support free people who are resisting attempted subjugation by armed minorities or by outside pressures"

20. The quote above was made by which of the following in reference to the growing sphere of influence in Eastern Europe?

   (A) Winston Churchill
   (B) Joseph Stalin
   (C) Harry Truman
   (D) Franklin Roosevelt
   (E) George Marshall

"From Stettin in the Baltic to Trieste in the Adriatic, an iron curtain has descended across the Continent"

21. The quote above was made by which of the following in reference to the growing sphere of influence in Eastern Europe?

    (A) Winston Churchill
    (B) Joseph Stalin
    (C) Harry Truman
    (D) Franklin Roosevelt
    (E) George Marshall

22. Josip Tito was a revolutionary that led the Communists in a sociopolitical overthrow in which of the following nations?

    (A) Czechoslovakia
    (B) Hungary
    (C) Romania
    (D) Yugoslavia
    (E) Poland

23. Which of the following nations left Palestine in 1947 triggering the eventual formation of Israel and would lead to continuous war and resentment that we continue to see today?

    (A) Germany
    (B) France
    (C) United States
    (D) Great Britain
    (E) Russia

24. The European decolonization and independence of much of Africa occurred during which of the following time periods?

    (A) 1930s–1940s
    (B) 1940s–1950s
    (C) 1950s–1960s
    (D) 1960s–1970s
    (E) 1970s–1980s

25. Which of the following European nations was involved in the First Indochina War, which lasted from 1946 to 1954?

(A) France
(B) Russia
(C) Germany
(D) Great Britain
(E) United States

26. The Maastricht Treaty (1992) resulted in a major economic change in the global economy because it provided for

(A) the formation of independent states following the collapse of the Soviet Union.
(B) the unification of Germany with the collapse of the Berlin War.
(C) the formation of the North Atlantic Treaty Organization.
(D) the establishment of the euro as a common currency in Europe
(E) the formation of the European Economic Community (EEC)

27. The Treaty of Rome (1957) resulted in the formation of which of the following?

(A) European Union (EU)
(B) European Coal and Steel Community (ECSC)
(C) North Atlantic Treaty Organization (NATO)
(D) European Economic Community (EEC)
(E) Organization for European Economic Cooperation (OEEC)

28. All of the following nations are part of the European Union EXCEPT

(A) Germany
(B) Latvia
(C) Hungary
(D) Italy
(E) Turkey

29. The National Health Service (NHS) was instituted in the United Kingdom following the success of which of the following political parties in elections in 1945?

(A) Labour Party
(B) Conservative Party
(C) Liberal Party
(D) Unionist Party
(E) Green Party

30. Bloody Sunday refers to an engagement between civil rights marchers and military of which European nation in 1972?

(A) Ireland
(B) Italy
(C) Germany
(D) Great Britain
(E) France

31. Margaret Thatcher instituted major economic changes as Britain's first prime minister. Her policies held close to those of her political party, which was the

(A) Labour Party
(B) Conservative Party
(C) Liberal Party
(D) Unionist Party
(E) Green Party

32. The Berlin Airlift was necessary to get much-needed assistance and supplies to Berlin after which nation blockaded the city?

(A) France
(B) Great Britain
(C) United States
(D) Soviet Union
(E) Italy

33. Prior to the formation of the Berlin Wall, there was a large exodus of people across the two regions of Germany. Which direction did they primarily travel?

(A) North to South
(B) South to North
(C) East to West
(D) West to East
(E) There was equal movement in all directions.

34. Which of the following nations witnessed the most Jewish civilian deaths at the hands of the Nazis during the Holocaust?

(A) Germany
(B) Hungary
(C) Poland
(D) Russia
(E) Romania

"We welcome change and openness; for we believe that freedom and security go together, that the advance of human liberty can only strengthen the cause of world peace. There is one sign the Soviets can make that would be unmistakable, that would advance dramatically the cause of freedom and peace. General Secretary Gorbachev, if you seek peace, if you seek prosperity for the Soviet Union and Eastern Europe, if you seek liberalization, come here to this gate. Mr. Gorbachev, open this gate. Mr. Gorbachev, tear down this wall!"

35. Which of the following leaders made the speech above in front of the Brandenburg gate?

(A) John F. Kennedy
(B) Winston Churchill
(C) Ronald Reagan
(D) Helmut Kohl
(E) Margaret Thatcher

"Gas! GAS! Quick, boys! – An ecstasy of fumbling,
Fitting the clumsy helmets just in time;
But someone still was yelling out and stumbling,
And flound'ring like a man in fire or lime ...
Dim, through the misty panes and thick green light,
As under a green sea, I saw him drowning."

36. The poem above was written by Wilfred Owen describing the horrors of which of the following wars?

(A) World War I
(B) World War II
(C) Cold War
(D) Vietnam War
(E) War in Afghanistan

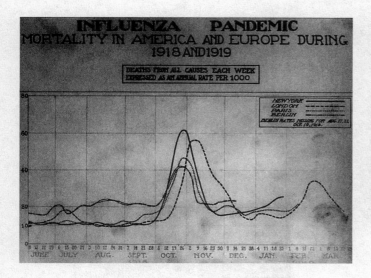

37. The image above depicts the amount of deaths each week due to the Spanish flu pandemic in America and Europe. How did the total mortality due to Spanish flu compare to the mortality associated with World War I?

   (A) There was approximately the same number of deaths during World War I as there were due to the Spanish flu pandemic.
   (B) World War I resulted in more deaths than the Spanish flu pandemic.
   (C) The Spanish flu pandemic resulted in more deaths than World War I.
   (D) Spanish flu was not the same as influenza and therefore it remains unknown what exactly was the cause of the pandemic.
   (E) It is unable to be determined, as accurate numbers of deaths from both the Spanish flu and World War I were not kept.

38. The image above depicts a wartime propaganda poster to recruit British troops during World War I. Which British leader is depicted?

   (A) Winston Churchill
   (B) Edward VII
   (C) George V
   (D) Edward VIII
   (E) Neville Chamberlain

The Allies — "Onward to Victory"

39. The image above is a British war propaganda poster released to generate nationalist pride during which of the following wars?

(A) Cold War
(B) World War I
(C) World War II
(D) Korean War
(E) Falklands War

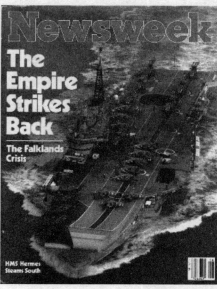

Newsweek, 1982

40. The magazine cover above references the Falklands War between Great Britain and what other nation?

(A) Brazil
(B) Argentina
(C) South Africa
(D) Namibia
(E) France

41. The image above depicts the Yalta conference (1945). All of the following are pictured in this image EXCEPT

(A) Charles de Gaulle
(B) Winston Churchill
(C) Franklin Roosevelt
(D) Joseph Stalin
(E) George Marshall

42. The image above depicts the public's disapproval at a mass demonstration in May 1919 in protest to the Treaty of Versailles. Where was this image taken?

(A) Paris
(B) London
(C) Rome
(D) Berlin
(E) Amsterdam

Whatever the weather
We must move
together

43. The image above depicts a poster generated to promote
the Marshall plan in Europe. All of the following nations
received financial assistance from the United States
EXCEPT

(A) West Germany
(B) Great Britain
(C) France
(D) Greece
(E) Russia

Free-Response Questions

44. Compare and contrast how fascism was able to take control over the peoples of Italy and Germany following World War I.

_____

_____

_____

_____

_____

_____

_____

_____

_____

_____

_____

_____

_____

_____

_____

_____

_____

_____

_____

_____

_____

_____

_____

_____

_____

_____

_____

45. The Spanish flu was one of the deadliest single events in human history resulting in over 500 million affected and at least 30 million deaths. Critically evaluate the following statement and provide evidence for your conclusion:

The high mortality of Spanish flu was due to perfect timing at the end of World War I.

_____

_____

_____

_____

_____

_____

_____

_____

_____

_____

_____

_____

_____

_____

_____

_____

_____

_____

_____

_____

_____

_____

_____

_____

_____

_____

Chapter 21
1900–Present:
Social and
Economic
Answers and
Explanations

ANSWER KEY

1.	C	23.	D
2.	A	24.	C
3.	D	25.	A
4.	B	26.	D
5.	B	27.	D
6.	A	28.	E
7.	B	29.	A
8.	A	30.	D
9.	C	31.	B
10.	C	32.	D
11.	A	33.	C
12.	A	34.	C
13.	D	35.	C
14.	B	36.	A
15.	C	37.	C
16.	B	38.	C
17.	D	39.	B
18.	C	40.	B
19.	C	41.	A
20.	C	42.	D
21.	A	43.	E
22.	D		

ANSWERS AND EXPLANATIONS

1. **C**   In 1900, Sir Arthur Evans rediscovered much of the Minoan culture on the island of Crete. His work shed new light on early civilizations and culture in the Mediterranean during the first millennium B.C.E.

2. **A**   Influenza had caused pandemics before, including the Russian flu pandemic of 1889–1890, which killed over a million people. However, the Spanish flu pandemic was significant for its increased incidence of mortality and rapid spread worldwide. Trench warfare (B), the end of the war (C), and increases in transportation technology (D) facilitated the reach and potency of the virus. Virology (E), or the study of viruses, was still in its infancy at the time of this outbreak.

3. **D**   Throughout the war (including after the abdication of the throne), Russia remained committed to the Triple Entente (allied with Great Britain and France). This played a major role in Russians remaining in the war (albeit only for a short time) despite a revolution on the homefront. By 1917, Russia faced nationwide food shortages (A), the promotion of many incompetent leaders within the tsarist regime (B), and significant losses to Germany in the war effort (C). These issues compounded with the economic collapse of the Russian state pushed the many revolutionary groups in the nation (E) towards the revolution.

4. **B**   The United Kingdom (which included Ireland at the time) and Germany provided women's suffrage at the conclusion of World War I (both in 1918). This was in large part due to the valuable contribution that women made at the home front during the war. Spain would provide suffrage in 1931. France would not provide suffrage until 1945.

5. **B**   Germany remained after the Treaty of Versailles; however, they were forced to make war reparations (A), they lost many of the territories that they had acquired over the last century (C), and faced years of high inflation and an economic meltdown in the 1920s. All of these factors led to the growth of the Nationalist Party (Nazis) in the late 1920s and eventual power of Adolf Hitler.

6. **A**   The rise and public support for the National Socialist Workers' Party (or Nazis) ultimately triggered the collapse of the Weimar Republic. The Nazis grew out of the publically supported views that the Treaty of Versailles was an offense to the national pride of the state and that the Germans lost the war only because a variety of hate groups which "stabbed them in the back" including Jews and Communists. Although in the early years of the Weimar Republic, Germany was in financial ruin, the Republic became much more financially stable in the late 1920s (B). The Weimar Republic had collapsed by the onset of WWII (D). Italian fascism did not have a major role in the collapse of the republic, though rising Nazism did.

7. B   To aid Germany in its postwar recovery, the United States loaned the nation large amounts of money tying the German economy directly to the U.S. economy. When the stock market crashed in the United States, the contraction of available credit made the German economy led to widespread job loss, a return to high inflation, and demand for change (which ultimately opened the door to fascism and the Nazis).

8. A   Keynes argued that governments should increase deficit spending thus providing jobs, public assistance, and most importantly getting money recalculating within the private sector.

9. C   During the Great Depression, approximately one-third of the available workforce was unemployed in Germany. This major struggle opened the door to fascism and the death of the republican institutions that had revitalized the state.

10. C   The S.A. were the Nazi political army which had allowed Hitler to gain power over Germany. However, Hitler viewed them as a threat to his absolute rule and had their leader Ernst Rohm and other leaders killed to reduce their influence and strength and gain control of the army. Hitler had not yet turned his efforts towards the Jewish (A), European Roma (D) communities, or homosexuals (E).

11. A   Vladimir Lenin was the leader of the Bolshevik party and engineered the fall of the Romanov monarchy in 1917. His party would ultimately gain control and implement what would later be called Leninism in Russia.

12. A   The Treaty of Versailles brought an end to World War I and demarcated the new boundaries and territories following the war. In addition, it outlined the war reparations that would be made by Germany and ultimately would tie American finances to the tattered economies of Europe.

13. D   Through the Marshall plan, the United States would make billions of dollars available to rebuild Europe following the war. Although only Western Europe accepted American assistance, it did have a stabilizing role in helping reestablish the Western European economies.

14. B   The newly formed Lenin government signed the Treaty of Brest-Litovsk with the Germans to remove Russia from the war and allow them to focus on domestic control and stability. Though the treaty was never enforced with the Germans losing the war, it would have provided Germany with immense territorial gains in Eastern Europe.

15. C   Hitler's "Final Solution" targeted all social and religious groups that he felt undermined the German state and were inferior to his "Aryan" race. Millions of people of the Roma (Gypsy), homosexual, Jewish, and Jehovah's Witnesses were executed by the Nazis during World War II. The hostility and brutality of this effort wasn't realized until the Allied forces began freeing the concentration camps throughout Nazi-controlled Europe.

16. B   Dr. Josef Mengele was a notorious Auschwitz physician that made decisions regarding selection for the gas chambers and performed brutal and sadistic human experiments with captured Jews. Following the war, he fled to Brazil to evade capture for war crimes.

17. **D** 1945 marked the darkest point in their history for most Germans. The country was in complete disarray, the Nazis had fallen, nearly every city in Germany lay in rubble and ruin, and the "Final Solution" was open and exposed to the international community. It would take many years for Germany to reestablish itself and rebuild following the war.

18. **C** In 1941, Roosevelt and Churchill discussed their vision following the war and signed a statement known as the Atlantic Charter which would create an international commission to oversee the problems of the world. This was later signed by the leaders of the Allied nations in 1942 and manifested itself as the United Nations in 1945.

19. **C** The Tocqueville quote has often been recited as having predicted the Cold War. Both Russia and the United States (Anglo-Americans as he referred to them) would ultimately seek to gain control politically and diplomatically over the world and found themselves at odds following the end of World War II.

20. **C** The quote was from Truman's speech to the American congress that "it is the policy of the United States to support free people who are resisting attempted subjugation by armed minorities or by outside pressures." This speech was directly aimed at the growing Soviet threat in Eastern Europe.

21. **A** Churchill's "Iron Curtain" speech delivered at Westminster College is arguably his most famous and described the extant of Soviet control over Eastern Europe. Churchill understood the threat of Soviet influence over Eastern Europe and spent many years trying to prevent continued Soviet expansion across Europe.

22. **D** Josip Tito was a Yugoslav revolutionary who led the Communists gaining control of Yugoslavia in 1946.

23. **D** The British left Palestine after an agreement could not be reached between the Arab and Jewish factions in the region. Ultimately, Israel would be formed in the vacancy left by the British and war ensued immediately by the Arabs who were seeking an Arab Palestinian state.

24. **C** Over 30 separate African nations gained independence from European nations during the 1950s and 1960s. In many of these nations, independence was achieved without any fighting.

25. **A** The French fought to remain in control of Indochina following the defeat and withdrawal of the Japanese in World War II. Primarily, the war was fought between the French and the Viet-Minh, the latter who were led by Ho Chi Minh. After a long-fought war, the Viet Minh eventually won and the region is split into several states including Northern and Southern states of Vietnam.

26. **D** The Maastrict Treaty (1992) led to the establishment of the euro as a common currency with coins and banknotes going into circulation in 2002. The euro changed the economic climate of the world and has become a major traded currency worldwide.

27. **D** The Treaty of Rome established the European Economic Commision (EEC), which would be a precursor to the European Union. The EEC lifted nearly all trade restriction between member states and the passing of the European Single Act in 1986 led to free movement of capital, labor, and services between member states.

28. **E** Turkey, despite many attempts to join the EU, has yet to be accepted due to concerns over economic targets and meeting necessary benchmarks for human rights.

29. **A** The Labour Party achieved a great victory in 1945, in part because they sought widespread reforms on the domestic front following the war. One of the most critical was an overhaul of the health system. They established a social welfare program highlighted by the establishment of the National Health Service (NHS), which remains active today.

30. **D** Social and political unrest in Northern Ireland resulted in the British moving troops into the province. On January 30, 1972, British soldiers fired on civil rights marchers killing thirteen in what became known as Bloody Sunday. This triggered increased violence and support for breakaway and anti-British occupation groups.

31. **B** Margaret Thatcher was the leader of the Conservative Party and pushed for many conservative economic changes including cuts to public spending, cutting taxes for the wealthy, and tighter control of the money supply to curb inflation.

32. **D** The Berlin Airlift provided resources and supplies to Berlin after the Soviet Union blockaded the city and prevented Westerners from entering. The airlift went on for nearly eleven months until Stalin lifted the blockade in 1949.

33. **C** Prior to the establishment of the Berlin wall, there was a major exodus of the educated elite from East Germany to West Germany. To prevent this emigration, the Soviets formed the Berlin Wall, which divided the city and largely the country into two.

34. **C** Approximately 3 million Polish Jews were executed by the Nazis during the Holocaust or approximately 40 to 50% of all Jews executed in total during the war. By the end of the war, 90% of Jews in Poland had been executed.

35. **C** Ronald Reagan declared that Gorbachev tear down the Berlin Wall at the Brandenburg Gate in 1987. This famous speech would go on to represent the eventual collapse of the Soviet Union and the fall of the Berlin Wall.

36. **A** Wilfred Owen's poem was written describing the horrors of chemical weapons during World War I. This excerpt is from his famous *Dulce et Decorum Est*.

37. **C** The Spanish flu pandemic was caused by a high mortality strain of influenza that spread worldwide. At least 30 million deaths are attributed to the pandemic, far more than the number of dead during World War I (the death toll was 17 million, with 10 million combatant and 7 million civilian casualties). Accurate numbers were accessible at this time (evidenced by this graph) and

Spanish flu or influenza was the primary source of this illness (there remains no ambiguity about the causative agent of this outbreak).

38. **C** King George V ruled the British kingdom throughout the war. He would not die until 1936.

39. **B** This is an example of a British World War I propaganda poster. Note the presence of Japan as an ally during the war. The British and Japanese would fight on opposite sides during World War II.

40. **B** In 1982, Great Britain went to war with Argentina over possession and control of the Falkland Islands. The British and Argentines have continued to lay claim to the islands today. However, the British colonized the islands and quickly won the war to maintain their governance of them.

41. **A** Charles de Gaulle, leader of the French resistance forces, did not attend the Yalta conference in 1945. The image shown depicts the leaders of Britain (Churchill, left), the United States (Roosevelt, center), and Russia (Stalin, right) along with military leaders of several countries including George Marshall (behind Churchill).

42. **D** This image was taken in 1919 in front of the Reichstag in Berlin, Germany following the signing of the Treaty of Versailles. The Treaty was particularly harsh towards the Germans, and the German public carried much resentment and anger regarding this Treaty with them into World War II.

43. **E** The Russians rejected the Marshall plan viewing it as an effort of the United States to control and expand their influence over other nations in Europe. West Germany, Great Britain, France, and Greece received financial assistance from the United States (their flags are also represented in the fan depicted).

The Free-Response Essay Questions Explained

Question 44

44. Compare and contrast how fascism was able to take control over the peoples of Italy and Germany following World War I.

Essay Notes

Fascism makes use of extreme nationalism to destroy the notion of the individual and enforce the concept of community. In your essay, there are many similarities and differences between the rise of fascism. In particular, note below how the people fell on hard times and how fascism (or nazism) picked them up.

Fascism in Italy:

- Following World War I, Italy underwent a political transformation whereby parties would be given seats in legislature based on percentages of the national vote. This encouraged political parties to grow and attempt to seize as many votes as possible.

- Around the same time there were many factory occupations, which triggered unrest in the people, and many viewed democracy as the cause of problems. This opened the door to other social and political movements.
- Mussolini formed the National Fascist Party and quickly formed paramilitary squads (called Black-shirts) to enforce his party's policy and collect money for their political aspirations. By 1921, the Fascists had started to fill seats in Italian parliament.
- In 1922, Mussolini forced King Victor Emmanuel III to provide him and his officers with seats of power. Instead of using military force to put down the Fascists, the King made Mussolini the Prime Minister. Within a few years, Italy was completely under Mussolini's power.

Fascism in Germany:

- The Germans were very angry with the Treaty of Versailles, as it was brutal on the state following the war. As a result of the war and the war reparations, Germany sank into a deep depression.
- The National Socialist Party (originally named the German Workers' Party) formed after World War I and were a small extremist group. Hitler, an unknown member of the party at the time, attempted to stage a revolt in Germany referred to as the Beer Hall Putsch. However, this was largely unsuccessful and he was imprisoned for the effort where he wrote his famous *Mein Kampf*.
- The Nazis (as they came to be called) refocused their efforts on addressing the concerns of the people at the time when unemployment and inflation was high and sentiment towards the Western nations was at a low. They advocated for social reform and development of jobs and were able to slowly gain control within the Weimar Republic.
- Similar to the Italian Fascist, they also used enforcement groups to fight for their power and control.
- However, in contrast, the Nazis also deflected blame for economic woes on disliked groups such as the Jews, Communists, and opposing socialist groups. They also used propaganda to boost their own nationalist pride in being German.
- By 1933, the Nazi leader Adolf Hitler had become chancellor of Germany and used his power to destroy opposing factions and gain complete control.

Question 45

45. The Spanish flu was one of the deadliest single events in human history resulting in over 500 million affected and at least 30 million deaths. Critically evaluate the following statement and provide evidence for your conclusion:

The high mortality of Spanish flu was due to perfect timing at the end of World War I.

Essay Notes

This essay asks you to "critically evaluate" the statement. Therefore, you must assess whether or not you agree with the statement and provide evidence in support AND against the statement, before coming to a final conclusion.

Evidence in Support:

- Spanish flu emerged in 1918 at the end of World War I.
- The close proximity of troops in the bunkers and trenches made for rapid transmission or spread of the virus from person to person.
- The war brought people from many different parts of the globe to one place; thus the influenza virus was likely able to infect a contingent of several different countries before they returned to their respective countries.

- The rapid movement of troops and supplies during and immediately after the war resulted in efficient travel of the virus over long distances.

Evidence Against Support:

- The origin of the virus remains unknown and its name "Spanish flu" refers to the spread of the disease to Spain, a country that had not seen much (if any) fighting during the war.
- This was not the first influenza pandemic, though it did result in a higher than usual amount of deaths.
- The disease symptoms were far more severe than previous viruses and thus the mortality rate was likely due to a more virulent virus rather than increased spread (due to the war effort).
- Independent of the war effort, advances in transportation technology helped the virus spread all throughout the globe, including parts that had no connection to the war.

Part V
Practice Test

Chapter 22
AP European
History
Practice Test

AP® European History Exam

SECTION I: Multiple-Choice Questions

DO NOT OPEN THIS BOOKLET UNTIL YOU ARE TOLD TO DO SO.

At a Glance

Total Time
55 minutes
Number of Questions
80
Percent of Total Grade
50%
Writing Instrument
Pencil required

Instructions

Section I of this examination contains 80 multiple-choice questions. Fill in only the ovals for numbers 1 through 80 on your answer sheet.

Indicate all of your answers to the multiple-choice questions on the answer sheet. No credit will be given for anything written in this exam booklet, but you may use the booklet for notes or scratch work. After you have decided which of the suggested answers is best, completely fill in the corresponding oval on the answer sheet. Give only one answer to each question. If you change an answer, be sure that the previous mark is erased completely. Here is a sample question and answer.

Sample Question   Sample Answer

Chicago is a   Ⓐ ● Ⓒ Ⓓ Ⓔ
(A) state
(B) city
(C) country
(D) continent
(E) village

Use your time effectively, working as quickly as you can without losing accuracy. Do not spend too much time on any one question. Go on to other questions and come back to the ones you have not answered if you have time. It is not expected that everyone will know the answers to all the multiple-choice questions.

About Guessing

Many candidates wonder whether or not to guess the answers to questions about which they are not certain. Multiple-choice scores are based on the number of questions answered correctly. Points are not deducted for incorrect answers, and no points are awarded for unanswered questions. Because points are not deducted for incorrect answer, you are encouraged to answer all multiple-choice questions. On any questions you do not know the answer to, you should eliminate as many choices as you can, and then select the best answer among the remaining choices.

THIS PAGE INTENTIONALLY LEFT BLANK.

EUROPEAN HISTORY

SECTION I, Part A

Time—55 Minutes

80 Multiple-Choice Questions

<u>Directions:</u> Each of the questions or incomplete statements below is followed by five suggested answers or completions. Select the one that is best in each case, and then fill in the corresponding oval on the answer sheet.

1. Humanism consisted of all of the following aspects EXCEPT

(A) admiration and emulation of the Ancient Greeks and Romans
(B) philosophy of enjoying this life, instead of just waiting for the next one
(C) the glorification of humans and the belief that individuals can do anything
(D) the desire to prove the superiority of Catholic dogma
(E) the belief that humans deserved to be the center of attention

2. In 1500, the papal states were most concerned about a French invasion of the Italian peninsula for which of the following reasons?

(A) The French king was not Catholic.
(B) The pope didn't have the troops to adequately defend Rome against the French army.
(C) Other Italian city-states might decimate their armies fighting the French.
(D) The English would renounce the Catholic Church.
(E) The pope was afraid it would affect his power over the French cardinals.

3. Which of the following documents is most closely associated with the Protestant Reformation?

(A) Declaration of the Rights of Women
(B) The Treaty of Villafranca
(C) The Augsburg Confession
(D) The Pragmatic Sanction
(E) The Maastricht Treaty

4. The War of the Roses resulted in

(A) the establishment and strengthening of the Tudor Dynasty
(B) the strengthening of the English nobility
(C) the enclosure movement
(D) the first agricultural allotments in English history
(E) overwhelming support for the noble class from the peasantry

5. The fact that nineteenth-century English workers experienced rising income without damaging national productivity disproved

(A) Napoleon's Continental System
(B) the Reform Bill of 1832
(C) the Midlothian Campaign
(D) the Treaty of Paris
(E) Ricardo's Iron Law of Wages

6. In the nineteenth century, the new theory of germs influenced the work of all of the following thinkers and scientists EXCEPT

(A) Louis Pasteur
(B) Robert Koch
(C) Joseph Lister
(D) Sigmund Freud
(E) Edwin Chadwick

7. Which of the following thinkers did NOT contribute to evolutionary theory?

(A) Jeremy Bentham
(B) Charles Lyell
(C) Jean Baptiste Lamarck
(D) Charles Darwin
(E) Herbert Spencer

GO ON TO THE NEXT PAGE.

8. The most important reason that Russia waged the Crimean War in 1853 was for the purpose of

   (A) protecting the Orthodox Christians under Ottoman rule

   (B) gaining a foothold on the Mediterranean Sea, which would help it become a power on the European stage

   (C) securing the wheat fields of the Ukraine for its people

   (D) demonstrating its tough stance on crime

   (E) putting its prisoner population to work

9. The person most responsible for creating and maintaining the Triple Alliance was

   (A) Tsar Nicholas II

   (B) Otto von Bismarck

   (C) Neville Chamberlain

   (D) Louis Napoleon Bonaparte

   (E) Woodrow Wilson

10. The First and Second Balkan Wars were fought in the

   (A) sixteenth century

   (B) seventeenth century

   (C) eighteenth century

   (D) nineteenth century

   (E) twentieth century

11. In the 1960s, many of the revolts in Europe were headed by

   (A) housewives tired of the rising price of bread

   (B) middle-class burghers afraid of losing their positions in society

   (C) elderly people who had suffered cuts to their state benefits

   (D) university students who subscribed to radical political philosophy

   (E) religious figures urging change

12. The American writer Betty Friedan was renowned in Europe for her stance on

   (A) economic self-determinism

   (B) anti-Semitism

   (C) women's issues

   (D) French cuisine

   (E) growing consumerism

13. Which one of the following nations was NOT absolutist in the seventeenth century?

   (A) Russia

   (B) Prussia

   (C) France

   (D) Poland

   (E) Austria

14. The Holy Roman Empire and the Ottoman Empire were similar in that each was characterized by all of the following EXCEPT

   (A) decentralized structure

   (B) weak army

   (C) multiple religious and ethnic groups

   (D) haphazard taxation

   (E) a single language

15. The Pragmatic Sanction of 1713 was written to

   (A) provoke war with the Hohenzollern dynasty that ruled Prussia

   (B) ensure that the Habsburg hereditary possessions could be inherited by a daughter

   (C) influence people to adopt a more logical, realistic view of natural laws

   (D) weaken the Venetian resistance to Austrian-Hungarian rule

   (E) strengthen the power of the Viennese nobility

16. The artistic term *rococo* (meaning delicate, florid, and graceful) was a reaction against the characteristics of what previous artistic movement?

   (A) Romanticism

   (B) Classical

   (C) Neoclassical

   (D) Baroque

   (E) Surrealism

17. The Great Trek refers to

   (A) the march of the Chinese Communists to escape attack from the Nationalists

   (B) the retreat of Dutch settlers from the English in South Africa

   (C) Napoleon's ill-fated winter attack on Russia

   (D) the Catholic pilgrimage along the Camino de Santiago in northern Spain

   (E) the English habit of taking aimless rambles on the weekend

GO ON TO THE NEXT PAGE.

18. Justification for colonization in Africa did NOT rest upon which of the following?

    (A) Social Darwinism
    (B) The "white man's burden"
    (C) New technologies such as the machine gun
    (D) The desire to project power to fellow European countries
    (E) The need for new resources

19. Key figures in the German romantic movement did NOT include

    (A) Erwin Rommel
    (B) Richard Wagner
    (C) Johann Wolfgang von Goethe
    (D) Johann Fichte
    (E) Novalis

20. In a famous front-page article entitled "J'Accuse," what writer accused the French government of anti-Semitism and obstruction of justice regarding Alfred Dreyfus?

    (A) Voltaire
    (B) Émile Zola
    (C) Guy de Maupassant
    (D) Honoré de Balzac
    (E) Marquis de Sade

21. During World War I, the United States declared war on Germany as a direct result of

    (A) the sinking of the Lusitania
    (B) the Battle of the Marne
    (C) the interception of the Zimmermann note
    (D) the Treaty of Brest-Litovsk
    (E) the Schleiffin Plan

22. Scandinavian countries responded most effectively to the Great Depression because

    (A) they insisted on balanced budgets
    (B) they were social democrats and used large deficits to finance public works
    (C) they ended the gold standard to keep their currency competitive
    (D) they renounced the Kellogg-Briand Pact
    (E) they exercised the "right of first refusal"

23. The term *fin de siècle* refers to

    (A) the transition from bicycles to automotives in the early twentieth century
    (B) a small glass of dessert wine enjoyed by *philosophes* in Parisian salons
    (C) the rubble of many European cities after World War II
    (D) a period of decadent art near the turn of the twentieth century
    (E) the Romantic view of the glory of warfare following World War I

24. The sense of isolation experienced by many twentieth-century Europeans was reflected by all of the following novelists EXCEPT

    (A) Marcel Proust
    (B) Franz Kafka
    (C) Percy Bysshe Shelley
    (D) Thomas Mann
    (E) James Joyce

25. The dominant school of economic thought from the fifteenth to the eighteenth centuries was

    (A) mercantilism
    (B) microeconomics
    (C) communism
    (D) manorialism
    (E) classicism

26. All of the following terms are associated with Renaissance Italy EXCEPT

    (A) civic virtue
    (B) scholasticism
    (C) secularism
    (D) individualism
    (E) vernacular

27. The Protestant Reformation did NOT feature the ideas of

    (A) Ulrich Zwingli
    (B) John Calvin
    (C) Martin Luther
    (D) John Knox
    (E) Ignatius Loyola

GO ON TO THE NEXT PAGE.

28. Girolamo Savonarola was most famous for his

   (A) textual analysis proving that the Donation of Constantine was a forgery
   (B) denouncement of papal corruption and calls for Christian renewal
   (C) painting of the Sistine Chapel
   (D) authorship of the *Decameron*, a collection of one hundred tales
   (E) belief in a division between the perishable world of humans and the eternal world of forms

29. The English naval officer who repeatedly defeated the French fleet during the Napoleonic Wars was

   (A) Horatio Nelson
   (B) Duke of Wellington
   (C) Winston Churchill
   (D) Joseph Trafalgar
   (E) William Harvey

30. Pierre-Joseph Proudhon is closely tied to the history of which nineteenth-century philosophy?

   (A) Romanticism
   (B) Naturalism
   (C) Nationalism
   (D) Anarchism
   (E) Socialism

31. Metternich's famous observation that "Italy is only a geographical expression" would eventually be proven wrong by which two political leaders?

   (A) Sophia Loren and Gina Lollabrigida
   (B) Victor Emmanuel I and Giuseppe Garibaldi
   (C) Filippo Brunelleschi and Leon Battista Alberti
   (D) John and Sebastian Cabot
   (E) Pope Pius XI and Cosimo d' Medici

32. King Louis Philippe is known for all of the following EXCEPT

   (A) his reputation as the "bourgeoisie king"
   (B) refusing demands for broader suffrage from liberals
   (C) forbidding public meetings
   (D) abdicating the throne and fleeing to England
   (E) being captured while trying to regain his throne at the Battle of Waterloo

33. The "scorched earth" policy refers to

   (A) periodically burning fields to increase nutrient load in the soil
   (B) Russia's practice of retreating while burning its own crops, effectively depriving invaders of resources
   (C) Metternich's unwillingness to tolerate revolutions during his time as the head of the Concert of Europe
   (D) innovations in the production of iron kettles during the early Renaissance period
   (E) the Prussian army's tendency to blacken its own clothing with soil following a swift victory

34. The depiction of the density of the poverty in this slum most likely reflects the author's concern about

   (A) the immediate effects of the Continental System
   (B) the changes wrought by the Second Industrial Revolution
   (C) feminists' desire to educate the populace about birth control
   (D) the evils of alcohol consumption
   (E) the bright future of a nation that has so many young people

35. The assassination of the Archduke Francis Ferdinand is most notable because

   (A) it ushered in a new era of peace in Eastern Europe
   (B) it showed the world that, in the twentieth century, the nobility were beginning to lose hold of their economic domination of the peasantry
   (C) anarchists were finally able to express their political beliefs
   (D) it triggered a series of wartime alliances that led to the outbreak of World War I
   (E) it led to more severe gun control laws throughout the continent

GO ON TO THE NEXT PAGE.

36. The term that best described the strategy that guided warfare during World War I is

    (A) Pyrrhic victory
    (B) attrition warfare
    (C) asymmetric warfare
    (D) guerilla warfare
    (E) Mexican standoff

37. All of the following are considered twentieth-century philosophies EXCEPT

    (A) Structuralism
    (B) Marxism
    (C) Nationalism
    (D) Existentialism
    (E) Logical positivism

38. The anti-utopian theme of helpless individuals crushed by powerful hostile forces is portrayed in the works of all of the following writers EXCEPT

    (A) Oswald Spengler
    (B) George Orwell
    (C) Franz Kafka
    (D) Aldous Huxley
    (E) Francis Fukuyama

39. The last czar of Russia, Nicholas II, found his power being usurped by

    (A) his daughter, Anastasia
    (B) his cousin, Emperor Wilheim II
    (C) the Duma, the legislative body of Russia
    (D) his wife, Alexandra
    (E) his wife's advisor, Rasputin

40. The European belief in reason, societal progress, and individual rights was greatly weakened following

    (A) the Thirty Years' War
    (B) the French Revolution
    (C) the Revolutions of 1848
    (D) World War I
    (E) the birth of the European Union

41. The event that spelled the end of England's policy of appeasement was Hitler's

    (A) burning of the Reichstag
    (B) signing of the non-aggression pact with Poland
    (C) efforts to create *Anschluss*
    (D) invasion of the Sudetenland
    (E) invasion of Poland

42. The Price Revolution of the sixteenth century is generally attributed to

    (A) the removal of Dutch tariffs
    (B) the unrest among the Protestant citizens of northern European cities
    (C) the influx of gold and silver from the Spanish treasure fleet
    (D) the discovery of new methods of determining the value of precious stones
    (E) the invention of double-entry bookkeeping

43. The belief that national wealth is derived primarily from the development of agriculture is attributed primarily to

    (A) Adam Smith
    (B) The Physiocrats
    (C) David Ricardo
    (D) Henri Comte de Saint-Simon
    (E) Robert Owen

44. Written by Edward Gibbon, *The History of the Decline and Fall of the Roman Empire* (1789) reflected the typical Enlightenment

    (A) suspicion of religion
    (B) celebration of intuition
    (C) indifference to modern scholarship
    (D) reverence for classical methodology
    (E) racial hostility

GO ON TO THE NEXT PAGE.

45. The Marquis de Lafayette, often considered the most important link between the French and American Revolutions, did NOT

    (A) serve in the Continental Army underneath George Washington
    (B) propose the meeting of the Estates-General that led to the creation of the National Assembly
    (C) consult Thomas Jefferson when drafting *The Declaration of the Rights of Man and Citizen*
    (D) lead the Girondins against the rise of Robespierre
    (E) decline the offer to become dictator of France following the July Revolution in 1830

46. The overall English reaction to the fall of the Bastille and the establishment of a constitutional monarchy in France initially consisted of

    (A) the publication of well-reasoned but pessimistic editorials
    (B) street demonstrations reflecting exuberant joy
    (C) friendly encouragement from the prime minister
    (D) an angry sense of marginalization
    (E) the immediate erection of trade barriers

47. The most important purpose of the politics of Prince von Metternich was to promote

    (A) growing nationalistic fervor among student groups
    (B) Russia's imperialistic policies in Eastern Europe
    (C) support for liberalism across the continent
    (D) the European balance of power after the Napoleonic era
    (E) southern Europe's respect for the power of the Catholic Church

48. The Irish potato famine of 1846 resulted in all of the following EXCEPT

    (A) the island's population decreasing by nearly one-third
    (B) a heightened desire to end British domination and establish an Irish republic
    (C) the ban of all food exports during the famine
    (D) a massive Irish diaspora throughout the western world
    (E) an increase in the number of evictions

49. The most important European spokesman for liberalism in the nineteenth century was

    (A) Count di Cavour
    (B) John Stuart Mill
    (C) Edmund Burke
    (D) King Leopold II of Belgium
    (E) William Gladstone

50. The European population sharply increased in the second half of the nineteenth century as a result of all of the following EXCEPT

    (A) higher levels of immigration
    (B) improved health care
    (C) increased food supply
    (D) an increasingly urban population
    (E) a younger average age of marriage

51. During the revolutionary era of the early nineteenth century, Hungarians living under Austrian rule demanded all of the following EXCEPT

    (A) a free press
    (B) a national guard
    (C) reparations from the Hapsburgs
    (D) the abolishment of feudal obligations
    (E) the power to levy taxes

52. Which condition did NOT lead to the birth of the Italian Renaissance?

    (A) Because of the Crusades and new trade routes, Italians began to come into contact with other, more advanced civilizations.
    (B) Due to recent scandals in the Catholic Church, the pope was losing his authority in the eyes of the residents of the peninsula.
    (C) The lay piety movement led to a new appreciation of paintings of Madonna and Child.
    (D) The new middle-class wealth led to the philosophy of enjoying earthly life instead of waiting for rewards in a heavenly one.
    (E) Competition between wealthy people for status led to more artistic sponsorships.

GO ON TO THE NEXT PAGE.

53. Sigmund Freud is known primarily for

   (A) studying a wide variety of patients
   (B) inventing the field of psychoanalysis
   (C) stating that people were driven by their superegos
   (D) proposing the idea of the collective unconscious
   (E) refining the technique of interior monologue

54. Which of the following scientists did NOT challenge the tenets of modern science in the early twentieth century?

   (A) Serge Kirov
   (B) Ernest Rutherford
   (C) Edward Morley
   (D) Max Planck
   (E) Werner Heisenberg

55. In the decade of the 2000s, the anti-immigrant movement was best typified by which French leader?

   (A) Francois Mitterand
   (B) Jacques Chirac
   (C) Nicolas Sarkozy
   (D) Segolene Royal
   (E) Patrice de Mac-Mahon

56. The Berlin blockade of 1948–9 ended when

   (A) Harry Truman threatened Stalin with massive retaliation
   (B) Josef Stalin ended lifted the blockade with no preconditions
   (C) Winston Churchill delivered his famous "iron curtain" speech
   (D) negotiations at the Potsdam Conference resulted in an acceptable compromise
   (E) Italian Prime Minister Pietro Badoglio successfully intervened in the standoff

57. The Italian "economic miracle" of the 1950s and 1960s is NOT owed to

   (A) the role of the Institute for Industrial Reconstruction
   (B) the land reform that broke up the large estates of the south
   (C) the cheap labor supply provided by six million southern Italians who moved to the industrial north
   (D) the new dominance of Antonio Gramsci and the unusual flexibility of the Italian Communist party
   (E) its early commitment to the Common Market

58. Boris Yeltsin's decision to move the Russian economy towards a free-market economic system resulted in all of the following EXCEPT

   (A) short-term dislocation followed by greater economic expansion
   (B) more governmental transparency
   (C) hyperinflation
   (D) the creation of a new class of oligarchs
   (E) transfer of government assets to private hands

Cathédrale de Chartres.

oldbookillustrations.com

59. The cathedral pictured above is considered an excellent example of which type of European architecture?

   (A) Norman
   (B) Gothic
   (C) Baroque
   (D) Neoclassical
   (E) Romantic

GO ON TO THE NEXT PAGE.

60. As the leader of the Renaissance Neoplatonists, Marsilio Ficino believed in

    (A) the dignity and the immortality of the human soul, as evidenced by Plato's works
    (B) the impossibility of different religious philosophies to share common principles
    (C) the belief that platonic friendship was a higher calling than romantic love
    (D) the re-evaluation of Italian dishware, particularly plates
    (E) a reasoned argument against the allegory of the cave

61. The Decembrist Revolt was

    (A) held by a group of radicals in Montenegro who protested the assassination of the Archduke Francis Ferdinand
    (B) a failed plot by Russian liberal intelligentsia to set up a constitutional monarchy
    (C) a peasant uprising during the French Revolution, caused by chronic shortages of bread
    (D) a group of Oxford professors who resisted the Parliamentarians during the English Civil War
    (E) the first successful labor strike, which occurred in London in the late nineteenth century

62. The Dutch East India Company was NOT

    (A) the first multinational company in modern history
    (B) in sole control of the spice trade in the East Indies
    (C) given the right to imprison and execute convicts
    (D) allowed to coin money and establish colonies
    (E) subject to the native laws of Indonesia

63. All of the following were famous figures during the Age of Discovery EXCEPT

    (A) Prince Henry the Navigator
    (B) Bartolomeu Dias
    (C) Vasco da Gama
    (D) Antonio Salazar
    (E) Hernando Cortés

64. The term *lebensraum*, meaning "living room," is a term that the Nazi party used to describe

    (A) the "showers" that were used to gas Jews in the concentration camps
    (B) the desire to improve the general standard of living following the hyperinflationary era of the Weimar Republic
    (C) the need for German territorial expansion to relieve overpopulation
    (D) the appointment of Adolf Hitler to the office of Chancellor in 1933
    (E) the encouragement of outdoor exercise as a method of improving the health of the Aryan race

65. The textile factory owner and political philosopher who provided Karl Marx with hard data for his book *Das Kapital* was

    (A) John Stuart Mill
    (B) Vladimir Lenin
    (C) Immanuel Kant
    (D) Friedrich Engels
    (E) J. W. F. Hegel

66. The Dadaist movement

    (A) urged blonde men in Germany to become fathers, thus populating the homeland with more Aryan blood
    (B) rejected traditional artistic standards, employing a sense of the irrational, absurd, and outrageous
    (C) resulted in the enshrinement of more civil rights for men in the Napoleonic Code
    (D) was a group of androgynous painters that formed in Moscow after the disruptions of the Russian Revolution
    (E) began in the Ottoman Empire and spread to Russia via the Crimean War

67. The roots of the twenty-first century European Union can be traced directly back to the

    (A) Royal Society
    (B) Estates-General
    (C) Treaty of Brest-Litovsk
    (D) European Coal and Steel Community
    (E) European Economic Community

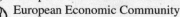

GO ON TO THE NEXT PAGE.

68. The Fabian Society is notable for all of the following EXCEPT

   (A) laying the foundation of the Labour Party
   (B) influencing the shape of modern government during the era of decolonization that followed World War II
   (C) enjoying widespread acclaim of its principles across the European continent
   (D) advancing the principles of socialism via gradual means, such as elections
   (E) often allying itself with a social democratic viewpoint

69. The Fourteen Points offered at the Treaty of Versailles did NOT include

   (A) annexation of the Turkish portion of the Ottoman empire
   (B) freedom of navigation
   (C) reduction of national armaments
   (D) restoration of Belgian sovereignty
   (E) the return of the Alsace-Lorraine to France

70. Otto von Bismarck is remembered for all of the following EXCEPT

   (A) instituting an anti-Catholic policy of *kulturkampf*
   (B) delivering the famous "blood and iron" speech
   (C) engineering brief but powerful wars with both Austria and France
   (D) reducing the amount of governmental support for workers
   (E) forming the modern German state

71. Unlike other European nobles, Italian nobles of the Renaissance tended to

   (A) live in densely populated urban areas
   (B) feel threatened by powerful monarchs
   (C) resent the growing power of the middle class
   (D) live on inherited wealth
   (E) defend the dogma of the Catholic Church

72. The French leader who, following a *coup d'état*, crowned himself the ruler of the Second Empire was

   (A) Napoleon Bonaparte
   (B) Napoleon II
   (C) Napoleon III
   (D) Louis Philippe
   (E) Charles X

73. The Hanseatic League was

   (A) a group of Catholic rulers of largely Protestant principalities in southern Germany
   (B) a commercial and defensive confederation of merchant guilds that dominated trade along the coast of northern Europe
   (C) a group of Germanic tribes who attacked the Danes throughout the twelfth to sixteenth centuries
   (D) a group of Nordic villages that created the first organized sporting league in modern Europe
   (E) a gang of elite pickpockets who operated in London slums during the early nineteenth century

74. The quotation "From each according to his abilities, to each according to his needs" describes the political philosophy of

   (A) John Knox
   (B) Edmund Burke
   (C) Thomas Hobbes
   (D) John Maynard Keynes
   (E) Karl Marx

"If we take in our hand any volume; of divinity or school metaphysics, for instance; let us ask—Does it contain any abstract reasoning concerning quantity or number? No. Does it contain any experimental reasoning, concerning matter of fact and existence? No. Commit it then to the flames: for it can contain nothing but sophistry and illusion."

75. In which era would the quotation above most likely have been stated?

   (A) Medieval
   (B) Renaissance
   (C) Reformation
   (D) Enlightenment
   (E) Age of Revolutions

GO ON TO THE NEXT PAGE.

76. Adam Smith and John Locke both agreed on the importance of

(A) government intervention
(B) private property
(C) mercantilism
(D) the need to improve others' lives
(E) storing large amounts of wealth

77. All of the following occurred during the radical phase of the French Revolution EXCEPT

(A) the storming of the Bastille
(B) the king's attempt to secretly flee Paris
(C) the outbreak of war with Austria and Prussia
(D) the division of the National Assembly into Political Factions
(E) the rise of the *sans-culottes*

78. The painting above does NOT represent which of the following artistic and intellectual movements?

(A) Nationalism
(B) Liberalism
(C) Romanticism
(D) Symbolism
(E) Conservatism

79. The Chartist movement favored a repeal of the Corn Laws because

(A) workers in factory towns such as Manchester depended upon the import of grains
(B) working-class radicals demanded more economic protections
(C) the Corn Laws imposed a tariff upon imported grain and were a symbolic representation of aristocratic landholdings.
(D) the Chartists objected to the artificially low price of bread that the Corn Laws created
(E) they worried about the growing power of the conservative faction of Parliament

80. The European Union was established under its current name in 1993 by

(A) the Brussels Treaty
(B) the Treaty of Paris
(C) the Bonn Agreements
(D) the Maastricht Treaty
(E) the Treaty of Rome

STOP

END OF SECTION I

IF YOU FINISH BEFORE TIME IS CALLED, YOU MAY CHECK YOUR WORK ON THIS SECTION.
DO NOT GO ON TO SECTION II UNTIL YOU ARE TOLD TO DO SO.

GO ON TO THE NEXT PAGE.

EUROPEAN HISTORY

SECTION II

You will have 15 minutes to read the contents of this essay question booklet. You are advised to spend most of the 15 minutes analyzing the documents and planning your answer for the document-based question in Part A. You should spend some portion of the time choosing the two questions in Part B that you will answer. You may make notes in this booklet. At the end of the 15-minute period, you will be told to break the seal on the free-response booklet and to begin writing your answers on the lined pages of that booklet. Do not break the seal on the free-response booklet until you are told to do so. Suggested writing time is 45 minutes for the document-based essay question in Part A. Suggested planning and writing time is 35 minutes for each of the two essay questions you choose to answer in Part B.

BE SURE TO MANAGE YOUR TIME CAREFULLY.

Write your answers in the <u>free-response</u> booklet with a <u>pen</u>. The essay question booklet may be used for reference and/or scratchwork as you answer the free-response questions, but no credit will be given for the work shown in the essay question booklet.

DO NOT OPEN THIS BOOKLET UNTIL YOU ARE TOLD TO DO SO.

GO ON TO THE NEXT PAGE.

GO ON TO THE NEXT PAGE.

EUROPEAN HISTORY

SECTION II

Part A

(Suggested writing time—45 minutes)

Percent of Section II score—45

<u>Directions:</u> The following question is based on the accompanying Documents 1–10. (Some of the documents have been edited for the purpose of this exercise.) Write your answer on the lined pages of the free-response booklet.

This question is designed to test your ability to work with historical documents. As you analyze the documents, <u>take into account both the sources and the author's point of view</u>. Write an essay on the following topic that integrates your analysis of the documents; in no case should documents simply be cited and explained in a "laundry list" fashion. You may refer to historical facts and developments not mentioned in the documents.

1. Discuss the ways in which attitudes towards food and drink reflected changes in European society from the fifteenth to the nineteenth centuries.

Document 1

A Nobleman Picnic, from *The Hunting Book of Gaston Phébus,* fifteenth century, France

GO ON TO THE NEXT PAGE.

Document 2

—*Noble family,* Tudor dynasty, sixteenth century, England

Document 3

—*The Interior of a London Coffee House,* 1705

GO ON TO THE NEXT PAGE.

Document 4

In order to describe the queen's private service intelligibly, it must be recollected that service of every kind was honor, and had not any other denomination. To do the honors of the service, was to present the service to an officer of superior rank, who happened to arrive at the moment it was about to be performed: thus, supposing the queen asked for a glass of water, the servant of the chamber handed to the first woman a silver gilt waiter, upon which were placed a covered goblet and a small decanter; but should the lady of honor come in, the first woman was obliged to present the waiter to her, and if Madame or the Countess d'Artois came in at the moment, the waiter went again from the lady of honor into the hands of the princess, before it reached the queen.

—*Memoirs of the Private Life of Marie Antoinette,* Madame Campan, 1818

Document 5

Man is a carnivorous production,
And must have meals, at least one meal a day;
He cannot live, like woodcocks, upon suction,
But, like the shark and tiger, must have prey.
Although his anatomical construction
Bears vegetables, in a grumbling way,
Your laboring people think beyond all question,
Beef, veal, and mutton better for digestion.

—*Don Juan,* Canto II, Lord Byron, 1819

Document 6

In a nation where the affluence is sufficient to balance, by the decrease which it causes amongst the rich, the increase arising from the poor, population will be stationary. In a nation highly and generally affluent and luxurious, population will decrease and decay. In poor and ill-fed communities, population will increase in the ratio of the poverty, and the consequent deterioration and diminution of the food of a large portion of the members of such communities. This is the real and great law of human population...

—*The True Law of Population Shewn as Connected With the Food of the People,* by Thomas Doubleday, 1843

GO ON TO THE NEXT PAGE.

Document 7

The Reports of the Inspectors of the Prisons have furnished abundant evidence of the errors committed by magistrates in the dieting of criminals. Debility, diarrhea, scurvy, and other evils known to be consequences of defective nutriment, have prevailed in many of the prisons of this country to a serious and alarming extent.... Place the individual, as an offender against the law, in a small, cold, ill-ventilated cell; a prey to his own reflections, or, what is worse, with his mind almost a vacuum, cut off from all real social intercourse, subjected to the irksome, uninteresting labour of treading a wheel or picking oakum; it is in this condition, I contend, that the stimulus of animal food becomes indispensable for his support against the inroads of low and debilitating diseases.

—*A Treatise on Food and Diet,* by Charles Alfred Lee, 1843

Document 8

The abuse of spirituous liquors is fatal to the European transported to the burning climate of the West Indies; the Russian drinks spirituous liquors with a sort of impunity, and lives to an advanced age amidst excesses which an inhabitant of the south of Europe would sink.

—*Illustrations of Eating,* by George Vasey, 1847

Document 9

Anything like an accurate knowledge of the chemistry of milk was unknown before the close of the eighteenth century. There was indeed a very early acquaintance with butter, curd, and whey; but this information remained for many centuries nearly all that was known regarding it.

It is only during comparatively recent years that the composition and properties of the several characteristic substances found in milk have been fully investigated, and their proportions in the various kinds of milks accurately estimated.

—*The Chemistry of Foods: With Microscopic Illustrations,* by James Bell, 1883

GO ON TO THE NEXT PAGE.

Document 10

That which is remarkable in these Egyptian feasts is the preponderance of women represented. It is evident that in these remote times, ladies were not consigned to the galleries to look on whilst their lords and masters enjoyed the good things provided by Egyptian cooks, but were allowed their fair share both of the comestibles and of the table talk.

—*Our Viands: Whence They Come and How They Are Cooked,* by Anne Walbank Buckland, 1893

END OF PART A

GO ON TO THE NEXT PAGE.

EUROPEAN HISTORY

SECTION II

Part B

(Suggested writing time—70 minutes)

Percent of Section II score—55

<u>Directions:</u> You are to answer TWO questions, one from each group of three questions below. Make your selections carefully, choosing the questions that you are best prepared to answer thoroughly in the time permitted. You should spend 5 minutes organizing or outlining each answer. In writing your essays, <u>use specific examples to support your answer</u>. Write your answers to the questions on the lined pages of the free-response booklet. If time permits when you finish writing, check your work. Be certain to number your answer as the questions are numbered below.

Group 1:   Choose ONE question from this group. The suggested writing time for this question is 30 minutes.

   1.   Describe the changes on the Iberian peninsula during the second half of the fifteenth century.

   2.   Discuss the causes, events, and outcome of the Thirty Years' War.

   3.   Describe the extent of the success of Louis XIV's attempts to create a more prosperous France.

Group 2:   Choose ONE question from this group. The suggested writing time for this question is 30 minutes.

   4.   Analyze the actions taken towards the Catholic Church during the French Revolution.

   5.   Describe the effects of World War I upon European society.

   6.   Analyze the reasons for the disintegration of the Soviet Union in the late twentieth century.

END OF EXAMINATION

Chapter 23
AP European
History
Practice Test
Answers and
Explanations

ANSWER KEY

1.	D	41.	E
2.	B	42.	C
3.	C	43.	B
4.	A	44.	A
5.	E	45.	D
6.	D	46.	C
7.	A	47.	D
8.	B	48.	C
9.	B	49.	B
10.	E	50.	A
11.	D	51.	C
12.	C	52.	C
13.	D	53.	B
14.	E	54.	A
15.	B	55.	C
16.	D	56.	B
17.	B	57.	D
18.	C	58.	B
19.	A	59.	B
20.	B	60.	A
21.	C	61.	B
22.	B	62.	E
23.	D	63.	D
24.	C	64.	C
25.	A	65.	D
26.	B	66.	B
27.	E	67.	D
28.	B	68.	C
29.	A	69.	A
30.	D	70.	D
31.	B	71.	A
32.	E	72.	C
33.	B	73.	B
34.	B	74.	E
35.	D	75.	D
36.	B	76.	D
37.	C	77.	A
38.	E	78.	E
39.	E	79.	C
40.	D	80.	D

ANSWERS AND EXPLANATIONS

1. **D** Humanists, while sometimes religious, were not in any way apologists for the official teachings of the Catholic Church. Erasmus, for example, the most famous of the northern humanists, was a faithful Catholic who also issued blistering attacks on official church teachings.

2. **B** The overriding concern of the pope was how to defend the treasures of Rome from the French army. He wasn't concerned about other city-states, French cardinals, and certainly not the religion of the French king (which was Catholic). And England was irrelevant to the question.

3. **C** Choice (A) is incorrect because the feminist movement grew out of the eighteen-century Enlightenment movement. (B) is incorrect because the treaty ended the Austrian-Sardinian War in the nineteenth century. (D) relates to the passing of power within the Austro-Hungarian Empire in the eighteenth century. (E) was signed in 1991 to create the European Union.

4. **A** The War of the Roses was waged between the houses of Lancaster and York. It resulted in a greatly weakened nobility and a stronger throne. Answers (C), (D), and (E) are imaginary. Note well: If you see a question with two answer choices that are diametrically opposed (as in A and B), one of them will probably be correct.

5. **E** Ricardo's Iron Law of Wages stated that all wages will ultimately drop to the lowest possible level necessary to sustain life to the worker. However, as the people's reaction to Industrial Revolution continued throughout the century, and as politicians jumped into the process (because mass voting now guaranteed their careers), ordinary workers saw their incomes increase.

6. **D** Freud was the father of psychoanalysis and was unconcerned with germs. Koch developed immunization, Lister built the antiseptic principle, Chadwick said that disease and death caused poverty, and Pasteur literally invented the germ theory.

7. **A** While Jeremy Bentham promoted utilitarianism (the greatest good for the greatest number of people) he did not contribute to the idea that human society advanced itself by weeding out the unfit. In fact, that runs counter to his philosophy of helping the masses survive. The other four thinkers were all believers, or the founders of, evolutionary theory.

8. **B** While Russia nominally told the world that it was protecting Orthodox Christians suffering under Ottoman rule, the real story was quite different. It was using the religion as a pretext to serve its own expansionism under Tsar Nicolas I. Britain saw this and realized that a Russian presence in the Middle East would present challenges to its own dominance in the region, and so it assembled a coalition of European powers to defend the Ottomans.

9. **B** Bismarck, the man who unified Germany, understood the necessity of defending his new nation from a war on two fronts: France and England to the west, Russia to the east. He managed to prevent this by engineering a defensive agreement—the Triple Alliance—with Austria-Hungary and Italy. It's no coincidence that Germany did find itself in that very nightmare scenario in both World War I and World War II.

10. **E** One of the minor skirmishes in Europe's long history of warfare, the Balkan Wars were fought in 1912 and 1913. The first one succeeded mainly in expelling the Ottoman Turks from the peninsula. The second occurred when Bulgaria attacked Macedonia in the name of expansion, but it was defeated, and Turkey and Romania seized most of the lands Bulgaria had been granted in the First Balkan War.

11. **D** If there's one thing you can depend on during the late twentieth century—and even in earlier times—it's the role of university students in fomenting revolution. From Europe to South America to North America to Asia, colleges have become hotbeds of social protest. In Europe, the student revolt in Paris in 1968 was a perfect example of this.

12. **C** Betty Friedan was the author of *The Feminine Mystique* and the godmother of second-wave feminism in the United States. She was the head of the National Organization of Women and spearheaded many other feminist groups during the late twentieth century. In Europe, she was also considered a feminist icon, and inspired a generation of women to react to male-dominated institutions.

13. **D** Throughout its history, Poland has been ruled not by a single regent, but by a class of nobles who often met in a diet, and who had strong restrictive power upon the king as well as one another. (That's why the phrase King of Poland doesn't really roll off the tongue) The other countries, particularly France and Russia, are classic examples of consolidated absolute power.

14. **E** The Ottoman Empire, while using Turkish as its official language, was weakened by the various languages used by its people, such as Farsi, Arabic, Greek, and eventually French and English. Because of its constantly shifting borders, the Holy Roman Empire faced similar problems over the centuries, as its languages included German, French, Dutch, Italian, Czech, Polish, and others.

15. **B** Because Charles VI had no male heirs, the throne of the Austro-Hungarian Empire was in doubt in the early 1700s. Sensing the vultures starting to circle, he issued a document claiming that female inheritors (such as his daughter, Maria Theresa) had the same claim to the throne as male heirs. It also ordered neighboring powers to stand down during the transition period. Despite this precaution, it didn't stop Prussia from ignoring the document and waging the War of the Austrian Succession.

16.   **D**   During its day, the Baroque movement, while greatly respected today, was seen as being perhaps too inflexible in its artistic criteria. The counterpoint used in the compositions of J.S. Bach was beautiful, but its strict demands of symmetry and grandeur were criticized for being a little too cold. Rococo paintings of fat cherubs, in contrast, were typically ornamental, playful, and merely entertaining.

17.   **B**   The Dutch had settled South Africa as far back as the seventeenth century, and were soon joined by French Huguenots escaping from persecution. By the 1800s, the English had won control of the colony as a result of the Napoleonic Wars. Resentful of this new domination, the Boers decided to escape by simply walking deeper into Africa.

18.   **C**   This is a trick question. While new technologies such as the machine gun were certainly used to conquer native Africa peoples, these technologies were not the reason for the conquering. They were a means, not an end. The AP test will occasionally try to confuse causes and effects.

19.   **A**   Unlike the other nineteenth-century artists and writers, Erwin Rommel ("The Desert Fox") was a German Field Marshal in World War II. He commanded the North African campaign as well as the Nazi resistance to the Allied invasion at Normandy. It should be noted that though he was a Nazi commander, he was a Nazi commander with a conscience—he routinely ignored orders from Berlin to kill Jews, and he treated his prisoners humanely. In fact, in 1944, he was caught plotting a coup against his own boss, Adolf Hitler, and was forced to swallow a cyanide tablet, which ended his life.

20.   **B**   Émile Zola was incensed by the cover-up that the French government was instituting in the case. His article, which was published as an open letter to the president of France, demanded that the proper channels of justice be followed in the Dreyfus case. The reaction was huge: It divided France deeply between the reactionary army and church and the more liberal commercial society.

21.   **C**   The trap answer was the sinking of the Lusitania. While that angered many, the United States continued to remain neutral in the conflict. The Zimmermann note, on the other hand, was a cable sent from Germany to Mexico, urging that country to invade the United States. As a reward, Germany promised to return to Mexico all American land that had been taken during the Mexican-American War. (In the note, Germany also hilariously urged Mexico to ask Japan for assistance.) When the United States discovered this note, involvement in World War I could no longer be avoided.

22.   **B**   Modern economic policy dictates that the best way to combat a major depression is to engage in deficit spending. In other words, borrow and spend money you don't have, just to keep things moving. This was the innovation of John Maynard Keynes, and it was used to great effect in the Scandinavian countries. (A) is the opposite of what occurred. Whether (C) is true or not is irrelevant, since so many countries were giving up the gold standard during this time that the benefits of doing so were erased. (D) and (E) are nonsensical and off topic.

23. **D**   The fin de siècle was an artistic movement found primarily in France and England during the 1890s and 1900s. Its characteristics include symbolic mysticism, a willful sense of decay, and rejection of social order. In literature, its major figures were the inimitable Oscar Wilde and Arthur Rimbaud. In painting, it is represented by *In the Moulin Rouge* by Henri Toulouse-Lautrec—not to mention the ubiquitous *The Scream* by Edvard Munch.

24. **C**   One of the major Romantic writers, Percy Shelley lived in the early nineteenth century, and focused mostly on poetry. His wife, Mary, was the author of *Frankenstein*. The other writers were all towering figures of the twentieth-century European Modernist movement.

25. **A**   Mercantilism is a national economic policy aimed at accumulating monetary reserves through a positive balance of trade, especially of finished goods. High tariffs, especially on manufactured goods, is a typical feature of the policy. It was a cause of frequent wars and also motivated colonial expansion. Bourbon Spain and France are great examples of this policy in action.

26. **B**   Scholasticism was the preferred method of investigating the world during the medieval era. Its adherents, centered at Europe's first universities such as Paris and Oxford, believed in using deductive reasoning and inference to arrive at truth. Unfortunately, this led to several extended dialectics on such compelling topics such as "How many angels can dance on the head of a pin?" It did exist during Renaissance Italy but doesn't define that era.

27. **E**   Ignatius Loyola was the founder of the Society of Jesus (the Jesuit order of Catholic priests), who at the time represented one of the three arms of the Counter-Reformation (the others being the Council of Trent and the Inquisition). He was quite obviously not part of the Protestant Reformation.

28. **B**   Savonrola was a Dominican friar who assumed great power in Florence, booting the ruling Medicis out the door for four years, and eventually getting himself burned at the stake by Pope Alexander VI. The other choices describe Lorenzo Valla (A), Michelangelo (C), Boccaccio (D), and Neoplatonism (E).

29. **A**   Horatio Nelson defeated Napoleon's fleet at the Battle of the Pyramids, the Battle of the Nile, the Battle of Trafalgar, and others. The Duke of Wellington fought primarily on land. Churchill wouldn't be born for another century. Nelson's Column now stands in Trafalgar Square, but Joseph Trafalgar is imaginary (it commemorates a cape on the Spanish coastline). William Harvey was the discoverer of the circulation of the blood.

30. **D**   Proudhon was a proud anarchist, remembered largely today for two reasons. One, his masterpiece, *Property is Theft!* (exclamation mark included), predated and influenced the ideas of Karl Marx by nearly forty years. The two men were in fact friendly, until Marx tried to argue the older Proudhon's ideas. Two, Proudhon is reputed to have invented the famous anarchy symbol: an A inside of a circle.

31. **B**   In the north, King Victor Emmanuel II of the Kingdom of Piedmont persuaded and even forced all the many northern Italian states towards accepting unification. He was steered largely by his prime minister, the Count of Cavour, who later became Italy's first prime minister for three short months. In the south, the radical revolutionary Garibaldi led a group of "red shirts" to demand Italian unification from the north. In 1860, they met, and after a tense negotiation, modern Italy was born.

32. **E**   While Louis Philippe did abdicate the throne as a result of the July Revolutions (imagine shouting Frenchmen standing on barricades while waving the tricolor), he never attempted to return. The Battle of Waterloo was, in fact, Napoleon I's last stand.

33. **B**   As joked in the movie *The Princess Bride*, don't get involved in a land war in Asia. Napoleon's invasion of Russia with his Grand Army stands as a textbook case of the foolishness of this. As the Russians retreated into their vast land mass, Napoleon unwisely followed, stretching his own supply lines to thousands of miles long because of the pesky Russian habit of burning their own country to deprive him of looting. They even burned their own capital, Moscow, shortly before he entered. Later the Grand Army was destroyed by cold weather and attrition, losing approximately 85% of its army.

34. **B**   The drawing, which is of Dudley Street in the Seven Dials neighborhood of London, is most properly viewed as a critique of the massive influx of families into the city to work in factories. The exploitation of child labor was an unfortunate aspect of life in London at this time, many of whom were orphans. Charles Dickens expertly captured the bleakness of this world in his many novels.

35. **D**   The assassination of the Archduke Francis Ferdinand by the anarchist Gavrilo Princip was the first event in the chain reaction that precipitated World War I. Following the event, Austria demanded an ultimatum from Serbia that Serbia couldn't accept, so Germany rushed to Austria's aid. This caused Russia to assist Serbia.

36. **B**   Attrition warfare is a military strategy in which a belligerent side attempts to win a war by wearing down its enemy to the point of collapse through continuous losses in personnel and supplies. The war will usually be won by the side with greater such resources. World War I stands as the best example of this strategy.

37. **C**   Nationalism was born in the revolutions of the nineteenth century and died in the rubble of World War II. It was defined by the belief that your identity lay, at its core, in your identification with your homeland (and, to a certain extent, your race). The twentieth century was better defined by the other four terms, even Marxism, which reached full flower in the 1910s.

38. **E**   Fukuyama is best known for his book *The End of History and the Last Man*, which argued that the worldwide spread of liberal democracies and free market capitalism of the West and its lifestyle may signal the end point of humanity's sociocultural evolution and become the final form of human government. This is clearly not a dystopian vision of the future; it's an announcement that the future will be free of any conflict.

39. **E** Grigori Rasputin was a peasant and a mystic, though he belonged to no church. After miraculously curing Alexandra's son of leukemia, he became an instrumental part of her inner circle, with some claiming that he ran Russia while Nicholas II was sick. Ultimately, he was murdered, but his legendary influence lives on.

40. **D** World War I utterly changed Europe's view of itself. Where warfare had once been heroic individualism, a way to prove one's manhood, it now became impersonal mass slaughter. After such horrific encounters such as the Battle of the Somme, in which hundreds of thousands perished to secure a mile or two of advancement, Europeans began to wonder if their worldview really was leading to the greatest happiness for the greatest number of people.

41. **E** The invasion of Poland was the fourth of four major events leading to England's ultimate declaration of war. First was the annexation of Austria (Anschluss); second was the invasion of the Sudetenland; third was the invasion of Czechoslovakia. The last straw was the invasion of Poland, which explicitly broke the non-aggression pact they had signed (B).

42. **C** The silver found in places such as Bolivia and Mexico contributed greatly to changing the economic environment of Europe during the 1500s. With many newly rich people chasing relatively few consumer goods (remember, this is before the advent of mass production), prices skyrocketed by a factor of six, initially in Spain but eventually throughout the continent.

43. **B** The Physiocrats, a group of eighteenth-century French thinkers, are now regarded as the very first scientific school of economics. A collection of outspoken agrarians, these men promoted the idea that holding large tracts of land, and carefully cultivating the crops, was the only way to build wealth. They also believed in typical Enlightenment ideas such as logic, self-interest, and disciplined labor. Their ideas have since become antiquated, especially since Adam Smith and, later, the Industrial Revolution.

44. **A** During the twenty-odd years that it took to research and write his masterpiece, Gibbon came to the realization that the decline of the Roman Republic was due in part to the loss of civic virtue. He attributed this to the birth of Christianity, which he saw as significant in that it taught its adherents to ignore their present earthly conditions and to focus instead on the promise of heavenly rewards.

45. **D** A major figure in French history, the Marquis de Lafayette really did serve in the U.S. Constitutional Army (Lafayette Square in Washington, D.C. is named for him), really was buddies with Jefferson, and really did turn down the dictatorship of France in his elderly years. However, he did not spend the French Revolution in France; while attempting to escape the country, he was captured by the Austrians, and spent five years in prison.

46. **C** On the eve of the French Revolution, Prime Minister William Pitt publicly stated his support for the changes that were under way across the channel, as did other members of Parliament. The English were quite excited to put an end to the rivalry between the two nations, and to perhaps improve both economies with increased trade. Enthusiasm soon changed to horror, and a strongly reactionary movement gripped the country, as exemplified by Edmund Burke (who had opposed the revolution from the beginning).

47. **D** One of history's most famous conservatives, Metternich was anything but liberal, having used spy networks to squash countless liberal revolutions across Europe during his time as the Austrian chancellor. Neither was he a fan of nationalism, especially since nationalists were often liberals at this time. Mostly, he wanted stability, and that meant a return to pre-1789 policies. It is worth noting that his policy was successful; there were no major wars in Europe during the first half of the nineteenth century.

48. **C** One of the sad ironies of history is that, during the Great Famine, the British crown continued to use Ireland to export massive amounts of grains (wheat, barley, and oats) and livestock (calves, bacon, ham) to their own country. Since nearly one million Irish people died, and since it was preventable (though at an economic loss), many experts view this event as an indirect form of genocide.

49. **B** John Stuart Mill, a famous philosophe, supported freedom of thought, universal suffrage, and collective action by workers. His most famous work is even called *On Liberty*. Cavour unified Italy, which is an expression of nationalism. Burke was a famous conservative thinker. King Leopold was a promoter of imperialism. (E) might have tempted you, but remember that Gladstone's liberal influence was limited mostly to England, whereas Mill's philosophical influence was more diffused.

50. **A** During this time, the immigration to the European continent was nowhere as strong as the emigration away from it. The United States, for example, absorbed fourteen million immigrants, mostly eastern and southern Europeans, between 1860 and 1900. The other four answers were all quite true, however. Better medical practices, agricultural technology definitely helped grow the population, as did the newly urbanized population who benefitted from the absence of a traditional property requirement for marriage.

51. **C** The young Hungarian revolutionaries made all of these demands (except C), which caused the Viennese youth to demand similar measures of self-rule. The members of the Viennese court watched in horror as crowds rose up. Ultimately, Metternich resigned, censorship was abolished, a constitution was promised, and universal male suffrage was given. This caused a chain reaction: Hungarian autonomy caused similar demands from the Czechs in Bohemia, the Croatians in Croatia, and the Romanians in Transylvania. The original revolutionaries, ironically, had no tolerance for other smaller revolutions, so ultimately everything fizzled out without any major changes.

52. **C**   The lay piety movement was part of the northern Renaissance, which occurred after the Italian Renaissance, and therefore could not be a cause. Furthermore, the ubiquitous paintings of Madonna and Child were a staple of medieval art (the church wouldn't allow much else) and Renaissance artists largely turned their backs upon what was viewed as clichéd material.

53. **B**   Freud, a Viennese psychologist, single-handedly invented the field of psychoanalysis. He opined that the human mind is composed of the id (instinctual urges), ego, and superego (conscience). He also stated that repression of memories led to neuroses, and he conveniently urged people to speak about their troubles with professionals as much as possible. Many of his ideas have been discarded by modern medicine, partly because he used only mentally ill women as subjects.

54. **A**   Serge Kirov wasn't a scientist; he was a proud Stalinist who was ironically assassinated by Stalin himself, on the pretext that he was becoming too popular. Ernest Rutherford associated radioactivity with the breakdown of atoms; Edward Morley challenged the old principle that the universe was filled with ether. Max Planck challenged Newtonian physics by showing that energy was emitted in quanta and displayed many of the same characteristics of matter, and Werner Heisenberg summed up the coming century neatly in his Uncertainty Principle.

55. **C**   Not the fairest question in these pages, it's testing your knowledge of modern French politics. The only people who were French leaders in the 2000s were Jacques Chirac and Nicolas Sarkozy. Chirac followed a typical liberal openness towards foreigners, while Sarkozy promoted the opposite.

56. **B**   Berlin had been a hotly desired commodity following World War II, with England and the United States vying with the Soviets for possession. When the United States and England introduced their own currencies to the city, Stalin reacted badly, setting up a blockade around the city. Following that, however, the United States used a previously agreed upon airspace to begin ten months of lifting supplies to the people trapped within the Soviet blockade. In May of 1949, Stalin inexplicably lifted the blockade with no preconditions.

57. **D**   The Italian Communist party was doomed to permanent second-class status after World War II. For the next forty years, in fact, Italy was ruled by the Christian Democrats. It is interesting that the flexibility of the Communist party did, in fact, lead to its continued existence. Compare that with the utter destruction of communist political parties in every other developed Western country.

58. **B**   Governmental transparency refers to how easy it is for the public to monitor the government's actions. Unfortunately, governmental transparency didn't increase under Putin's administration; it remained just as opaque as it had been underneath the Soviets. All of the other choices are also unfortunate results of the end of the Soviet system—a system which has created a class of superrich oligarchs who control the burgeoning oil companies. Today, in fact, Moscow has more billionaires than any other city in the world.

59. **B**   Gothic architecture, while slightly outside the range of this test, is such an integral part of European history that it's worth at least one question. Marked by spires, intricate facades, clerestory windows, and flying buttresses, the cathedral seems to leap into the air. A UNESCO World Heritage site, it marks the high point of medieval European religious architecture.

60. **A**   The Neoplatonists have existed for thousands of years, from Plotinus (ancient philosopher) to Maimonides (medieval Spain) to Renaissance Italy (Ficino) and even to the present day. This intellectual tradition eschews civic activism for deep contemplation of eternal things, especially the human soul. It was deeply inspired by Plato's world of Forms.

61. **B**   Caused by Tsar Nicolas I's assumption of the Russian throne following the renunciation of his older brother Constantine's claim, the Decembrist Revolt was led by a group of army officers leading about 3,000 soldiers. They were brutally suppressed by Nicholas I, with many being cast into frozen rivers, and several were publicly hanged (the last such imperial hanging in Russia). Their dedication to their causes, such as the abolition of serfdom, served as an inspiration for the next century.

62. **E**   At the time of the chartering of the Dutch East India Company, which occurred in 1602, the nation of Indonesia didn't exist. It wouldn't form until the twentieth century, after the company had long since collapsed. Still, the Dutch East India Company was astoundingly powerful, unrestrained by most laws, able to act with total impunity, and utterly dominant over the spice trade for two hundred years.

63. **D**   During the fifteenth and sixteenth centuries, the Age of Discovery was dominated by Portugal (Prince Henry, Dias, da Gama) and Spain (Cortés, plus others). Antonio Salazar, while Portuguese, actually lived during the twentieth century. He was the authoritarian, right-wing leader of that country for nearly forty years until 1968.

64. **C**   "Living room" refers to the Nazi belief in the need for superior people to occupy land that is inhabited by inferior people. This of course was seen in racial terms, and the Nazis justified it by pointing out that their own Aryan people were overpopulating their meager land (whose borders had been drawn by other European powers at the Treaty of Versailles). This philosophy was subsequently used to justify their invasions of Austria, the Sudetenland, Poland, and other nations.

65. **D**   Friedrich Engels was more than just a textile factory owner and intellectual; he was a lifelong friend of Marx. Together, they coauthored *The Communist Manifesto*. The factory had belonged to his father; he began as a clerk and worked his way up to partner, eventually retiring young and dedicating the rest of his life to political and philosophical pursuits.

66. **B**   The Dadaist artistic movement grew up in Switzerland and then spread to Germany during the tumultuous interwar years. Their work reflected the uncertainty of the moral and economic crisis that was being experienced at the time. Marcel Duchamp's famous urinal-as-art is a perfect example of its work.

67. **D** Common sense should eliminate (A), (B), and (C), all of which were either too early or not international in nature. The remaining two choices were both international economic communities, but the ECSC was founded about seven years earlier than the EEC. Its purpose: to facilitate the trade of coal and steel between France and West Germany, rendering them so economically interdependent that future wars would be unthinkable. The ECSC was eventually absorbed into the EEC.

68. **C** While the Fabian Society was highly influential across the former members of the British Empire, it never gained much traction in continental Europe. Those nations, of course, did adopt largely social democratic governments as the twentieth century wore on, but this wasn't explicitly due to the Fabian Society, which remains Anglocentric.

69. **A** Quite the opposite: Sovereignty for the Turks was point 12, just before Polish independence (point 13) and a call for a general association of nations (point 14). That last one was the stickiest; though it had been suggested by U.S. President Woodrow Wilson, his enemies in Congress refused to ratify it, concerned about being drawn into an entangling alliance overseas.

70. **D** Otto von Bismarck, despite his hostile foreign policy of *realpolitik* and his even more rabid hostility towards Catholics, actually extended the governmental support for German workers. In fact, it's not too far-fetched to say that he created the first modern welfare state through his creation of retirement accounts, accident insurance, medical insurance, and unemployment benefits.

71. **A** The Italian peninsula, particularly in the north, was unusual in that the wealthy aristocrats often walled themselves into dense towns, right alongside the peasantry. In other countries, nobles often lived on remote manors, far from the urban areas. Historians attribute this one difference as crucial for the development of the Renaissance in Italy first.

72. **C** It's sometimes difficult to keep the nineteenth century French leaders straight, but remember this: it began with Napoleon Bonaparte, skipped his son (who never ruled), went to Louis XVIII, then to Charles X (who was deposed by the July Ordinances fiasco), passed to the "bourgeoisie king" Louis Philippe (who abdicated during the revolutions of 1848), then finally was handed to Napoleon III (who declared himself emperor after he was blocked by the Constitution from running for a second term).

73. **B** The Hanseatic League, which existed from the thirteenth to the seventeenth centuries, was created to protect economic interests and diplomatic privileges in the cities and countries and along the trade routes the merchants visited. The Hanseatic cities had their own legal system and furnished their own armies for mutual protection and aid. Despite this, the organization was not a city-state. Today its name lives on many places' names in northern Europe, including the excellent Lufthansa Airlines.

74. **E** Marx, the godfather of communism, based his worldview upon the fact that competition was causing the proletariat to be exploited by the bourgeoisie. Therefore, he proposed to end competition by abolishing private property, declaring that whatever a person could contribute to society would be enough, and that all would share equally in whatever bounty resulted. This redistribution of this wealth would be controlled by the government, thus ensuring an end to economic inequality.

75. **D** The suspicion of divinity and metaphysics, the insistence upon reasoning, experiments, and facts—these are hallmarks of the Enlightenment. This particular quote was written by David Hume, the ultimate European skeptic, in his *Enquiry Concerning Human Understanding*.

76. **D** Both men abhorred unnecessary government intervention (A). Smith disagreed with mercantilism as a viable national economic policy (C) and Locke was silent about the duty we have to improve one another (D). While both agreed that the pursuit of wealth was important, neither one really promoted the idea of sitting on top of large piles of cash.

77. **A** Believe it or not, during the violence that occurred at the Bastille—when 98 people were killed and the heads of the governor and his guard were paraded on spikes through the city—the Revolution had not yet entered a violent phase. That would begin two years later, in 1791, and would be far, far worse, with approximately 70,000 murdered and many, many more than that imprisoned.

78. **E** *Liberty Leading Her People*, by Eugène Delacroix, commemorates the July Revolutions of 1830 that toppled Charles X. He was the leader of the Romantic school of painting, and it was liberalism that he was trying to symbolize in the female figure (known throughout France as Marianne). Nationalistic fervor had not yet been unhooked from liberalism, so that was evident here too, especially in the French tricolor. And yes, it's the same painting on the cover of that one Coldplay album.

79. **C** The union between the Chartists, a political group dedicated to egalitarianism, and the anti-Corn Law movement wasn't always easy, but they shared the same basic goals: to provide more freedoms and more rights for the common English person. While Chartists concerned themselves with political goals such as the expansion of male suffrage, they did see the wisdom in fighting for economic freedoms too. This is why they supported the repeal of the Corn Laws.

80. **D** The Maastricht Treaty allowed for the creation of a new currency, one that wasn't bound to national borders: the euro. The EU started off somewhat slowly with only a few members, but soon there was significant momentum, and as of this writing, it boasts 28 different member nations.

THE DBQ EXPLAINED

The DBQ in this practice test uses food and drink as a lens through which a person can view European history. This question is definitely broader than an ordinary DBQ question, since it covers 400 years, but it therefore allowing you to demonstrate your knowledge of European history as a whole (and not of one particular era).

That can be a blessing or—if you haven't studied the big picture—a curse.

Protocol tells you to brainstorm outside information about a DBQ question *before* looking at the documents. That might prove to be difficult here. How much do you really know about European diets and methods of food preparation throughout history? Those things typically aren't covered in AP European History classes. It will make much more sense—for this question only—to read the documents and *then* see what associations you can make.

The fullest possible essay, however, will definitely contain three things:

- Visual analysis of the paintings (Documents 1, 2, and 3)
- Outside information that connects each document to the era in which it was written
- Acknowledgement of at least three authors' bias

Here are a few thoughts that might have occurred to you in the time you had to look over the documents.

The Documents

Document 1

A Nobleman Picnic is rife with visual cues that decent food was a splurge in medieval Europe, a luxury that only the nobility enjoyed. The healthy horses tethered to the trees on the left, the wealthy fur robes worn by the noble at the top of the frame, the golden flagons filled with wine or mead in the lower left—and this was all for a casual outdoor picnic. This picture also reflects the manorial system, feudalism. You could also point out that the absence of any peasants is significant.

Document 2

It might be worthwhile to compare and contrast the *Noble family* with Document 1. Unlike the raucous *A Nobleman Picnic*, these people seem much more restrained; even the smallest child on the left resembles a small adult. The children look nearly identical to one another and, more importantly, well-fed. It's no accident that this family posed itself sitting around the simple victuals on its dinner table. It's possible that these people are Puritans of some sort, and you could associate this painting with all sorts of outside knowledge, such as the War of the Roses, Elizabeth I, and even the Puritans who arose following the end of the Tudor reign.

Document 3

The Starbucks phenomenon had a precursor in the London coffeehouse scene of the seventeenth and eighteenth centuries. After centuries of people spending most or all of their days partially drunk, a new beverage was introduced (thanks to the Age of Discovery)—coffee. As a stimulant, it helped people to stay awake, and being seen at the coffeehouse suddenly became all the rage for men, since women weren't typically allowed. A lot of politics was discussed (see the newspapers on the table in the painting), and witty conversation became much more common, as evidenced by the rise of cleverly humorous eighteenth-century writers such as Pope, Dryden, and Swift. It's not too much to say that the discovery of caffeine changed the course of European social life (as did the invention of electric lighting later).

Document 4

A description of the mind-boggling layers of servants that a simple glass of water needed to pass through before reaching Marie Antoinette, this document stands as perfect evidence of the ineffectiveness of the French monarchy on the eve of the French Revolution. Anything related to the Ancien Regime or the moderate phase of the French Revolution could be tied here—as could the fact that Marie Antoinette kept a fake village on the ground of Versailles so that she and her ladies-in-waiting could "play peasant."

Document 5

Unlike Document 4, this document begins a string of three documents in which food is shown to be a major concern of those who worry about the overall health of mass industrial society. In this poem, Lord Byron shows a bit of the old-fashioned *noblesse oblige* by pointing out that the working classes really like to eat meat. It's no coincidence that this document dates from the earliest days of the Second Industrial Revolution, when working classes in the dark industrial hellholes of London, Manchester, and elsewhere were often subsisting on gruel and vegetables.

Document 6

Doubleday points out that as a society grows poorer, its families paradoxically have more children, thereby degrading the quality of their food. Since the English population had doubled during the eighteenth century, this was a real worry. This should evoke many associations with the ideas of nineteenth-century population theorists such as Thomas Malthus (specifically his *Essay on Population*), David Ricardo (the iron law of wages), Jeremy Bentham (utilitarianism), and John Stuart Mill (*On Liberty*). You could also bring up the earlier Agricultural Revolution, which introduced scientific farming to Great Britain. Jethro Tull advocated iron plows and planting by drilling, and Charles Townshend innovated a new form of crop rotation that maintained the nutrient level of the soil.

Document 7

Here, Lee plays the role of the nineteenth-century social reformer (a common figure at this time in history), pointing out that proper nutrition could avoid a host of diseases suffered by those in prisons. You could connect a myriad number of outside pieces of information to this observation, such as the Poor Law of 1834, which forced destitute to enter workhouses where conditions were purposefully miserable.

Document 8

This document is significant in that the author shows an awareness of the problems that liquor consumption presents. It can be tied to the various movements that had grown in England, spearheaded by middle-class women, to limit the vicious effects of alcohol upon the poorest in society.

Document 9

James Bell displays the newly scientific bent of society, but this time applied to nutrition. While science had been around since the establishment of the Royal Society in 1660, Europe in the late nineteenth century was experiencing a boom in the number of scientific discoveries. Anthropology, sociology, and archaeology came into being, while synthetic dyes, man-made fertilizers, and dynamite were all invented. Pasteur's microbes, Lister's disinfectant, Michael Faraday's electromagnetism, Joule's laws of thermodynamics, Mendeleev's periodic table, Curie's isolation of radium, Rutherford's nucleus, Planck's quanta, Darwin's theory of evolution—the list of scientific breakthroughs from this era goes on and on.

Document 10

Feminism enters into the picture in the late nineteenth century as well, and this document registers the outrage that more middle-of-the-road suffragists undoubtedly felt as they chafed against the constrictions of the cult of domesticity. Connect this document to the more militant suffragettes, such as Emmeline Pankhurst and her Women's Social and Political Union. In prison, she went on hunger strikes that only ended with her being force-fed.

Choosing a Thesis Statement

The most difficult part of this DBQ would be to find an appropriate thesis sentence that is broad and yet says something significant. Here are two possible ideas:

- *The changing European attitude towards food and drink reflects the continent's slow transformation from a medieval feudal structure into a solidly middle-class industrial society.*

Or

- *The changing European attitude towards food and drink reflects the decline of nobility and the rise of mass society from the fifteenth to the nineteenth centuries.*

You should be aware of these themes already—the story of European history is largely the rise of more rights (economic, political, social) for more people. Martin Luther King, Jr. had it right when he said that the moral arc of the universe is long, but it bends towards justice.

Remember, it's not necessary to use every document provided; don't feel like you *have* to stretch to find a use for, say, Byron's poem in Document 5. That desperation will show in your essay. Better to use fewer documents (no fewer than two-thirds, though) and create a much more unified essay.

And though it may be tough, always try to find a bias in the documents, even if it's as simple as pointing out that since Document 10 was written by a woman, readers should be suspicious of her opinions about feminism. This is historiography, and graders want to see that you don't blindly swallow every primary source you're fed.

The Free-Response Essay Questions Explained

Question 1

1. Describe the changes on the Iberian peninsula during the second half of the fifteenth century.

Essay Notes

Occasionally, the AP testers will dance around the actual terms that you're supposed to write about. This question is a good example of that. Hopefully you recognized that *Iberian peninsula* referred to Spain and Portugal, and hopefully you also connected the *second half of the fifteenth century* with two towering figures: King Ferdinand and Queen Isabella.

This question, therefore, is essentially asking for a description of the many efforts that this famous power couple took to unify the disparate regions of their peninsula, which led to the creation of what we call modern-day Spain.

Your essay should include some (or all, if you can write quickly) of the following points:

- **Ferdinand and Isabella's marriage** itself, in 1469, united the northern kingdoms of Castile and Aragon. It provoked a ten-year civil war waged by the nobles, who felt their power being threatened. The monarchs eventually won and instituted a new system of government.
- They overhauled the entire administration by insisting upon **meritocracy**: ability, not social status, should determine appointments. (This was three hundred years before Napoleon did the same thing in France.) At the local level, they replaced the nobles as local administrators with people from a lesser class of nobility called the *hidalgos* (similar to gentry in England) who occupied positions called *corregidors*. Each province was allowed to keep its own representative assembly, called a *cortes*.
- The pope granted them the power to run an independent **Inquisition**, for the purpose of weeding out non-Christians. They tapped a man named Torquemada to serve as the Grand Inquisitor. The Inquisition tortured many in a ruthless search for non-believers.
- They famously ejected the **Moors** (Muslims who had ruled the southern portion of the peninsula for seven hundred years) from the southern lands. The culminating moment was the recapture of Granada, and its grand fortress, the Alhambra. Following that, they ejected all **Jews** from Spain as well.
- As a result of this *reconquista* (reconquest), the pope allowed the monarchs the power to make their own appointments. This gave them power over the Catholic Church in their own land, which is no small accomplishment.
- They instituted a **sales tax** to raise revenue without the consent of the *cortes*.
- They instituted a **new system of Castilian law** across the peninsula. It was similar to Roman law.

Question 2

2. Discuss the causes, events, and outcome of the Thirty Years' War.

Essay Notes

This is a wicked question that wise students will avoid. The reason: The Thirty Years' War was a staggeringly complex conflict with multiple causes, multiple conflicts, shifting alliances, and no real outcome. Many history teachers don't even understand it themselves, and it often gets glossed over in lectures.

However, if you're brave enough to attempt to answer the prompt, here are a few key points that you should hit:

- Fought from 1618 to 1648, the war was initially caused by the **Habsburgs**—the Holy Roman Emperors Ferdinand II and Ferdinand III in Austria, along with their Spanish cousin Philip IV.
- The Habsburgs' opponents varied during the thirty years, but included the Danish, the Dutch, and of course France. Sweden also played a role.
- It was also a **German civil war**. The principalities that made up Germany took up arms for or against the Hapsburgs. The reason: many Catholics felt that the **Peace of Augsburg** wasn't being honored, as newly Protestant leaders were scooping up Catholic holdings. On one hand, the pro-Catholic Habsburgs were full of Counter-Reformation zeal, as was Maximilian I of Bavaria, who formed the pro-Catholic League. On the other hand, leaders such as Frederick V of the Palatinate formed significant Protestant alliances.

- Conflict between these groups erupted in the **Bohemian phase** of the war, which was initiated by the **defenestration of Prague**. That's a big word meaning "to throw a person out of a window," which is exactly what happened to Catholic officials by a Protestant group.
- The **Palatine phase** saw the Protestant Frederick V, with the help of the Dutch, attempt to wrestle control of the Palatinate away from the Spanish.
- The **Danish phase** of the war saw France, England, and the Dutch support Denmark in its attack upon the Catholic Habsburgs. The Danish were crushed, and the Holy Roman Emperor issued the Edict of Restitution, demanding all lands that had been taken since 1550 to be returned.
- The **Swedish phase** of the war commenced when King Gustavus Adolphus attacked some of the Catholic German states, but were repelled by the combined Austrian and Spanish forces. Adolphus was killed.
- During the **French phase** of the war, France declared war on Spain and seized the Alsace region. The Swedes returned to the German area and seized more land.
- The war was finally concluded with the **Peace of Westphalia**. Within the German portions of the Holy Roman Empire, religion was nullified, and all Catholic-Protestant issues supposedly laid to bed. The Habsburg territories of Bohemia and Austria stayed under the control of the Catholic Habsburgs, which they always had been. Sweden received a cash indemnity for its trouble. In short, nothing changed.

Question 3

3. Describe the extent of the success of Louis XIV's attempts to create a more prosperous France.

Essay Notes

Louis XIV, who ruled France from 1643 to 1715, is by far the most absolute monarch in European history. It's important to remember that being an absolute ruler isn't the same thing creating a healthy society. It's fair to say that some of his policies worked (even at the expense of his own people), while others didn't. The blackest mark on his historical record was his foreign policy, which dragged down his efforts to improve the domestic economy.

An essay on Louis XIV should contain some or all of the following points:

- As a boy, his family was killed in Paris. This occurred during the **Fronde**, a rebellion by the nobles, during which time the country was being run by **Cardinal Mazarin**. It also explains why he never lived in Paris again.
- To achieve his goals of usurping power from the nobles, he built a pleasure palace, **Versailles**, just outside of Paris. As the center of French culture, it was a palace of temptations that the nobility found impossible to leave, and subsequently there was a power vacuum in their home districts, which Louis filled with his own hand-picked provincial **intendants**. As the king's representatives in the farflung regions, they monitored Louis's refinements of the French military, including the institution of a merit promotion system and a policy of military enlistment limited to four years and single men. They also collected taxes and put down peasant rebellions.
- He also tried to create religious uniformity under the Catholic Church with less success. He **revoked the Edict of Nantes** in order to "cleanse" the country of Huguenots. Later, he also tried to get a papal bull to condemn the Jansenists, a Catholic faction, but Louis XIV died before he could put the policy into effect. In attempting to unify the country through religion, Louis XIV simply alienated his people.

- His economic advisor, **Colbert**, recommended that tax money go towards building a navy so that France could engage the Netherlands in battle, whom Colbert viewed as France's biggest economic enemy because it dominated overseas trade. Louis listened to him, built a navy, fought the Dutch, and promptly lost.
- Another advisor, **Louvois**, said that land wars were a better option. Louis listened to him, built a bigger army, conquered some new parcels of land, and then was promptly defeated by a **Grand Alliance** (spearheaded by England and, surprise, the Dutch).
- The biggest foreign policy disappointment was the **War of Spanish Succession**, which was intended to gain the Spanish throne for Louis's grandson, Philip. However, Louis himself had refused to promise to open Spain to trade, and so the offer was revoked. A war ensued, and France was defeated. At the Peace of Utrecht, Philip was once again offered the throne of Spain, but with one condition: He couldn't hold both Spanish and French thrones. He agreed, and became the king of Spain. The war marked the end of French hegemony, and it was a large waste of money for the French, because it put added stress upon the peasantry in the form of more taxation. This pattern culminated, decades later, in the French Revolution.

Question 4

4. Analyze the actions taken towards the Catholic Church during the French Revolution.

Essay Notes

This should be an open-and-shut essay. You should remember that one of the goals of the French Revolution was the de-Christianization of France.

A good essay should touch upon some or all of the following points:

- The historical strength of the Catholic Church is worth mentioning, perhaps in the introduction. The Catholic monarchy had been unfriendly to the Hugenots for well over a century, **revoking the Edict of Nantes**, even killing thousands in the **St. Bartholomew's Day Massacre**.
- The Ancien Regime had institutionalized the authority of the clergy in its status as the **First Estate**. Its power was legendary. As the largest landowner in the country, the Catholic Church controlled properties which provided massive revenues from its tenants; it also had an enormous income from the collection of tithes. Since the Church kept the registry of births, deaths, and marriages and was the only institution that provided primary and secondary education and hospitals, it influenced all citizens.
- This is why, after the dissolution of the First and Second Estates, the new **National Assembly confiscated all Church lands**. Because the government was bankrupt, the National Assembly was forced to use the money derived from the sale of these properties as insurance for the brand-new paper currency, the assignat. This currency was accepted by foreign creditors, and therefore was used to pay down the French government's enormous debts.
- The National Assembly also signed the **Civil Constitution of the Clergy**, which stripped clerics of their special rights—the clergy were to be made employees of the state, elected by their parish or bishopric, and the number of bishoprics was to be reduced. It also required all priests and bishops to swear an oath of fidelity to the new order or face dismissal, deportation, or death.
- Three bishops and two hundred priests were killed by a mob in the **September Massacres**.
- Statues, crosses, bells and other religious iconography were removed from places of worship and often destroyed.

- The new government instituted the **Cult of Reason** (and later the Cult of the Supreme Being under Robespierre), a brand-new belief system inspired by Enlightenment principles. It was intended to replace the Catholic Church, and its goal was to lead all humans towards logical perfectability. The Cathedral of Notre Dame was transformed into a Temple of Reason.
- The Gregorian calendar, which had been commissioned by the papacy, was replaced by a new **French Republican calendar**, which abolished the sabbath.
- Priests were routinely deported to penal colonies.
- After the Revolution ended, Napoleon signed the **Concordat of 1801**, which returned Catholicism as the majority church of France, and made the Catholic Church into an arm of his government. This would be appropriate for the conclusion of the essay.

Question 5

5. Describe the effects of World War I upon European society.

Essay Notes

This is an incredibly broad question, . . . but the upside is that you don't have to go into too much detail, since the so-called "Great War" had so many different effects upon the continent.

A good essay will use some (or all) of the following points:

- The **Russian Revolution** of 1917. Stimulated in part by food shortages caused by the war effort, the Bolsheviks, led by Lenin, took over the country and decided to abandon the war, which they did in the **Treaty of Brest-Litovsk**, surrendering Poland, Ukraine, Finland, and the Baltic provinces to Germany. Internally, of course, this revolution resulted in the formation and growth of the Soviet Union, and that eventually led to the Cold War, which defined the second half of the twentieth century.
- The **influenza epidemic** of 1918, most of which technically occurred after the war had ended, was found by a team of English virologists to have to begun in a hospital camp in France. (The term "Spanish flu" is a misnomer; the Spanish, being neutral in the war, were simply the first to freely report on the epidemic, and were unjustly tagged by the world with having started it.) Since 50 million people died worldwide as a result, it's fair to say that this was an effect of the unsanitary conditions of the war.
- The Allied occupation of Istanbul led to the official collapse of the **Ottoman Empire**, often called "the sick man of Europe."
- The English found themselves economically crippled. Though they had been the world's biggest investor before the war, they found themselves saddled with nearly a half billion pounds worth of **war debts**. To their credit, they paid off their debts in a relatively short few years.
- An entire generation of young people grew up devastated (and lopsided, since far more men than women had perished). This became known as the **Lost Generation**, described accurately by writers such as Ernest Hemingway.
- The war also accelerated the **women's suffrage** movement in England. Women had served capably in factories during the war effort and, combined with the shortage of available young men, provided the momentum to reach a critical tipping point. In 1918, Parliament gave Englishwomen over age thirty the right to vote.
- The **Treaty of Versailles** deserves a full paragraph, mostly for the famously punitive restrictions it placed upon Germany. That country was forced to make an annual payment of $5 billion in reparations, relinquish its overseas colonies, return the Alsace-Lorraine to France, limit its own standing

army, and accept full blame for the war. This created the conditions that led to severe economic deprivation in the 1920s, hyperinflation, a desperate populace, and the eventual rise of the Nazi party.

- The Treaty of Versailles also provided for the founding of the first international council: **the League of Nations**.
- The constellation of various ethnicities that formed Austria-Hungary was finally shattered, and new countries were formed out of its ethnic pieces, including Hungary, Czechoslovakia, and Yugoslavia (the last two of which themselves splintered in the 1990s).
- The many **overseas colonial troops** who fought for the French returned home and, tired of being treated as second-class citizens even after their French military service, began the first pro-independence movements in areas such as North Africa, Senegal, Madagascar, and Indochina.

Question 6

6. Analyze the reasons for the disintegration of the Soviet Union in the late twentieth century.

Essay Notes

Provided that your teacher made it to the late twentieth century, this should be a fairly easy question to answer.

A good essay should include some (or all) of the following points:

- The most important underlying reason was **economic privation**. For decades, the Soviets had put their own political and ideological needs ahead of the people's need to eat decently, live warmly, and learn efficiently. During the four decades of the Cold War, the Soviets had always struggled to keep up with the United States' level of defense spending, known as the **arms race**, and they did so at the expense of things like bread and potatoes.
- The **invasion of Afghanistan** in the early 1980s was a major contributor to the breakup. It placed unprecedented economic and emotional stress upon the system, exposing its deep weaknesses. In short, it broke the Soviet bank.
- The disaster at **Chernobyl**—the total meltdown of a nuclear reactor in the Ukraine—affected Soviet morale.
- What finally changed was a new generation of leaders, exemplified by **Mikhail Gorbachev**, who had spent time in the West. He decided to restructure the economy (an effort called **perestroika**) and then urged the people to adopt **glasnost** (openness to new ideas). He challenged the Soviet people to wean themselves off the central government, to seize control of their own lives.
- If Gorbachev struck a match, then it started a brush fire in the various Soviet satellite states. The first to demand independent elections was **Poland**, where **Lech Walesa** and his political party, **Solidarity**, began demanding a free election. The Communist party reluctantly gave up its monopoly on political power in that country, and in December 1990, Walesa was elected president, and the Polish people began a long, difficult conversion to democratic capitalism. This began a chain reaction that included the **Velvet Revolution** in **Czechoslovakia**, which saw poet and playwright **Václav Havel** elected president.
- The grand finale to the disintegration of the satellite states was the collapse of the **Berlin Wall** and the reunification of Germany, which was televised. East Germany was annexed quickly by West German Chancellor **Helmut Kohl.**

- Near the end, Gorbachev attempted to broker an agreement between all the states. Called the **Treaty of the Union**, it would have declared all the former Soviet states to be part of a loose confederation. Hardline communists, however, tried to oust him at this point, and the coup was averted by a leader named **Boris Yeltsin**, who positioned himself between the communist military tanks and the parliament building. Gorbachev resigned, and Yeltsin became the next premier.

The Princeton Review

Completely darken bubbles with a No. 2 pencil. If you make a mistake, be sure to erase mark completely. Erase all stray marks.

1
YOUR NAME: _____
(Print)   Last   First   M.I.

SIGNATURE: _____   DATE: /   /

HOME ADDRESS: _____
(Print)   Number and Street

_____
City   State   Zip Code

PHONE NO.: _____
(Print)

IMPORTANT: Please fill in these boxes exactly as shown on the back cover of your test book.

2. TEST FORM

6. DATE OF BIRTH

Month		Day		Year	
⊂ ⊃ JAN					
⊂ ⊃ FEB					
⊂ ⊃ MAR	⊂0⊃	⊂0⊃	⊂0⊃	⊂0⊃	
⊂ ⊃ APR	⊂1⊃	⊂1⊃	⊂1⊃	⊂1⊃	
⊂ ⊃ MAY	⊂2⊃	⊂2⊃	⊂2⊃	⊂2⊃	
⊂ ⊃ JUN	⊂3⊃	⊂3⊃	⊂3⊃	⊂3⊃	
⊂ ⊃ JUL		⊂4⊃	⊂4⊃	⊂4⊃	
⊂ ⊃ AUG		⊂5⊃	⊂5⊃	⊂5⊃	
⊂ ⊃ SEP		⊂6⊃	⊂6⊃	⊂6⊃	
⊂ ⊃ OCT		⊂7⊃	⊂7⊃	⊂7⊃	
⊂ ⊃ NOV		⊂8⊃	⊂8⊃	⊂8⊃	
⊂ ⊃ DEC		⊂9⊃	⊂9⊃	⊂9⊃	

3. TEST CODE   4. REGISTRATION NUMBER

⊂0⊃	⊂A⊃	⊂0⊃	⊂0⊃	⊂0⊃	⊂0⊃	⊂0⊃	⊂0⊃	⊂0⊃	⊂0⊃	⊂0⊃
⊂1⊃	⊂B⊃	⊂1⊃	⊂1⊃	⊂1⊃	⊂1⊃	⊂1⊃	⊂1⊃	⊂1⊃	⊂1⊃	⊂1⊃
⊂2⊃	⊂C⊃	⊂2⊃	⊂2⊃	⊂2⊃	⊂2⊃	⊂2⊃	⊂2⊃	⊂2⊃	⊂2⊃	⊂2⊃
⊂3⊃	⊂D⊃	⊂3⊃	⊂3⊃	⊂3⊃	⊂3⊃	⊂3⊃	⊂3⊃	⊂3⊃	⊂3⊃	⊂3⊃
⊂4⊃	⊂E⊃	⊂4⊃	⊂4⊃	⊂4⊃	⊂4⊃	⊂4⊃	⊂4⊃	⊂4⊃	⊂4⊃	⊂4⊃
⊂5⊃	⊂F⊃	⊂5⊃	⊂5⊃	⊂5⊃	⊂5⊃	⊂5⊃	⊂5⊃	⊂5⊃	⊂5⊃	⊂5⊃
⊂6⊃	⊂G⊃	⊂6⊃	⊂6⊃	⊂6⊃	⊂6⊃	⊂6⊃	⊂6⊃	⊂6⊃	⊂6⊃	⊂6⊃
⊂7⊃		⊂7⊃	⊂7⊃	⊂7⊃	⊂7⊃	⊂7⊃	⊂7⊃	⊂7⊃	⊂7⊃	⊂7⊃
⊂8⊃		⊂8⊃	⊂8⊃	⊂8⊃	⊂8⊃	⊂8⊃	⊂8⊃	⊂8⊃	⊂8⊃	⊂8⊃
⊂9⊃		⊂9⊃	⊂9⊃	⊂9⊃	⊂9⊃	⊂9⊃	⊂9⊃	⊂9⊃	⊂9⊃	⊂9⊃

7. SEX
⊂ ⊃ MALE
⊂ ⊃ FEMALE

The Princeton Review
© TPR Education IP Holdings, LLC
FORM NO. 00001-PR

5. YOUR NAME

First 4 letters of last name				FIRST INIT	MID INIT
⊂A⊃	⊂A⊃	⊂A⊃	⊂A⊃	⊂A⊃	⊂A⊃
⊂B⊃	⊂B⊃	⊂B⊃	⊂B⊃	⊂B⊃	⊂B⊃
⊂C⊃	⊂C⊃	⊂C⊃	⊂C⊃	⊂C⊃	⊂C⊃
⊂D⊃	⊂D⊃	⊂D⊃	⊂D⊃	⊂D⊃	⊂D⊃
⊂E⊃	⊂E⊃	⊂E⊃	⊂E⊃	⊂E⊃	⊂E⊃
⊂F⊃	⊂F⊃	⊂F⊃	⊂F⊃	⊂F⊃	⊂F⊃
⊂G⊃	⊂G⊃	⊂G⊃	⊂G⊃	⊂G⊃	⊂G⊃
⊂H⊃	⊂H⊃	⊂H⊃	⊂H⊃	⊂H⊃	⊂H⊃
⊂I⊃	⊂I⊃	⊂I⊃	⊂I⊃	⊂I⊃	⊂I⊃
⊂J⊃	⊂J⊃	⊂J⊃	⊂J⊃	⊂J⊃	⊂J⊃
⊂K⊃	⊂K⊃	⊂K⊃	⊂K⊃	⊂K⊃	⊂K⊃
⊂L⊃	⊂L⊃	⊂L⊃	⊂L⊃	⊂L⊃	⊂L⊃
⊂M⊃	⊂M⊃	⊂M⊃	⊂M⊃	⊂M⊃	⊂M⊃
⊂N⊃	⊂N⊃	⊂N⊃	⊂N⊃	⊂N⊃	⊂N⊃
⊂O⊃	⊂O⊃	⊂O⊃	⊂O⊃	⊂O⊃	⊂O⊃
⊂P⊃	⊂P⊃	⊂P⊃	⊂P⊃	⊂P⊃	⊂P⊃
⊂Q⊃	⊂Q⊃	⊂Q⊃	⊂Q⊃	⊂Q⊃	⊂Q⊃
⊂R⊃	⊂R⊃	⊂R⊃	⊂R⊃	⊂R⊃	⊂R⊃
⊂S⊃	⊂S⊃	⊂S⊃	⊂S⊃	⊂S⊃	⊂S⊃
⊂T⊃	⊂T⊃	⊂T⊃	⊂T⊃	⊂T⊃	⊂T⊃
⊂U⊃	⊂U⊃	⊂U⊃	⊂U⊃	⊂U⊃	⊂U⊃
⊂V⊃	⊂V⊃	⊂V⊃	⊂V⊃	⊂V⊃	⊂V⊃
⊂W⊃	⊂W⊃	⊂W⊃	⊂W⊃	⊂W⊃	⊂W⊃
⊂X⊃	⊂X⊃	⊂X⊃	⊂X⊃	⊂X⊃	⊂X⊃
⊂Y⊃	⊂Y⊃	⊂Y⊃	⊂Y⊃	⊂Y⊃	⊂Y⊃
⊂Z⊃	⊂Z⊃	⊂Z⊃	⊂Z⊃	⊂Z⊃	⊂Z⊃

Start with number 1 for each new section. If a section has fewer questions than answer spaces, leave the extra answer spaces blank.

1 ⊂A⊃ ⊂B⊃ ⊂C⊃ ⊂D⊃ ⊂E⊃	21 ⊂A⊃ ⊂B⊃ ⊂C⊃ ⊂D⊃ ⊂E⊃	41 ⊂A⊃ ⊂B⊃ ⊂C⊃ ⊂D⊃ ⊂E⊃	61 ⊂A⊃ ⊂B⊃ ⊂C⊃ ⊂D⊃ ⊂E⊃
2 ⊂A⊃ ⊂B⊃ ⊂C⊃ ⊂D⊃ ⊂E⊃	22 ⊂A⊃ ⊂B⊃ ⊂C⊃ ⊂D⊃ ⊂E⊃	42 ⊂A⊃ ⊂B⊃ ⊂C⊃ ⊂D⊃ ⊂E⊃	62 ⊂A⊃ ⊂B⊃ ⊂C⊃ ⊂D⊃ ⊂E⊃
3 ⊂A⊃ ⊂B⊃ ⊂C⊃ ⊂D⊃ ⊂E⊃	23 ⊂A⊃ ⊂B⊃ ⊂C⊃ ⊂D⊃ ⊂E⊃	43 ⊂A⊃ ⊂B⊃ ⊂C⊃ ⊂D⊃ ⊂E⊃	63 ⊂A⊃ ⊂B⊃ ⊂C⊃ ⊂D⊃ ⊂E⊃
4 ⊂A⊃ ⊂B⊃ ⊂C⊃ ⊂D⊃ ⊂E⊃	24 ⊂A⊃ ⊂B⊃ ⊂C⊃ ⊂D⊃ ⊂E⊃	44 ⊂A⊃ ⊂B⊃ ⊂C⊃ ⊂D⊃ ⊂E⊃	64 ⊂A⊃ ⊂B⊃ ⊂C⊃ ⊂D⊃ ⊂E⊃
5 ⊂A⊃ ⊂B⊃ ⊂C⊃ ⊂D⊃ ⊂E⊃	25 ⊂A⊃ ⊂B⊃ ⊂C⊃ ⊂D⊃ ⊂E⊃	45 ⊂A⊃ ⊂B⊃ ⊂C⊃ ⊂D⊃ ⊂E⊃	65 ⊂A⊃ ⊂B⊃ ⊂C⊃ ⊂D⊃ ⊂E⊃
6 ⊂A⊃ ⊂B⊃ ⊂C⊃ ⊂D⊃ ⊂E⊃	26 ⊂A⊃ ⊂B⊃ ⊂C⊃ ⊂D⊃ ⊂E⊃	46 ⊂A⊃ ⊂B⊃ ⊂C⊃ ⊂D⊃ ⊂E⊃	66 ⊂A⊃ ⊂B⊃ ⊂C⊃ ⊂D⊃ ⊂E⊃
7 ⊂A⊃ ⊂B⊃ ⊂C⊃ ⊂D⊃ ⊂E⊃	27 ⊂A⊃ ⊂B⊃ ⊂C⊃ ⊂D⊃ ⊂E⊃	47 ⊂A⊃ ⊂B⊃ ⊂C⊃ ⊂D⊃ ⊂E⊃	67 ⊂A⊃ ⊂B⊃ ⊂C⊃ ⊂D⊃ ⊂E⊃
8 ⊂A⊃ ⊂B⊃ ⊂C⊃ ⊂D⊃ ⊂E⊃	28 ⊂A⊃ ⊂B⊃ ⊂C⊃ ⊂D⊃ ⊂E⊃	48 ⊂A⊃ ⊂B⊃ ⊂C⊃ ⊂D⊃ ⊂E⊃	68 ⊂A⊃ ⊂B⊃ ⊂C⊃ ⊂D⊃ ⊂E⊃
9 ⊂A⊃ ⊂B⊃ ⊂C⊃ ⊂D⊃ ⊂E⊃	29 ⊂A⊃ ⊂B⊃ ⊂C⊃ ⊂D⊃ ⊂E⊃	49 ⊂A⊃ ⊂B⊃ ⊂C⊃ ⊂D⊃ ⊂E⊃	69 ⊂A⊃ ⊂B⊃ ⊂C⊃ ⊂D⊃ ⊂E⊃
10 ⊂A⊃ ⊂B⊃ ⊂C⊃ ⊂D⊃ ⊂E⊃	30 ⊂A⊃ ⊂B⊃ ⊂C⊃ ⊂D⊃ ⊂E⊃	50 ⊂A⊃ ⊂B⊃ ⊂C⊃ ⊂D⊃ ⊂E⊃	70 ⊂A⊃ ⊂B⊃ ⊂C⊃ ⊂D⊃ ⊂E⊃
11 ⊂A⊃ ⊂B⊃ ⊂C⊃ ⊂D⊃ ⊂E⊃	31 ⊂A⊃ ⊂B⊃ ⊂C⊃ ⊂D⊃ ⊂E⊃	51 ⊂A⊃ ⊂B⊃ ⊂C⊃ ⊂D⊃ ⊂E⊃	71 ⊂A⊃ ⊂B⊃ ⊂C⊃ ⊂D⊃ ⊂E⊃
12 ⊂A⊃ ⊂B⊃ ⊂C⊃ ⊂D⊃ ⊂E⊃	32 ⊂A⊃ ⊂B⊃ ⊂C⊃ ⊂D⊃ ⊂E⊃	52 ⊂A⊃ ⊂B⊃ ⊂C⊃ ⊂D⊃ ⊂E⊃	72 ⊂A⊃ ⊂B⊃ ⊂C⊃ ⊂D⊃ ⊂E⊃
13 ⊂A⊃ ⊂B⊃ ⊂C⊃ ⊂D⊃ ⊂E⊃	33 ⊂A⊃ ⊂B⊃ ⊂C⊃ ⊂D⊃ ⊂E⊃	53 ⊂A⊃ ⊂B⊃ ⊂C⊃ ⊂D⊃ ⊂E⊃	73 ⊂A⊃ ⊂B⊃ ⊂C⊃ ⊂D⊃ ⊂E⊃
14 ⊂A⊃ ⊂B⊃ ⊂C⊃ ⊂D⊃ ⊂E⊃	34 ⊂A⊃ ⊂B⊃ ⊂C⊃ ⊂D⊃ ⊂E⊃	54 ⊂A⊃ ⊂B⊃ ⊂C⊃ ⊂D⊃ ⊂E⊃	74 ⊂A⊃ ⊂B⊃ ⊂C⊃ ⊂D⊃ ⊂E⊃
15 ⊂A⊃ ⊂B⊃ ⊂C⊃ ⊂D⊃ ⊂E⊃	35 ⊂A⊃ ⊂B⊃ ⊂C⊃ ⊂D⊃ ⊂E⊃	55 ⊂A⊃ ⊂B⊃ ⊂C⊃ ⊂D⊃ ⊂E⊃	75 ⊂A⊃ ⊂B⊃ ⊂C⊃ ⊂D⊃ ⊂E⊃
16 ⊂A⊃ ⊂B⊃ ⊂C⊃ ⊂D⊃ ⊂E⊃	36 ⊂A⊃ ⊂B⊃ ⊂C⊃ ⊂D⊃ ⊂E⊃	56 ⊂A⊃ ⊂B⊃ ⊂C⊃ ⊂D⊃ ⊂E⊃	76 ⊂A⊃ ⊂B⊃ ⊂C⊃ ⊂D⊃ ⊂E⊃
17 ⊂A⊃ ⊂B⊃ ⊂C⊃ ⊂D⊃ ⊂E⊃	37 ⊂A⊃ ⊂B⊃ ⊂C⊃ ⊂D⊃ ⊂E⊃	57 ⊂A⊃ ⊂B⊃ ⊂C⊃ ⊂D⊃ ⊂E⊃	77 ⊂A⊃ ⊂B⊃ ⊂C⊃ ⊂D⊃ ⊂E⊃
18 ⊂A⊃ ⊂B⊃ ⊂C⊃ ⊂D⊃ ⊂E⊃	38 ⊂A⊃ ⊂B⊃ ⊂C⊃ ⊂D⊃ ⊂E⊃	58 ⊂A⊃ ⊂B⊃ ⊂C⊃ ⊂D⊃ ⊂E⊃	78 ⊂A⊃ ⊂B⊃ ⊂C⊃ ⊂D⊃ ⊂E⊃
19 ⊂A⊃ ⊂B⊃ ⊂C⊃ ⊂D⊃ ⊂E⊃	39 ⊂A⊃ ⊂B⊃ ⊂C⊃ ⊂D⊃ ⊂E⊃	59 ⊂A⊃ ⊂B⊃ ⊂C⊃ ⊂D⊃ ⊂E⊃	79 ⊂A⊃ ⊂B⊃ ⊂C⊃ ⊂D⊃ ⊂E⊃
20 ⊂A⊃ ⊂B⊃ ⊂C⊃ ⊂D⊃ ⊂E⊃	40 ⊂A⊃ ⊂B⊃ ⊂C⊃ ⊂D⊃ ⊂E⊃	60 ⊂A⊃ ⊂B⊃ ⊂C⊃ ⊂D⊃ ⊂E⊃	80 ⊂A⊃ ⊂B⊃ ⊂C⊃ ⊂D⊃ ⊂E⊃

DO NOT MARK IN THIS AREA
⊂ ⊃ ⊂ ⊃ ⊂ ⊃ ⊂ ⊃ ⊂ ⊃ ⊂ ⊃ ⊂ ⊃ ⊂ ⊃ ⊂ ⊃ ⊂ ⊃ ⊂ ⊃ ⊂ ⊃ ⊂ ⊃

The Princeton Review

Completely darken bubbles with a No. 2 pencil. If you make a mistake, be sure to erase mark completely. Erase all stray marks.

1

YOUR NAME: _____
(Print)   Last   First   M.I.

SIGNATURE: _____ DATE: __ / __ / __

HOME ADDRESS: _____
(Print)   Number and Street

_____
City   State   Zip Code

PHONE NO.: _____
(Print)

IMPORTANT: Please fill in these boxes exactly as shown on the back cover of your test book.

2. TEST FORM

6. DATE OF BIRTH

Month		Day		Year	
⊂ ⊃ JAN					
⊂ ⊃ FEB					
⊂ ⊃ MAR	⊂0⊃	⊂0⊃	⊂0⊃	⊂0⊃
⊂ ⊃ APR	⊂1⊃	⊂1⊃	⊂1⊃	⊂1⊃
⊂ ⊃ MAY	⊂2⊃	⊂2⊃	⊂2⊃	⊂2⊃
⊂ ⊃ JUN	⊂3⊃	⊂3⊃	⊂3⊃	⊂3⊃
⊂ ⊃ JUL		⊂4⊃	⊂4⊃	⊂4⊃
⊂ ⊃ AUG		⊂5⊃	⊂5⊃	⊂5⊃
⊂ ⊃ SEP		⊂6⊃	⊂6⊃	⊂6⊃
⊂ ⊃ OCT		⊂7⊃	⊂7⊃	⊂7⊃
⊂ ⊃ NOV		⊂8⊃	⊂8⊃	⊂8⊃
⊂ ⊃ DEC		⊂9⊃	⊂9⊃	⊂9⊃

3. TEST CODE   4. REGISTRATION NUMBER

⊂0⊃	⊂A⊃	⊂0⊃	⊂0⊃	⊂0⊃	⊂0⊃	⊂0⊃	⊂0⊃	⊂0⊃	⊂0⊃	⊂0⊃
⊂1⊃	⊂B⊃	⊂1⊃	⊂1⊃	⊂1⊃	⊂1⊃	⊂1⊃	⊂1⊃	⊂1⊃	⊂1⊃	⊂1⊃
⊂2⊃	⊂C⊃	⊂2⊃	⊂2⊃	⊂2⊃	⊂2⊃	⊂2⊃	⊂2⊃	⊂2⊃	⊂2⊃	⊂2⊃
⊂3⊃	⊂D⊃	⊂3⊃	⊂3⊃	⊂3⊃	⊂3⊃	⊂3⊃	⊂3⊃	⊂3⊃	⊂3⊃	⊂3⊃
⊂4⊃	⊂E⊃	⊂4⊃	⊂4⊃	⊂4⊃	⊂4⊃	⊂4⊃	⊂4⊃	⊂4⊃	⊂4⊃	⊂4⊃
⊂5⊃	⊂F⊃	⊂5⊃	⊂5⊃	⊂5⊃	⊂5⊃	⊂5⊃	⊂5⊃	⊂5⊃	⊂5⊃	⊂5⊃
⊂6⊃	⊂G⊃	⊂6⊃	⊂6⊃	⊂6⊃	⊂6⊃	⊂6⊃	⊂6⊃	⊂6⊃	⊂6⊃	⊂6⊃
⊂7⊃		⊂7⊃	⊂7⊃	⊂7⊃	⊂7⊃	⊂7⊃	⊂7⊃	⊂7⊃	⊂7⊃	⊂7⊃
⊂8⊃		⊂8⊃	⊂8⊃	⊂8⊃	⊂8⊃	⊂8⊃	⊂8⊃	⊂8⊃	⊂8⊃	⊂8⊃
⊂9⊃		⊂9⊃	⊂9⊃	⊂9⊃	⊂9⊃	⊂9⊃	⊂9⊃	⊂9⊃	⊂9⊃	⊂9⊃

7. SEX
⊂ ⊃ MALE
⊂ ⊃ FEMALE

The Princeton Review
© TPR Education IP Holdings, LLC
FORM NO. 00001-PR

5. YOUR NAME

First 4 letters of last name				FIRST INIT	MID INIT
⊂A⊃	⊂A⊃	⊂A⊃	⊂A⊃	⊂A⊃	⊂A⊃
⊂B⊃	⊂B⊃	⊂B⊃	⊂B⊃	⊂B⊃	⊂B⊃
⊂C⊃	⊂C⊃	⊂C⊃	⊂C⊃	⊂C⊃	⊂C⊃
⊂D⊃	⊂D⊃	⊂D⊃	⊂D⊃	⊂D⊃	⊂D⊃
⊂E⊃	⊂E⊃	⊂E⊃	⊂E⊃	⊂E⊃	⊂E⊃
⊂F⊃	⊂F⊃	⊂F⊃	⊂F⊃	⊂F⊃	⊂F⊃
⊂G⊃	⊂G⊃	⊂G⊃	⊂G⊃	⊂G⊃	⊂G⊃
⊂H⊃	⊂H⊃	⊂H⊃	⊂H⊃	⊂H⊃	⊂H⊃
⊂I⊃	⊂I⊃	⊂I⊃	⊂I⊃	⊂I⊃	⊂I⊃
⊂J⊃	⊂J⊃	⊂J⊃	⊂J⊃	⊂J⊃	⊂J⊃
⊂K⊃	⊂K⊃	⊂K⊃	⊂K⊃	⊂K⊃	⊂K⊃
⊂L⊃	⊂L⊃	⊂L⊃	⊂L⊃	⊂L⊃	⊂L⊃
⊂M⊃	⊂M⊃	⊂M⊃	⊂M⊃	⊂M⊃	⊂M⊃
⊂N⊃	⊂N⊃	⊂N⊃	⊂N⊃	⊂N⊃	⊂N⊃
⊂O⊃	⊂O⊃	⊂O⊃	⊂O⊃	⊂O⊃	⊂O⊃
⊂P⊃	⊂P⊃	⊂P⊃	⊂P⊃	⊂P⊃	⊂P⊃
⊂Q⊃	⊂Q⊃	⊂Q⊃	⊂Q⊃	⊂Q⊃	⊂Q⊃
⊂R⊃	⊂R⊃	⊂R⊃	⊂R⊃	⊂R⊃	⊂R⊃
⊂S⊃	⊂S⊃	⊂S⊃	⊂S⊃	⊂S⊃	⊂S⊃
⊂T⊃	⊂T⊃	⊂T⊃	⊂T⊃	⊂T⊃	⊂T⊃
⊂U⊃	⊂U⊃	⊂U⊃	⊂U⊃	⊂U⊃	⊂U⊃
⊂V⊃	⊂V⊃	⊂V⊃	⊂V⊃	⊂V⊃	⊂V⊃
⊂W⊃	⊂W⊃	⊂W⊃	⊂W⊃	⊂W⊃	⊂W⊃
⊂X⊃	⊂X⊃	⊂X⊃	⊂X⊃	⊂X⊃	⊂X⊃
⊂Y⊃	⊂Y⊃	⊂Y⊃	⊂Y⊃	⊂Y⊃	⊂Y⊃
⊂Z⊃	⊂Z⊃	⊂Z⊃	⊂Z⊃	⊂Z⊃	⊂Z⊃

Start with number 1 for each new section. If a section has fewer questions than answer spaces, leave the extra answer spaces blank.

1 ⊂A⊃ ⊂B⊃ ⊂C⊃ ⊂D⊃ ⊂E⊃	21 ⊂A⊃ ⊂B⊃ ⊂C⊃ ⊂D⊃ ⊂E⊃	41 ⊂A⊃ ⊂B⊃ ⊂C⊃ ⊂D⊃ ⊂E⊃	61 ⊂A⊃ ⊂B⊃ ⊂C⊃ ⊂D⊃ ⊂E⊃
2 ⊂A⊃ ⊂B⊃ ⊂C⊃ ⊂D⊃ ⊂E⊃	22 ⊂A⊃ ⊂B⊃ ⊂C⊃ ⊂D⊃ ⊂E⊃	42 ⊂A⊃ ⊂B⊃ ⊂C⊃ ⊂D⊃ ⊂E⊃	62 ⊂A⊃ ⊂B⊃ ⊂C⊃ ⊂D⊃ ⊂E⊃
3 ⊂A⊃ ⊂B⊃ ⊂C⊃ ⊂D⊃ ⊂E⊃	23 ⊂A⊃ ⊂B⊃ ⊂C⊃ ⊂D⊃ ⊂E⊃	43 ⊂A⊃ ⊂B⊃ ⊂C⊃ ⊂D⊃ ⊂E⊃	63 ⊂A⊃ ⊂B⊃ ⊂C⊃ ⊂D⊃ ⊂E⊃
4 ⊂A⊃ ⊂B⊃ ⊂C⊃ ⊂D⊃ ⊂E⊃	24 ⊂A⊃ ⊂B⊃ ⊂C⊃ ⊂D⊃ ⊂E⊃	44 ⊂A⊃ ⊂B⊃ ⊂C⊃ ⊂D⊃ ⊂E⊃	64 ⊂A⊃ ⊂B⊃ ⊂C⊃ ⊂D⊃ ⊂E⊃
5 ⊂A⊃ ⊂B⊃ ⊂C⊃ ⊂D⊃ ⊂E⊃	25 ⊂A⊃ ⊂B⊃ ⊂C⊃ ⊂D⊃ ⊂E⊃	45 ⊂A⊃ ⊂B⊃ ⊂C⊃ ⊂D⊃ ⊂E⊃	65 ⊂A⊃ ⊂B⊃ ⊂C⊃ ⊂D⊃ ⊂E⊃
6 ⊂A⊃ ⊂B⊃ ⊂C⊃ ⊂D⊃ ⊂E⊃	26 ⊂A⊃ ⊂B⊃ ⊂C⊃ ⊂D⊃ ⊂E⊃	46 ⊂A⊃ ⊂B⊃ ⊂C⊃ ⊂D⊃ ⊂E⊃	66 ⊂A⊃ ⊂B⊃ ⊂C⊃ ⊂D⊃ ⊂E⊃
7 ⊂A⊃ ⊂B⊃ ⊂C⊃ ⊂D⊃ ⊂E⊃	27 ⊂A⊃ ⊂B⊃ ⊂C⊃ ⊂D⊃ ⊂E⊃	47 ⊂A⊃ ⊂B⊃ ⊂C⊃ ⊂D⊃ ⊂E⊃	67 ⊂A⊃ ⊂B⊃ ⊂C⊃ ⊂D⊃ ⊂E⊃
8 ⊂A⊃ ⊂B⊃ ⊂C⊃ ⊂D⊃ ⊂E⊃	28 ⊂A⊃ ⊂B⊃ ⊂C⊃ ⊂D⊃ ⊂E⊃	48 ⊂A⊃ ⊂B⊃ ⊂C⊃ ⊂D⊃ ⊂E⊃	68 ⊂A⊃ ⊂B⊃ ⊂C⊃ ⊂D⊃ ⊂E⊃
9 ⊂A⊃ ⊂B⊃ ⊂C⊃ ⊂D⊃ ⊂E⊃	29 ⊂A⊃ ⊂B⊃ ⊂C⊃ ⊂D⊃ ⊂E⊃	49 ⊂A⊃ ⊂B⊃ ⊂C⊃ ⊂D⊃ ⊂E⊃	69 ⊂A⊃ ⊂B⊃ ⊂C⊃ ⊂D⊃ ⊂E⊃
10 ⊂A⊃ ⊂B⊃ ⊂C⊃ ⊂D⊃ ⊂E⊃	30 ⊂A⊃ ⊂B⊃ ⊂C⊃ ⊂D⊃ ⊂E⊃	50 ⊂A⊃ ⊂B⊃ ⊂C⊃ ⊂D⊃ ⊂E⊃	70 ⊂A⊃ ⊂B⊃ ⊂C⊃ ⊂D⊃ ⊂E⊃
11 ⊂A⊃ ⊂B⊃ ⊂C⊃ ⊂D⊃ ⊂E⊃	31 ⊂A⊃ ⊂B⊃ ⊂C⊃ ⊂D⊃ ⊂E⊃	51 ⊂A⊃ ⊂B⊃ ⊂C⊃ ⊂D⊃ ⊂E⊃	71 ⊂A⊃ ⊂B⊃ ⊂C⊃ ⊂D⊃ ⊂E⊃
12 ⊂A⊃ ⊂B⊃ ⊂C⊃ ⊂D⊃ ⊂E⊃	32 ⊂A⊃ ⊂B⊃ ⊂C⊃ ⊂D⊃ ⊂E⊃	52 ⊂A⊃ ⊂B⊃ ⊂C⊃ ⊂D⊃ ⊂E⊃	72 ⊂A⊃ ⊂B⊃ ⊂C⊃ ⊂D⊃ ⊂E⊃
13 ⊂A⊃ ⊂B⊃ ⊂C⊃ ⊂D⊃ ⊂E⊃	33 ⊂A⊃ ⊂B⊃ ⊂C⊃ ⊂D⊃ ⊂E⊃	53 ⊂A⊃ ⊂B⊃ ⊂C⊃ ⊂D⊃ ⊂E⊃	73 ⊂A⊃ ⊂B⊃ ⊂C⊃ ⊂D⊃ ⊂E⊃
14 ⊂A⊃ ⊂B⊃ ⊂C⊃ ⊂D⊃ ⊂E⊃	34 ⊂A⊃ ⊂B⊃ ⊂C⊃ ⊂D⊃ ⊂E⊃	54 ⊂A⊃ ⊂B⊃ ⊂C⊃ ⊂D⊃ ⊂E⊃	74 ⊂A⊃ ⊂B⊃ ⊂C⊃ ⊂D⊃ ⊂E⊃
15 ⊂A⊃ ⊂B⊃ ⊂C⊃ ⊂D⊃ ⊂E⊃	35 ⊂A⊃ ⊂B⊃ ⊂C⊃ ⊂D⊃ ⊂E⊃	55 ⊂A⊃ ⊂B⊃ ⊂C⊃ ⊂D⊃ ⊂E⊃	75 ⊂A⊃ ⊂B⊃ ⊂C⊃ ⊂D⊃ ⊂E⊃
16 ⊂A⊃ ⊂B⊃ ⊂C⊃ ⊂D⊃ ⊂E⊃	36 ⊂A⊃ ⊂B⊃ ⊂C⊃ ⊂D⊃ ⊂E⊃	56 ⊂A⊃ ⊂B⊃ ⊂C⊃ ⊂D⊃ ⊂E⊃	76 ⊂A⊃ ⊂B⊃ ⊂C⊃ ⊂D⊃ ⊂E⊃
17 ⊂A⊃ ⊂B⊃ ⊂C⊃ ⊂D⊃ ⊂E⊃	37 ⊂A⊃ ⊂B⊃ ⊂C⊃ ⊂D⊃ ⊂E⊃	57 ⊂A⊃ ⊂B⊃ ⊂C⊃ ⊂D⊃ ⊂E⊃	77 ⊂A⊃ ⊂B⊃ ⊂C⊃ ⊂D⊃ ⊂E⊃
18 ⊂A⊃ ⊂B⊃ ⊂C⊃ ⊂D⊃ ⊂E⊃	38 ⊂A⊃ ⊂B⊃ ⊂C⊃ ⊂D⊃ ⊂E⊃	58 ⊂A⊃ ⊂B⊃ ⊂C⊃ ⊂D⊃ ⊂E⊃	78 ⊂A⊃ ⊂B⊃ ⊂C⊃ ⊂D⊃ ⊂E⊃
19 ⊂A⊃ ⊂B⊃ ⊂C⊃ ⊂D⊃ ⊂E⊃	39 ⊂A⊃ ⊂B⊃ ⊂C⊃ ⊂D⊃ ⊂E⊃	59 ⊂A⊃ ⊂B⊃ ⊂C⊃ ⊂D⊃ ⊂E⊃	79 ⊂A⊃ ⊂B⊃ ⊂C⊃ ⊂D⊃ ⊂E⊃
20 ⊂A⊃ ⊂B⊃ ⊂C⊃ ⊂D⊃ ⊂E⊃	40 ⊂A⊃ ⊂B⊃ ⊂C⊃ ⊂D⊃ ⊂E⊃	60 ⊂A⊃ ⊂B⊃ ⊂C⊃ ⊂D⊃ ⊂E⊃	80 ⊂A⊃ ⊂B⊃ ⊂C⊃ ⊂D⊃ ⊂E⊃

DO NOT MARK IN THIS AREA
⊂ ⊃ ⊂ ⊃ ⊂ ⊃ ⊂ ⊃ ⊂ ⊃ ⊂ ⊃ ⊂ ⊃ ⊂ ⊃ ⊂ ⊃ ⊂ ⊃ ⊂ ⊃ ⊂ ⊃ ⊂ ⊃ ⊂ ⊃ ⊂ ⊃

NOTES

NOTES

NOTES

NOTES

NOTES

NOTES

NOTES

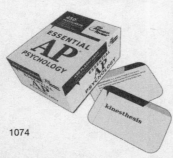